HOME LIFE IN FLORIDA

BY

HELEN HARCOURT

Author of Florida Fruits and How to liaise Them etc., Editor of "Our Some Circle" in the Florida Farmer and Fruit Grower.

Originally published by

LOUISVILLE, KY.

JOHN P. MORTON & COMPANY.

1889

www.yesterdaypress.com

Jupiter, Florida

2022

Home Life in Florida. Helen Harcourt.

Copyright 2022, Yesterday Press

This work is in the public domain in the United States. Any user may copy, distribute, adapt, display, or broadcast it without restriction.

Preserving history…one story at a time…

Yesterday Press is dedicated to reprinting titles that are in the public domain and offering them to the public in order to share history and preserve the stories and records of the past.

All reprints are carefully matched against the originals and with the exception of minor font and formatting changes to fit the current day, all spellings, paragraph breaks, chapter headings, etc. are preserved from the original.

DISCLAMIER: This document was originally written in 1889 and reflects the societal norms and prejudices of that time period. The publisher, editor, and transcriptionist do not necessarily hold the same views. For the sake of historical accuracy, they have not omitted or altered the content of the original author's words.

Transcription and Layout: Karen Yvonne Hamilton

Cover: Image extracted from page 1 of Home Life in Florida, by HARCOURT, Helen. Original held and digitized by the British Library. Copied from Flickr.

ISBN: 978-1-7347858-5-2

LA MARQUE ROSE, BEARING ONE THOUSAND ROSES, AT THREE AND A HALF YEARS OLD: RESIDENCE OF MRS. S. B. WARE??, MONTCLAIR, FLA.

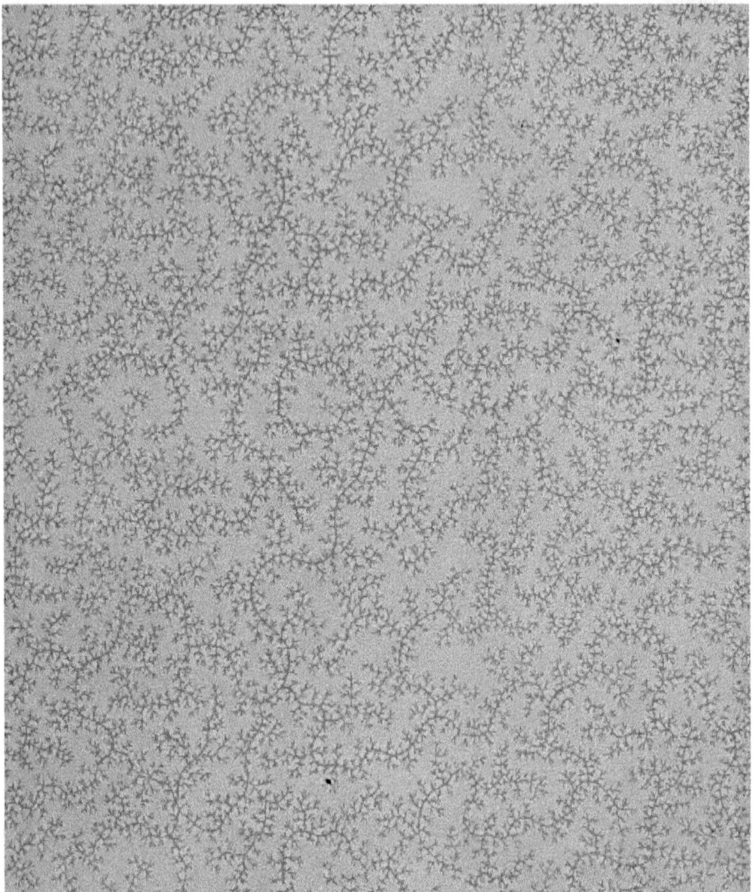

PREFACE.

It is not well to venture into unknown regions blindfold, as it were. That sound old admonition to "Look before you leap" is full of good common sense, and yet it is passed by unheeded more frequently than one can well realize.

We doubt if, in all the globe, there is any one spot concerning which more has been written, pro and con, than of our beloved Florida ; much that is true, much more that is untrue.

An injudicious friend has more power to harm than an open foe — and thus has it been with Florida : some of her friends, misled by eager enthusiasm, have painted her in colors unnaturally brilliant, such as belong not to this world, all light, no shadows ; enemies, moved by self interest to turn the great tide of immigration to other quarters, have portrayed Florida in somber tints, dark and forbidding enough to deter any but the most courageous from crossing her borders.

We love Florida; of our fair State it may well be said that "to know her is to love her," but we hold that her truest interests are best served by a plain statement of facts, not fancies; of realities, not theories; "the truth, the whole truth, and nothing but the truth."

Not only throughout the United States, but in Europe, thousands of home seekers are eagerly turning their eyes toward Florida, and questioning as to what manner of life, what measure of comfort and success await those who elect to cast in their lot with hers.

To answer these eager questioners, to cast a clear, honest light upon the paths they will be called upon to tread, to reveal the truths and possibilities of home life in Florida, this is the task we have set our pen to perform ; and if, as the reader closes the following pages, he is not satisfied that an honest, industrious man or woman need have no fear of not " making a living" and a comfortable home in Florida, with less outlay of capital and hardship than elsewhere, then has this volume been written in vain.

Profiting by the experience of a former work (Florida Fruits and How to Raise Them) in which several articles valuable to settlers were referred to, but no address given where they might be procured, an omission which called forth numerous inquiries from readers, the present volume will be found to contain all the information relative to each article mentioned which is necessary to enable the reader to procure it direct, thereby immensely enhancing its practical value to the settler whose interests it seeks to serve.

That this humble work, which may at least claim to be honest and candid, may be the means of winning many to test the peaceful content and comfort of home life in Florida is the earnest hope of

THE AUTHOR.

TABLE OF CONTENTS.

PREFACE.

TABLE OF CONTENTS.

    CHAPTER I. WHAT FLORIDA OFFERS.   1

Comfort and Competence for the Honest and Industrious. Increase of Prosperity, and Population of the State. Good Investment for both Capital and Labor. Health for the Invalid.

    CHAPTER II. A BACKWARD GLANCE.   14

Why Florida is called "A New Country." A Glimpse of her History

    CHAPTER III. CLIMATE.   30

Proved by Comparison and Statistics to be the Finest in the World. Scientifically "Moderately Dry:" Variation of Temperature Just Sufficient for Health and Comfort.

    CHAPTER IV. HEALTH.   41

The First Consideration. Statistics Prove Florida to be the Healthiest State in the Union. Safe to Settle at all Times of the Year. Purity of the Air. Points in Locating: Water, Wells, and Filters

    CHAPTER V. TEMPERATURE. WINTER. SUMMER   60

Violent Changes almost unknown. Mild Winters. Cooler in Summer than in the Northern States.

    SUMMER.   66

    CHAPTER VI. PINE LANDS AND HAMMOCKS.   72

Diversity of Soil and Surface. Relative Value in Productiveness and Healthfulness.

    CHAPTER VII. "WHERE SHALL I SETTLE?"   81

Northern, Middle (including West), and South Florida. Varied Products and Climatic Differences of the Several Sections.

CHAPTER VIII. "WHAT WILL IT COST?" 95

Prices of Land: According to Location and Quality. Cost and Methods of Clearing Land. Solid and Increasing Value of a Bearing Orange Grove. Overproduction Impossible.

CHAPTER IX. MAKING THE HOME. 115

Attractive Locations. Beautiful Water Views. About Windmills.

CHAPTER X. HOME SURROUNDINGS. 127

Grass Lawns. Vines and Flowers. Shade-trees and Arbors. Shade for Poultry-yards.

CHAPTER XI. "WHAT SHALL I NEED?" 144

Warm Clothing and Carpets Desirable. Cool Weather. "The Dark Days of January, 1886." Whether to Bring or Buy in Florida the Household Furniture. Hints for Shipping Goods.

CHAPTER XII. "WHAT SHALL I EAT?" 158

Deprivations in New Neighborhoods. The Provision Closet. Conveniences and Food Supply Constantly Increasing.

CHAPTER XIII. HOME SUPPLIES. 167

Fish, Flesh, and Fowl to be had for the Catching. The Gopher Tortoise.

CHAPTER XIV. "OUT OF THE DEPTHS." 178

A Boat the first Requisite. Methods of Fishing for Trout or Bass. Salt-water Fish, Clams, and Oysters. Methods of Catching Fresh-water Turtle; Curious Quality of their Flesh.

CHAPTER XV. THE DAIRY QUESTION — OLD STYLE. 190

The Native Florida Cow. Methods of Milking. How to Make a Cowpen. Best Plan for best results in Fertilizing the Soil by Cow-penning. Treatment of the Florida Cow.

CHAPTER XVI. THE DAIRY QUESTION — THE COMING STYLE. **210**

Native Stock to be Improved by Crossing with Thoroughbreds and Proper Treatment. Acclimated Thoroughbreds should be Bought of Florida Breeders

CHAPTER XVII. PASTURAGE. **223**

Bermuda, Johnson and Para Grass. Beggar's Weed or Indian Clover

CHAPTER XVIII. FLORIDA POULTRY. **233**

Nearly all Varieties do Well. How to Treat them Successfully

CHAPTER XIX. THE POULTRY YARD. **255**

Shade, Grass, and Pure Water Requisite. The Nursery. How to guard against Hawks. Movable Coops and Fences.

CHAPTER XX. POULTRY PATIENTS. **269**

How to Treat the Few Diseases Florida Poultry are subject to

    ERYSIPELAS. **273**

    DOUGLASS' MIXTURE. **275**

CHAPTER XXI. FIRING THE WOODS. **277**

Permitted by Law for the Benefit of Cattle; but will soon be a Thing of the Past. A Most Pernicious Custom, Injurious to Soil and Property. How to Fight Fire.

CHAPTER XXII. ALL ABOUT FENCES. **283**

The Fence Law. Repeal Urgent. Injury done by allowing Stock to roam at Large, and compelling the Agriculturist to Fence against Them. How to Make Good and Cheap Fences. Wire Fences Made at Home

CHAPTER XXIII. HOUSEHOLD HELP. **299**

Housekeeper's Trials. Florida Negro Servants. Amusing Experiences. Importance of the Problem of Domestic Help. How it may be solved.

CHAPTER XXIV. TRIALS AND TRIBULATIONS. **319**

Insect Foes, and How to Eight Them. Harmless Lizards and Frogs. The "Bugaboo" of Snakes.

CHAPTER XXV. MAKING THE BEST OF IT.   350

Compensations for Drawbacks. How to Make the New Home Happy.

CHAPTER XXVI. HELPFUL HINTS.   357

How to Paint Houses. Recipes for Cheap Paints. About Horses, Wagons, and Harness. How to Renovate Carriages. Home-made Furniture, Rugs, and Refrigerators. To Preserve Food.

THE AMATEUR HOUSE PAINTER.	357
MILK PAINT.	359
ANOTHER DURABLE PAINT	360
FIRE-PROOF PAINT.	360
THE HORSE AND ITS ADJUNCTS.	361
TO PRESERVE HARNESS.	369
HOME-MADE FURNITURE.	370
BED-ROOM FURNITURE.	370
THE ROSS NOVELTY RUG MACHINE.	375
THE BARREL CHAIR.	377
A HOME-MADE REFRIGERATOR.	379

CHAPTER I. WHAT FLORIDA OFFERS.

Comfort and Competence for the Honest and Industrious. Increase of Prosperity, and Population of the State. Good Investment for both Capital and Labor. Health for the Invalid.

A little bird has come tapping at our study door, bearing in its beak a message from the North, East, West, and Southwest, and from "beyond the seas," which reads thus:

"We have read of Florida's fruits, of her cotton, her cane, her climate; we have heard glowing accounts of what has been and can be done through all the length and breadth of the noble 'Land of Flowers;' but nowhere have we read or heard of the thousand and one details of the every-day life that must be met and lived by the settler before he attains the grand sum total of independence.

How do he and his wife live and work and pass their time? What do they wear? What do they eat? What does it cost? What can they raise? Tell us of these things, so that all the thousands of us who are coming to Florida seeking homes may know to what we are coming, and see some clear rays of light shining through the obscurity of vague generalities. Things known to you old settlers are unknown to us; things familiar to you are enigmas to us.

We know that your ways are not as our ways, but we do not know the details of the difference, nor how to prepare to meet them. We are thirsty for information of the little things that go to make up the daily life of the settler.

Give us to drink of the fountain of knowledge, that we may be strong to meet the life we must face in our future homes."

And so, having been taught that it is as impolite to ignore a message as to refuse to notice a verbal question, we "take our pen in hand to let you know "of Florida" the truth, the whole truth, and nothing but the truth."

Florida's climate has been spoken of, and justly, by the most eminent scientists as one of the finest, and, away from the miasmas of the swamps, as one of the most healthful in the world, and we, who know her well, know that she has no need of exaggerated statements to plead her cause, and we propose to make none.

We who dwell and have dwelt for years within her borders know that our beautiful State has no need of overdrawn, rose-colored pictures.

It is better to understate rather than overstate the truth; it is better to climb up than fall down. Human nature is apt to fly to extremes, to expect too much, and then, not finding it, to shut the eye to the good that really nestles amidst the evil. And so it has fared with hundreds who have gazed on highly-colored pictures of Florida life, pictures tinted with rainbow hues, not a shadow or a flaw anywhere; and, so gazing, have hastened there with pockets empty, yet full of anticipations of a quick and easy fortune to be obtained without time, or work or patience, or deprivation, and then finding that Florida is only an earthly country after all, not a paradise, and that orange trees are so unreasonable and willful as to decline to grow up, increase, bear, gather, and ship their fruit of their own volition while their owner sleeps, they turn their backs upon the prospective golden fruit and draw a black brush over the rainbow-hued picture that had drawn them Florida-ward.

We hardly know what our own ideas of Florida life were until the realities were before us; for, in fact (like many another, doubtless), we hardly had time to think about it at all.

> "Jack and gill went up the hill
> To get a pail of water;
> Jack fell down and broke his crown,
> And gill came tumbling after,"

and never stopped until they landed in the midst of a young orange grove, which some day will surely carry Jack and gill up hill again in a gold and green chariot, if only they are patient and energetic.

But there were some of us, we remember, who thought the trees had only to be stuck in the ground anyhow and then left severely alone for two or three years, when they would be found full of glorious fruit. Visions of special steamers to be chartered, of whole trains of cars loaded with the produce, floated before the glowing imagination; and as for vegetables, they were to be had for the scattering of the seed, all the year round, if, indeed, they did not spring up and grow of their own accord.

It is curious to find, in collecting the preconceptions of "Florida fever" patients, how wildly just such ideas as these obtain credence. Very rarely, indeed, do we find a settler who has not formed impossible expectations, and is therefore "gwine to be disappinted," and in the rebound to see his future home in darker hues than it deserves.

And all this comes of the unwise laudations of the enthusiastic friends who have done more actual harm to our beautiful State than all her foes collectively.

To clear away the mists and throw in the shadows that all earthly paintings must accept as part and parcel of themselves, and to tell the honest truth, and in such shape as to do the most practical good, is the earnest object of this present work.

Throughout the length and breadth of these United States, north, south, east, and west, and scarcely less in Great Britain also, there are at this moment thousands of hearts turning wistfully toward Florida as a haven of refuge and of hope from financial storms or from untimely death and disease. These inquirers are eager to know the real, substantial advantages she holds out to those who elect to cast their lot with hers, and the Floridian who sets forth these advantages side by side with the ever-attendant disadvantages, giving publicity to facts and not to "vain imaginings," will do his State more real service than he who willfully misleads by false statements impossible to be credited by any reasonable thinking being.

We hold that our beautiful State has no need of exaggeration, no need of that which is bright to be painted brighter. She only wants the truth to be known to mark her out as thrice blessed among her sister States. She has her drawbacks and deprivations, of course, though these are fewer than those of any other new country that we know of. Take notice that we use the word "new," for there are those who come to Florida ignoring the fact of its very recent opening up to settlers, and then grumble because things are not conducted in the old well-worn grooves they have been accustomed to in their old homes, whose rescue from the wilderness dates back for many years, even to the hundreds. There are plenty of such unreasonable, unreasoning, impractical people in the world, and occasionally they edify and amuse their wiser brethren by holding forth on the subject of imaginary grievances.

Florida has seen a goodly number of them, and some of them not being known outside her borders in their true character have done her considerable injury. Many a man has come to our beautiful State, lured by glowing descriptions and rose-colored pictures of impossible perfections, with his expectations wrought to the highest pitch, and finding no paradise of ease and plenty awaiting his picking up without working or waiting, has turned his back upon her and gone back whence he came, to revile her as a fraud, a sham, a " trap to catch sinners."

Surely it is better for Florida that her settlers should come to her with moderate, reasonable expectations, and find their ideas lower than the reality; far better this way than the opposite of expecting too much, and meeting bitter disappointment, and such a revulsion of feeling that the good that really lies before them is swallowed up in the gloom. Florida desires nothing but the truth to be told of her wealth and virtues—the plain, sober truth, in facts and figures, of deeds done and work accomplished, of what has been and is, not of the theoretical "might be," this should be enough to satisfy an energetic, reasonable man; and she wants none other. She is beautiful, but is not a paradise; her climate, both summer and winter, is delightful, but it is not perfection; the summer days and nights are cooled by such breezes as are seldom known at the North. The heat is therefore less oppressive than the same season in any other State, in the North or South, but the warm weather continues longer. The winter has no snow, but sometimes there is ice, a thin skim that forms during the night and usually vanishes in the morning, but stays long enough to nip tender vegetables; so that the truck gardener must hasten to plant again in order not to lose the cream of the early Northern markets. And sometimes there is a drought that shrivels up the vegetables and keeps back the earliest shipments.

So you see there do exist drawbacks and discouragements, but they are not always nor all the time, and the man of pluck and energy who has made up his mind to act on that grand old adage, "If at first you don't succeed, try, try again," is certain to triumph in the end.

We heard the other day of a man (and this is only one instance out of hundreds) who came to Florida a few years ago with six hundred dollars' capital, borrowed money, every dollar of it. In five years he had repaid the money, including a heavy interest, and had three times as much in the bank, besides being the owner of forty acres of land, a young orange grove and peach orchard, two horses, half a dozen cows, and a comfortable house. He wisely located on a line of railroad to secure quick transportation, instead of settling in some place where his products could not find a market, and then he rolled up his sleeves and went to work like a man, to raise vegetables. He was new to the business, had been a hard-worked book-keeper, struggling vainly to support his family even in the most frugal manner. He knew nothing of farm life, but he studied, used his eyes and his brains as well as his hands, questioned his neighbors, did not disdain to take advice from men less educated but better informed in agriculture than himself, and so he succeeded, as every man will who follows his example— one of true worth and manliness. His cucumbers brought him from four to six dollars a crate, his tomatoes from two to six dollars, and peas, beans, beets, potatoes, and cabbages in like proportion; and he blessed the day that he resolved to turn his back on the office desk and seek his fortune in fair Florida's outstretched hand.

It was not all plain sailing, be it understood. He worked faithfully and intelligently in spite of discouragements. Sometimes frost killed his young plants; sometimes dry weather did it. Insects helped them, dishonest commission men robbed him, but he kept steadily on, planting a new crop as fast as the old one was killed or gathered. Neither he nor the ground were allowed to remain idle.

To-day he is in possession of as pretty a home as one need wish to see. His wife and children are well and happy, and his life is full of contentment. "What a contrast," he exclaims, "to what it was eight years ago!" And all because he had the nerve to drag himself out of the old worn-out groove and the pluck to hammer out a new one.

This is no fancy picture, but one that every energetic man may make a reality for himself if he will but seize and hold Florida's royal bounty. And this man, take notice, was a gentleman, educated and trained as a bookkeeper—one of a vast army who struggle on from day to day, overworked, underpaid, or not paid at all.

Take up any one of the newspapers of our great cities, and what do we see? The same old story that has been told over and over again for years past. "A merchant advertised for a clerk at ten dollars a week, and eight hundred applied for the position." "There are now no less than seven thousand book-keepers out of employment in this one city alone!" Is not that a pitiful showing? and in "one city alone." Think of it then all over the country! Now why is it that so many young men prefer the precarious life of a salaried clerk, book-keeper, or salesman, shut in-doors all day and every day, from morning till night, earning barely enough to keep up appearances before the world, laying by nothing to meet the rainy season, sure to come—if "out of employment," "on the sick list," " too old to work"— to the free, manly life of the farmer or fruit-grower, breathing God's pure air, uncontaminated by the dust and smoke of cities, living a life of comfort and freedom from care, even if one of honest daily toil, and storing up for the future a sufficient independence for himself and his family? Why is it? Is it because in these days of ultra civilization and refinement manual labor has come to be looked upon as unworthy of a "gentleman"?

Fie upon it! If this is the reason of the surplusage of clerks and book-keepers, and the scarcity of young farmers and horticulturists and artisans, why then let us hasten back to the good old times of barbarism, and be happy and prosperous because we are not educated above a good, honest, hard day's work!

"Do ye not perceive," saith the Great Ruler of us all, "that whatsoever thing from without entereth into the man, it can not defile him?" But "that which cometh out of the man, that defileth the man." And so it is not the work that a man does that lowers him, but his manner of doing it. A sturdy, intelligent tiller of the soil, free to come and go, to breathe the pure air and join in the joyous hymns of the birds, doing his work cheerfully, energetically, and in the best manner, is surely the full equal of the salaried book-keeper, sitting at his desk, at the call of another, and liable to be thrown out on the world penniless after years of steady application to work that is certainly less elevating, free, and manly than that of the farmer or fruit-grower.

Florida holds forth her hand in hearty welcome, not only to the capitalist and manufacturer, whose gold is a magnet to draw forth yet more of the precious metal from amidst her hidden treasures and mysteries, and to utilize those resources of which we already know. Not only these does Florida welcome, but also, with just as much earnestness, the poor, honest man, be he *ci-devant* clerk, bookkeeper, mechanic, artisan, or farmer, who comes to her seeking a comfortable home, and is neither ashamed nor too lazy to work for it. She wants good men and true—men of intelligence, of mind, and of muscle, with willing hands to convert her vast forests into rich fields and fruitful groves, and to fill their own treasure chest with the well-earned reward of honest toil judiciously expended. She has ample room for the skilled workman, the industrious mechanic, the day laborer, the farm hand, the truck farmer, the fruit-grower, the merchant, the blacksmith, and all the "many men of many trades" who go to make up our busy, hard-working world. It is a noble, bounteous gift that she holds out to such as these, who flee to her from the crowded, icy North. It can all be summed up in one word—a veritable *multiim in 'parvo.*

Comfort! a glorious boon, is it not?—a comfortable climate, a comfortable home, a comfortable competence, a comfortable life for all their days to come, and a comfortable fortune for their children after them. It is all here waiting for the self-chosen ones, who elect to take advantage of the gift so freely offered to those who have manhood enough to grasp it and make the best use of it. But mark well that proviso, 'to grasp it and make the best use of it." For there are some who take and hold it in a feeble, half-hearted sort of way, and do not, by any means, make as good use of it as they might, and others who are so blind that they may gaze straight into bonnie Florida's outstretched palm and see nothing there but the sand that has got into their eyes and affected their vision with a curious obliquity and color-blindness that changes all the fair landscape to one deep shade of blue.

Aye! it is a most generous offer—comfort—a boon for which weary thousands upon thousands are seeking all their lives long and never find it, not for an hour or a day—a most noble gift indeed, but not made to sloths nor sluggards, nor to men who expect to reap where they have not sowed, to gather without planting, to thrust an orange tree into the ground one day and see the golden fruit drop into their pockets the next; nor to men who possess neither patience nor energy, neither perseverance nor "backbone," who prefer sharp practice to honesty, falsehood to truth. For such men as these Florida has no gifts to offer; she does not want them, has no room for them, and gives them small encouragement to encumber her fair fields and forests.

Not only in our own dear country, but in England, Scotland, Ireland, Norway, Sweden, Germany, there are thousands upon thousands of men and women, many of them too in the higher walks of life, struggling day by day to meet the daily, never-ending problem of how to live and how to clothe and educate their children. Ah! did they but know of the peaceful, comfortable home that fair Florida holds forth for their acceptance!

When the cold, chilling breath of the Ice King sweeps over the land of the North, and suffering—suffering from cold, from starvation, from sickness—presses its heavy hand upon the downcast, "out of work," poverty-stricken toilers of the earth, we of sunny Florida read the sad story with aching hearts; we look out upon our own bright surroundings and clear, warm sky, upon trees loaded with golden fruit, ground green with growing crops, chickens and ducks merrily chasing insects; birds, rabbits, fish, turtle, and, on the coast, oysters and clams to be had for the catching; upon our own lightly clad forms, our small wood fires, some days not even called into requisition; upon cord after cord of heat-giving, life-giving wood lying rotting on the ground; upon master builders, carpenters, artisans of all kinds crying out, "We can not work faster because we can not get workmen enough." We of bonnie Florida look out upon all these things, and the contrast in the lives of those wretched, suffering masses of the North, as it is, with what it might be if they would but accept the comforts that Florida freely offers them, fills our hearts with a yearning compassion and desire to point out the open road that lies before them, did they but see it. And we are thankful, intensely thankful to know that the number of those who do see it is daily increasing—increasing, too, just as we would have it, in exact proportion as the veil of mystery is lifted from Florida's beautiful, genial form, and she stands revealed, her true self, the refuge, the benefactor of the struggling multitude.

The weary, anxious father and mother, whose hard, unremitting toil scarce suffices for the present needs of their little ones, and who, so long as they creep on in the same old groove, are able to lay by not one dollar for the future or for the "rainy day," so certain to come to all sooner or later, need but to transplant their household treasures to a genial Florida home to find in the present, comfort, and in the future competence, if nothing more; and this, too, with less toil and hardship, less anxiety from day to day than they endured in the old life behind them. And many are awakening to this truth.

Here, there, everywhere, we see colonies forming, neighbors joining hands and fleeing in a body from the icy winters of their old homes to seek an easier, more prosperous life in sunny Florida, making in themselves a community bound together by mutual associations in the past, giving to each other hope, support, encouragement in the present and future.

To the honest man willing to work, with a wife or children willing to lend a helping hand, there can be no such word in Florida as "fail." Even the despairing widow with little children dependent upon her, if she is able to work and can but get together enough money to carry her to one of the growing Florida towns, secure an acre or half acre of land (there are some who donate several acres to actual settlers), and erect a little frame house thereon, will find plenty of work to do, and reduced expenses for clothing and fuel; profit, too, in raising a few chickens and vegetables; and meantime, for the future, may have growing on her little property a few well-cared-for orange and other fruit trees. For mark well this fact: a few trees properly tended will pay better and quicker than five times the number only half nourished and cultivated.

One acre of land set with choice orange trees, say fifty of them, with peach, fig, and pear trees in the diamonds and corners, and vegetables raised between them, will in a few years go far toward supplying the wants of any reasonable family. And there are very few who could not acquire this much of landed property in bonnie Florida.

Florida offers opportunities for the energetic and industrious in every class of life, from the great capitalist down to the common day laborer. In all her towns workmen of every kind are in request at excellent wages, with less expense for clothing and fuel and house rent to be met than at the North. In every one of the numerous towns springing up all over the State, wherever and whenever the fast spreading net work of transportation lines- reaches out its life-giving arms—in every one of these numerous towns there are openings ready and waiting for all who choose to grasp them. For the man or woman who would embark in mercantile pursuits, with only a small capital to start with; for the merchant, the dressmaker, the tinsmith, the milliner, the baker, the washer and ironer, the blacksmith, the carpenter—for each and all, in fact, Florida has a welcome and a home.

The day has gone by when there was employment in Florida only for builders and those connected with horticultural pursuits. "Many men of many minds" can now find plenty of opportunities to ply their several callings with profit. Merchants, manufacturers, capitalists are coming in day by day, and as to the future resources and possibilities of our infant State no one now living dares fix their limit, for the simple reason (by way of illustration) that no one dare say that Edison, the great electrician, can proceed no further than his last wonderful invention, that of telegraphing to and from a railroad tram going at full speed. Year by year, month by month, as the tide of immigration and travel flows across the border m a steadily augmenting stream, some new resource some new indication of Florida's future greatness is discovered when her most despised productions develop into fresh resources of wealth and channels of industry. Witness, in passing, the much condemned scrub or saw palmetto, found here, there, every where. Its fiber proves to be very valuable for manufacturing brushes and brooms and various other things, while its sturdy roots are found to be richer in tannin than the much-vaunted oak, and hence invaluable in tanning leather. Ground fine or burned, it is also a valuable fertilizer. The long gray moss which drapes the hammock trees is coming into extensive use for mattresses and upholstery; and so we might go on swelling our list indefinitely. Tobacco factories are already in operation at several points, ice factories are numerous, the manufacture of textile fibers has commenced, fruit and vegetable canneries are springing into being, cotton mills coming to the fore, cattle ranches are close at hand.

But it is not the purpose of this present work to enter in detail into the various methods that Florida offers of winning home and competence to the industrious and intelligent toilers of the world. Enough that we have indicated the roads that lie open to the "Home Life in Florida" and its possibilities. As to the means that shall support that home, it is for the settler to choose according to his means or inclination. Our sole object is to show what the Florida home may be made, what the settler must expect to meet, and how to make the best of his or her surroundings. We want the every-day realities of the new home to be known, so far as it is possible for our humble pen to reveal them, and in the telling of it all it shall be our earnest endeavor to adhere strictly to facts and to point out all sides of Florida life, good, bad, and indifferent. Happily we can truthfully say that the former largely predominates. Those who come to Florida "to stay," seek health, wealth, and a happy home, and these they will find if they are sought for in a reasonable, sensible spirit. We trust that when our readers lay down the pages of this book they will have gained a correct idea of Florida home life.

Very many still hold to the same utterly unjust and erroneous opinion of Florida's true inwardness that was once uttered concerning her by that most eccentric statesman and senator, John Randoph, of Roanoke. It was when the question of the purchase of Florida from Spain was being considered by the United States Senate, and Randolph was bitterly opposed to it. "What is Florida?" he exclaimed. "A land of swamps, everglades, filled with frogs, tadpoles, snakes, terrapins, alligators, mosquitoes, gallinippers, and ague and fever! Why, sir, a man would not emigrate to that county, even from purgatory! What, then, do we want with Florida?" And all the John Randolphs are not dead yet, but they are dying rapidly. Florida kills them all off, one after the other, as fast as they look upon her fair, honest face. One glance does it; but the trouble is that so many do not take that one glance, and hence, if they pay any attention to the subject at all, are liable to be deceived, whether they believe all or believe nothing. Those who know Florida as she is, are those who love her best, and are most willing to tell the truth about her, without fear or favor.

Not yet is she appreciated by the world at large as she should be and will be in the near future; but she is better known now than she was two or three years ago, and is to-day considered as one of the most valuable sections of our great nation—the only part on the eastern side of our country where snows never fall, and where, in literal truth, "perpetual spring abides and never-fading flowers." False statements, deliberate, unblushing, malicious, have been made time and again, with the one set purpose of doing our beautiful State an injury, and other statements have been made also with a very different intent, yet scarcely less untrue because the picture they drew of ease, comfort, and rapid wealth are penciled in colors too bright to be realized in this world, inasmuch as they are promised without the prelude of waiting or working. And yet, in spite of the assaults of unscrupulous foes and injudicious friends, Florida prospers with an exceeding prosperity, because the truth is ever triumphant; and here are a few figures that go to prove what she has done in the last few years, which we clip from a current newspaper:

"The census returns show that the people of Florida are getting richer very rapidly. During the five years since the census of 1880 the population increased at the rate of about 13,000 yearly, or from 269,494 to 334,146, while the value of property has increased from $30,000,000 to $60,000,000 in round numbers. Thus twice the values represented by the population in 1880 are represented now by a population increased less than one sixth, and, averaging the property *per capita*, makes each individual of to-day worth nearly twice as much as he was five years ago. These figures are even more satisfactory than those showing the increase of population. There are a good many more of us, and we are much richer."

CHAPTER II. A BACKWARD GLANCE.

Why Florida is called "A New Country." A Glimpse of her History

The question is frequently asked, "How is it, if Florida is so desirable a country as a home, a fruit orchard and vegetable garden, that people have been so long in finding it out? Why was it not thickly settled long years ago?"

And the query is natural enough if one has not paid much attention to the records of Florida's history; but when one pauses to look backward into those strangely romantic pages, the wonder ceases. Not one amidst all the various units that go to make up the noble sum total of our United States can boast of a story so full of marked events and tragic romance that savors of the olden times as can the beautiful "Land of Flowers," which, even from the first moment of its discovery, seemed to be set apart from the rest of the continent to undergo an experience all its own. The very fashion of that discovery was out of the ordinary track of common events.

Dating from the ever memorable year 1492, when the immortal Columbus revealed the existence of another continent to the astonished denizens of the "Old World," each year had witnessed the departure from the shores of the latter of one or more expeditions fitted out for the double purpose of discovery and conquest. But though the several voyagers had sailed all along the eastern shores of the new continent, from the Carolinas northward, and had landed here and there, exploring the country, its rivers and harbors, yet none had set foot on the Florida coast, although one or two had sailed within sight of its eastern shores. No good harbor for their ships offering, however, they passed it by unheeding. Somehow, as we have intimated already, the southernmost extremity of North America seems from the first to have been, by common consent, set apart for "future consideration." Nature had, in a measure, placed it by itself, and man was disposed to follow her example. Oddly enough, it was decreed that the saying, "the last shall be first, and the first shall be last," should be verified in this instance.

While other lands to the north and west of Florida were being drenched in the blood of conquered and conquerors and settlements formed and as quickly abandoned, the fair land so long neglected was destined to have and to hold the first permanent settlement on the whole continent for, as every one knows, the quaint little town of St. Augustine, still bearing the imprint of its Spanish origin, antedates all others in America.

But it was with no thought of future St. Augustine or any other settlement that Juan Ponce De Leon turned his prow toward the fair land of Florida. The discovery of the "New World" had drawn to its shores hosts of adventurers in search of fame, gold, and conquest, many of them seeing them, too, under the guise of religion—the promotion of the cause of the church and the conversion of the heathen. But of none of these things thought Ponce De Leon. He sought a personal benefit, it is true but of a widely different kind. The heyday of his youth had passed, but not, as he now fondly hoped, forever. He had heard wondrous tales of a marvelous spring wherein one's youth might be regained, and this, this alone, was the object of his quest—the realization of a new, strange hope. Juan Ponce De Leon had served his country during the wars in Granada with no slight distinction, and when Columbus sailed on his second voyage to the "New World" he had discovered, De Leon went with him in search of a fresh field for adventure. On this expedition he added not a little to his reputation as a skillful, daring soldier, and his services were rewarded by the appointment to the governorship of Bimini, one of the Bahama Islands lying nearest to the great continent.

De Leon lived in an age of comparative ignorance, and therefore superstition held full sway over the minds of the masses of all ranks, from the highest to the lowest. Particularly was this the case with the traveler, who witnessed much that he could not understand, and consequently set it down to the account of an agency not "of the earth, earthy." Ponce De Leon was not an exception to the general rule. He had journeyed far and often, over sea and land, and had seen many wonderful things which he attributed to supernatural causes. In the new land in which his lot was now cast there was much to astonish the rough, ignorant soldier. The very existence of this great country was in itself a thing to marvel at. Altogether poor De Leon was in a proper frame of mind to be victimized, or, rather, to victimize himself; and that is just what he did, aided not a little therein by the wondrous tales brought to his credulous ears by those of his comrades in arms who had penetrated into the wilds of the continent.

Now, among the aborigines of Bimini and of the adjacent islands there was a legend which had been handed down from father to son from time out of mind, and none could tell its origin beyond tracing it to a certain great cacique. It was hardly a legend either, for its whole purport was to the effect that he who bathed in the stream should renew his youth. It was, in fact, only a different version of our own saying that "cleanliness is next to godliness." The far-away cacique, dead so long ago that his very name was forgotten, who impressed this maxim on his people, was certainly a wise old gentleman, and worthy of more renown than has fallen to his lot. The strength and vigor of youth is a boon cherished by all; hence, to preserve it, or to recover it when lost, the natives bathed frequently, and by so doing did much to attain their object, since cleanliness is certainly a great promoter of health, and health simulates youth. This was, doubtless, the full and entire extent of the wise cacique's meaning, and as such the great majority of his people received it; but here and there one might be found who took the matter less literally, and held fast to the belief that the cacique's words referred to one particular spring or fountain, which, it was true, they had not yet discovered, but only because it had not been perseveringly searched for.

With sundry of these believers the veteran De Leon took counsel, and at once decided in his own mind that the Fountain of Youth was an actual, tangible fact, somewhere; therefore, that it could be discovered, and that Ponce De Leon was the happy man destined to accomplish this great feat and to be the first to profit by it. Week after week, month after month, the Governor of Bimini brooded over this wonderful fountain, until he became a man with but one idea, a monomaniac. He boldly avowed his firm belief that any man, no matter how worn out with age he might be, who should dip his body into the waters of this mighty spring, would emerge restored to the full bloom of youth and strength. Imbued with the idea that his own lost youth might be regained did he but make the effort, the sturdy warrior at length threw prudence to the winds, and with a few followers embarked on a voyage among the neighboring islands, determined to find the lifegiving fountain, if he spent years in the search; for of what value were years upon years when once the wonderful youth restorer were discovered? In the light of our modern knowledge and contempt of superstition, it is pitiful to think of a strong man, a renowned soldier and leader, thus wasting his energies in the vain quest of a supernatural boon on earth.

Long and weary were the days and weeks that followed his departure from Bimini. Buffeted about by wind and wave, De Leon persevered in his search for that which did not exist, landing on every island and every little point of terra firma, exploring every hill and hollow, tramping through weary miles of tangled underbrush, and plunging into every stream, every spring, and every hole containing water, no matter how slimy or muddy it might be. But from none of these many baths did he rise up one whit the younger; on the contrary, the historians tell us, what one would naturally suppose would be the result, that all this toil and exposure and fatigue, coupled with continual anxiety and disappointment seriously affected De Leon both in mind and body, so that he never afterward displayed his wonted energy or judgment in thought or deed.

Hither and thither sailed poor, deluded Ponce De Leon, wearied and disheartened, yet still convinced that the Fountain of Youth existed and that in time he should find it. So magnificent a boon to mankind would naturally be difficult of access. Men hid their best treasures, oftentimes; then why not Dame Nature?

Suddenly, on the 27th of March, 1512, while beating about on the ocean, De Leon unexpectedly sighted land, and, sailing cautiously nearer, perceived that it was an extensive country, heretofore unknown, and very different from the small islands of the Bahamas. Slowly he crept along the coast, seeking a harbor for his ships, and at last he landed on the spot where now stands the oldest city in the United States, St. Augustine. Splendid forests of pine trees, immense oaks, cypress, magnolia, palm, and bay trees rose grandly toward the sky, adorned to their very tops with the long gray moss now so familiar to us all. From the ground at their feet peeped forth, amidst a rank growth of coarse grass, flowers of all colors ; and even away up toward the tree tops climbing vines bedecked the green foliage with yellow and white and scarlet flowers, all gleaming and glinting in the sunshine, with the graceful, sober-tinted moss waving to and fro in their midst, and altogether forming a scene so weirdly strange and beautiful that Ponce De Leon and his followers with one accord named this new land "Florida"—blooming or flourishing. And thus was our fair peninsula christened for all time by the Spanish adventurer.

So elated was the old warrior by the grand discovery he had accidentally made that even the long-cherished dream of the Fountain of Youth was relegated to the background; and although one might naturally suppose that here in this fairy-like land, if any where, the wondrous fountain might well be located, yet now De Leon turned suddenly from his chimera, and instead of wasting still more of his valuable time in any further search, he at once proceeded to investigate the extent of this new island, as he believed it to be.

Knowing as we do, at this present day, all the many visible and hidden dangers and intricacies of navigation among the Florida reefs, and violent currents produced by the Gulf Stream in flowing among the numerous islands or "keys," it is a marvel that De Leon was able to follow the coast in safety, as he did, from the site of St. Augustine southward, finally rounding the southernmost point and sailing northward a short distance along the western shore.

Although still believing the land he had discovered to be an island, he was now well assured that it was very large and important. He therefore hastened to Porto Rico and thence to Spain, where he laid before the king the particulars of his discovery, and received as a reward authority to conquer and govern the country, under the high-sounding title of *Adelantado*. Returning to the West Indies, he immediately commenced extensive preparations for an expedition of conquest and settlement. The building and arming of ships and the enlistment of the proper kind of men for such work consumed a considerable time, and it so happened, unluckily for Ponce De Leon, that he was in the interval called upon to suppress an insurrection of the Caribs, who, having long patiently borne with the wanton cruelty of their conquerors, were at last roused to resistance. And now the physical results of that direful search over sea and land for the Fountain of Youth revealed themselves more unmistakably than ever. De Leon, the renowned soldier, had lost his cunning. He led his men through swamps and jungles, with a reckless disregard of probable ambuscades and entanglements more suited to a young, inexperienced volunteer than to a disciplined, war-hardened veteran. His soldiers died from sickness brought on by needless exposure and fatigue, their ranks were thinned by unseen foes who lurked behind the trees and underbrush, ever and anon sending a fatal arrow into their midst. Instead of securing, as they expected, an easy victory over the untaught savages, one reverse after another overtook the devoted band, until they were compelled to abandon the expedition, the whole burden of its failure being justly ascribed to the want of skill and judgment of its leader.

The effect of this reverse was disastrous to the future fortunes of De Leon. His *prestige* was gone forever, and men feared to trust to his leadership. The result was that nine years elapsed before he succeeded in collecting even a small force to accompany him to the beautiful land of which he was nominally *Adelantado*. Before that unfortunate expedition against the Caribs Ponce De Leon could have filled a dozen ships with enthusiastic followers. Now he could with difficulty find enough men willing to accept his leadership to fill two ships. With these, however, he finally set sail once again for the flowery shores of Florida, still believing his promised domain to be a large island.

Landing, he spent some time in explorations with a view to locating a colony, the *nucleus* of his government.

The natives, astonished at the sight of the white strangers, kept carefully aloof during these preliminary proceedings; but, coming at length to the conclusion that their presence boded themselves no good, they determined to drive them away.

Had Ponce De Leon been the soldier he once was, their resolves had been made in vain; but here again, as with the Caribs, he neglected the most ordinary precautions, and conducted all his operations with culpable carelessness, despising the naked heathen too much to guard against his attack. Strange that he had not yet bought experience!

The Indians collected in large numbers, and while De Leon was busily engaged in planning the site for his colony, he and his men were boldly attacked and completely routed by their savage foes.

De Leon himself was severely wounded by an arrow, and this accident tended not a little to the demoralization of his force. Carrying their leader with them, they fled to their ships, returning with all haste to Cuba.

Here, soon after Ponce De Leon, the deluded, baffled soldier, laid down his arms forever. The wounded body and broken spirit proved too heavy a burden for a life that once had deemed no deed of valor impossible.

And thus ended the first scene in the history of Florida.

The disastrous result of De Leon's expedition had, as might be supposed, a dampening effect on the ardor of those sturdy adventurers whose minds were set on the discovery and conquest of "golden countries," and for a time Florida was relegated to her wonted quiet and obscurity.

Individual merchants, however, made repeated visits to her shores, and on one of their expeditions a certain Diego Miruelo obtained a considerable quantity of gold. We are not told how much nor in what shape, but, however it was, the fact was sufficient to revive all the old delusive stories of Florida's fabulous wealth in gold and silver.

These Spaniards, be it remembered, had before their eyes the solid facts of the enormous wealth in these metals already, "in sight" of the recent conquests in Peru and Mexico, and readily conceived that other lands might prove as rich. Not only so, but by this time they had learned from communications with the Indian inhabitants that Florida, so far from being the island they had supposed, was only a small section of a vast country, and therefore so much the more worth conquering. They accordingly claimed as "Florida," and the property of the Spanish Crown, the whole continent of North America, even including Quebec.

In February, 1528, the second would-be Spanish conquerer of Florida, the Adelantado Narvaez, landed on her beautiful coast and took possession for Spain with solemn ceremonials. Noticing some golden ornaments in the possession of the Indians, and learning that they had obtained them at "Apalachen, a country in the interior," Narvaez, despite of his total ignorance of the land he was to penetrate, of the difficulties and foes he might encounter, took up his line of march for the interior, with only one day's provisions.

The history of that march is pitiful indeed. Unspeakable hardships awaited the adventurers; a third of their number perished by the arrows of the Indians, and more than another third died from exposure and fatigue. Finally, after reaching the coast and not finding their fleet awaiting them, they built rude boats, sewed their shirts together as sails, and made ropes of the fibers of palm trees. They were hunting for the ships they had left to await their return, but it was like "hunting for a needle in a hay-stack," ignorant as they were where to look.

Hither and thither they sailed, without aim or result. Some died of disease, some of starvation, after vainly endeavoring to preserve life by eating the bodies of their dead comrades.

Finally, from five boats holding forty men each, the once proud expedition was reduced to one boat, containing six men and a boy! One of these men was the hapless veteran, Narvaez. Near the mouth of the Perdido River his soldiers went ashore to seek provisions, while he himself, with a sailor and the boy, remained in the boat. During the night a violent wind drove the boat out upon the Gulf; and there, either by drowning or starvation, the life-light of the once brilliant soldier went out. Neither the boat nor its occupants were ever heard of again.

The four soldiers, left thus on shore in the midst of enemies, fared but little better. They finally succeeded, however, after seven years of misery of all kinds, slavery to the Indians included, in reaching Mexico, and were there rescued by their own countrymen. Meantime the ships that should have met them on the Florida coast returned to Spain, having given up their comrades for lost.

Thus ended the second scene in Florida's history.

In the year 1539 came Fernando De Soto to try his fortune in Florida, and landed at Tampa Bay, which he named Espiritu Santo. He had a thousand men at his back, and three hundred and fifty horses. His search was not so much for conquest as for gold.

Marching onward, the Indians opposed his advance at Ocali (now Ocala, Marion County), the cacique, Vitachuco, met and fought the Spanish invaders, but of course was utterly routed by the superior weapons and discipline of his foes.

De Soto marched on through Florida into Alabama, his troops meeting hardships, death by arrows, death by disease, starvation, fatigue; but no gold. Then, while at the Indian village of Mawvilla (presumably Mobile), their leader heard that not far away, at Ochuse, now Pensacola, his ships were waiting his arrival; but so infatuated, so resolute to find gold or die, was this fated soldier, that he carefully kept the news from his many followers, and straightway led them further into the interior. And there, less than four years after his enthusiastic landing at Tampa Bay, with his thousand troopers, Fernando De Soto, one of the most brilliant soldiers of his time, was laid to rest beneath the waters of the Mississippi River, lest, if buried on land, his Indian foes should find the grave, and, freed from their fear of the great warrior, destroy his followers. This sad duty performed, the disheartened remnant of the expedition started on the march for Mexico, three hundred and eleven survivors out of a thousand having marched five hundred miles and wasted four years of their lives for no result.

And so closed the third scene in Florida's history, leaving her just where Juan Ponce De Leon had found her thirty years before, except indeed that her soil was the richer for Spanish blood and Spanish bones.

And now one would have thought that at last the adventurous Spaniards would have been content to abandon Florida to its fate.

But the fact is, that those rugged old soldiers of bygone days were very much as we find the human family at the present time: each one thought himself smarter than his predecessor, and that he would succeed where the latter had failed. Moreover, each was searching for another Peru or Mexico, with their marvels of health.

Consequently, just twenty years after the landing of Fernando De Soto at Tampa Bay, another force, even more splendid in equipments and greater in numbers, landed at the then Bay of Santa Marie, now Pensacola, fifteen hundred men, and a large number of priests to christianize the natives, under the leadership of Don Tristan De Luna.

The expedition was ill-omened from the start, for within a few days after their arrival a hurricane wrecked every one of their ships, together with the greater portion of their provisions. Nothing daunted, however, they built a ship from the remnants of the fleet, and, sending it back to Cuba for more stores, set forth into the interior to look for gold, and convert the natives by conquest and oppression and chains.

Some of the Indians were friendly, but there is such a thing as trespassing on the hospitality of our friends, and "wearing out our welcome."

Wearied and worn, the Spanish troops, coming to a pleasant spot and finding generous hosts, sat them down for a good long period of rest and enjoyment. It was all very well at first, but soon the poor Indians found themselves likely to be eaten out of house and home. They were not rich; in fact, it was rather hard times with them, because (we suppose) the "factory hands had struck for higher wages," the railroad freights had "eaten up the profits on vegetables," and the pigs had rooted up their sweet potatoes, and the savings bank had gone all to pieces.

At all events, whatever the inducing causes might have been (there are some who may not credit the above as such), the friendly Indians felt that they had "too much of a good thing." They could not invite their unwelcome elephants to leave by force of arms, so they got rid of them by a strategem worthy of the most august court in Europe.

One morning an ambassador from the most powerful King of Coosa arrived to interview the great white warrior. He was most gorgeously arrayed in paint and feathers, and accompanied by a large number of attendants. His errand was to convey a most pressing invitation from the King of Coosa (Alabama) to visit him forthwith, bringing all his troops with him.

Nothing loth, the valiant De Luna set forth for Coosa, guided by the ambassador, and after several days of hard traveling he awoke one morning to find the ambassador and his suite vanished, and himself—sold, a fact he speedily realized.

He, however, pushed on toward Coosa ; as well there as any where. Hardships pursued the adventurers; they grew ill-tempered and quarreled and mutinied; they suffered from hunger, lived upon roots, berries, and acorns; and at last, with a few followers only left of all the brave fifteen hundred, Tristan De Luna made his way back to Santa Marie or

Pensacola, and there found ships awaiting him, with orders to return to Mexico forthwith.

And so ended the fourth Spanish attempt to wrest golden conquest from Florida.

There was, in very truth, a golden conquest to be made in that beautiful country, but it was not to be won by force or the sword; rather by peace and the plow.

Possibly, after this, the Spaniards might have let Florida alone as an unlucky country, but there is a good deal of the dog-in-the-manger disposition in human nature.

The French Huguenots, under the direction of the famous Admiral Coligni, conceived the project of a settlement in the New World, and, after several unsuccessful attempts, finally built Fort Caroline, on the St. John's River, at a point, it is supposed, now called St. John's Bluff.

All this stirred up the Spaniards once more, and under a fierce, bigoted leader, Don Pedro Menendez, an expedition was fitted out to drive the accursed heretics out of Florida. This force landed at St. Augustine, as Menendez named the settlement he at once founded as a basis of supplies, and thus, in the year 1565, was started the first settlement in Florida, and the oldest in the United States.

The French commander, Ribault, hearing of his enemies' approach, resolved to become the assailant. Taking five hundred men, and leaving less than one hundred in the fort, he sailed for St. Augustine; but before reaching the mouth of that river a storm drove his ships out to sea, and then drove them on shore, leaving them total wrecks, and himself and his men three hundred miles from their fort.

After nine days of constant marching and hardships they arrived in sight of their longed-for haven, to see the Spanish flag floating over the rampart! It was a cruel blow.

Ribault justly distrusted the assurances of Menendez; but his men were worn out, unable to retreat, unable to fight, and the only thing left to do he did—surrendered to Menendez, on his promise of safety. Then the treacherous Spaniards, taking their prisoners into the fort (from across the river), thirty at a time, tied their hands behind their backs and mercilessly slaughtered them, heaping useless cruelties and indignities upon them, while the military band played its loudest and merriest to drown the cries for mercy.

And so the poor Frenchmen were murdered, each detachment ignorant of the fate of its predecessors. Ribault, pleading for his men, was stricken down, stabbed in the back, and covered with wounds. And then Menendez, not satisfied with his demoniacal work, hung up the mangled bodies to a tree and wrote above them, "Not as Frenchmen, but as heretics."

But it was not long before retribution came: "As ye mete, it shall be meted unto you."

A French warrior, De Gourges, his heart burning to avenge his countrymen, equipped an expedition at his own expense, sailed from France, reached Florida, and was there joined by a large body of the natives, who had learned to love the more gentle Frenchmen as much as they hated the Spaniards.

De Gourges was fortunate in every movement. He surprised and captured the Spanish forts on the St. John's, and hung their garrisons on the very same trees from which the mangled remains of his unfortunate countrymen had been suspended, writing above them, "Not as Spaniards, but as traitors, robbers, and murderers."

Menendez, the arch-murderer, escaped, because he was in Spain at the time of De Gourges' vengeance.

From this time forth the Spaniards held to their settlement at St. Augustine, fighting off and on all the time with the English, who now began to settle along the Carolina and Georgia shores, which Spain claimed as also "Florida."

In 1696 the Spaniards began to colonize the western coast of Florida, and built a fort at Pensacola, besides establishing missions at various points.

Finally, in 1763, by a treaty, Spain ceded Florida to England in exchange for Havana, which heretofore had belonged to the British Empire. The result of the Spanish claim to Florida, held since 1512, being two small military settlements.

The new English possessors at once proceeded to make a very different use of their prize. General James Grant was appointed Colonial Governor, immigration was invited, land grants made to officers and soldiers upon condition of settlement, books descriptive of Florida were issued and distributed, good roads built (some still remaining), agriculture was fostered, the culture of indigo encouraged.

During the Revolution no less than seven thousand tories and loyalists found refuge in Florida, which remained under English supremacy.

In 1780 Governor Tonyn called together the first General Assembly of Florida.

And now the beautiful State at last was prosperous. Indigo culture was a splendid success; the turpentine product was very valuable. Florida's fame as a manifold agricultural country was slowly spreading, and immigration was rapidly on the increase. But nature in those days was not done playing football with genial Florida.

England had lost all the rest of her American possessions south of Canada, so she did not care now to keep Florida, consequently she tossed her over into the lap of Spain once more. The English settlers, all their cherished labors come to naught, being allowed eighteen months to rise up and go back home to the "old countree."

So once more poor Florida was put to bed and to sleep in the Spanish cradle, dreaming realistic dreams of border warfare, fights with Indians, broils among adventurers, and runaway convicts. Once, in 1812, a party of Georgians resolved to annex Florida, and govern it their own way, and they marched down to St. Augustine to take it. But on complaint of the Spaniards, the young United States Government sat down on the Georgians, and sent them home in disgrace, like naughty boys.

The United States already owned that portion of Florida lying west of the Perdido River. Spain had ceded it to France, and the latter, as a part of Louisiana, sold it to the American Government in 1803. Having this much, the Georgians, like

Oliver Twist, wanted "more, more," hence their action in the premises.

Spain, like England, at length concluded that Florida was an elephant it would be well to get rid of, as costing more than it earned; so, in 1821, it was formally handed over to the United States, and in 1822 East and West Florida were consolidated into the Territory of Florida, under an organized government, and soon after the site of the former Indian settlement of Tallahassee was selected as the capital.

And now, as the rich agricultural possibilities of the country and its wonderful climate began to be understood at last, and more and more immigration crossed the borders, the Indians became an important factor in the case.

They occupied some of the best portions of the State, and naturally resisted the advance of the whites, whom they waylaid, murdered, and plundered continuously. In one Indian village alone, when General Jackson, in 1818, captured it, were found three hundred fresh scalps of men, women, and children.

The burning of plantations, the carrying off of stock, the murder of their owners were every-day occurrences; and at last it became imperative to remove the Indians from the country, or abandon the fairest of all the United States to their sole use and benefit. Until this was done, and, as every one knows it cost seven years of war and massacre to do it, it is no wonder that the settlement of Florida was slow.

It was not until 1842 that the settlers felt safe and could draw a long breath of relief, freed forever from their enemies. But still the development of the country was necessarily slow. It lay outside the usual line of travel, and transportation facilities were few and far between. But these points were rapidly improving, and Florida was once more striding forward when the unhappy civil war broke out, and again her onward progress was checked. But not for long.

After three hundred and seventy years of playing football to Spain, France, England, Indians, Florida is now herself again, and is blossoming out into one of the most noble, most beautiful flowers in the giant bouquet held by Uncle Sam—the United States.

In growth, in improvements, in developments, in possibilities, Florida stands among the first and foremost. The infant has awakened from her long sleep, a very giant of wonders, and will yet be known as one of the wealthiest among her many powerful sisters, as she will ever be the fairest.

CHAPTER III. CLIMATE.

Proved by Comparison and Statistics to be the Finest in the World. Scientifically "Moderately Dry:" Variation of Temperature Just Sufficient for Health and Comfort.

Going back to its Greek derivation, we find that the word *climata* means literally, "the slope of the earth from the equator toward the pole." In its modern meaning it signifies the condition of a place in relation to the various phenomena of the atmosphere, as temperature, moisture, and other properties of the same nature, which may either directly or indirectly affect animal life and more notably that of man.

Florida has many, very many attractions, not fanciful nor ephemeral, but real, solid, lasting, and amid them all the brightest jewel in her crown of brilliant gems is her climate. The "Italy of America" is a title frequently applied to our fair State, but those who know Italy, and also know Florida, assert that the inference is very far from flattering to the latter. While Italy and Southern France enjoy a winter climate far milder than that of the rest of Europe, still it is incomparably inferior to that of Florida. And as to their spring time, here is what an eminent physician, who has made the subject one of special study, says of that, in concluding a winter contrast by no means to the advantage of our trans-atlantic neighbors: "I will say nothing of their spring, for no one who has ever tried it, or who has inquired of any reliable authority about it, would trust himself there after the first of March. Even in the most sheltered localities, as at Cannes and Mentone, a change on one of the most pleasant days from the sunny to the shady side of the street often produces a shiver, and renders necessary for an invalid an extra covering. At sunset one must rush home and in-doors for his life; nor does any prudent man dare to ride out in the afternoon without the wraps he would require in his northern home. Such is the case even in Algiers, which is a superior climate to that of the north shore of the Mediterranean."

In Nice, that much-vaunted resort for those Europeans who seek a mild climate, the same physician tells us that, "In winter there is a difference of 12° to 24° between the temperature of places exposed to the south and the north, between those in the shade and in the sun," and traveling from Nice to Italy we find in the latter a significant saying that, "Only dogs and strangers go on the shady side."

And here, in contrast, let us notice one more brief quotation, this also from the pen of a well-known physician:

"In Florida during most of the warm and pleasant days one may not only be out at sunset on land, but with equal comfort on the water. I have frequently called the attention of persons to this contrast with the European climates, when we were returning from a row at sunset in mid-winter, some of us in our shirt-sleeves. Had there been any considerable dampness in the air this would not have been prudent or comfortable."

From the earliest visitors, and from the numerous adventurers who once landed on Florida's shore, came enthusiastic reports of her climate, and from that time to this the cry has been taken up and echoed and re-echoed all over the world, a paraphrase of the Mussulman's watch-word, "Florida! Florida! there is but one Florida!"

Why, would you ask?

In the first place, our State is a peninsula almost in its entirety, and from the earliest days of civilization peninsulas have always been preferred as favorite residences, and resorted to in the winter by those living in the cold, inland countries, because their climates are always milder, and have a peculiarity all their own, in the fact that the heat rising from the vast bodies of water lying on either side, tempers and modifies every cold current of air that passes over their surface. This during the winter season. In the summer time the same force is at work; the cooler waters absorb a portion of the heat contained in the warm air sweeping across their bosom and store it up for their genial winter service to their landward neighbor.

For these reasons the climate of a peninsula varies greatly from that of inland countries, even in the same section and same latitude.

We have already noted the fact that Florida now confessedly holds the front rank before all other peninsulas or seaside countries. There are very good reasons for this.

Not one of them all has the same latitude, the same slope to the winter sun, the same topography, and the same features.

The Apennine Mountains, with their lofty snow-capped summits, chill the air that circulates over the Mediterranean and Atlantic seas. In Mexico, in Southern California, in Spain, in France, every where, save in our bonnie Florida, we find mountain ranges towering aloft, their white peaks covered with snow, their hollows with ice, cooling off the air faster than the sun can warm it, obstructing the pressure of the winds in summer and in winter, keeping the kindly breezes in check during the one season, and sending down cold, cutting winds during the other.

Now, Florida has nothing like this, so far as such experiences go. Her surface is comparatively level, having only a gentle rise between the ocean on one side and the gulf on the other, so that the breezes, warmed by her outlying waters in the winter season and cooled by them during the summer, are ever free to play back and forth over her beautiful bosom. And when we say that her surface is comparatively level, we do not mean to be understood that it is actually and entirely flat, though we know this is the generally received opinion, and quite on a par with some of the other ideas that are wafted across land and sea concerning our sunny Florida. "Low and damp, and generally malarial," those are the terms a supposed-to-be-reliable professor applied to her not very long ago in the columns of a magazine that should have more carefully guarded its pages against the crime of "bearing false witness against its neighbors." We shall have more to say about that charge by and by, for we intend to look thoroughly into this question of Florida's climate, since upon this point hinges the whole subject of her suitability as a home—a healthy, happy home worthy of the name.

But just now we have to do with her surface, which is by no means uniformly level; in fact, one of its greatest and oddest features is its picturesque lack of uniformity of any kind, for it is all one strange mixture of rock and sand, hill and flat woods, pine land, and hammock land, rivers and lakes, interior and coast line, fruits of the tropics, the semi-tropics, and the temperate zones; trees of the equatorial regions, and of the colder climes, and vegetables of the most tender as well as the most hardy kinds.

Florida is more than seven times as large as Massachusetts. It is larger than the States of New Hampshire, Vermont, Massachusetts, New Jersey, Maryland, Delaware, and Rhode Island combined. Florida is one fourth larger than the great Empire State of New York, and fifty per cent greater than the State of Ohio with its population of three millions. Stepping across the Atlantic, we find it covering considerably more territory than Greece, Belgium, and Switzerland, and it goes squarely over the whole of England by a surplus of nine thousand square miles.

Florida is one of the largest States in the Union; the very largest east of the Mississippi River. It embraces 37,913,600 acres of good, solid land, and 4,440 square miles of water, and has over 1,200 miles of coast line. So you see there is plenty of room for variety of all kinds, especially so when we note the fact that her length from north to south (that is, from the southern point of the peninsula to the Georgia line) is 380 miles, and her breadth in what is called the mainland portion, is 345 miles from the Atlantic Ocean to the Rio Perdido. The average breadth of the peninsula is less than one hundred miles, and that of the strip between the Gulf of Mexico and the Georgia and Alabama Hues is less than forty miles, consequently there is no portion of the State so far removed from the vicinity of the sea air as not to feel its modifying influences.

South Florida—and by this term we mean those counties that have an undisputed claim to the title which is often erroneously bestowed on others that should more properly be termed the "Central Belt." South Florida, represented by the counties of Dade, Monroe, Brevard, Manatee, Lee, Hillsboro, Hernando, Osceola, Citra, and Polk are noted for their generally "level" surface, prairies, and flat woods, with the exception of Polk and Citra, which are the proud possessors of numerous beautiful, clear water lakes, formed by a rather undulating country—"high sand hills," as they are termed, only they are not really "high" at all, that is, to a resident of a true hill country; but locally the name is correct, although non-residents are apt to be misled by its application. High hammock, low hammock, high sand hills, flat woods, all these are localisms well understood by those acquainted with the State. It is not height above the sea that is indicated, but location with regard to natural drainage.

Down through the center of Florida runs a decided ridge or backbone; not mountainous, but rising gently from the sea-coast on either side until the middle, running north and south, is reached, and here at some points the "divide" is so sharp that the little streams taking their rise in one of the small lakes will flow to the east on one side and toward the west on the other.

A phenomenon similar to this was witnessed by the writer a few years ago on the summit of the high ridge dividing the Isthmus of Panama. There is a space three or four feet long where the water in the railroad drain lies perfectly still, while at each end it flows rapidly in opposite directions, one toward the Atlantic, the other toward the Pacific Ocean.

Crossing Florida's peninsula from east to west, or vice versa, is like ascending gradually a series of terraces, the one blending into the other, until a gently undulating plateau is reached at the highest point, continuing for a distance varying from six to twenty or more miles across, and then commencing another terraced descent on the other side.

Probably the greatest elevation in Polk Count, which is the highest in South Florida, is not over but rather under two hundred and thirty-five feet above the sea.

Passing northward from South Florida we find the face of the country gradually changing; instead of the rolling lands being the exception they become the rule; and not only so, but the undulations are more decided, real, genuine "hills" being frequently found, for here, in the vicinity of the backbone of the State, is its greatest elevation, about three hundred feet above the sea.

While the general opinion prevails that "Florida is low," very few are aware of the fact that her highest elevation is also that of all the States on the Atlantic coast, their general elevation, with some local exceptions, being actually less than three hundred feet.

Florida's average level above the sea, according to Toner's Dictionary of Elevations is sixty feet, while that of Louisiana is seventy-five feet; no very great difference, you see, yet no one looks askance at Louisana on that account, even though it necessitates the construction and maintenance at an immense expense of a levee to keep the land from being inundated at times by the "Father of Waters," an effort, as we all know, not always successful either.

But enough for the present of the surface of Florida. We have seen sufficient to prove that, while she has no mountain ridge to cool the air with snow and ice and sudden blasts of wind, yet neither can she be justly described, as she has so often been by her enemies, as "one vast expanse of swamps and flat woods."

"Low," as regards elevation above the sea, in comparison with many countries, Florida undoubtedly is; but compare her with some others and her lowest lands become high lands.

Look across the ocean, for instance, at the Old World. The valley of Jordan is no less than one thousand feet below the level of the Mediterranean Sea. The countries lying along the Caspian Sea are lower than its surface; and why is it that a large portion of Holland has to be defended by a system of dykes against the inroads of the waters? Not, surely, because her lands lie higher than the waves that beat against her shores. Yet these countries we have named are healthy and fertile, and thickly populated, and no one thinks of casting their lowly station in their teeth.

"Chiefly low, and generally damp and malarial," those are the words we quoted a while ago as applied to Florida by a certain professor who had not even done her the justice of investigating the truth or crossing her borders. We have effectually disposed of the first charge, now let us attack the second, "generally damp."

We suppose he meant "humid," as that term applies to the atmosphere or climate, while "damp" indicates "moisture" or "slightly wet," and if this quality refers to the soil, accompanied by warmth and fertility, it is very far from being objectionable to any farmer or fruit-grower.

Taking humidity, then, to be the word that should have been employed as applied to the degree of vapor held in the atmosphere and not perceptible to the human senses, let us see how it stands.

Well, in the first place, humidity is by no means unhealthy when accompanied by sunshine and fresh air, and if these are to be had any where on earth it is in bonnie Florida.

In the second place we will compare the degree of moisture held in the Florida atmosphere with that of some other places, and note how she bears the comparison of scientific and authorized facts and figures.

Here are some items from the Signal Service reports, as cases in point:

The mean humidity for Jacksonville, Punta Rassa, and Key West for the five coldest months of the year is 72.7; for the same months in the three principal cities of Minnesota the mean was 74.3; while, crossing to Southern France, we find the humidity for the same period to be 2.4 at Cannes and Mentone. That shows a difference in favor of Florida of 1.6 against Minnesota, and an advantage of only 0.3 in favor of the French cities, and the difference in both these readings would have been still more upon Florida's side had the observations been taken in the interior of the State at a higher altitude instead of, as they were, on her lowest grounds and on the bank of the St. John's River and the Gulf of Mexico. As a matter of fact the relative humidity of Florida year by year is less than that of five out of eight of the most celebrated European health resorts.

The beautiful *Tillandsia usneoides*, or Spanish moss, which adds so much to the beauty and grandeur of our Southern forests, and is one of the most admired among the many novelties that attract the attention of a newcomer, is often quoted as a proof of the excessive moisture in Florida's atmosphere. Now it is quite true that in those spots where this graceful drapery is found in the greatest abundance there is a very moist local atmosphere; note that word, local, for in that lies the explanation of the seeming contradiction. Some people have an idea that the moss itself creates the dampness while in truth it finds already there the moisture it requires for its daily food, and by living upon it and taking it up out of the air actually lessens the amount and so performs valuable sanitary service. Its presence in large quantities—which is always in low hammock lands—indicates the existence of superabundant moisture, but has the opposite effect to increasing it; and yet it is frequently found scattered about here and there, forming a most luxuriant drapery on isolated trees, growing on high and dry lands, but here its presence is no indication of dampness. The sunshine pours down on it all day long, and water may not be any where near it, but it thrives, nevertheless, on the same principle that one man can live upon less than two.

The great scientist, Vivenot, has carefully classified the degrees of relative humidity as follows: "It being understood that here as elsewhere, the basis of all such figures is the air saturated so that it can hold no more moisture in invisible suspension. This point is marked as one hundred per cent; then, if the air of a certain place is only half saturated it is marked as fifty per cent; one quarter saturated as twenty -five per cent."

Here then is Vivenot's classification: "Moderately dry, 56 to 70; moderately moist, 71 to 85; excessively moist, 86 to 100."

We have already seen that the humidity of certain points in Florida during the five coldest months is 72.7, which just brings it under the heading of "moderately moist."

But take the whole State and the whole year, and then the figures change to 69.6, and this at once places Florida's climate where it belongs, under the classification of "moderately dry."

She has reason to be thankful that it is not any drier than it is, for if her atmosphere contained less moisture her greatest charm would be gone. Why, do you ask?

Simply because a certain amount of moisture is absolutely necessary to prevent great and sudden ranges of temperature, a thing which is quite as deleterious to health as an excess of humidity.

Who that has sat in a dentist's chair to have a tooth filled does not recall with a shudder the intense aching caused by the little bellows which dries the cavity to be filled? It must be very dry, and it is this absence of moisture, producing an intense cold by rapid evaporation, which causes the excess of pain.

We see the same principle at work in the air. For instance, if Florida did not possess a certain amount of moisture and a consequent deposit of a certain amount of dew, then, instead of a night and day variation of 13° or 14° (often less) in temperature, there would probably be a difference of 30° or 40°.

In the desert of Sahara, where the dryness is absolute and radiation at night entirely unrestrained, the temperature changes from an almost unendurable heat during the day— 100° or over in the shade—to no less than 32°, the freezing point, at night.

In Upper Egypt the range is 40°, and out on our own western prairies there is not infrequently a difference of 60°, so that one is scorched by day and frozen at night.

Let us be thankful then that Florida has just enough moisture to temper the heat during the day by condensation, and during the night by retarding radiation sufficiently to keep the cold in check. Her climate is just as it ought to be to secure health and warmth.

A few practical, every-day illustrations of the proof of our statements, and we close our study of Florida's climate so far as humidity goes.

One of the scientific tests of a "moderately dry" climate is the dessication of meats and their slow decomposition. Now, it is a fact that causes much surprise to newcomers, that beef when hung up in a current of air will keep fresh much longer than in the same or even lower temperature in the more northern States; and venison, which has naturally less moisture than beef, wall harden and dry on the surface and continue good much longer than beef.

Another test is, "matches will take fire with certainty, even in unheated rooms." Here, also, the writer has noted a marked difference between, for instance, Maryland, New Jersey, New York, or Pennsylvania, and Florida, and decidedly in favor of the latter. It is very seldom indeed that a match is found to have absorbed enough moisture to crumble or miss fire.

Unless during the prevalence of several days' rain (an infrequent occurrence) ladies find that their hair will remain in crimps or curls for days together; this, as is well known, is an unfailing proof of dry air.

If pianos are kept closed on rainy days when not in use, and occasionally thrown wide open—that is, the entire lid raised—at other times, little if any trouble is found in keeping them in tune, especially in the interior of the State, which is very far from being the case in very moist countries.

During the rainy season, from June to August inclusive, it is difficult to keep table salt dry; but no more so than in the majority of the States under similar circumstances, and the writer has frequently seen in Philadelphia and New Jersey salt-cellars actually full of liquid salt, but never more than very moist in Florida.

Clothing that has been wet and "salted" with perspiration, even though dry when taken off at night, will often be found quite damp in the morning, the salt having absorbed moisture during the night. But clothing not so salted, even though left by an open window, will be perfectly dry. Of how many of our States can this be said during a long "rainy spell"?

Even during the rainy season, when showers fall more or less copiously every day (the sun shining in the interval), the air is not saturated. It never comes under Vivenot's classification of "excessively moist," a fact that is proven by the continued, though diminished evaporation of water, for, as every one knows, this would be an impossibility if the atmosphere already contained as much moisture as it could hold in suspension.

In the lower St. John's fogs are quite frequent and heavy, but in most other localities they seldom occur, and then are light and quickly vanish as the sun rises higher.

And now we hope that the facts we have given so far will refute effectually the erroneous idea that generally prevails concerning "Florida's moist climate."

The charge of unhealthfulness or "malaria" remains, and this too we shall presently lay in its grave, along with sundry other untruths and misconceptions, and cover them away out of sight forever, from the sight of those who peruse these pages.

CHAPTER IV. HEALTH.

The First Consideration. Statistics Prove Florida to be the Healthiest State in the Union. Safe to Settle at all Times of the Year. Purity of the Air. Points in Locating: Water, Wells, and Filters

One of the very first questions that confronts the intending settler is that of health, and so it should be, paramount to all others; for what is wealth, or life itself, without the capacity for enjoying them? And we all know from bitter experience, either in our own persons or in that of those dear to us, that there can be no pleasure, whether in riches or in life, if they are accompanied by sickness and pain.

So in selecting a home the question of its healthfulness should be the most important of all. The first and foremost to be considered, even at the possible cost of sacrifice in some minor points; we say minor advisedly, because all other points are minor to this, and the wise man will subordinate them to it first and last.

It is a well-known, but none the less to be lamented, phase of human nature, that the moment a country or individual becomes prominent among the rest, by reason of superior merit or advantage, that moment hosts of enemies, bitter and unscrupulous, arise and assail them with a venom born of that "envy, hatred, malice, and all uncharitableness," from whose evil dominion we pray for deliverance.

For years upon years our sunny Florida lay perdue, as it were, too humble and insignificant to attract the notice of the busy, struggling thousands scattered all over the rest of the world. Why this was so is easily understood by any one who pauses to look back upon her history, as we have seen. Only within a comparatively few years has general attention been bestowed upon this hidden gem of the Union.

The cry was, "Go West, young man!" and many a young man obeyed; and some remained rejoicing, and some departed in a different frame of mind. But enough went, and enough continued to follow in their footsteps to enrich the land speculators. And it was like the falling of a bomb-shell into their midst when Florida, bonnie Florida, with her sunny smile and warmth of welcome, stepped forward into the light, offering far more than all the much-vaunted West could bestow, even after years of toil and exposure to the inclement storms of winter and the terrible gales of summer.

And then straightway arose a host of foes, striking blindly at the formidable rival looming up so suddenly in their pathway. She endangered all their cherished plans, and so she must be struck down by slander, falsehood, misrepresentations, malice, by any and every weapon, so that only their end was attained. But it never was, for Florida was too powerful in her charms, and truth, like murder, "will out," providing that one searches for it. Yet still, as we have seen, a great many are satisfied to accept as truth every chance statement they may happen to see or hear, whether for or against, without reaching down below the surface, much less seeking "at the bottom of the well" for it.

This is the reason why such charges as we have quoted in these pages gain headway. They are carelessly read, and repeated from one to the other, and no one stops to ask, "How much is true? how much is false?"

We have proven by facts and figures that Florida is not "low," in the usual acceptation of the term, and that her climate is not "damp," and now let us put to rout that other charge, that she is "generally malarial."

We have dealt it a heavy blow already, for every one knows that a "moderately dry "climate, and undulating lands, with distinct ridges here and there, such as we have shown Florida to possess, and malaria are antagonistic, and that therefore the reign of the latter must be local, and on a small scale. We do not for one moment intend to assert, or wish it to be believed, that there is no malaria in Florida. She is "of the earth, earthy;"

not by any means a paradise, not without drawbacks nor imperfections; but only better, balancing all things pro and con, than any other land we know of.

Yes, Florida has malaria. Can you name a country or a State that has it not in some localities? Can you point to districts low, marshy, where vegetation is alternately covered by water and exposed to the air and sun, and say that such districts are healthy and fit for human habitations; that malaria, in all its many phases, finds no foothold there?

If a man chooses to locate his home in such spots as these, either in Florida or any other land, when all around him are high, dry, healthy lands, then he really deserves to lose his health and his life; but we pity his family, and counsel them to rise up in rebellion while yet they may.

We know a man here in Florida, whose home was in the pine woods, as healthy a location as could be found any where, and his family grew and flourished apace. But there came a day when work was offered a few miles away, and he preferred taking his family to leaving them at home. He rented a house that had been deserted by its owner because of the malaria lurking around it. It was built in a low, wet place, surrounded by swamp and low hammock; but it was lower in rent, as well as position, than any other offering. So the family dwelt in this "Black Hole" while the husband and father went off to his work on a high pine ridge a mile or two away, so that the malaria affected himself but little. What was the result? The wife and children were stricken down with fever, one of the latter died, and almost another. Then they went back to their healthy home with shattered health, one and all, and soon the poor wife followed her child, thankful to be at rest, yet sorrowful too for those who remained behind. And all this did not come of ignorance of the probable results either, but was just a deliberate "tempting of Providence" to save a few dollars.

But when the accounts were footed up, to the two lives lost were added also many dollars lost as well. There is a moral to this story, and "He who runs may read," and if he is wise, "He who reads will run" from low places every where.

Florida is like every other country on the face of the earth; there are spots totally unsuited to human habitation, others moderately good, others desirable, and still others yet more desirable.

And yet during the dry winter months even the most malarial of these localities become almost healthy, because the excess of moisture and the poisonous gases from decaying vegetation are taken up far above the earth by the absorbent power of the atmosphere and wafted far away by the constant breezes. But during the warm, rainy months the decay is too rapid and the moisture too great to permit this beneficial factor to do its work so effectually, although even then it is still powerful enough as a general rule to rob the fever fiend of much of its deadly strength.

What says the report of the United States Army Surgeon-General: "The statistics of this bureau show that the diseases which result from malaria are of a much milder type in Florida than in any other State in the Union, and the number of deaths there to the number of cases of remittent fever has been much less than among the troops serving in other portions of the United States."

Let us glance for a moment at the ratio of deaths from remittent fever in the various divisions of the United States, and note how they stand the test of official statistics.

In the Middle States there is one death to thirty-six cases, in the Northern States one to fifty-two, and in the Southern one death to fifty-four cases, the Western States not being given.

So much for these three great divisions. The South has the best of it, you see, although such is not the general impression.

And now here are three representative States: In Texas the death-rate in remittent fever is one to seventy-eight cases, in California one to one hundred and twenty-two, and in Florida only one to two hundred and eighty-seven.

Then taking all diseases together: In New York State the ratio is one death out of every two hundred and fifty of the population, while in Florida it is only one in fourteen hundred. What a contrast! Yet no one calls New York an unhealthy State, neither "low, and generally damp and malarial." Why not? If Florida is, then New York must be nearly six hundred per cent worse, according to the official statistics, and certainly ought to be forever quarantined and suppressed.

It is the usual impression among those not "to the manor born" that one or two years of that half-sickness, which is harder to bear than a severe illness, is the least that one must expect in becoming acclimated to the Southern States.

Undoubtedly it is true in some localities, but we do not believe it is generally so. It is human justice, because one member sins to call the whole family sinners.

At all events we know of our own experience that it is not so of Florida. Here it is perfectly safe to come at all times of the year. One portion of the writer's family arrived at their new Florida home, in the midst of the pines, in April, and the remainder in June, yet all from that day to this—nearly eleven years—have enjoyed better health than they could boast of in their old home. Two who suffered for years with severe headaches, lasting for days together, have not had one such attack since breathing the balmy air of Florida. Another, for whom the fiat seemed to have gone forth—and indeed had done so—bade farewell to hemorrhages and coughs after the first year of the new home life, and now is able to get through with no inconsiderable amount of literary work. We feel, therefore, that we have good reason to love bonnie Florida's sunny face, and defend her by telling the truth concerning her.

With the same amount of prudence, or even less than is or ought to be practiced at the North, neither malarial fever, nor the less dreaded but decidedly miserable "chills and fever," need be feared at all. And it soon comes to be noticed by the new settler, that in Florida one's feet may get wet time and again with impunity, even from a drenching in the rain, if one keeps in motion so as not to become chilled before dry clothes can be obtained, and that no ill effects are apt to follow.

It is a matter of daily and increasing wonder to those new to the State to note how much more exposure of this kind they can endure without injury than they had ever before deemed possible in their old homes, be they where they might.

What few fevers there are, as we have seen, are usually of a mild type and easily controlled.

Diphtheria and scarlet fever are almost unknown, and cases of pneumonia are rare and seldom fatal.

Those who suffer from rheumatism and kidney diseases are always relieved, and not infrequently cured entirely by a continuous residence in this healthful piney woods.

As to the benefit accruing to those with lung trouble, consumption, asthma, catarrh, we need not speak, for in this Florida's reputation is world-wide.

Children who are racked and nervous, and stand at death's door, from the attacks of measles, scarlatina, or whooping-cough, almost invariably recover rapidly if they are brought to Florida, and that too with little if any medical treatment.

In the adult nervous dyspepsia, which is becoming more common every year, finds immediate relief and generally cure in the quiet, peaceful, out-of-door life of Florida.

There is one widespread disease, for it really amounts to that, for which, as Dr. Lente tells us, "Florida affords as healing a balm as for the pulmonary variety" of consumption. Dr. Lente calls it "cerebral consumption," but fifty years ago it was described thus by James Johnson, and no one can fail to recognize the picture: "There is a condition of body, intermediate between sickness and health, but much nearer the former than the latter, to which I am unable to give a satisfactory name. It is daily and hourly felt by tens of thousands, but I do not know that it has ever been described. It is not curable by physic, though I apprehend it makes much work for the doctors, ultimately, if not for the undertakers. It is the wear and tear of the living machine, mental and corporal, which results from overstrenuous labor and exertion of the intellectual faculties rather than of the corporal powers, conducted in anxiety of mind and bad air."

For such as these, victims of nervous prostration, Florida does indeed offer a healing balm and a bower of rest and quiet.

Is it not with good reason that we claim for our sunny Florida that none need fear to trust their lives in her hands, when both facts and figures—the former widely known, the latter official—proclaim that "Florida leads the list of healthy States"? Is not the false charge of "generally malarial" dead and buried?

We have not yet referred to the singular purity of the Florida air, a constituent of climate which has not until recently been regarded worthy the attention it certainly merits.

The usual idea of "pure air" is simply air that is free from disagreeable odors; but this is so far from being correct, that the gases from which these odors emanate are the least serious of the impurities of the atmosphere, and very seldom exist in sufficient quantities to do any harm to human beings.

Carbonic-acid gas, which is popularly supposed to be the most dangerous of all, is rarely found in injurious quantities even in a crowded room, and is not in itself poisonous.

What makes the difference between "country air" and "city air"? Not, as is generally believed, the presence of poisonous gases to an injurious extent in the latter, as exhaled from the multitude of chimneys, workshops, and animal bodies, living and dead.

The celebrated Angus Smith tells us that the amount of gases present in the air of a city and in that of the pure and unadulterated country are very nearly the same. To prove his assertion he makes a calculated statement of the actual amount, which overturns one's previous ideas as to the relative purity of city and country air.

For instance. Lake Geneva, in 100 volumes of air, has 0.439 parts of gas, while in the city of London the analysis shows 0.420 in the same amount of air.

Who has not read with a thrill of horror the sad story of the poisonous air of the "Black Hole" of Calcutta, where two hundred and sixty out of three hundred prisoners died like dogs "because they were compelled to inhale air poisoned by carbonic-acid gas and destitute of oxygen"? But the cause thus given for this wholesale slaughter is another of those world-wide mistakes that modern science is revealing day by day. It has been proven of late that these unfortunate men, shut up like rats in a trap, without light or ventilation, died not from too much carbonic-acid gas or too little oxygen, but from the presence of organic matter in the air, diseased germs, too minute to be visible, yet all powerful to sow the seeds of malaria broadcast, and contaminate all with which they came in contact.

That country air is purer than city air is universally conceded, but, as we have just observed, it is not the absence of gases to a greater degree in the former that gives it the advantage. No, not in the gaseous, but in the solid portions of the atmosphere do we find the mischief-maker enthroned.

"It has been established beyond all doubt," says Shroeder, "that these organic substances, be they the gaseous products of putrefactive processes in the animal or vegetable kingdom, floating in the atmosphere, do reach the lungs in the currents of air inspired, and are there capable of doing great mischief."

So we see that it is these germs, or "seeds of disease," as they have been appropriately termed, that cause the trouble and contaminate the air, and these are found, as would seem most natural, in much greater quantities in the atmosphere of the cities than in that of the country. In the one thousands of agencies are at work to produce and encourage their presence; in the other the leaves of the trees, the grass, the growing crops, the sparkling river or lakes, all serve to keep the air pure and sweet. But of course these "seeds of disease" do exist in some localities, even in the open country, for they are the direct cause of malarial affections which, be it understood, do not always manifest themselves simply as fevers, but assume many and varied forms, attacking always the weakest parts of the individual.

Wherever vegetation is undergoing the process of decay and fermentation, there look out for the breeding places of these fatal germs. It does not matter whether the locality be north or south, at the equator or the north pole, given certain conditions such as the above, and the same result will follow.

There are some places in Canada, and some in New York, and some in Pennsylvania, some in California, in Texas, in Georgia, in Florida, where we would not build our home for all the wealth of the United States, because we could not live to enjoy them, neither we nor any one else. But these places are self-evident; no one is compelled to live there, or even to try to; there is room enough for all in healthy localities.

Where, however, this presence is known or suspected, a thin cotton screen in the windows and doors—cheese-cloth for example—will prove a great safeguard, as it has been proven by frequent tests that the disease germs can not pass through cotton; the fine loose films catch and hold it.

This is a fact well worth remembering by those who have unhappily "cast their lines" near low, swampy ground, where these germs "most do congregate."

Nor is this cotton screen the only barrier that may be interposed between these fatal atoms and their intended victims. A thick belt of forest trees or of sunflowers, or where the climate is mild enough, the eucalyptus tree, all these serve as efficient body-guards and hold the enemy in check. This is especially true of the latter tree, which acts is a double manner; first, by evaporating moisture from the soil, for there is no other that is such a "hard-drinker" as the eucalyptus tree, and consumes such large quantities of water; and, second, the peculiar aroma which exhales from its leaves seems to possess the qualities of an antiseptic, and destroys all the seeds of disease that come within its influence.

There is a district in Persia, reaching for miles back from the banks of a river, a district large and exceedingly fertile. Until twelve years ago it was esteemed an accursed spot, and was shunned as a pest-house, because no one could live—all died—who sought to dwell there. But now it is all changed as by magic. The king ordered eucalyptus trees to be planted thickly along the river banks, and in groups here and there all over the district, and nobly they did the work they were set to do. They grew rapidly, as they have a way of doing, and drained the excess of moisture, while the aroma from their leaves killed the disease germs floating in the air. The whole district is thickly populated now, and no part of Persia is more healthy than this.

So this shows, one instance among many, what the eucalyptus can do for humanity. Better than a drug store, a doctor, or a watch-dog is a grove of these trees around a house where the malaria fiend lurks near by.

Until the discovery of these germs in the air it was a matter of increasing perplexity as to why some diseases should rage with violence in certain localities, and in others adjoining be almost unknown; often, too, being most violent, as in diphtheria or scarlet fever or cholera, in the homes of the wealthier classes where one would least expect to find them. But when the existence of the disease germs and the cause of their presence in greater or less quantities became known the mystery was solved. In the better class homes, where water-pipes, drains, and sinks were improperly made or allowed to become uncleanly, the malaria fiend grew and flourished, and performed its deadly work unsuspected, while in the humbler homes these breeding places were missing.

It was also found that experiments on the air from different places, but all of them "country air," gave different results. Sometimes the same methods used for the destruction of the germs failed to have that effect. This was the case with the air of Florida, taken from various localities away from the low or swampy lands or along the low margins of lakes or rivers. Why? Because the germs were not there to be killed; because the air was absolutely pure, in its deepest and widest sense.

In the low hammocks or wherever decaying vegetation lay on the surface of the ground, there, as must be expected, the malaria fiend was discovered, "seeking whom he might devour," stronger in summer than in winter, but seldom, as we have seen, as powerful here for evil as in other similar localities, because of the lack of excess of moisture to feed upon.

But in the undulating lands, or even in the flat woods, where the soil is sandy and the tall pine tree towers aloft, as it does on more than three fourths of the land surface of the State, where the lakes have clear, sandy shores, there the malaria fiend meets his death the moment he seeks to enter the charmed circle.

One of the most important factors both in producing and in preserving the remarkable purity of the Florida atmosphere is her much-abused "sandy soil," which has so often been held triumphantly aloft by her enemies, to be pointed at in ridicule, as an evidence of the falsity of her claims to luxurious vegetable production.

For the character of the soil has a very great influence on the health or otherwise of those who dwell upon it, and on the purity of the air that surrounds them. A clay soil that retains too much moisture, or one that will not retain it at all, are equally injurious and detrimental to health.

In his "Manual of Practical Hygiene," Parkes, the celebrated scientist, uses these words: "Sand absorbs very little, clay ten or twenty times more, and humus, or common surface soil, more than forty or fifty times as much as sand."

Now, when we consider that it is the excess of moisture lying on or near the surface that causes vegetable decay, and that the latter is the most powerful agent in breeding the malaria germ, we see at once why it is that the latter holds high carnival wherever soils retentive of moisture are found. And, considering further that a certain amount of moisture is absolutely necessary to preserve health and a moderate equality of climate, we perceive also why soils impervious to moisture are inimical to human life.

Well may Parkes remark that "the sands are therefore the healthiest soils in this respect."

It is evident then that a permeable soil is the most healthful soil, and nowhere in the world is this quality more prominent than on the sandy surface of Florida, which, however, be it noted in passing, is not only and all sand pure and simple, but disintegrated rock, finely comminuted shell, coral, lime, and other productive ingredients.

Dust is another factor in producing disease, whose influence is too often overlooked and underestimated.

On clay or humus or surface soils, the element of dust, when they are dry, is ever present and ready to rise up into baleful activity on the slightest provocation, as a breath of wind, or even a passing footfall of man or beast.

And here is another of Florida's safeguards. Her soil is generally sandy, and sand produces dust fine enough to be held in suspension in the air in such small quantities as to become immaterial as to any harm it can do. There is less of that "impalpable dust," the taste of which we all know, because we have all been compelled to breathe it more or less, there is less of this prevailing lung-irritant in Florida than in any other country we know of.

So we see that our bonnie Florida has cause to bless the sands that lie so thickly scattered over her bosom; to their sanitary work she owes no small part of her superlative healthfulness.

Quite as important as any other point in the selection of a home that will be a healthy one is that of the water-supply. For water, good, bad, or indifferent, must be had.

It is one of the things that a family must have, no matter what else they have not. Water and air—we can no more dispense with the one than with the other. That Florida has an abundance of the latter, pure and wholesome, we have already seen. Now, how about the water? This too must be pure and sweet, for there is no source more fruitful of disease than bad water. Says an eminent physician, "Did people know the nature and extent of the terrible impurities in the water they drink they would wonder that they are still alive."

Medical men every where assert that the vast majority of diseases are directly traceable to the results of some sporadic germ, unseen, unsuspected, unknown, but none the less surely existing, and by some means, either of air or water, drawn into the human system, and of these two means of conveyance the most powerful factor is the water we drink.

No one who has arrived at the age of maturity needs a physician to tell him that water which contains vegetable organic matter or minerals, like salts or lime for example, will cause dysentery or diarrhea.

But while this fact is generally known, there is another equally true, but so recently proven as not yet to be universally admitted; that is, that impure water may also cause malarial fevers, and not only may but does frequently so cause them to a greater extent than any other one factor.

If a certain place is known to have malaria in the air during the summer months because of conditions which do not exist in the winter season, all danger would be considered as passed so soon as the cold winter set in. And just here is where many a serious mistake has been made. Because the winter air does not contain the malarial germs, that is no proof that they are not still dangerously near.

The water of that contaminated spot holds within itself the seeds of disease, and these are just as active in winter as in summer. Impure water is always dangerous, and fevers induced by its use are more fatal than others.

Those who drink water coming from marshes, whether in Florida or elsewhere, will be subject to fevers at all times of the year, while those who are careful to drink only pure, clean water, even in malarial districts, very rarely have fever outside of the late summer or autumn, and then the water is not responsible. This has been repeatedly proven in all parts of the world, and is a fact well worthy of note, dwell where we may.

In respect to her water-supply Florida as a general rule is favored, as she is in most other things. In most localities, whether drawn from lake, river, spring, or well, her waters are "soft," that is, destitute of lime, and for all purposes as pleasant to use as rain-water. In a few less favored spots, however, the well-water is "hard," being charged with lime and magnesia, an excellent drink for growing children, who need these bone-making materials, but hardly so desirable in other ways.

There is a difference in "hard" water wells. Some are charged with magnesia and sulphate of lime, and others with magnesia and carbonate of lime; the one is permanently hard and utterly intractable, crying out, "The more you try me the more I won't come—soft;" the other is more obedient and only temporarily hard. But understand when we say "temporarily" we do not mean that the character of the water in the well itself is subject to change, that it fluctuates, and is sometimes hard and sometimes soft; not this at all, but only that by certain processes the hardness may be removed and the water rendered as soft as rainwater. Of course there is a reason for this. The sulphate of lime contained in the permanently hard water is deserted by it and becomes one of its constituents, and then when you rub soap in it the stearic acid in the latter combines with the lime and magnesia and forms a chemical compound that the water can not dissolve, and so instead of a pleasant cleaning lather, an ugly, disagreeable curdiness results.

On the other hand, the carbonate of lime, which is found in the temporarily hard water, is not, and can not be dissolved, like the sulphate, by pure water, and hence it is only held in suspension, not permeating or becoming an inseparable constituent of the water.

How does the carbonate get there, then, you ask? The explanation is simple; all natural waters, but especially those obtained from wells or springs, contain more or less carbonic-acid gas in a state of absorption, and when thus charged are capable of dissolving the carbonates.

Thus we see that, while pure water will not dissolve the carbonates, water that contains a certain proportion of carbonic-acid gas will do so. But expel the latter gas, and the carbonate will be at once precipitated. This expulsion is easily accomplished by boiling, and the incrustation found at the bottom and sides of the kettle shows what has become of the carbonate. Try the water now, and you will find it soft and fit for any purpose.

Boiling, however, is not the only way to treat this class of waters; stir into a tubful of it a little slaked lime, and allow it to settle; in ten or twelve hours, perhaps less, there will be a white deposit at the bottom of the tub, and the water will be almost as soft as rain-water. How and why? Because the lime you added combined with the free carbonic-acid gas and destroyed it, and then the carbonate, being insoluble in water without the presence of this gas, was precipitated to the bottom of the tub.

Where hard water is encountered, either in Florida or elsewhere, these simple tests will prove which sort it is, and if they render the water soft, the well owner may rejoice in having the less intractable servant of the two.

Some scientists aver that rain-water is the only safe water to use any where, and even that only after being filtered; this is doubtless true in part, that is, as regards some sections of country, but it does not apply to Florida as a rule, although in a few exceptional cases it maybe found the safest to use for drinking purposes.

Almost all over the State, however, the chief supply is obtained from wells, and purer, more crystal-like water no one need wish for.

As to the depth at which it will be found, that depends entirely upon circumstances, whether the spot selected for the well lies much higher than the level of the surrounding country, or lower, or whether dug in the wet or dry season.

It is always better, when possible, to have it sunk toward the end of the latter, or winter season, as then the water is at its lowest level, and the maximum depth of the well can be reached at once; otherwise several deepenings will be necessary, or the well will "go dry" as the waters recede in the lakes and streams.

Generally, Florida wells are cased with yellow pine boards, because they are every where obtainable; but where other material can be procured we would strongly advise against this.

The objections are, first, non-durability; every three or four years a new casing is required, the boards rotting away; and if not carefully watched, or repairs are postponed, a heavy shower is apt to "cave in" the well.

Sometimes the rotting of the casing is so complete and sudden that nothing can be done except to fill in the well and make a new one elsewhere.

The pine boards generally used are not heavy enough; that is the chief trouble; instead of half or three quarters of an inch, let them be at least two inches thick, and then, if they must be employed in the absence of preferable material, they will at least last long enough to pay for the work done on them.

The second objection is, fortunately, one that does not continue very long, not over a month or two, if the well is emptied of its water two or three times in this interval; we refer to the taste of the turpentine in the yellow pine, which, until it has all passed out into the water, causes the latter to foam and to taste and smell decidedly unpleasant; this is true, however, in a much lessened degree where the lumber used has been seasoned by exposure to wind and water for some weeks or months.

But where lumber just sawed is employed, as is usually the case, it will shorten the turpentine period greatly if the boards as soon as received are immersed in the waters of a lake or stream (one or the other is most likely to be at hand), and left there for several days, or longer if possible; a large portion of the turpentine taste and odor will be got rid of in this way.

Now, however, that our beautiful State is being traversed in all directions, further and further day by day, with the wonder-working rails of steel, and great throbbing steamers, speeding over land and water, the days of yellow pine casings, like many other things tolerated of necessity in the past, are rapidly passing away, except in localities far from transportation lines, and these are not so many, even now.

Artesian wells, with their iron pipes, circular wells, bricked or cemented, these are the coming wells of Florida, furnishing pure, clear water from the very first of their being.

Settlers who have been accustomed all their lives to the free use of ice during the warm months find the summer temperature of the Florida water-supply one of the greatest crosses they have to encounter in their new homes; they get used to it after a while, but where ice can not be had to cool it, and either spring-water at a temperature of 80°, or well-water, if drawn from as much as thirty feet below the surface, at about 70°, is all one can get to quench thirst, the contrast at first is hard to bear.

The writer found it so years ago, when there were no ice factories in the State; but there are many now, and but few places on the line of transportation where ice can not be procured, and that, too, at very reasonable rates, from one half to one cent per pound.

While the Florida waters are generally pure, it does not by any means follow that they are so because they look clear and have no unpleasant taste or odor; this is usually considered the test, but never was a greater mistake made.

Water, not only here, but any where, may possess these qualities, and yet be utterly unfit for use, because containing the germs of disease in mineral ingredients, and other water, like that of the St. John's and Ocklawaha rivers, for instance, may be tinged brown or yellow, because it has percolated through vegetable matter, and yet be wholesome, especially to those who are accustomed to its use.

Place nothing on the same side of the house with the well that can possibly pollute its water; do not rely on the soil acting as a filter to the water before it reaches the well; if you do, you make a mistake that may prove fatal to one or more of your family.

Hear what the National Board of Health, of New York, has to say on this subject, after a series of careful experiments, and their report, we may add, only confirms the opinion of every sanitarian in the civilized world, and proves that natural soil, while it is a good filter for impure air, is worthless where water is concerned:

"From these results it appears that sand interposes absolutely no barrier between wells and the bacterial infections from cesspools, cemeteries, etc., lying even at great distances in the lower wet stratum of sand. And it appears probable that a dry gravel, or possibly a dry, very coarse sand interposes no barrier to the free entrance into houses built upon them, of these organisms, which swarm in the ground air around leaky drains," etc. Other experiments have shown that ground air will take up infectious germs from water that is disturbed.

And here, from a physician resident in the State, comes still another warning:

"If you have a well for household purposes near orange trees, do not fertilize with commercial manures; such trees should have only cotton seed, tobacco leaf, or pure chemicals to feed upon. Animal fertilizers of any kind will yield a poison to the water through our porous soils. You can not be too careful, with our light soil, how you contaminate the surface of the ground about your wells. Bad water is a fruitful source of bowel troubles. Our water here can not be excelled, and let us see that we keep it sweet and pure."

It is an easy matter to test the purity of water, no matter whence drawn, and here is the *modus operandi*: Fill a pint bottle three quarters full of the water; dissolve in it one half teaspoonful of the best white sugar; set it away in a warm place for forty-eight hours. If the water becomes cloudy it is unfit to drink; if not, you are perfectly safe in using it freely.

There are also some safeguards that it is well to know.

The use of lemon juice or citric acid, even in the proportion of one two-thousandth part, will destroy any microscopic animalcules that may be in the water, and in about three minutes from the time the citric acid is used they will be found dead at the bottom of the vessel.

But bear in mind the citric-acid solution must be freshly made, or it will lose its power.

This citric acid would be an excellent thing for tourists or hunting parties, and still better is a filter that is within the reach of every one, light and portable, and always ready for use.

For such a filter as this, which is also very cheap and perfectly effective, we are indebted to the State Geologist of New Jersey; here are the directions he gives: "It is the bottle filter, and is made by tying a string wet with turpentine around the bottom of a quart bottle and breaking out the bottom. This is done by lighting the string, and, when the flame has encircled the bottle, dipping it in cold water. Layers of fine cotton batting must then be placed in the bottle until a wad is collected that rests on the shoulders of the bottle and its neck. Now dissolve a cup of alum in hot water and pour the solution into a cup of cold water. This makes a filtering substance. I use alum, because it is the only thing which will precipitate all the impurities of the water to the bottom. For every gallon of water that it is desired to purify, add a teaspoonful of the filtering fluid, and stir it until every particle of the amimalculæ is precipitated. This usually takes five minutes. Then run your gallon of water thus treated through the filter, and you will have your water free from all impurities."

To make a filter with a wine barrel, procure a piece of fine brass wire cloth of a size sufficient to make a partition across the barrel. Support this wire cloth with a coarser wire cloth under it, and also a light frame of oak, to keep the wire cloth from sagging. Fill in upon the wire cloth about three inches in depth of clear, sharp sand; then two inches of charcoal broken finely, but no dust; then on the charcoal four inches of clear, sharp sand. Fill up the barrel with water, and draw from the bottom.

Sometimes, after heavy rains, the well-water is found to have sediment in it; in such cases drop into it powdered alum, in the proportion of one tablespoonful to a hogshead of water.

Or, if alum is not at hand, borax will do, two ounces to about twenty barrels of water.

In either case stir the water for a few moments, and the impurities will in a few hours settle to the bottom, but more entirely so with the alum than with the borax.

Neither affects the taste of the water.

We have been thus minute in dealing with this subject, not because the settler is at all likely to have any trouble in procuring pure water, for, as we have said, this is only so in Florida in exceptional localities, but rather on the principle that "an ounce of prevention is worth a pound of cure."

The sugar test will quickly settle the matter of pure or impure water not one in one hundred will find it the latter.

CHAPTER V. TEMPERATURE. WINTER. SUMMER

Violent Changes almost unknown. Mild Winters. Cooler in Summer than in the Northern States.

And now we come to the last phase of the constituents of climate as regards fair Florida—a phase upon which we have not so far touched, yet one which is more frequently quoted, and to the superficial observer or tourist is more important than any other, as more directly affecting one's physical comfort—and that is, temperature.

It is this feature that is usually meant when passing allusions are made to the Florida climate; it is this that is called "charming," "incomparable," "glorious," "delightful."

These are the adjectives most frequently met with as applied to this subject, and, strong as they are, we think few who have experienced in their own persons the striking contrast between the climate of Florida and that of any other State, nay, of any other known country, will object to them as being too expressive.

Certain it is that thousands do indorse them, and among these is the writer, who, having spent in Florida ten consecutive summers and winters, with better health and more uniform comfort than any preceding years at the North, ought to be in a position to judge somewhat of their justice.

Florida's climate compared with perfection is not perfect, but compared with other climates it is perfect, and nothing less; no other can approach it, as we have previously shown.

Florida's temperature is not monotonous, not equable.

The time has been, and not so long ago either, when this fact would have condemned her in the eyes of medical men, for it was then considered that equability of temperature was, for an invalid, one of the first and foremost points to be insisted upon.

But all that is changed now-a-days, like many other things, as science advances, undoing and correcting our views and our knowledge.

Says a distinguished English physician, "A long residence in a very equable climate is not favorable to health, even with all the advantages of exercise in the open air: a moderate range of temperature and of atmospheric variation seem to be necessary for the preservation of health."

And another recent authority asserts, in speaking of the dread that persons in weak health experience of cold weather:

"If our invalids could indeed find a lotus-eater's land,
  "In which it seemed always afternoon,
  All around the coast the languid air did swoon,

I would predict that the results on their health would be rather pernicious than otherwise, and loss of appetite and diarrhea would probably be induced."

Now, just here is the difference between Florida and Africa, or the West Indies: the one is semi-tropical, the others are wholly tropical; the one has decided changes of temperature, the others have none—it is always the same, an unchanging, wearying heat, the only variation being from the wet to the dry seasons.

No, we do not claim that Florida's climate is entirely equable; on the contrary, we should regret very much having to admit that it was so: happily, we can "hold fast to the truth" and yet deny it emphatically; from the northern to the southern boundary, even down to the extreme point of Dade County, the temperature changes decidedly, according to the seasons; there is nothing monotonous or debilitating about it.

And yet these variations are rarely violent, as they so frequently are in all other countries; they are not of a nature to produce illness from exposure, or sudden shocks to the system, but, on the contrary, are entirely beneficial, even to the most delicate, acting as a wholesome, stimulating tonic rather than the contrary; it is the absence of these changes which, as we have seen, render tropical climates so enervating and ultimately injurious.

The usual range of temperature for Florida during the day, according to observations carefully conducted for more than forty years by Government officials, is only 13° to 14°; and for the night season only a little more; it changes just enough to be refreshing, seldom more or less.

The ideas that until recently obtained almost universal credence, and are still prevalent to a great extent regarding the mildness of a Florida winter, may be summed up in the often-heard phrase, "No winter clothing required."

And this is hardly to be wondered at when some of the most prominent land companies scatter broadcast over the country pamphlets containing such sentences as these:

"You can live in comfort all winter in tents;" "You need not bring your winter overcoats, it will only be an incumbrance;" "No carpets required hence a great expense saved."

And these and others also claim that bananas, pineapples, grapes, limes, and other tender plants can be raised to profit, even almost to the northern border, and "need no winter protection."

There is exactly one grain of truth in these statements, the last one quoted; for certainly the plants mentioned "need no winter protection" in the sections indicated, because it would do no good; tropical fruits can not be grown with profit in regions swept every winter by air that is frosty, even if it does not actually touch the freezing point.

Florida is over four hundred miles long, and her temperature varies more from one degree to another than is usual for equal distances on the main land; plants that will flourish in ordinary winters as far north as Orange County, for instance, are unreliable for crops a little further north, and regularly, winter killed yet a little more to the north.

Some poor, deluded people were actually trying to "live in comfort all winter in tents" down on the Gulf coast at the very time that the unprecedented cold wave of January, 1886, came rushing down from the north pole on its way to astonish Cuba; these good people had not been very happy before this cold wave interviewed them; they felt still sadder (and madder) afterward, and it was not long before, learning wisdom by experience, they had good substantial walls and roofs to shelter them and good honest fires to warm them, and then for the first time they ceased to regret and began to rejoice that they had selected Florida as their future home.

Others too had followed directions and left behind them the comfortable winter overcoat and the cosy carpets which they were not to require, and even before those few bitterly cold days they found out how little dependence is sometimes to be placed in flaming circulars set afloat by interested parties.

Those few days in January, 1886 (which will never be forgotten by the many who, in person or in property, felt the force of the blast), are not to be set down to the account of the Florida climate, or their effects quoted as those of even an "unusually severe winter," as this is commonly experienced; it was simply something abnormal, outside altogether, a fierce incursion into an unoffending country by an armed horde of marauders from the north pole, who carried destruction in their path over the whole United States, and even invaded Cuba and Europe.

The "January freeze" has no more to do with the climate of Florida than the bursting of a reservoir, or the flooding of a river, or the horrors of a cyclone have to do with the usual characteristics of any country in which these misfortunes may chance to occur in the course of the passing years.

It was literally a "passing strange" experience for fair Florida, and while its injurious effects will quickly pass away its salutary lessons will forever be remembered.

And now, that we may have a full and clear idea of the actual winter temperature, as Florida winters ordinarily run one with another, let us look at some of the facts and figures collected by years of observation by scientific men:

	Autumn.	Winter.
Jacksonville, ...	70°	56°
St. Augustine, ...	71°	58°
Palatka, ...	70°	57°
Indian River, ...	62°	60°
Florida (average), ...	71°	60°

These figures, as you will see, refer to different parts of the State. How do they compare with the autumns and winters elsewhere? Surely not to Florida's disadvantage.

Let us examine more in detail into the actual temperature of this famous winter of 1886, which was the most severe all through of any ever experienced in the State, and not at all likely to recur during the lifetime of its present population.

From observations taken during 124 days, from November to March, we find that the highest point reached by the thermometer was 87° and the lowest (for two days only) 16°; this latter, of course, during the reign of the "cold wave" king.

There were 102 days when the maximum temperature was between 55° and 80°; there were 89 days when the lowest point ranged between 34° and 54°; several more when the minimum was 70°, and only three when it was cold enough to freeze water at noon. Of sunshiny days during this same period there were no less than 82; showery days, 28; cloudy, 13; rain all day, 4.

Now this is the daily record of the most unpleasant winter Florida has ever known. What do you think of its contrast to that of the mildest winter at the North?

Note also the fact that these temperature markings were made at Jacksonville, and that the record further south would show still higher points.

As an ordinary thing the Florida autumn and winter weather is very like the typical May or September of the North, or the famous "Indian Summer," which every one calls "delightful."

The mornings and evenings are cool enough as a rule to make a brisk wood fire quite cosy and comfortable, and sometimes for several days together it is very acceptable all day long; in truth, necessary to comfort.

And then again there are times, many of them, when no fire at all is wanted, but rather summer clothing outside the heavy under flannels that wise people wear, even though it be balmy Florida; we have dressed at Christmas tide in thin white outer garments, and again in heavy blue flannels.

"Variety is the spice of life," and it is this very quality that saves Florida's climate from being enervating.

In ordinary winters, days when the thermometer reaches a maximum of 76° are not rare, but those in which the highest point is 60° or 65° are more frequent, while a minimum of 40° is of common occurrence, but these variations are seldom so sudden as to be violent, and when they are it is the chilling northwest wind that is responsible, rushing down without warning or welcome, with a snow storm at its back and a rain storm for Florida in its hand.

There has been a great deal of foolishness, both written and spoken, about something that does not exist in our beautiful State—"the frost line." It is true that some sections and some localities are less liable to damage from this cause than others, but none can claim certain and uniform exemption, if they "cling to the truth."

The frost weaves that occasionally sweep across the State are erratic—they travel by no known route, are governed by no known law.

For instance, a few years ago, during the march of one of these unwelcome visitors, the thermometer at Tampa marked 39°, while at Fernandina, two hundred miles further north, it recorded at the same day and hour 54°.

During the same cold wave tomato vines in Alachua County on the north side of a lake were uninjured, while those over two hundred miles farther south, with water protection, were killed outright.

Experience has abundantly proven that the effect of cold is dependent on currents of air, and is much modified by water protection. There is no use in trusting to lines of latitude for exemption, for they will surely fail sometimes; a frost that visits a locality one time and spares another close by, may do the opposite on its next visit.

The "frost line" is a myth, and if any claim to be uniformly "below it" in Florida "the truth is not in them."

SUMMER.

If there is any one point concerning Florida which is subject to more misapprehensions than any other, it is that of her summer climate. Ninety-nine persons out of a hundred would at once jump at the conclusion that a climate which is so much milder than that of others during the winter, must be correspondingly hotter during the summer season.

But put the question to those who live in Florida all the year round, "What of the climate in summer?" and the answer will be, "In winter the climate is pleasant, in summer it is delightful."

This is the almost universal verdict of all who spend a summer or two in the State; astonishment at first, then delight.

When the mildness of the winter is taken into consideration, and also the fact that the line of latitude included in Florida is also that embraced by Northern Africa and a part of the Desert of Sahara, where, as we have seen, the temperature ranges during the day about 100° in the shade and falls to freezing at night, it is not to be wondered at that the Florida summer should be regarded with suspicion by those who judge from the process of natural induction and are without knowledge of the facts.

Those who know Florida at all, are well aware that no such heated air as reigns perpetually during the day over the Sahara ever sweeps, even transiently, over fair Florida.

The same peculiar location of our treasured peninsula which influences the winter temperature has also its effect upon the summer. The very fact that it is a peninsula, with a great ocean to the east and south and a mighty gulf to the west, tells its own tale if one but pauses to interpret it, for it is simply impossible that such a long, narrow strip of land, its shores bathed by a great body of water on three sides and constant winds sweeping over it, their extremes tempered by its influence, should be either as cold or as hot as land in the same latitude not so located.

In the winter the winds passing over the Gulf-stream before touching the land lose a great portion of their sharpness; during the summer the current of cold water that passes between the east coast and the Gulf-stream, tempers and cools the warm air sweeping across it.

That is one reason why Florida is so favored in summer as well as in winter. Another (that also operates in the latter season, as we have already noted) is the absence of neighboring mountains to check the constant and even circulation of the air. The result is that Florida is never without a breeze, morning, noon, or night; first from the one great body of outlying waters, then from the other, a constant succession of pure, life-giving breezes are playing back and forth over her broad bosom. Of all the many summers the writer has spent in Florida, the first unbearably hot day or night has yet to appear!

We do not claim that Florida summers are not warm, very warm in the sun or in violent exercise, just as elsewhere, but we do claim, and ninety-nine out of a hundred of her citizens will bear us out in the assertion, that her summer is more pleasant and less oppressive than that of any other State, north or south.

Who has not suffered from the oppressive heat of the northern summer season with the thermometer ranging high up among the nineties, and not a breath of air stirring to cool the fevered pulse and throbbing head!

In our own old home, Philadelphia, we have many a time marked the thermometer at 96°, 98°, 100°; even occasionally 104°, and this too in the shelter and shade of the interior of a large brick dwelling, where it should have been cool if any where; we have seen the same thing also in other parts of Pennsylvania, in New Jersey, in New York, in Maryland, and with it all there was a close, sultry "feel" in the air that seemed to sap one's life away and to make the very effort of breathing too great for endurance.

Even in the country, with open fields all around us and a great river near by, we have experienced, night after night, heat so intense, so close, that it seemed as if we must suffocate; sleep, rest even, was impossible, and while wandering over the house in the vain hope of finding a "shadow of a breeze," we have noted our neighbors wandering likewise in the dead of night about their gardens, looking more like uneasy ghosts than merely unhappy mortals, slowly melting away in the vain search for a breeze.

That is a search that no one need ever take in Florida; it is more of a problem how to get out of the breeze than how to get into it; it is always on the *qui vive* and never waits to be hunted for; it hunts for you in every crack and corner.

It frequently happens that it is too cool to sit on the porches in comfort when the thermometer actually marks 90° or 92°, and common sense tells you that you ought to be feeling very warm, and would be excessively so with the same temperature in any other State.

It looks mysterious, does it not? but it is true, nor is the mystery very deeply hidden.

In Florida during all the long summer the thermometer and the breeze are perpetually warring with each other; they quarrel night and day, and have a lively time together, to the incalculable benefit of all living creatures.

The thermometer says one thing, the breeze says another; for instance, the former declares the true marking to be 96°, the latter insists that it is not over 82°, and hardly that. And the breeze is nearer the truth, at least so we should decide did we consult our feelings rather than the thermometer.

The reason is self-evident if one stops to think about it; when we have no ice and want to cool some water to drink we set it in the shade and in the breeze; the latter passing over it causes a rapid evaporation that at once produces the desired effect.

Exactly in the same way the breeze striking a moist skin produces that sensation of coolness which is so refreshing and so vainly sought for when there is no such kindly, stirring friend near by.

We have never once seen the thermometer in Florida rise higher than 98°, and that only two or three times, in the hottest part of the day, and even then the gentle breeze that never fails cools the heated air like an immense, invisible fan, so that it is not oppressive or a source of discomfort; unlike the North, there are cool places to be found in plenty, so long as you keep in the shade and at rest.

Of course it is hot in the sun. Was there ever a summer any where where it was not? If there is such a place, woe unto its grains, its grasses, its fruits.

Yes, the Florida sun is hot during the hot season, but not one whit more so than elsewhere.

And men, white men, unaccustomed to such work are seen toiling in the full glare of the sun, and declaring that they feel the heat less than if they had been quietly rambling along the road at their old homes with the thermometer at the same height.

It is a fact that men are able to work out-doors in the Florida summer in a higher temperature than they could possibly endure elsewhere.

Of course there is a reason for this; nay, two of them.

In the first place, the bountiful breeze, one of fair Florida's coolest yet best friends, is a very important factor in fanning the worker and preventing overheating; in the second place, the dryness of the atmosphere promotes profuse perspiration, which of itself is one of nature's cooling processes.

Sunstroke is utterly unknown in Florida. The reason of this unwonted exemption from one of the most common casualties of the Northern summer being this very fact of so profuse a perspiration; it is a safety valve, as every one knows or should know, and its sudden stoppage or absence is the direct cause of sunstroke and other serious illnesses.

Now and then (but very seldom) a man may attempt too much and overtax his strength, and consequently is overcome, not so much by heat as by exhaustion; but these attacks are very different from sunstroke, and are rarely serious.

One reason why the Florida summer is so pleasant and comparatively cool is that rains fall nearly every day, not all day, but in showers, usually in the afternoon or morning, and often when it is not actually raining the sun is veiled by clouds, so here are still other factors at work, you see, to cool the atmosphere. June, July, and August are the "rainy months," but of course it does rain at other times also.

The only objectionable feature of the Florida summer that we have ever heard quoted is its length. It is true that it begins sooner and ends later than the Northern summer, but even so it is not very much longer, and it is cooler and more uniform in temperature, and hence more healthful.

The warm season usually sets in about the middle of May and continues until the middle of September, when a sensible difference will be noticed.

And now, as to the nights during the Florida summer, they are invariably cool and refreshing. Here no one ever rises in the morning worn out with a night of restless tossing and inability to sleep because of heat and sultriness.

There is always the breeze ready to dance through your rooms, if allowed, and fan you to sleep, a good, sound, refreshing sleep, and no one who knows Florida will retire without having some extra covering lying convenient at the foot of the bed, for it is almost certain to be needed before morning.

Now, how does this record compare with the summer nights elsewhere?

Florida is in the far South, it is true, but she neither roasts nor boils her honest citizens who stand by her, not only in winter but in summer. Let the doubters come, see, and feel for themselves; let them come from the land of snow and ice, and hot, sultry days and stifling nights; from the land of storms and clouds and tornadoes and blizzards, and compare with these things Florida's mild winter and cool summer, her refreshing nights, her average of three hundred clear days out of the three hundred and sixty-five, and her gentle, invigorating breezes.

Having now, as we trust, proven beyond dispute by facts and figures that the climate of Florida is the most healthy, as it certainly is the most pleasant in the world, and therefore unsurpassed so far in the "raw material" that goes to make up a home full of happiness and contentment, we will pass on to the consideration of those points that must influence the settler in the locality he shall select for his new residence.

CHAPTER VI. PINE LANDS AND HAMMOCKS.

Diversity of Soil and Surface. Relative Value in Productiveness and Healthfulness.

Florida, it must be remembered, is a large State; so large and so varied in its productions that, to avoid confusion, it has been by common consent and Governmental authority subdivided into sections. Northern, Middle, and South Florida.

In each of these the character of the soil and landscape is exceedingly diversified; nowhere is it all pine or all hammock, all lake or all river, all flat or all undulating.

The report of one of the Florida Commissioners of Immigration speaks truly in saying: "There is one feature in the topography of Florida which no other country in the United States possesses, and which affords a great security to the health of its inhabitants; it is that the pine lands, which form the basis of the country and which are almost universally healthy, are nearly every where studded at intervals of a few miles with the rich hammock lands. These hammocks are not, as is generally supposed, low, wet lands; they do not require ditching or draining; they vary in extent from twenty acres to forty thousand acres."

In no one respect has Florida been more systematically misrepresented, both in malice and ignorance, than in the matter of her soil.

Unhappily, tourists as a rule see but little except that which lies on the surface, and as a consequence their report is almost invariably of a one-hued, "sandy, and unproductive" nature.

This is to be regretted, not only because it is only partially true, but because it at once prejudices those who are accustomed to dark, loamy soils, and have a dread of "hungry, leachy sands."

While it is true that in the surface soil sand predominates, yet in many parts of the State the soil is a firm, sticky, clay-like loam; sometimes of that rich dark red, which, as every one knows, is an indication of exceeding fertility.

Such, to a great extent, are the lands of Middle Florida, as we shall see in the future.

Before going further let us dive below the surface and bring to light some of the (literally) bottom facts that underlie the State.

In the older geographies, gazetteers, encyclopedias, every where, in short, where the subject is mentioned at all, you will read that Florida is of a comparatively recent formation, and upraised from the ocean on a coralline formation.

This statement, however, like so many others, as we have seen, has been proved to be a complete mistake, the result of judging merely by surface indication, Florida having been one of the few States that has never had the advantage of a regular geological survey.

At this present writing, however, this important work is at last going forward and a preliminary survey is being made by the new State Geologist, which has already revealed the truth above stated, although yet in its earliest stages and very far from complete in any respect.

The rocks that underlie Florida are of the same geological formation as those of the territories that rest on the heights of the Rocky Mountains, and the observations so far made render it not at all improbable that the same upheaval which raised the Rocky Mountains also lifted Florida from the depths of the ocean to become one of the most sparkling gems of our sisterhood of States.

So far from coral being the corner-stone on which she rests, the main rock beds that have been reached by the borings for her first artesian wells are those of the lignite and flint beds that belong to the eocene tertiary, and this too at a very moderate depth,- from one hundred and fifty to two hundred feet, and in some sections these rocks are actually outcrops.

The indications as to what riches and mineral wealth the thorough survey soon to be made will reveal are simply startling in their promise to those who have heretofore been satisfied to consider Florida as "all on the surface."

Near Tallahassee, for instance, rich specimens of iron ore have been found cropping out on the surface, and the probabilities are that the hills around that beautiful city are underlaid with this ore in paying quantities.

An eminent mineralogist, who some time since made careful and patient research in South Florida, found on the dividing ridge an outcropping of "over seventy tons in sight and unknown quantities beneath the surface" of an ore which, carefully assayed, proved to contain fifty-four per cent of pure lead and fifty-two ounces of pure silver to the ton, in addition to traces of gold in paying quantities, and this result was obtained from random specimens taken from the outcroppings.

Indications of gold have also been found in Northern Florida, and this same mineralogist declares that there are at least three extensive coal deposits, one in Northern, one in Middle, and one in South Florida.

"Mining, he says, "will be one of Florida's great future industries."

Already the preliminary geological survey has shown rich deposits of phosphates, equal in value to the famous Charleston phosphate rocks, and these appear to exist all over the State, as they have been found in widely separated districts; extensive marl beds and the best quality of limestone for manufacturing purposes are also among the preliminary revelations of the geological wealth of Florida.

The surface soil, to the consideration of which we now return after our excursion "into the depths," is composed all over the State of deposits—"recent" as compared with the age of the underlying rocks—of sand, clay, and marl, which in themselves contain finely comminuted marine shells, coral, phosphates, calcareous materials, salts, deposited by the sea that once swept over them all, and vegetable humus, which necessarily is the most recent addition of all and is constantly accumulating.

So varied is the quality of this soil that, like the State itself, it has been subdivided and classified as follows, in order that it may be spoken of understandingly: First, second, and third-class pine lands; high hammock, low hammock, and swampy lands; no less than six grades.

The first-class pine lands of Florida are not like any other lands found in any of her sister States; in fact, it is doubtful whether their counterpart exists in any country.

Their surface is covered for several inches with a rich, dark, vegetable mold, beneath which lies a chocolate-colored, sandy loam several feet in depth, and beneath this again is a substratum of marl, clay or limestone.

This soil, as may be seen, should be very fertile, and so it is, exceedingly so, and moreover wonderfully durable; for instance, there are several sections where for eighteen years the land has been cultivated in successive seasons without the addition of a particle of manure, and yet it has yielded, and still yields, four hundred pounds of Sea Island cotton to the acre; and how much longer these lands will continue thus productive "deponent sayeth not," because no one can tell; they have not yet begun to fall off.

These first-class pine lands are elevated, almost with "high hills" in some localities, but as a rule merely undulating in a degree pleasant to the eye and conducive to health and beauty of landscape.

The timber is large, tall, and straight, with occasional giant oaks; and in many localities where there is but little, underbrush, and the clear, sparkling waters of the lakes that are thickly scattered through these beautiful pine lands, with their clean, white beaches, peep at one here and there, the scene is full of a quiet, peaceful, home feeling that is inexpressively soothing and restful.

The greater portion of these superior lands—where they are found in the largest bodies we mean—is in the more northern and western sections, where are found some of the richest and most attractive portions of the State.

When we consider what has been raised on this first-class pine land (we could give some marvelous figures did our present purpose permit), and that it has been accomplished by the rather hap-hazard methods of cultivation that are still too much in vogue, and then consider what results thorough cultivation, intensive farming, and deep plowing and fertilizing would bring forth, we become lost in wonder at the possibilities of the despised Florida sands, as represented by her first-class pine lands.

Frequently clay is found close to the surface, intermingled with rich vegetable mud, and these lands are eminently adapted to the growth of almost every thing—oranges, lemons, long and short staple cotton, sugar-cane, corn, potatoes, oats, rye, turnips, vegetables, fruits of all kinds; and in the northern sections, wheat, barley, and some varieties of apples, and every where, also, grasses and cattle ad libitum.

There is more second-class pine land than first-class. Fully two thirds of all the Florida homes are located on this grade of land, and although rated as "second," their quality and productiveness in actual cultivation is little, if any, below that of the first-class.

Second-class pine land is timbered with a medium size growth of pine trees, with here and there a solitary black oak; a great many willow oaks, as bushes or small trees, and an occasional clump of palmetto in the lower spots, but elsewhere there is little underbrush.

These lands are frequently rolling and, like their superior grade, interspersed with crystal lakes.

Many of the finest orange groves in the State are located on the second-class pine lands. The famous Spear grove for one, the Ginn grove for another.

And now we come to a class of lands much abused and heretofore despised, but like many other things, especially in a new, progressive country, improving on acquaintance. These are the third-class pine or black-jack lands.

They do look poor and discouraging enough, and unfortunately these are the lands that lie along the lines of several of Florida's main railroads, in full view of the traveler, who naturally judges from what he sees rather than from a hidden reality.

The surface soil is light yellow, sometimes even white; the wire-grass is short and thin, and often missing altogether; the pine trees are stunted in height and their foliage sprawling, often only thirty or forty to the acre, with plenty of crooked, gnarled black-jack oak trees and sprouts, sickly clumps of palmetto, and altogether a tired, out-of-heart, don't-care sort of look.

This land costs less to clear than any other, and when put under cultivation and the same fertilizers, no more, given to it that are bestowed on the two superior grades, its productiveness is wonderful, and it takes a very close observer to detect much difference in the ultimate results.

Some of the most famous old groves are on "black-jack," or third-rate pine lands; the Belair grove, at Sanford, is one, the De Forest grove another.

If the "black-jack" soil shows the least tint of yellow (and very little of it does not), it will come out all right if properly fertilized and cultivated.

It should be noted that red or yellow soils contain iron in a greater or less degree, and this under cultivation combines with tannic and other acids, and so in a few years the yellow soil becomes dark and rich, but the white sands lack iron and will never darken.

"Hammocks" are tracts of land which, lying rather lower than the surrounding country or else along the banks of the larger lakes and rivers, are constantly moist, and have, therefore, escaped the annual visitation of the destructive fires which every spring sweep from one end to the other of Florida's piney woods. We shall have more to say upon this subject by and by.

Thus year after year the falling leaves of the hickory, oak, and other deciduous trees which grow so luxuriantly in these damp places remain to decay upon the ground, thus steadily enriching it and forming a rich humus in which a luxuriant undergrowth springs up, adding more and more to the fertility of the soil by its falling leaves and branches; such an undergrowth as has no opportunity to establish itself in the piney woods on account of these same annual fires we have mentioned.

This, we are convinced, is the true origin of the Florida hammocks, where the wild orange groves are invariably found, and where the rankest tropical luxuriance of vegetable life is the most striking characteristic; through one of these true Florida hammocks it is impossible to make one's way without the constant use of axe and hatchet.

The writer has seen the giant trees and wondrous wealth of vegetation of the tropical regions, those of South America, yet even there the rich, dense undergrowth of our genuine Florida hammocks is not excelled.

It is the high hammocks that are usually meant when a "Florida hammock" is referred to in a general way; these are on high ground, are often decidedly undulating, almost hilly, in fact; their soil is a fine vegetable mold with a sandy loam, and underneath, from two to five feet, is usually found a substratum of marl, limestone or clay—we saw a piece of this substratum the other day—a hard, rock-like substance underlying one of the finest (one time wild) groves of Lake Harris, and had we not known otherwise we should surely have declared it to be a fragment of the famous coquina wall of St. Augustine.

These soils seldom suffer from too much water, but they are frequently affected and their trees droop under a drought that passes harmlessly over their piney-woods neighbors.

"Hammocks" are very rich and fertile, no doubt; their large trees, dense undergrowth, the luxuriant growth of orange trees and splendid yield of sugar without the use of manures proves this fact.

Low hammocks may be said to be a cross between the high hammock and the swamp lands, and in truth, this fact is recognized in the odd kind of local name often used to designate them, which is "swammocks;" they are not less fertile than the swamp lands, but their good qualities are not so durable; the soil is deep and tenacious and the surface usually level, so that ditching is sometimes a necessity—not often, however.

Low hammock lands are not so plenty as the swamp lands, and it was on these tracts that the great bulk of the sugar plantations of the old regime were located.

Let it not be supposed that all of Florida's rich lands are "hammock" lands, nor that all hammock lands are alike. This is the most diversified State in the Union, not only as regards climate, but soil and the unique distribution of the different kinds of the latter.

Most people regard Florida's hammocks as her richest and best land; this is not the case, however. The richest of the rich lands are those technically called "swamp lands;" they are of alluvial formation, and are constantly being added to in extent year by year. These tracts, varying from twenty to two hundred acres, sometimes more, were originally depressed basins, which have become gradually filled in by the washings from the higher surrounding lands; for centuries, the broken branches, rotting wood, leaves, grass, and debris of all kinds have been steadily accumulating in these basins, which we may well term Dame Nature's compost heaps—heating, fermenting, decaying, and becoming vast store-houses of the richest plant-food. So that these swamp lands are really the most valuable in the State; not only because they are richer than the hammocks at the outset, but because their fertility is much more lasting.

But, and "there's the rub," these swamp lands are like gold mines, you know the richness is there, but you must have money in your pocket to get at it. You invest ten dollars and reap fifty or one hundred in return, but you must first have the ten dollars to use as a lever; if you have it, you are all right; but most people who immigrate to Florida have it not, and it is for this reason, because these rich swamp lands must be carefully ditched and drained before they can be made available, that today there still remain for sale nearly one million acres, which may be had for from two dollars downward per acre.

We have said nothing about the healthiness of living on these same lands—is it necessary? Swamp lands all over the world are the fever-breeders, and those who cultivate these lands should know enough to locate their homes several miles from them on higher ground.

Where, however, these lands are thoroughly and permanently drained in large bodies, as, for instance, by such enormous operations as those undertaken by the great Okeechobee Drainage Company, they become as healthy spots for residences as can be found any where, a fact that hundreds of people already settled on these wondrously rich "Reclaimed Lands" can testify.

Hundreds of thousands, nay, millions of acres of productive lands are thus being added to Florida's available resources as the result of one of the greatest enterprises of the age—a "howling wilderness" and waste of shallow waters converted into a veritable "Land of milk and honey."

CHAPTER VII. "WHERE SHALL I SETTLE?"

Northern, Middle (including West), and South Florida. Varied Products and Climatic Differences of the Several Sections.

The very first question that arises and imperatively calls for a decision, after the great question of "to be or not to be" a Floridian has been answered in the affirmative, is:

"Where shall I settle?"

In its narrower sense the query is quickly and emphatically answered: "In the piney woods—never in the low hammocks." In its broader sense the answer is not so ready, and, Yankee-like, must be primarily answered by another question:

"What is your special object? The best climate for a consumptive?"

Then locate in South Florida, by all means.

Do you want to raise oranges, lemons, guavas, bananas, pineapples?

South Florida again.

Is it merely your object to secure a climate less boisterous than that of the more northward Southern States, where you can raise peaches, pears, plums, and put early vegetables into the northern markets? where you can raise the regular farm products, oats, corn, rye, and potatoes?

Then Northern or Middle Florida will suit you just as well, if not better, than the more tropical divisions. Their soil is richer as a rule, and the two or three hundred miles of distance saved in time and freight make a respectable item in the balancing of accounts.

And now it strikes us that we have used the term of Northern, Middle, and South Florida, and it is not likely that one in ten of our readers will understand what these terms signify. Let us explain.

Florida is a very large State, embracing an area of over sixty thousand square miles, and all varieties of climate, from a tropical to a temperate, consequently the general term of "Florida" is too sweeping in its application, and the necessity for a more particular descriptive title has been met as above.

South Florida proper embraces the country south of twenty-eight and a half degrees of latitude.

Middle Florida lies between this and the thirtieth degree, while Northern Florida (embracing also "West Florida") claims the remainder of the State.

As we have indicated, this latter is the section to suit the settler whose main object is not the cultivation of the citrus family.

Here is the Florida for live stock, corn, wheat, grapes, figs, peaches, and all the products of a more rigorous climate, and a few of the hardier southern fruits; it is not tropical, it does not pretend to be, but it is beautiful, and more like the North we have left behind us than any other portion of the State; and better live stock and crops, at so little expense and so great a profit, can be produced nowhere, than in Northern Florida. Frosts are of no infrequent occurrence and the winters are quite cool.

Middle Florida lies between the twenty-eighth and thirtieth parallels, and its products are those of the semi-tropics.

Here one may see the vegetation of the temperate and the tropical zones growing side by side; only the long summer is sometimes hard upon the former, and an occasional winter frost chills the ardor of the latter.

The orange, lemon, lime, grape, fig, guava, peach, and all garden vegetables grow and flourish in close proximity all the year round, with the occasional mishaps before alluded to.

Cotton, cane, cow-peas, and rice, pay best of the field crops; but wheat, corn, and oats, are less profitable than in the more northern portions of the State.

Lakes are few, except in the central portion, where, in the "Santa Fe and Eustis Lake regions," are a number of very fine sheets of pure, clear water, full of fish, and frequently framed by bold, beautiful bluffs.

Here the large orange groves flourish, and hundreds of new groves are being set out, while settler after settler rolls up his sleeves, and goes to work with a will in the truckfield; sending on crate after crate, barrel after barrel, of green peas, tomatoes, cucumbers, beans, onions, spinach, egg-plants, celery, lettuce, beets, and the host of other garden vegetables to the great Northern and Western markets all through the months of January, February, March, and April.

It is a business that, as a rule, pays handsomely, though some seasons, owing to "cold snaps" or drought, it fails. It is no uncommon thing to see from five hundred to a thousand dollars cleared on one acre of some special crop that has matured and reached its destination at a fortunate moment.

One of the special crops is the strawberry, and often the profit on these little berries is so fabulous as to be fairly startling.

And now we come to South Florida, where the semi-tropical and truly tropical productions stand side by side; here heavy frosts seldom come, and when they do come the damage they do is usually light, chiefly affecting tender vegetables.

Every tree, plant, and shrub of the subtropics is at home here, especially in the southernmost parts; in the more northern portions some slight winter protection is given to pineapples, bananas, and guavas, a rude shelter of boughs, during two or three winter nights, when the thermometer threatens to fall below 36°. This may be necessary once or twice in several successive years, or it may not be needed at all in several seasons; of course, the further south one goes the more can yearly tender fruits be depended on. Key West, and thereabouts, is the home of the pineapple, banana, cocoanut, bread-fruit, sugar apple, and the host of more tropical fruits, but it is not the home of the orange, or lemon, or cane, or cotton.

Even from this cursory review of the different divisions of Florida, you can readily see that never was a greater mistake made than to suppose, as so many do, that all parts of the State are alike in soil, climate, and production.

Why is it that Norfolk, Virginia, vegetables and strawberries find their way to the markets of New York and Philadelphia several weeks earlier than they can be supplied from their own vicinity?

Simply because Norfolk is several hundred miles south of New York and Philadelphia; for the same reason Charleston beats Norfolk, and Florida leads them both.

Look at New Jersey: at Cape May spring is two weeks earlier than it is at Orange, only one hundred miles distant.

In New York snow and ice are on the ground in St. Lawrence while the trees are blooming in Queen's County, and when the fields are green at Chappaqua, Ogdensburg, two hundred and fifty miles away, is shivering with a foot or two of snow on the ground.

Now, Florida is nearly four hundred miles long from its southwestern-most point to its northern or Georgia boundary line; and who, after giving the subject even a passing thought, can not see the absurdity of the idea that her seasons, temperature, and productions, are alike over all her length and breadth? In fact, they are widely diverse, as we have already seen.

It is often charged against our State papers that they indulge in "sectionalizing," holding up one locality as better than others. Now we would respectfully suggest that this is rather an unjust accusation; true, the State has been "sectionalized," but it is the Creator who has done it, not poor, finite human beings. God sectionalized Florida when he laid down one portion several hundred miles nearer to the equator than the other, just as He has sectionalized Southern and Northern California, New York and the Hudson Bay territory.

What is it that the settler from the North and West seeks in coming to Florida for a home? Health, semi-tropical fruits, and a warm winter climate.

Well, the northern parts of the State can give him health, no doubt, and a far milder winter than he has left behind him, but very few semi-tropical fruits, and these with the ever-pressing danger of being killed, "root and branch," by the frequent winter frosts and icy nights. Having said this, we need not say much on the warm winter question.

Still, to those who seek only mild, not constantly warm, winters, and other occupations than semi-tropical fruit-growing, the more northern portions of Florida are very attractive, indeed, preferable.

Let us take Leon County as a type of the rest, and see how it is there.

Tallahassee, the quaint old capital of the State, is in this county, and the country thereabouts and around Pensacola was one of the earliest settled.

Only a few years ago cotton was the one staple production; a great deal of sugar-cane was raised, a little tobacco, some upland rice, corn, and here and there a planter—we mean the good old-fashioned, wealthy "Southern planter"—could boast of raising his own meat; but right here the production halted.

King Cotton reigned supreme, and according as the coming crop was full or short, so the merchant laid in a large or full stock of goods, for his pay must come from the royal hands of the reigning sovereign, the king aforesaid, so there followed the inevitable high prices consequent on long credits.

But now some of the stirring Northern element has crept in and things are changed in these as well as in the other portions of Florida. Truck-farming is the great winter business of three fourths of the people, and right royal is the attendant revenue, unless, as does sometimes happen, some unexpected mishap befalls the crops.

The planting, cultivating, gathering, and shipping of garden vegetables keeps the truck-farmer busy from November to May, or even June.

We have elsewhere referred to the live stock of this portion of Florida, and the majority of our Northern brethren, who have been reared in the idea that "there is neither beef or butter, nor grass in Florida," will be surprised to learn that dairy farming is hereabouts rapidly assuming noticeable proportions.

Improved stock has been imported, several genuine dairy farms, with pastures of Bermuda, Para, Guinea, and other grasses, have been established, and now, in the first infancy of this enterprise, three or four farms in Leon County, alone, are sending from seven hundred to one thousand pounds of first-class butter each week to the Jacksonville market, and the demand is far beyond the supply; this butter brings the owner thirty cents a pound.

Those who -inaugurated this new field of industry for Florida are reaping large profits, and each year sees their herds increased and their pastures enlarged. Even creameries are being established.

One half-blood or even three-quarter-blood Alderney or Jersey cow, they tell us, gives more and richer milk than four of the common breed, and eats only one fourth as much.

And now the dainty little Guinea cow is rapidly becoming a favorite. Success to the pioneer dairymen of Florida! More on this subject later on.

Another new enterprise is the drying and shipping of blackberries. This fruit is indigenous to the South, and in Florida we find it every where, by the roadside, in old and new fields, in the hammocks, in the piney woods—fine, large, plump berries, tempting and delicious.

Years ago North Carolina awoke to the wealth scattered broadcast over her wild lands, and now she sends out from her borders, each year, dried blackberries to the value of $100,000! Florida can do the same, "only more so." With a small, inexpensive fruit-drier, and berries bought, as they can be and are in some localities, at two cents a quart (and at this rate the pickers make from seventy-five cents to one dollar a day), the profit attained by the shipper is very handsome.

Then there is another business looming up for the upper divisions of Florida, one that has already, in its infancy, assumed immense proportions in California, and is quite as well if not better adapted to Florida. We allude to the raising and drying of figs. The fig is a paying fruit wherever grown, and nowhere can it be brought to greater perfection than in our State, wherever a clay or marl subsoil lies within three or four feet of the surface.

The tree is easily raised from cuttings, is a rapid grower, once started; it requires no pruning, fruits at an early age, and is a prolific bearer; it is not subject to blight or disease, and the process of drying the fruit for market is not a difficult one. The same fruit-drier that is used for blackberries, peaches, huckleberries, will answer the same purpose for figs also.

We have no fears of proving a false prophet in predicting that the time is not far distant when "Florida figs" will be quoted in the New York markets and will bring the highest prices.

Peach-growing is another important industry. Here this fruit flourishes as it rarely does in South Florida and marvelous prices are obtained for the early sorts, all the way from ten to forty dollars per half-bushel crate. It seems incredible and more like a fairy story, but it has been done more than once—single peaches sometimes selling in the large Northern cities at from one to two dollars each. The later kinds, too late for the Northern markets, find a ready home sale at two dollars per bushel, and any surplus can be dried and a handsome profit reaped therefrom.

Then the northern portion of Florida (in common with South Florida) has just been reached by a "boom that is destined to echo and re-echo over the land as loudly as the "orange boom" of the latter.

Every body knows what a stir the LeConte pear has been making these last few years in Georgia, where thousands of acres are being set out in this tree. Well, this same noble fruit has proved itself admirably adapted to Florida; as a rule, pears sought to be raised here do not behave well, their conduct is out of all reason and propriety; they put out their blossoms at uncanny times, when they should have known enough to stay at home, and then they are nipped in the bud by the chill weather, or drop their fruit before maturity. But this is not the case with the LeConte pear, it roots from cuttings, and bears three years thereafter; it is a vigorous grower, never sheds its fruit, but ripens it two to three months earlier than the earliest of other varieties; it ships well and brings splendid prices in the Northern markets; it is no unusual thing either for a tree to mature a second crop, and half mature a third, during the year; add to this, that it is free from blight and disease, and is a very handsome tree, and what more can we ask of a fruit tree!

Vineyards, too, are profitable; and last, not least, there is no country in the world better adapted to the culture of the mulberry tree, and consequently the production of silk. The people are awaking to this fact, and many an acre is already set out in the great silk-worm food, by private individuals and by corporations.

In fact, after long years of dormant energies, paralyzed by the rule of the *"ancient regime"* which has opposed all innovations and clung to old grooves, the northern and older settled portions of Florida are rousing up to new life and energy, and a prosperous future looms up ahead.

In concluding our review of this section, we need only to add, its health is all one could ask, and the face of the country such as to offer, not only comfortable, but picturesque homes, while the fine roads make driving a pleasure, and contribute not a little to sociability among its people. Game is abundant, and fish are plentiful.

We have, we trust, presented the northern divisions of the State in a fair and honest light; and, as you see, that light is not altogether dimmed by the more brilliant gleam of the southern sections.

Next in order, in our examination of types, comes the "Santa Fe Lake Region," which is receiving a goodly share of immigration; it is a picturesque country, with high, rolling hills, good roads, clear water lakes, deep to the very shores, and clean sandy beaches, beautiful mirrors enframed by green-mantled bluffs, with cosy homes nestling on their sides.

The key of this locality and port of entry, as it were, is Waldo, a thriving town on the line of the Atlantic and Gulf Transit Railroad, about midway between Cedar Keys and Fernandina, the termini of the road.

The country hereabouts owes its prosperity, present and future, in a great measure to the Santa Fe Canal, which, projected and pushed to completion only a few years ago by a few energetic capitalists, now connects, by means of a little steamer. Lake Santa Fe with Lake Alto, and this again with the Transit Railroad at Waldo, only sixty miles from Jacksonville.

The Santa Fe Canal thus affords an easy outlet for market to thirty miles of shore line, and one hundred thousand acres of good, rich land, both hammock and pine. This neighborhood is particularly adapted to raising early vegetables, and the transportation facilities afforded by the lakes and canal and railroad make it an especially desirable locality for the truck-farmer.

It is a very rare thing that orange or lemon trees are injured near these great lakes; many a severe frost has passed them by unharmed, while injuring and even killing to the ground these fruits a hundred miles further south!

And this remarkable exemption is due to the high lands, dry atmosphere, and the close vicinity of the lakes, whose gentle pleading softens and tempers the asperities of the rude north wind as he rushes over their placid bosoms.

The pine lands produce about fifteen bushels of corn to the acre, but, with a little manure and good cultivation, will easily yield double this amount; from one to two bales of cotton to the acre; oats and rye are also fair crops, and upland rice yields from forty to sixty bushels per acre; sugar-cane is also largely cultivated.

. Peaches, pears, grapes, figs, and strawberries, all these are destined to become staple crops.

This is true, not only of the Santa Fe or Central Lake Region, but also of a large portion of Northern Florida, where here and there some small orange groves are found, where a sheltered position can be obtained.

Lake Santa Fe is one of the most beautiful lakes in Florida, about twelve miles long and three to five wide; and, nestling cosily at its far southern extremity, around a little cove, lies one of the prettiest growing towns the State can boast of; as healthful as it is pretty, and surrounded by a beautiful hill and lake country, adapted to every variety of production peculiar to its section, possessing some of the oldest and finest orange groves in the State, Melrose is speedily destined to become one of the most flourishing towns in Florida; and with the one railroad connection it now has, and three others in progress, it can not fail to become a commercial center as well as a lovely home-site.

In Suwannee County and thereabouts, turpentine farms are in vogue and are very profitable.

Here we find no lakes or running streams of water, but many of these strange sinks to which we have alluded elsewhere, natural wells, we might call them, with perpendicular sides, and tunneled through the solid limestone rock, that crops up to the surface, or very near it.

And now we come to the Great Lake Region of South Florida, of which the rapidly-growing city of Leesburg is the commercial center.

This place, though by no means among the earliest settled in this section of the country, has, both owing to its location and the character of the land round about it, rapidly forged ahead of all the other portions of Lake County. It has two banks, several churches, a college, an academy, an ice factory, numerous stores, several railroads running north and south, and altogether has a bright future before it.

Lakes Griffin and Harris, the one twelve miles long, the other eighteen, are only separated from each other by a narrow strip of land, and on this neck, at a point where it is only half a mile wide, Leesburg is situated, thus securing a landing on both of these beautiful lakes, and the traffic of the hundreds of families who are scattered all along their shores, and for miles inland.

And now let us look at the country lying around these lakes. Griffin, Harris, and Eustis, as a type of the rest of this "piney woods" section, which includes no little hammock land as well.

The peninsula on which Leesburg stands extends northeast from the city for eight miles and is, at one point, several miles wide. Lakes Harris, Griffin, Eustis, and the Ocklawaha River, are its boundaries, and a remarkable tract it is, skirted along the water brink by rich hammock land, often a mile or a mile and a half wide, the center or backbone of the strip being pine ridges, overlooking beautiful little lakes.

On this weird peninsula were, a few years ago, the largest wild orange groves in the State, with the exception of one at Orange Lake; these have all been budded with the delicious fruit with which we are all so familiar.

And now, starting from a point two miles from Leesburg, on the shores of Lake Harris, one may see groves occupying hundreds of acres of trees in full bearing, and other hundreds of acres of younger trees, the whole extending in one unbroken line for several miles.

It is an impressive sight, especially when one remembers that only twenty years ago this whole region was one great tangled wilderness.

Then crossing this strip of land to Lake Griffin, what do we see there?

Another vast wild grove, reclaimed and civilized—nothing left as it was, except that the budded trees mostly stand where they grew, and the giant live-oaks stretch out their moss-draped arms with protecting care over their lowlier brethren.

In those localities where clay or marl crops up near the surface, within two or three feet, peaches grow thriftily, and nearly every where figs, pomegranates, guavas, bananas, grapes, and pineapples, flourish exceedingly, the latter needing occasionally a light winter protection.

Persimmons, plums, grapes, blackberries, huckleberries, grow wild and in great abundance. Cattle and hogs are kept in large numbers, and are very profitable to their owners, though the hogs, as we shall see in future chapters, are a terrible "thorn in the flesh" to the neighborhood in which they range. The cattle, as is too often the case in Florida, are valued less on account of the milk they yield than for the fertilization of the ground in the pens where they are confined during the night, their calves being retained as hostages by their owners to insure their coming home toward "sun-down." On this subject more hereafter.

There are only a few flocks of sheep and Angora goats as yet, and they are experimental; but the enterprise bids fair to prove successful and profitable, therefore it will quickly assume large proportions.

Of course, cotton and sugar-cane are staple crops; no where can they be grown in greater perfection; but still they are not supreme, the citrus is the royal family hereabouts.

The health of the people is excellent, whenever they have the good sense to avoid marshy localities, where; as every body knows, malaria is manufactured from the decaying vegetation, not only of Florida, but every where over the world.

As a general thing, the malaria of Florida marshes is not of a malignant type; the fever it gives is the regular old-fashioned chill and fever, or else a mild intermittent; it causes its victim to feel wretched and apathetic, but does not often kill, unless, as sometimes happens, it finds a sister disease ready to join forces with it.

Turning to the westward from Leesburg, we pass at once to the gentle, rolling country that is the characteristic type of the upper portions of South Florida. It is a pineywoods country, with a top soil of sand and a subsoil of red or white clay, marl, or shell-lime, sometimes cropping to the surface, at others two to ten feet below it.

Numerous small lakes break the monotony of the tall trees and green wire-grass that stretch for miles upon miles in all directions; these vary in size from a half acre to several hundred acres; nor is the extent of each lakelet always the same, but variable, according as the wet or dry season is paramount; their base is clear, pure sand; no marsh, no miasma here, no stagnant water, like our ponds of the North, with their muddy, slimy shores; and well is it that this is so, for scarcely can a piece of land containing twenty acres, be found in many localities, and most healthy ones too, without one or more of these little lakelets nestling in its midst, shimmering in the sunshine like a mirror set in a green frame.

Besides the various members of the citrus family, guavas, bananas, and pineapples grow here in great luxuriance, although they are occasionally "chilled in their ardor" by a winter frost; but a wrapping of moss will usually protect the banana if need be; the guava, even if it drops its leaves, soon starts out again, and a handful of moss dropped over the pineapple will insure its safety. This fruit is an extremely profitable one, a yield of four or five hundred dollars per acre being nothing uncommon, when the soil is rich and cultivation good.

Guavas are also very profitable, and will become a staple all over Florida, now that two species of this valuable fruit have been introduced that are frost-proof, as well as superior for jelly to the common sorts; these are the Cattley and Chinese guavas.

All of this family are very prolific, and bear in eighteen months from the seed, and the jelly made from them is superior to the far-famed "Guava jelly" of Havana, which is really marmalade. Florida guava jelly is jelly in reality, and is clear as crystal, having the appearance of crab-apple jelly.

And now we come to the Indian River Region, in describing which we virtually describe also the Tampa, Manatee, and other coastwise portions of South Florida. Let us take the country immediately around the Indian and Halifax rivers.

Oranges, lemons, and limes, head the list of fruits, and pineapples come next; then follow bananas, guavas, and other tropical and semi-tropical fruits; cotton and sugarcane are also largely grown.

This is pre-eminently a fruit-raising section; garden vegetables and several field crops are successfully raised, but they are only auxiliaries; there is more profit in fruit culture.

The climate is delightful; breezes from the neighboring ocean temper the summer heat and, as a rule, drive away the frosts of winter; the water fronts are often high banks with clear sandy beaches. Fish, oysters, turtle, waterfowl, deer, and other game, are to be had in profusion; mosquitoes are no more troublesome than in many places in the North, in some localities they are almost unknown, while in others they are "almost unendurable" during the summer season.

A very few homesteads, beautifully located, are still open to the settler; but many of the fortunate first-comers are dividing up their lands into lots for sale, both hammock and pine lands.

The country is very healthy, and full of great possibilities for the future; and now that the great iron horse has at last found his way into these regions, the Indian River, Manatee, Tampa, and Charlotte Harbor regions are already witnessing a rapid influx of settlers.

The Caloosahatchie and Peace rivers, emptying into Charlotte Harbor, are large, noble rivers, and numerous towns are springing up along their banks, of which the largest and oldest is Fort Myers, on the south bank of the Caloosahatchie, which river, for over forty miles from its mouth, is a mile or more in width.

This is one of the best locations in the State for tropical productions, and one of great healthfulness and beauty.

With these data in hand, we trust that our readers will find it an easy matter to select an objective point for settlement.

CHAPTER VIII. "WHAT WILL IT COST?"

Prices of Land: According to Location and Quality. Cost and Methods of Clearing Land. Solid and Increasing Value of a Bearing Orange Grove. Overproduction Impossible.

Having now discussed the important question, "Where shall I settle?" let us next look into the second, no less momentous one, "What will it cost?"

Now, this is a good deal like the far-famed query, "How big is a piece of chalk?"

There is no place in the civilized world, where men do congregate, where also money to any extent may not be got rid of by those so inclined, and Florida being in the above category, and not so near "the jumping-off place," either, as she was only a few years ago, is no exception to this rule. Money can be buried here as well as elsewhere; and the question of "What will it cost to settle?" may meet with widely different replies from as many stand-points.

We, however, are not writing for the benefit of those who have already an abundance of this world's goods; such need no advice from us, they can come and go, and settle as and where they list. Our items are meant for those who come to Florida seeking to improve their fortunes; who have but little to start with in their new life, except a wealth of hope, energy, and perseverance, and this is the best kind of wealth to possess, the world over. To such willing, earnest workers as these, the question of "What will it cost? comes home often with direful significance.

So, then, what we want to know, just now, is not the maximum (that is an uncertain quantity hard to determine), but the minimum cost of settling down in a new home in this genial clime. Of course, even here there is an extreme; some men, strong and sinewy, go out into the wild woods, how down the tall pines, build a little log hut to shelter their families, and then go out to work by the month or the day for wealthier or more enterprising neighbors; and thus keep on from year to year, without energy or ambition to work hard enough to improve their condition or insure the future comfort of their families; but such so-called "men" as these are few, thank Heaven! And, again, there are some who began their Florida lives just as cheaply and roughly as these, and yet kept pushing upward, until now they are among the richest and most influential men in the State. The majority who are coming to Florida in these days, however, are men who have a few hundred dollars in their pockets, and want to know how to make the best use of them for their present and future benefit.

The question of location settled in its broader sense, next comes that of the particular piece of land, both as to kind, quality, and locality. To those seeking permanent homes in Florida this is a subject so fraught with weal or woe, health or sickness, success or failure, that it can not receive too great care and study. And in this connection we can not too earnestly deplore the petty jealousies that are so frequently witnessed by would-be settlers, leading to the pitting of one section against another, and the decrying of one neighbor—especially of that neighbor's land—by another, to the harm and degradation of all.

The St. John's River man, meeting a stranger bound for the Ocklawaha and Lake Regions, will do his best to convince him that the only good, healthy land to be had, is that in which he is personally interested; the Indian River man will tell the stranger that his locality is the only right and proper one to settle in; the Lake Region man decries the St. John's River lands; the man with pine land to sell vituperates the hammocks; the hammock owner runs down the pine land, and each neighbor puts forward his own "bit of land" as" a "right smart chance better" for the purpose desired than any other tract thereabouts; and so this narrow, false-hearted, mistaken policy runs along the line, with of course here and there "the exception that proves the rule."

An amusing and instructive case in point was brought to our notice only a short time ago. A stranger, a man of wealth, energy, and intelligence—such a one as Florida most needs to develop her immense latent powers—agreed to purchase a certain piece of land, if, on seeing it, he found it as represented. Well, he saw the land, and was thoroughly satisfied; shortly thereafter he was accosted by a man living close by:

"Ho! stranger, I reckon you 're the man as 'lows to buy Chris Brown's land, eh?"

"Yes; it's a fine place, isn't it? "

Neighbor A, as we will call him, took off his cap, rubbed his head thoughtfully, looked up at the sky, then down at the stranger:

"I don't like to go agin a neighbor, ye know," he said slowly, with a significant wink.

"Why, what is the matter? Isn't it good land?"

"Well, that's as you takes hit; 'taint no good for cotton nor cane.

"I want it for oranges, lemons."

"Then hits as you find hit; 'taint never been tried. I know'd a man as 'clared he could play a flute; didn't know he could n't till he'd tried, you see, and then he just squeaked awful—was n't no good."

"But why do you think it is not fit for oranges?"

"Did n't say it twarent, stranger! I aint 'goin' to be on neighborly like, only I 'lows as wild oranges aint found only in swammocks, as that 'ud be the fittenest place for the sweet uns!"

There did seem to be some sense in this argument; so, as our stranger's contemplated purchase was not concluded, he went with neighbor A, who "didn't want to be onneighborly though," to view a "passel of hammock of his own."

The stranger approved of the tract, and had almost decided in its favor, when neighbor B met him.

"Stranger," quoth he, "I hear you're bound to take A's bit of sour swash."

"Sour swash?"

"Jes so! I don't want to make no trouble fer a neighbor, but it's easy to see that bit of land 's sour swash as 'ud pizen a 'gator! It's hammock, sure enough, but it ud take a fortun' to dreen it fer any use. Now, there's a bit of pine land, high and dry, that's just the thing you want; easy to clear and no dreenin'."

Had he, B, any of this vaunted high pine for sale?

"Well, yes, he had; and if the stranger wanted—he didn't like to be onneighborly; but if he must, why he must."

So the perplexed stranger looked at this pine land, and really liked it better than any he had seen yet; he was glad he had looked further. This land was all right, that was certain.

Then along came neighbor C, a better educated man than the others, capable of forming an opinion and giving a reason for it.

"Don't take that pine land," he advised. "There is hard-pan and clay under it; hard-pan kills the trees, and clay is cold; the worst of it is, you never can tell till your grove is old enough to bear, then the roots reach the hardpan or clay, and the trees just die, no help for them, and there you are, money and years all gone for nothing!"

Neighbor C (of course) had just the right kind of land to sell; but neighbor D quietly cautioned the stranger against it, as "scrub hammock, and no account nohow. He had some himself, though, first-class."

But the stranger shook his head sadly, and turned his back forever on that community, saying:

"No, I will have none of your lands. Any one of those tracts would suit me; I see thrifty, healthy trees on them all, but each one of you runs down his neighbor's honesty, and decries his neighbor's goods. I would not live and trade and visit among such men, if a grove was given me free."

Now, good reader, perhaps you think this is an imaginary experience. Unhappily, we can not plead guilty, it was an actual fact, and its counterpart may be met with any day.

"A word to the wise is sufficient," *prenez garde*.

The question is often asked, "What does good orange land cost?"

Well, as our friend, neighbor A, just referred to, remarks: "That's as you takes hit," whether your choice is pine land or hammock; remote from or near to good transportation facilities.

Our own experience and judgment, and that of the majority of Floridians, is decidedly in favor of pine land, as a general rule, for a permanent, healthy home, where one can be happy and contented.

An important consideration to most settlers, and one that would be paramount, were all other things equal, is the fact that it costs much less than hammock, not only in the actual purchase money or "first cost," but in the after preparations for the reception of the coveted orange grove, the Alpha and Omega of the Floridian's aspirations.

Hammock land is almost invariably found stretching back from the shores of the large rivers and lakes, joining a belt of rich land, varying in depth from a half mile, or less, to three or four miles. And here, and only here, are found the wild sour orange trees, either scattered thinly about amidst the giant oak, hickory, bay, magnolia, and palmetto trees, or else growing so closely together as to form those famous wild groves of which every one has heard and read so much in these latter years of the newly awakened interest in orange culture.

Happier than they knew were those fortunate first-comers, whose early appearance on the field enabled them to homestead the land on which these latent gold mines were "wasting their sweetness on the desert air." To them it was given to secure, for the nominal sum of fourteen dollars, one hundred and sixty acres of rich lands, frequently with hundreds or thousands of noble orange trees flourishing in their midst, and all they had to do was to clear away the underbrush, bud the wild stock with the sweet orange, and lo! in three or four years they were independent men, and in nine years rich men, with the smooth stream of their wealth constantly widening and deepening as time rolled quietly onward.

Those "good old times" are gone by; the area of wild groves was always limited, extremely limited—and now they are things of the past; tamed, domesticated, brought into subjection under the conquering march of civilization. A few, a very few, are left still, but they are scattering, and would not have existed so long, but that they lie so far away from transportation centers as to be useless for years to come. Hammock lands, after passing from the State and General Governments into private hands, have always been held at much higher prices than the pine barrens, and this not entirely because the former are the richer lands, but because also of a natural law which operates in the commercial world wherever man buys and sells.

When the demand for an article is in excess of the supply, the owners of that article reap the inevitable results of higher prices. Obviously, the supply of hammock land, especially of that accessible to transportation lines, is extremely limited, and even if the demand were much less than it actually is the supply would still run short; therefore hammock lands are always held at rates from five to ten times higher than pine lands, which exceed them in area in yet larger proportions.

The relative merits of these two classes of Florida lands is a question much agitated at present, with the great preponderance of opinion in favor of the pine lands.

Here and there we find tracts of high hammock on the borders of our great lakes where the shores are bold and sandy, and the miniature waves come rolling upon a clear white beach, from which the hammock land rises high and dry, with a mixture of sand in its loamy soil; no rotting, malaria-breeding vegetation here—no marsh, no low, wet spots.

Now, no one need to be afraid to reside on such a spot as this, if he will just clear ten or twenty acres of the dense growth around his dwelling, and give free admission to those revivifying influences, sunshine and pure air. We know of many such homes along the shores of Lakes Harris, Griffin, Eustis, Apopka, Kingsley, Santa Fe, and other of our large lakes, and they are healthy as our pine-land homes and very beautiful, with an outlook for miles over the clear sparkling waters of these lakes, with their emerald green borders rising abruptly from the shores. Only recently we stood on the portico of one of these favored dwellings, and gazed out over Lake Santa Fe, as on a beauteous picture of peaceful fairy land.

But not to every one, no, not to one in five hundred, is such a favored location possible. The majority must be and are content to dwell in the "piney woods," with their healthful, balmy fragrance, and the sparkle of small, clear water lakes or lakelets gleaming like mirrors through the pines.

Undoubtedly, hammock lands are the richer lands at the start, but their fertility is of a deceptive sort; that is, as we have already intimated, it is not lasting.

Trees and vegetables grow finely for several years, but after that every year increases the need of fertilizing hammock land, while with pine lands it is just the reverse; they are poorer at the outset, but improve steadily with each year's cultivation.

Then, too, as we have also said before, hammock land is much more expensive than the pine; where the latter can be had of the best quality, for from ten to twenty dollars an acre, the former is held at fifty to seventy-five or even several hundred dollars.

The expense of clearing the land preparatory to cultivation must also be taken into account.

The hammock is full of underbrush, young trees, vines, roots, and palmetto; all these must not only be cut down, and either burned or piled up to decay, and furnish by and by nourishing food for the future grove, but the numberless roots must be grubbed up at no slight expenditure of time or money; time, if the settler is a strong man, able and willing to work; money, if he has to hire the clearing done for him.

It does not cost less than thirty dollars, oftener fifty, to clear an acre of hammock land, as it should be cleared; and for a year or two afterward the fight against the upspringing roots must be waged unceasingly or else the clearing will go back to its original state, and all the toil and money already expended be thrown away.

In clearing a piece of hammock for a grove, it is only the underbrush that should be got rid of entirely; some of the grand old oaks should be left standing to flourish as of old, before civilization had dreamed of intruding upon their time-honored domains; the growing orange trees will need the protecting shelter of their wide-spreading arms as a shield from high winds, the too great mid-day heat, and from possible frosts. Very few realize the importance of this subject; we shall have more to say about it hereafter, in its proper place.

Two or three years ago pine lands could be bought in settled localities at from five to ten dollars an acre; now, they are held at twenty to one hundred in the same places and for the same lands.

There is an important point that should be borne in mind by every settler coming to this State, and that is, how he is to get his fruits and other crops to market, and where he is to buy the provisions necessary for his family.

These are questions that can not be too carefully considered, for of what use would the best lands and heaviest crops be to their owner, if he were compelled to let fruit and vegetables rot on the ground because there was no way of transporting them to a profitable market?

Or where would be the comfort of a home if every pound of coffee, tea, sugar, and the host of other things indispensable to the well-being of a civilized family, were only to be had by hauling them by horse power over rough sandy lands for many weary miles?

And so, if good lands, inaccessible to transportation lines, either in the present or in the near future, should be offered to an incoming stranger at five dollars an acre, we would say to him : "Refuse the offer, rather buy less land at quadruple the price, where the markets for your produce may be easily reached, where the necessities of life are at hand, and where you can obtain farming tools and fertilizers without ruinous freightage."

It is a fatal mistake to settle on land merely because it is nominally cheap; really desirable pine lands can not be bought now-a-days, as a rule, at least from private owners, for less than twenty to fifty dollars per acre.

There are still some good tracts of land scattered about to be bought from the State, or United States Government, for from one dollar and a quarter to two dollars and a half per acre; but these and homestead lands—for which a five years' residence entitles the settler to a warranty deed—are becoming scarcer every day.

In this matter of selecting lands upon which to make a home and a grove too much care can not be given.

The class of land which is the most available and also the most desirable in all respects is that called "high pine land." The growth of timber on this land is especially, as its name denotes, pine, with here and there small oaks, shrubs, wild persimmons, hickory, and a few other trees, sometimes solitary, but more frequently in groups, and when the latter occurs it is called "scrub hammock."

The rule is that when tall, straight pine trees are found, large in size, and about seventy to the acre, and no undergrowth but the famed wire-grass, and a little palmetto, the land is first quality; where the small oak trees are scattered thinly about, it is second rate; and where the oaks surpass the pines in number the land is less desirable, being third rate.

There is something to be said, however, as we have seen, even for the latter class. It is very poor at first, it is true, but it responds very quickly to fertilizers, and even the poorest of it can in time be brought into the highest state of cultivation and improved year by year.

One does not require as much land for a farm in Florida as at the North, for several crops may be taken from the same acre in one year. If a moderate sized grove, say of five acres, is the desideratum of the settler, and just enough land besides to raise fodder for his horse and vegetables for his family, ten acres, inclusive of the grove, will be ample.

There is only one way of clearing hammock land, and that we have already mentioned. There are, however, several ways of preparing pine land for cultivation. One way is to girdle the trees, which deadens them, and puts an immediate stop to the great drain their wide-spreading roots make upon the plant food contained in the soil.

The trees are left standing, and then the land is ready for fencing and plowing. In a few months the decaying bark and limbs begin to fall upon the ground, and continue to do so for several years, and the branches must either be carried away from time to time or else become an eye-sore and a constant annoyance in cultivation.

The first cost of this method of "clearing" is very little, only about two dollars an acre, or even less; but it is very likely to cost more in the end than it saved in the beginning.

After a few years' time, when the orange grove is fairly under way, the deadened trees will begin to fall; after heavy winds or a soaking rain down they crash, now here, now there, and, as they are not noted for judgment, they are just as likely as not to come down on an orange tree and put it beyond the pale of recognition. And then it must be chopped up, and either hauled away or burned; the expense and trouble of doing which are just as great as they, would have been at first, plus the loss of some of your best orange trees.

The claim that the dropping sap, bark, and branches of the pine trees, left to decay on the ground, furnish a valuable fertilizer, is a specious one; and, even if one is willing to have his grove strewn over with branches that trip up his horse and interfere with the plow, the amount of nutriment thus given to the soil is so small that a few cart-loads of rotten sap and grass, hauled from outside and spread around the orange trees, would far surpass it. We do not consider the gain, even considering the small first cost, at all compensates for the after-clap of falling pine trees and crushed orange trees.

Another and a better way is to cut down the trees, chop them up in convenient lengths, pile and burn them. This method costs from twelve to eighteen dollars per acre, according to the number of trees to be disposed of, and of the amount of "small deer," in the shape of bushes and young oaks, to be grubbed up by the roots.

But then the stumps of the pine trees are left in the ground, and it is a sad mistake to leave them there as so many do. They are not only a constant eye-sore—that is the least of it—but, no matter how often and how completely the field is cultivated, these stumps scattered all over the grove will harbor ants and weeds, especially that curse of many cultivated fields in the South, called maiden cane grass. It is very difficult to eradicate that grass where it becomes established; but it can be done by constant use of the cultivator for one or two seasons. Its roots penetrate the ground to the depth of several feet, and every joint makes a new plant. For this enemy the pine stumps afford a strong rallying point, and it is simply impossible to destroy it while the stumps remain.

Even if the maiden cane can be kept at bay as the orange trees grow, the stumps interfere with their proper cultivation. When the orange trees become large the stumps can not well be burned out on account of damage to the trees. They must be removed by cutting out, which is a very laborious and expensive.

Better, by far, to burn out the stumps before your trees are planted, and have your land clear and smooth with no broken lines in your avenues of orange trees. Stumps often stand just where you want to plant a tree; therefore it is always best to have a clear course. It will cost from fifteen to twenty cents each to get out the stumps, but it is cheaper in the end.

Another plan of removing trees, which costs less, and is quite as effectual as the other, is to attack the tree at once at the root. A hole is dug on one side of the tree, embracing about one half its circumference. The roots on that side are all cut off, fire is then applied, and when the tap root is burned off the tree topples over, dragging out the roots on the opposite side. So here are tree, stump, and roots got rid of all at one operation. It remains then to burn up the tree and fill up the hole, and the land is ready for the plow for all time to come; no more falling branches, no trees, no stumps.

This process costs from twenty to thirty dollars per acre; not more, not so much, indeed, as first cutting and burning the trees and then digging out and burning the stumps.

The land cleared, plowing comes next in order. This can be done for three dollars per acre, not a high charge for breaking up new land, as it is no easy or quick work even in our light Florida soil.

Rails for fencing are split from the pine trees, at a cost of one dollar per hundred. It is well to have the rails split before the trees are burned, as, among the trees cut down, there will be found many fit for splitting. No matter how plentiful wood may be for the time being, it is not wise to waste what will be needed later on. Another thing we would note in this connection: among the fallen pines will be found many logs suitable for household fuel, and these should be stacked up for future use.

Hauling the rails and building the fence will cost fifty cents per hundred. The total cost of fencing one acre is sixteen dollars and fifty cents.

And now, having answered the question of "What will it cost to clear and fence one acre?" let us look at the next query: "What will it cost to build a house?" This is a question difficult to answer, for the same reason that it is difficult to give the exact size of the proverbial "piece of chalk."

A poor man, one who is actually pressed by poverty, can do as many of our now wealthy settlers did—build a log house. No matter where or what land you may select, there is sure to be plenty of timber growing on it.

With the aid of a negro laborer—who can be hired for from seventy-five cents to one dollar a day, according as he is "found," or "finds himself," in food—a strong man can cut down the logs, "skin," "notch them," and put up a single-room house, ready for the roof, in one week. The boards for roofing can be rived out in two days more, from pine or cypress logs. The rafters can be made with young saplings, stripped of bark, and the laths to support the shingling boards from still smaller saplings. There are a number of houses so constructed in every new vicinity.

The roofing boards can be held down on the lathing by cross-pieces fastened by withes, but nailing is far better. Good riven cypress shingles, four and a half inches wide and eighteen inches long, can be had for four and a half dollars per thousand, delivered, within three miles. They make the best roof and will last a life-time. Unplaned boards for flooring can be had at the saw-mills for one dollar per hundred feet, hauling extra. The cost for a room, sixteen feet square, would be less than three dollars. A chimney can be put up against the house on the outside.

The cheapest ones are built of sticks about two inches square and thirty inches long. They are simply laid across each other, forming a square, reaching above the roof, and are plastered inside and outside with clay or with mortar.

Such a chimney can be built in one or two days at a cost not exceeding five dollars. Chimneys built of brick cost about thirty dollars for a one-story house. The preceding description applies to a rude and cheap house, but hundreds of families have lived comfortably in such for years, and hundreds are living so now, all over the State.

And now for a better class house: Lumber is to be had at the mills for eleven dollars per thousand feet; the hauling from three to six dollars per thousand, according to distance. Doors, sash, and blinds can be got from Jacksonville, Fernandina, Gainesville, whichever may be most convenient. The necessary hardware can generally be had at the nearest country store. The prices are about twenty per cent higher than those of Philadelphia or New York.

Carpenters' wages, by the day, range from two dollars to two dollars and seventy-five cents, according to the workman's skill; but building is usually done by contract.

It is much the best plan to supply all your own material and pay your own carpenters only for their work; if you leave them to find the building requisites, you will probably have to pay them a considerable profit over the cost-price of the article used.

Cypress shingles, as we have already said, are held at four dollars per thousand, delivered on the spot where they are to be used.

House-building in such a mild climate as Florida is a very different thing from what it is at the North. Here is no need for the thick walls and winter-proof dwelling so necessary there.

A tight roof is needed of course, but weather-proof walls are not indispensable, although desirable, as it is not always "summer time" even in Florida.

There are occasional days in every month, from November to March, when fires morning and night are very comfortable things, and there are days when a good wood-fire in the stove or open fire-place is extremely grateful all day long, and then one feels a transient wish for a weather-proof house. But it is not often that this happens; and all the rest of the year we want the pure fresh air to have access to every nook and corner of our semi-tropical homes.

We have no cellars in Florida, though we see no reason against their practicability, where the location of the dwelling is high, and drainage good; the houses are set up from the ground, one, two, or three feet, as we may choose, on stout pine blocks, segments of huge pine or oak trees sawed off horizontally. It is claimed that there is not enough cold weather to chill the soil, and so a cellar would not be as cool a place for provisions as is a closet built of slats, or a wire-net safe, where the breeze has free access at all times; and doing without a cellar makes building much easier and much cheaper. But we have seen one Florida cellar, and it was a cool, airy spot.

We think the best plan for a Florida home is one that gives a wide hall through the center of the house, with rooms opening into it on either side.

This same plan could be carried out in the second story, when such is desired, but, as a general thing, Florida houses are only one story, as there is always plenty of ground on which to "spread out" as much as one chooses, and downstairs rooms are the coolest and pleasantest.

Every house of the least pretension to comfort should have a wide porch on at least two sides, notably the south and west, and all the better if the porch be continued entirely around it. Our idea of what a true Florida house should be, is that of a broad-brimmed hat, and for the self-same reasons that make such a hat desirable in a warm, sunshiny day.

It will convey to our readers a clearer idea of the actual cost of erecting a neat, comfortable home in Florida, if we give here the dimensions of such a house and its cost.

A "box house" of rough lumber outside, and planed within, and battened inside and out, a porch on the east and south sides, a covered piazza, back, leading to the dining-room and kitchen, which are detached from the main building but join each other. This is the grand sum total of the building we will describe:

The house is thirty-two feet wide by twenty-four deep, ceiling twelve feet high, a hall ten feet wide and twenty-four in length runs through the center from front to back piazza.

Two rooms on each side open into the hall, the two front apartments are twelve by fourteen feet; the two back rooms, ten by twelve; each apartment has two windows and two doors, one into the hall, one communicating.

From the hall a staircase leads to an unfinished attic, to store away trunks and surplus goods, or it may serve for a servant's room, although, when one can afford it, a small outside room is preferable for this purpose; one measuring ten by twelve can be put up for thirty-five dollars.

Connecting the main building with kitchen and dining-room is a covered piazza twelve by fourteen feet, on which is built the provision closet, as aforesaid, and where also is the pump, close to the kitchen door.

Housekeepers will appreciate the convenience of this arrangement, which should be much more common than it is. Usually the supply of water for household purposes is obtained by hoisting it from a well outside, by crank or pulley, a heavy task for one who is not strong.

Crossing the piazza, we come to the kitchen, twelve feet by sixteen, and joining it at one end is the dining-room, fourteen by eighteen feet.

Such a house as is thus portrayed, as comfortable a Florida home as one need wish, will cost in the near neighborhood of one thousand dollars.

A smaller and rougher but very habitable dwelling can be built for one half this sum, however.

Lands, direct from the Government or State, may be purchased at from $1.25 to $2.50, and occasionally $7, per acre, but these chances are rapidly becoming things of the past.

Inquiries regarding State lands should be addressed to the State Land Office at Tallahassee, while those regarding the United States lands should be sent to the Register United States Land Office at Gainesville. For Government lands write to the Department of the Interior, Washington.

Railroad lands are still abundant, and the incoming settler would do well to turn his attention in this direction, as, all other points being equal, they are held at lower prices, from $2.50 to $7.50 per acre, sometimes $10 for the best locations, good lands, and near actual or projected towns.

By private owners all prices are asked, and what is more, obtained; it depends somewhat on the whim or necessities of the seller, but still more on the quality of the land and its location, the latter governing prices even more than the former. Poor lands may be made fertile with cultivation or drainage, but a poor, inaccessible location can not be changed.

Lands, pine lands, held by private owners, range in price from ten dollars to two or three hundred, while hammock ranges from one to five hundred dollars per acre.

As to the cost of orange groves, while it is not within the province of our present work to go into details on this point, which has been fully treated of in our previous work on "Florida Fruits and How to Raise Them," a few leading facts and figures with regard to an industry which is usually made the "backbone "of the Florida home will certainly not be out of place.

The State Land Commissioner, basing his statements on verified figures, puts the cost of five acres (a man of moderate means should not attempt more at first) set in trees, fertilized and cultivated for five years, at eight hundred and fifty dollars, and estimates the value of the property at that time, simply as an orange grove, at five thousand dollars. If the trees are choice budded fruit, and the location on a lake, or near transportation, or a town, its value is very much increased.

Now, this estimate takes into account the cost of constant cultivation, which is one of the heaviest expenses the orange-grower has to meet. That this item will in the near future be almost, if not entirely, a thing of the past we firmly believe.

Our own observations and experience, and those of others scattered here and there over the State, point conclusively to the future orange grove as one of beautiful, thrifty trees growing happily, their tender surface rootlets neither torn nor mangled by the cruel plow or cultivator, with a thick turf of Bermuda grass nestling close up to their trunks, protecting the ground from sun-bake, enriching it constantly and silently by the decay of its roots and tops, keeping down the noxious weeds, preserving an equal moisture and requiring only an occasional top-dressing and perhaps an annual hoeing around the tree.

This is the grove that we see looming up in perspective. We have seen it in practice on our own grounds ; the finest, most thrifty trees we have—orange, lemon, pear, fig—are those that have been left undisturbed for several years, not even touched by a hoe, with Bermuda grass growing thick and high all around them. Not only so, but the soil has perceptibly increased in rich dark humus simply from the natural decay of the grass, while a top-dressing gives all the fertilizing needed.

When this fact, and fact it is, comes to be generally recognized, the cost of raising a grove "to profit" will be reduced to less than one half the sum required by the usual methods now prevalent, and the trees will be more vigorous.

Now, as to purchasing a bearing grove: while the prices asked by the seller usually seem high to the purchaser, who is new to orange culture and does not, can not, realize the full and increasing value of that which he seeks to acquire, the latter may safely buy on a basis of one hundred dollars to a tree in full bearing. Ten thousand dollars is not a high price for one hundred bearing trees, and, if located near to transportation and in a healthy place, such a grove is really worth much more in actual money returns and advantages.

Not only is there a rapid increase in value from added age and yield of the trees, but the land itself becomes more valuable from year to year, even independent of the crops that may be raised on it.

There is no danger of the orange crop being "overdone," or of "prices going down below a paying point," which is a question frequently raised by the cursory observer.

The idea is an absurd one on the face of it; it would be just as reasonable to ask in real, sober earnest, if one acre of land was not in danger of raising more than the people of New York

City could eat, for that is about the proportion of orange lands to the people wanting to eat the fruit they produce.

Here is a calculation that speaks for itself, and shows what are really the available orange lands:

	Acres.
The State of Florida contains	38,000,000
Above the 30th parallel there are lands "too cold" for oranges as a market crop, and better adapted to early and profitable vegetables and other fruits than the orange,	16,000,000
In the Everglades, saw-grass region, and swamp lands of South Florida, there are, unfit for oranges and, if drained, far better for sugar, etc.	10,000,000
Then there are of third-class pine-lands, cypress and other swamps, waste pine barrens, areas of rivers, lakes, ponds, creeks, and flat lands, too wet, etc.	6,000,000
	32,000,000
Leaving available orange land	6,000,000

Of this but a portion will be planted in groves, for every one must leave land for house lots, gardens, and other crops of fruits besides oranges, and other plantings of various kinds, and towns must have lands, etc. Thus, actually, there is not more than 3,000,000 to 5,000,000 acres of land in Florida available for orange growing for market; and people holding land which they can afford to keep need have no anxiety, as the lands will soon be absorbed; and, while the population of the United States is increasing rapidly, the area of orange land remains unalterable.

The consumption of oranges is rapidly extending, and lands in Florida must advance to many times their present prices. The purchase of land here, for the next fifteen years, can not fail to be a paying investment, even if left to lie idle.

CHAPTER IX. MAKING THE HOME.

Attractive Locations. Beautiful Water Views. About Windmills.

It is now in order that we should proceed to the discussion of how to make a home.

We do not mean a house, we have already discussed that matter, but a real, true home. One may have a very fine house, fitted with every comfort, and with gorgeous furniture and beautiful grounds, and yet it may utterly lack that repose and harmony and sensation of "coziness" without which a true, heart-satisfying home can not be made any where, even if all the members of the family that occupy it are genial, good-natured, and affectionate, and, as every one knows, these qualities are so important that without them there can be no home life at all, but only a restless unhappiness and a passionate longing for peace and kindly fellowship.

They make up three fourths of a home, it is true, and with them one may be happy, even with the most incongruous surroundings, but still there will be a sensation of "something wanting."

There are costly houses scattered all over the country, elegantly furnished and full of luxury, but the moment you are ushered into their drawing-rooms, where the expensive furniture is carefully swathed in cold-looking linen, and books, if not altogether absent, are, because of their handsome bindings, practically labeled "touch not, handle not," being stowed away under glass covers to be seen, not read, you feel a chill sense of uneasiness and draw a sigh of relief as you pass out again into the free and untrammeled air.

Again, there are snug little cottages all about us, where every apartment, though furnished in the plainest manner, conveys an idea of comfort, ease, and home.

Now, though we have few very fine houses as yet in Florida, we find this same difference in full existence. We have seen houses well built, with large rooms, halls, and piazzas, and all necessary furniture, the dwelling-places of wealthy people, which conveyed not the faintest touch of that home feeling so dear to us all. We have seen the same thing in other houses, where the owners had dwelt for years and yet had planted neither tree, nor vine, nor flowers, around them; where chickens and pigs roamed in and out of the house at will, in and under the beds and tables; sometimes a rough rail fence suffices to keep cattle at a respectful distance from the house, but often the house is dropped down in the piney woods without any fence at all.

We passed such a house as the latter one day (our conscience forbids us to call it a home), and a woman arrayed in one scanty garment, a "kaliker" dress, was singing over the wash-tub, near the door, while a sow and three of her progeny were visible from our point of view (a saddle) inside the narrow entry; at the door, half inside, were a cow and calf, and, roosting contentedly on the window-sill, were a half dozen chickens.

The woman nodded at us with the customary "Howdy!" and we rode on with a wonder and a half-sigh—the wonder at the evident contentment of that woman under such a state of existence, and the half-sigh because some of the rest of us could not be content with it also—it involves so little work and so little expense—at least, until our groves come into profit; for that little significant word, "until," covers for many a Florida settler a multitude of weary days and months, aye, and years, if he has not the wherewithal to meet current expenses or raise other fruits and vegetables while waiting the happy climax to his labors.

It often happens to such an one to wish that human creatures could do as the alligators and water-turtles, namely, go down into the mud and lie dormant until the sun shines, or, what means the same thing here, until the grove has arrived at full bearing.

And now we hear a voice at our shoulder more truthful than complimentary, "Goosie, goosie gander, whither will ye wander?" It is true we have strayed from our path.

Let us go back to our present task of making a home, such an one, we mean, as we find here and there, with neat fences, clearly laid out walks bordered with oleander or other ornamental trees, with roses and other flowers scattered all around, with broad latticed piazzas, shaded and beautified by densely foliaged vines, mingled together in a joyous, happy-go-lucky fashion that is charming to see.

Bona nox, evening glory, yellow jasmine, coral honeysuckle, and trumpet creeper, beauties, all of them, and to be had for the digging in the hammocks all around. Thunbergia, cypress-vine, barclayana, evening jasmine, English ivy, honeysuckle, all these and many more, hobnob together in riotous exuberance, and the glory and fragrance of their loving embrace must be seen to be realized.

This is a type of the home we would have every lady to own who comes to live in our "Land of Flowers;" and she can easily have it, too, and in less time than one would suppose possible. To any one accustomed to the slow growth and yearly check for months of vegetable life in the North, the rapid, luxurious, and almost ceaseless, growth of Florida vegetation is simply wonderful.

If you own so much as twenty acres of land, in some sections, it will go hard if there is not at least one large or small lakelet on the tract. If it be a deep one, at least in the center, it will never go dry like a cow; build your house near by, not very close, else in wet weather the water may creep up to your door—but so as to have a full view of the clear, sparkling water, and the beautiful water-lilies that are either already there or can be brought from more favored lakelets in the neighborhood. A little water, in one pure, mirror-like spot, will do wonders for a landscape; in fact, one feels the want of a principal element of beauty, if it is not to be seen.

As we have intimated, there are few tracts of twenty, or even ten acres, in the Lake Regions of Florida, where a lake of some kind may not be found. From the second-story of a house at the writer's hand, for instance, no less than ten such sheets of water, some larger, some smaller, are visible, their extent altering greatly as the wet or the dry season prevails.

"Are they not unhealthy?" we are often asked. No, not at all; they are vastly different from the ponds scattered widely through many of our Northern States, which have mild bottoms, and in which the water becomes stagnant and malarial; our numerous Florida lakelets (we don't degrade them by calling them ponds) are formed by hollows of different sizes becoming filled with water during the copious rains of summer.

Sometimes they are originated and fed by springs; but, however this may be, the fact remains that their bottoms are composed entirely of sand, clean, pure, and unfouled by mud. The water constantly filters down through the sand, and a constant evaporation also takes place from the surface, so that its mass is always changing and never stagnates.

Many a time have we ridden through these little lakelets when the water was so deep as to necessitate lifting our feet to our horse's back, and yet the white sand and short grass at the bottom were almost as plainly to be seen as if uncovered.

When the dry time comes, and they begin to recede from their shallow margins, there is nothing left exposed to decay in the sun and air, as there is on the great lake shores, only clean sand, or perhaps a few blades of timid, slender grass, looking as if frightened to death at its return to dry land.

There are no healthier localities than those containing these numerous little sheets of water, and they are not only ornamental, as we have said, but useful also. The horses, cattle, chickens, ducks, dogs, all the domestic family, in fact, regard them with high favor as fashionable watering-places, and frequent them accordingly, especially during the summer season. The horses and cattle browse around their margins, and indulge in frequent baths, the chickens have a fine time chasing insects and hunting little frogs; the ducks paddle about to their hearts' content, only slightly demoralized when, once in a while, a wicked alligator pokes up his head and one of their number reluctantly accompanies him on his return trip to the bottom of the lake. The dogs lap up the pure, clear water and go their way rejoicing, and the cats, when disgusted with the table kept by their owners, go down to the shore and step on the damp ground with a comically reluctant, dainty tread, and sitting down at the water's edge, with a silent protest against such useless moisture, wait patiently, with pricked up ears and intent gaze, until a luckless fish swims within the fatal radius of those lurking claws, and then, presto! a paw goes under the water, like a flash, and the fish comes out, bewildered with its sudden rise in the world.

That last word gives another phase of the usefulness of even our smaller lakes, for there is scarcely one that lacks a supply of fish. The so-called trout, which are really black bass, are found in nearly all, and the bream, sunfish, warmouth perch and cat-fish, abound. They are all fine fish for the table, their flesh sweet and firm. The trout often attain a weight of from twelve to fifteen pounds, the others are smaller and good for frying; often also, in these small lakes, a small fish abounds, so tiny as to be cooked like the smelts, or frost-fish, of the Northern winter markets, namely, in one indiscriminate mass. They taste very much like them too.

Then there are turtle in these lakelets, real genuine turtle. We don't claim that they are green turtle, but nevertheless they are excellent eating, either in soup, a plain stew, or cooked *a la terrapin*. There are two kinds. One, a very handsome fellow, with an arched, hardshell back, boldly marbled in orange and black. He is a mild, inoffensive creature, and very pleasant to interview in the soup tureen. We can't speak so highly, socially, of his brother turtle, who is an unmitigated scamp, with a broad, flat, leathery back, hard in the center and pliable at the edges, and who wears a dirty, blackish, wrinkled coat. He is not mild nor inoffensive; try him once, and you will see in what manner he will dart his long, horny, tube-like snout at your fingers. He always receives very respectful treatment from his captors until the opportunity, carefully watched for, arrives, of cleaving the threatening snout from his ugly body, or, perchance, he ends his days in a pail of boiling water, which, after all, is the best and most merciful way of ending them.

The largest we have seen of either of these turtles weighed about ten pounds, and they, with the fish, are no despicable gifts from the little lakelets to the family table.

How are they caught? Well, we will come to that in due time.

Very often, too, water-fowl frequent their smooth waters, and from this source a sportsman can furnish many a welcome dish for the household. In front of our modest home, with a short avenue of oleander trees leading down to its grass-grown shore, is one of these little lakes we have been talking about. It does not cover an acre of ground at its largest, and in dry times it shrinks to a deep half-acre basin in the center, whose sides are evidently perpendicular like a well. It never contracts more than this, and is probably fed by springs.

The water is as clear as crystal, and in calm weather reflects the sun and clouds like a burnished mirror, while, in windy times, it is wonderful to see how the miniature waves rise up so as to thump and toss our little boat and curl their white caps all around it. Our circular water mirror has a veritable frame of its own of green and gold, a clear, unbroken circle, about six feet wide, of a curious aquatic plant with small leaves floating on the surface of the water, and bright yellow flowers rising above them, clearly defining the edge of the well-like, permanent basin.

"I would give five hundred dollars for a lakelet like that on my place," exclaimed a less fortunate neighbor whose water-mirrors will sometimes shrink away to nothing, leaving a grass-grown hollow that cattle delight in. And this wish is expressed, not on account of the beauty of that little shining spot, but because of its permanency, and hence its value to its owner, should he desire to water his grove or truck gardens in a dry time by the aid of a windmill, or use it for the supply of his house. In this connection, five hundred dollars is a low estimate of the value of a permanent lakelet, large or small, near one's grove and house.

Few persons realize the vast utility and comfort of possessing a sure, never-failing water-supply, by means of a windmill. A windmill, to the masses, is an "unknown quantity," a thing of complexity, of mystery, of heavy, unprofitable expense. But we would urge an earnest consideration of this subject upon our readers.

Even where not desired for large irrigating operations, a small size windmill would vastly increase the comfort of a whole household, ease the burdens of the housewife, and insure the safety of the house in case of fire.

It could also be utilized to bring water to the barn-yard, to irrigate the home vegetable garden or strawberry patch; in fact, the uses to which a never-failing supply of water could be turned are legion; yet any one of them would be worth the whole cost of obtaining such a supply.

The added comforts a windmill could contribute to the home life of the Florida householder are manifold and will be easily seen by any one who pauses to give the subject due attention.

Realizing its importance in this connection, we have looked well into the matter of windmills, and have found that while there are several makes on the market—all claiming (of course) to be the best—there is one that stands pre-eminent, as not only being more simple, durable and effective—moving and pumping, just as it is set to do, whether the wind blows a gale or a zephyr—but, has never yet been dismounted, even by the fierce western tornadoes, when every other kind of windmill exposed to them went down to the ground in sorrow and sadness. For this fact, and also for its superiority, we have the testimony of those who have proved its sterling qualities for years.

This particular windmill is rightly named the "Champion," and is manufactured by R. J. Douglass & Company, of Waukegan, Illinois, one of the oldest and most reliable establishments in the United States. They are also, we would remark, in passing, manufacturers of pumps of all kinds, and notably of the "Star" pump, which is unsurpassed for family use. Seeking reliable data, as to the actual cost of such a mill as would meet all the points we have named, we went to the "fountain-head," and here is the estimate furnished: "A windmill erected on a tower, thirty to thirty-five feet, which is high enough for Florida, would cost about sixty-five to seventy-five dollars. A tank to hold two hundred barrels of water, about fifty dollars. A pump, all complete, one of the best for a well twenty-five to thirty feet deep (or for a pond), about twenty dollars or thereabouts. Probably the total cost of this outfit would not exceed one hundred and fifty dollars. Of course larger mills, more tanks, and larger ones, can be put up at an additional cost. A person can bring his water-supply up into the thousands, or he can make it very cheap."

Those of our readers who desire still further information can obtain it from the manufacturers.

As a rule, the shores of Florida lakelets incline so gradually to the deep water in the center that fishing from the shore is out of the question, unless one chooses to follow the example of the small boy, and wade out waist-deep. A prettily painted skiff riding on the water adds much to its beauty, but where such can not be procured, a home-made flat-bottomed scow answers almost as well for fishing.

As we said awhile ago, it is better to put your house back a few hundred yards from the lakelet, not only for the reason then given, but because, if you have no other conveniently near, you will either have to shut out your chickens, horses, and calves from its enjoyment, or else lay aside all idea of building up a cozy, home-like surrounding.

Chickens, horses, and calves don't agree with flowers, trees, and vines. Fence off a small space around the house; if regularly made pickets can not be had (and this is the case in many parts of the State), shingling laths from the nearest saw-mill, cut into five-feet lengths, make an excellent substitute, painted or whitewashed. We say a small space advisedly, because unless one is able to keep a man or boy constantly employed among the flowers and small fruit trees and grass plats around the house, the weeds will gather headway and soon choke the more delicate plants to death, and that wicked, irrepressible sand-spur grass, with its tall tufts of sharp, stiff, hooked points, that puncture like a needle, and hold fast with a tenacity of purpose that we might admire under other circumstances, will quickly take possession of the territory and make pedestrians unhappy, especially those who are unfortunate enough to wear skirts. One might well liken these vandals of the Florida soil to an uneasy conscience, "their prick" is sharp enough surely.

They are called "spurs" rather sarcastically it would seem, since their effect is to retard progress rather than to spur it on. They are bad enough in the field or grove, but they become intolerable around the house, and so, since they and other obstreperous weeds flourish during nine months of the year, and require constant watchfulness to keep them under subjection, it is better to throw most of the battle upon the plow outside of the garden gate; for, in a family where the means are wanting to hire a man or boy by the month, the burden of keeping such "useless trash" as flowers or vines in order will be cast by the busy men folks upon their more delicate companions who are more alive to their actual utility as home attractions.

Those who have come from the old-settled, thoroughly civilized portions of the North or West, or indeed of the South, will almost inevitably experience a sense of dismay and hopelessness at the prospect of the long struggle before them, when they behold a wilderness of oak or pine trees rearing their heads aloft on the very spot selected for their home. Where a place can be purchased with improvements already started it is a great gain; but the majority can not secure such an one, and so must carve their own home out of the virgin forest. Nor is this such a dreadful undertaking as it appears at the outset, the trees and vines grow so rapidly, and it is such a pleasure to watch their increase and note how steadily order is forming out of chaos and comfort and beauty marching to the front.

We know all about it, because our own home was started amid a forest of tall, deadened trees, with a straggling field of corn growing in their midst, and sand-spurs so luxuriant that every step was painful and almost impossible until a plow had turned under the obnoxious vandals. The white, ghostly-looking trees had to be hewn down, cut up and rolled away in piles to be burnt, the stumps also grubbed and burned out, and the corn laid low before the carpenters could even lay the foundation for the house.

The kitchen, which is generally detached from the main house, was built first, and the two members of the family who preceded the rest in their flight from the chilly north lived therein, cooking on an oil stove out of doors for two months. The room was commodious enough, twelve by eighteen feet; but for a dwelling, after a large, three-story city house, with all modern conveniences, was a somewhat bewildering change, and the wild surroundings of a native forest, and the rat-tat-tat of hammers on the main house, and the thud of falling trees all day, the weird glare of a hundred fires illuminating the landscape at night, flashing back from that little mirror we have spoken of— all these things added not a little to the oddity of a novel scene, until irresistibly arose the recollection and personal application of the famous nursery rhyme, of the "Little old woman who fell asleep on the king's highway, who, bewildered by the curtailment of her skirts by a peddler while she slept, exclaimed:

"'If I be I, as I hope I be,
I've a little dog at home, and he knows me;
If I be I, he will wag his little tail.
If I be not I, he will bark and he will wail.'

"Home went the little woman, all in the dark,
Up jumped the little dog, and he began to bark;
The dog began to bark, and she began to cry,
'Oh, lawk! oh, mercy! this surely can't be I!'"

When the house was finished, every one went to work to "fix up" and transform the crude elements into a comfortable, home-like place; the stronger arms went to digging out and burning out stumps; and, in a few months, one pair of arms—unaccustomed to such work, too—disposed of over three hundred of these unsightly hindrances to cultivation. The weaker hands found full employment, first, in placing in order furniture, pictures, busts, brackets, and various knicknacks that tell so much of the refinements of a true home, wherever it may be or however humble; and, a little later, in directing the formation of flower-beds and walks around the house, and setting out roses and budding plants; in rooting and planting oleander slips; in sowing thunbergia and other rapid-growing vines; in procuring from the neighboring hammocks yellow jasmine, creepers, scarlet honeysuckle, bona nox, and other thrifty vines to the manor born.

They all looked very small and puny at first, and it seemed almost ridiculous to hope to see the oleanders become trees, or the vines cover the lattice-work around the porch, or to dream that the two-feet-high orange trees, set out from a grove near by, would ever be large enough to support one orange, not to say thousands of that luscious golden fruit. But, in three years from the time this work of creating a home out of the wilderness was commenced, the oleanders towered aloft higher than the roof and mingled their fragrant pink flowers across the carriage way.

The roses, that came to us in cigar-boxes, ran riot over frames and covered one end of the house, reaching above the attic window at the peak of the roof and disputing the march of a noble English ivy; verbenas covered the ground in luxuriant masses, petunias flourished and bloomed, sometimes becoming perennials, while, for six months or more of the year, phlox of all conceivable colors and shades made the ground one brilliant mass of color, sowing itself season after season, just as buttercups, dandelions, violets, and daisies dot the fields at the North. The vines had clambered to the very top of the lattice in one tangled mass and spread out below into a dense mass of foliage.

The evening jasmine towered above the piazza roof, shading one end completely, and filling the air with its delicate fragrance, almost too powerful, however, as the sun went down.

More important than all, the back-bone of a Florida home, the orange trees, had aspired above their two-feet stature into goodly trees of eight to ten feet high; lime trees, one foot high when planted, towered to the attic windows and were loaded with fruit; guavas, raised from seed sown two years before, bore fruit enough to supply the table; Florida lemon trees were loaded with yellow fruit, and some fine budded sorts were in bloom.

All this in three years from the wilderness, with no commercial fertilizers, and on exceptionally poor soil. So you see it is not so fearful a thing as it looks to be, this making a home in the Florida woods.

We have not thus related our own experience from egotism, but because we could better thus depict the methods and result of intelligent, refined labor, and so dispel the dread that is doubtless felt by many would-be Florida settlers at the idea of starting a new home out of virgin materials and on virgin soil.

As soon as the novelty wears off, and one "gets used" to the inevitable differences in the new mode of life, the work of carving out the home, with all its varied surroundings, becomes one of fascinating interest, which grows deeper month by month, as the plants and trees rise up and testify their thankfulness for kind treatment.

CHAPTER X. HOME SURROUNDINGS.

Grass Lawns. Vines and Flowers. Shade-trees and Arbors. Shade for Poultry-yards.

One of the hardest things for a Northerner to bear, on first coming to Florida, is the absence of the beautiful green turf and lawn so familiar to his sight that no country home seems half a home without this grateful resting place for the eyes. We are used to seeing it all around our old homes and in great fields all over the land, and because we do not see the same in this newly-settled country, the cry has been raised, "Grass will not grow in Florida."

Now that is a great mistake, and a great injustice done to a State that only wants a chance given her to show what she can do in the way of raising grasses.

If the fine lawn grasses, so abundant now in the old-settled Northern States, are indigenous and grow of themselves just where they are wanted, as some unreasonable people seem to expect they should do in Florida, how is it that the seedsmen advertise "lawn grass" seeds for sale, and the agricultural papers are so particular each year to give full directions as to the proper way of preparing the ground and sowing the seed for making lawns?

We have spent a great many months of our life in the country at the North, and we never yet saw a piece of woodland, that had never been cleared, plowed or planted, that could be utilized as a ready-made pasture sufficient for cattle. Where we see green fields and meadows, the grass has been sowed there; it has not sprung up by magic, and it has required a good many years and a great deal of care to make a good pasture at all. Yet much-maligned Florida, even in her uncleared virgin woodlands, does raise a grass that subsists hundreds of thousands of cattle all the year round, so that their owners are never at one dollar of expense to keep them.

This is the famous wire-grass that grows every where in the piney woods, tender and nutritious when young, but tough enough when old. It grows in tufts, starting out from the root in early spring, and keeps on growing as fast as the cattle eat it, until late in the fall, when it grows more slowly and the cattle are apt to leave it and seek the moss-draped hammocks for two or three months.

Florida has other grasses too that are destined before long to supply her with all the hay she needs, some native, others imported. We shall speak of them by and by, but at present we shall only speak of those that make a close, thick turf, and can be made important factors in the work of making home beautiful.

Carpet grass is one of them. It is a native of the country, and makes a low, tolerably close mat of green, but it does not grow evenly as a lawn grass should do, nor will it endure uninjured even our light winters, so we do not very much approve of carpet grass. We want something better and more permanent around our houses, and we find it in Bermuda grass. This is a fine, dark-green turfy grass that is yearly growing more and more in favor; the sole objection to it, either as lawn or pasture grass, being its habit of straying out of bounds, and this is a very small matter in comparison with its real value. We heard of Bermuda grass when we first came to Florida, and there chanced to be a small patch of it on our land, where a few roots, sent to the former owner from Kentucky, had been carelessly stuck down. The patch was not a yard square, and no more was to be had. But we wanted grass, no matter how little it might be. We felt lost without our plat of green to rest the eyes on when sitting on the porch, so two small plats of the sandy soil were leveled off and inclosed by a border of strips, one on each side of the broad path leading down to the lakelet, and then the few roots of Bermuda were .planted in spots about twenty inches apart. They looked very ridiculous at first, "little dried-up wisps of straw," somebody called them; with the bare sand dividing them from each other, it seemed hopeless to expect ever to see those desolate-looking plats covered with grass. But the " little dried-up wisps," as soon as they recovered from their astonishment at being moved, put up tiny green blades, and kept on trying to shake hands with their neighbors, until, in less than a year, they succeeded in embracing each other and uniting into one beautiful brotherhood of emerald-green turf. Another year, and so luxuriant was its growth, that the boundary strips were removed and leave given it to roam whither it would; so, now, a fine large plat of deep green stretches out before the house, where, only a few years ago, was nothing but rough, weed-infested sand, hard to walk on, ofttimes painfully hot to the feet and glaring to the eyes whenever the sun was shining. The horses rejoice to graze on it whenever permitted, the cows and calves eagerly munch the sweet hay it makes when cut, as it has to be several times each summer when it has grown up to be eight or ten inches high; children love to roll on it, and visitors exclaim, while wonderingly rubbing their feet back and forth on the short, springy turf, "I've never seen any thing like this in Florida." But there is no reason why it should not be seen all over the State, wherever there is a house occupied by people who want to make a home in the land of their adoption.

In the particular case we have referred to the creeping propensities of the one-time small plat of green turf are so far from being regarded with terror that they are being encouraged, and a few years hence, from present appearances, from house to lakelet will be one beautiful lawn, refreshing to the eyes and a thing of joy forever to the horses or calves that may be tethered thereon. There will be trees in its midst, orange, pear, peach, Japan plum, Japan persimmon; but we have no fears of their being injured by the grass, rather will their roots be shaded and the ground made richer by the turf that will decay around them, as nine years of experience has proved.

We used to be told that a lawn of grass was impossible in the piney woods of Florida, but we laugh at that idea now. The Bermuda looks well all the year round, though during the months of December and January it stands still, and sometimes looks a little weary of well-doing, it never dies down entirely; on poor soil it spreads slowly, on good ground, or with a top-dressing of stable-manure, ashes or bone-meal, it grows rapidly and tall. It crowds out obnoxious weeds, and altogether lends so pleasant and homelike an air to one's garden that we can not too strongly urge the Florida settler to plant Bermuda, or, as it is really named after its introducer, a sea captain, "Permudy" grass, close to their houses.

"Familiarity breeds contempt," and we are so accustomed to see grass around our houses at the North, wherever there is room for it, that we do not realize until we see an expanse of desolate, weed-grown sand, what a great factor it is in our lives.

Looking at the great oleander trees, with their stiff, dark-green leaves and bright pink flowers, growing so luxuriantly without care all the year round "out in the open," it is hard to realize that this is the same plant that is so highly prized and so tenderly cared for in our Northern homes.

There they are reared in boxes, and at the first approach of cold weather hurried off into the warmer cellars, a specimen six feet high being regarded as a great possession.

Here we see them every where, in every yard of any pretensions, towering to the height of thirty feet and loaded with blooms. Their growth is very rapid; in four years on poor soil, a slip rooted in a bottle will become a widespreading tree ten feet high. Delicate vines, that will hardly grow at all in the chilly North, here flourish in the wildest luxuriance, and in our milder winters do not even die down to the roots, and, when they do, set to work again in the spring just as if nothing had happened to them.

It is well known that the most beautiful roses are the most tender, and can not be raised in the open air at the North; but here they run riot, and not only so, but many of the tea-roses that are not supposed to be runners at all become regular runaways and clamber all over one's porch or lattice- work; the glorious, fragrant queen of flowers, peeping out here and there, amid a mass of tangled vines in such unexpected places that vague ideas of a return of the days of miracles float about in one's mind, until a close examination reveals the runaway rose branch hiding slyly amidst the dense foliage of another plant. In fact, the ways of the denizens of the vegetable world in Florida are full of surprises to the ignorant Northern mind, and their ways eccentric to the last degree.

Morning-glories, that grow so luxuriantly in the North, are apt to become curious dwarfs here, miniature plants that trail for two or three feet on the ground and bear flowers proportionate in size. Cypress vines, so tender and shy of growth in the North, in Florida run rampant, climbing to the tops of fences and lattice-work, and then drooping downward like beautiful feathery cascades of scarlet and green, or else ramble at will over the ground in wild beauty, running up to the tops of tall weeds, then down, and here and there and every where.

Tuberoses, lilies, and hyacinths, among bulbous roots, do well: and there are beautiful white lilies and pink lilies growing wild in the hammocks, that flourish when transplanted to a flower-bed. The *bona nox* (good-night) is a remarkably rapid-growing vine, with leaves shaped much like an ivy, set singly about three inches apart, on a slim, leathery, pliable stem; it is not only, as we have said, so rapid a grower that it is sometimes called "railroad ivy," but from the base of each leaf two or three stems start out, each of which seems to vie with the other as to which can travel the fastest. The result is a fine, dense shade in an incredibly short space of time, if one only has the patience to keep pace with the long, down-reaching stems that hang helplessly downward, waiting to be put up like long hair that has no curl to it.

The flower of the *bona nox* is as much of a curiosity as the vine itself. It is large and pure white, save for faint green bands that mark it off in several divisions. It is shaped like a shallow convolvulus, with tips so decidedly pointed as, when open, to present a star-like appearance. It is a handsome, waxy, showy flower; but the most curious thing about it is its manner of opening; it don't do it at all in the quiet, respectable way, so fashionable in the world of flowers. It reminds one of those jerky, excitable people who move through life on springs, who bounce and thump over every little unevenness in their path, who can not work quietly nor open a door save with a jerk. This is just the way the *bona nox* behaves; from the seed to the flower it growls with one continuous rush, as though running for a wager; and the flower—well, you see the long, white bud, just as the sun has put his night-cap on and gone to bed; it is about three inches in length, like a slender finger—you see it there among the thick, green leaves, lying *perdu*; but the moment the bright luminary sinks to rest the bud awakes to a sense of its own impoliteness to the god of day, and lo! in an instant, while you draw a breath, the bud is gone and in its place a broad, white flower is nodding '*bona nox*" "good night." It is like a transformation scene in a fairy tale, one moment a bud, the next, in the twinkling of an eye, the full-blown flower. So quickly does it open, that even when waiting on purpose to see it, one often fails, though sometimes a slight tremor is visible, as though a tiny elf were inside the bud, slyly casting loose its bonds. Opening at sunset, the flower remains open until the sun rises again. This curious vine is at the beck and call of every one, for it is a native of the hammock and readily propagated from the seed or root. It is the now famous "Moon Flower," recently introduced in the North and Europe.

Another native vine, also a strong grower, and bearing a pink, convolvulus-shaped flower and a pretty shield-like leaf, is the "evening glory." This, like the *bona nox,* opens after the sun has sunk low in the west, unless when the ay proves to be that rare thing in Florida, a thoroughly cloudy day, and then it remains open.

The yellow jessamine is another favorite for home decoration, and abundant in the hammocks; its quick growth, once it gets started, its abundant, permanent foliage and fragrant yellow flowers, and above all its scornful disregard of frosty weather, which makes sad havoc of the bona nox and evening glory, all combine to make it very desirable to train over our porches and arbors wherever needed.

The clematis, coral honey suckle, Virginia creeper, and trumpet creeper, that seems to have no particular name, are also to be found in the hammocks, and all of these native vines seem not to mind their transfer to pine lands, but thrive and grow apace.

The question of shade is of no small importance in a land where three fourths of the year is summer, and where the sun shines nearly every day. Occasionally the newcomer is fortunate enough to find a few large oak trees growing on the site he has fixed on for his house, and then, if the latter is built to the northeast of these and not very far away, their dense foliage will shield the southern and western rooms from the direct rays of the summer's sun, a blessing not to be despised.

As to the pine trees that may be on the building site, they must come down, every one of them—nay, we are wrong, a lightning-rod is wanted, and these tall pines make very effective ones; there should be one left standing on each side of the house, deadened of course, and so far away (but no farther) that, if some day they come toppling down before a lively breeze, they will not come

> Tap, tap, tapping at the door,
> Splintering that and something more.

In planting shade trees, and this is one of the first things that should be done, no more beautiful and no more rapid growers can be found than the Texas umbrella tree and its kindred, but less symmetrical tree, the *China-berry*. Their graceful, fern-like foliage adds not a little to the attractive looks of a Florida home.

The mulberry is another rapidly growing shade tree. Two or three of these set on the south side of a house will, in a few years, give as dense a shade as one need desire; but these trees have the disadvantage of being at a certain season almost stripped of their leaves by an ugly worm that takes possession of them and well-nigh skeletonizes them. The Russian mulberry, however, is exempt from this drawback, having no insect enemies. In the winter also they are apt to lose their leaves just as they do at the North.

Where porches can not be afforded, and trees are being waited for, an excellent plan is to put up an arbor such as is commonly used for grape-vines. Let it be parallel with the house, on the south or west, since these are the points where the summer's sun rests all the day long, and about eight to ten feet from it make a slatted roof sloping from the wall, and then plant rapid-growing vines of all kinds and train them up the arbor. It is really wonderful how quickly an efficient shade can be obtained in this simple way; and the effect is charming— the various shades of green, dotted all over with the buff, orange, and white of the thunbergias, the light yellow of the jessamine, and the vivid scarlet of the cypress; one or two of the swift-growing wild, or, better still, Scuppernong grape-vines will help greatly to make the green background for the vivid flowers, and by and by these grape-vines may be left in undisputed possession of the arbor, furnishing not only a leafy screen, but an abundance of grapes.

While the vines are growing up the sides of the arbor, how about its roof? We want shade under that too, want it at once to keep the sun, when high in the heavens, from peeping down inside our green wall and heating the wooden walls of our house.

An awning stretched over the slatted roof is just the thing, not a water-proof one either, but one which will ward off the fierce rays of the sun while allowing the rain to pass through it, because you want a flower-bed under your window, and flowers need rain.

Under such an awning as we have in our mind, and, we may add, shading our study, plants will grow that could not be raised in Florida without some such shelter; here, under the reflected sunlight that sifts down to the ground, hyacinths, pansies, violets, fuchsias, and geraniums wax exceedingly beautiful and grow apace under the sheltering care of bagging stuff; yes, just those coarse bags in which oats, coffee, and corn are sold; rip them open, sew them together, nail them ou your slatted roof, and the work is done.

Really, this subject seems inexhaustible, and in fact it is so, for there is none more important nor more susceptible of new ideas than this, of making a home that will satisfy heart, mind, and body, and conduce to content, cheerfulness, and health.

We have already wandered round considerably out of doors; that is a way we have of doing in Florida, three fourths of our time at least, and consequently we are not quite prepared to go in yet.

We have told somewhat of the wealth of beautiful flowers and vines that may be gathered around the house, and trained over the porches, but we have not yet mentioned one of the most important and by far the most fragrant, the evening jessamine. It is impossible for the Northern mind to conceive, from its home experience, the strong, thrifty growth of this much-prized plant in this genial clime. The plant, as it is known there, is a frail, delicate thing, of slow and precarious growth, almost impossible to rear outside of conservatories, "a pampered, aristocratic darling," over whose wayward blossoming there is much rejoicing and much boasting. We remember that, a few years back, our whole family was summoned one evening, in great haste, to the house of a neighbor to view the bloom of the cherished evening jessamine, growing in a small flower-pot, and to enjoy the delicious perfume it exhaled; we were made happy by the presentation of a slip for rooting, that we might "go and do likewise." But now, to see this same fragrant, delicate night-bird among flowers in Florida!

Three years ago a tiny slip, not six inches tall, rooted in a box, was set at the end of our ten-feet-wide piazza, fortunately, as the result proved, it was placed near the middle. At the present time, although several times it was killed back almost to the ground, that wonderful jessamine forms a dense, fan-shaped shade all over the end of the piazza a foot or more in thickness, and reaching several feet above the piazza roof. Almost all the year it is in bloom, and as darkness settles down upon the earth its little starlike flowers, gathered in clusters, peep out to see what the stars look like, and toss their fragrant greeting abroad in the air. Then, if never before, we understand what is meant by the "air being heavy with perfume." Sometimes it is almost too powerful, and then we indulge a wish that our much-valued jessamine was a little further away; but usually we are not disposed to quarrel with it.

Of course the various plants and vines are the better for suitable food. We don't expect people or horses to work on day after day without nutriment, yet some people do expect their vegetable servants, which are living things as well, to exist and grow without food. Their requirements are modest: on hammock land they will ask no help for a few years, but on pine land they will need more at first than later on. There, you see, is the difference between hammock and pine land, as those who are ahead of their times are beginning to discover; one, better at the start, deteriorates; the other, poor at the start, constantly improves. If some muck, rotten leaves, cow-chips, or stable-manure, can be spaded into the flower-beds, before setting out the plants, so much the better; but if the plants are ready first, this can be done later on, although of course more care must then be exercised not to disturb the newly anchored roots.

A wonderful tonic and invigorator of the growth of plants, not only in Florida, but every where, is a weekly or semi-weekly dose of liquid manure, made thus: two buckets, or twenty pounds, of stable-manure to one barrel of water; let it stand for twenty-four hours before using. It should be of the color of weak coffee when applied, and sometimes it is necessary to dilute it to attain this color. An ounce or two of carbolic acid is a great improvement, as it serves to discourage the "Meddlesome Matties" so numerous among the insect families.

A heavy mulch of leaves, grass, or pine needles, will be of double advantage, not only retaining moisture and an even temperature for the roots of trees and plants, but also preventing the continuous and excessive growth of weeds, which, proverbially rampant all over the world, are not backward in asserting themselves in Florida.

Weeds, we say; yet, after all, what are weeds? The fact is it all depends on where one stands. How we cherish and coax geraniums to grow, buying plants and seeds from the nurseryman; yet in Australia, their native land, they are weeds, and regarded as nuisances. Our Northern florists advertise, among others, the rose geranium, and their customers think highly of them; here, in Florida, they run rampant. Put a tiny slip from a bouquet into a Florida bed, and in a few months it will be trespassing on its neighbors' domains; it will travel right and left, and actually become a runner. It keeps one busy lopping off great arm-loads of straggling branches; but we don't quarrel with it after all. The leaves are fragrant and form a pretty addition to bouquets; the mass of green is always acceptable to the eye, and when a geranium is planted here and there about the grounds and trained into a mound-shape the effect is very pleasing; but still these geraniums are in a measure " weeds" in Florida.

And how the Northern gardener sows seeds year after year of the phlox and petunia. In Florida all that is necessary is to once sow a small paper of these seeds, and henceforth, year after year, phlox and petunias greet you every where, nodding their gay little heads in the grassplats, the flower-beds, and the corn-field; then, you see, they become "weeds;" it is the same with the cypress vine, the bona nox, and in fact with almost every plant that has seeds. It is wonderful how persistently they sow themselves broadcast. There is a miniature portulacca, with pink flowers about a quarter of an inch in diameter, a native of the soil, that is rather pretty, but becomes a nuisance because it degenerates into a weed and keeps one constantly on the war-path.

The ease with which delicate plants, guarded and cherished at the North, perpetuate themselves in Florida, and imitate the example of the famous Topsy, who was not brought up, but "just growed," is a source of surprise to natives of the more chilly States; but it is readily traced to its cause, no freezing to kill the germs of the tender seeds.

One of the most striking and distinctively tropical plants that one can find to set out in the Florida flower-garden is the native "yucca," or, as it is generally called, the "Spanish bayonet." This is a curious plant found in the hammocks, and bears transplanting to pine land very well. It is formed by a straight spine, as it were, on which are thickly set long, narrow, stifle-edged leaves, which droop downward and are armed at the point with a sharp spine, whence its name, "Spanish bayonet." It often attains a height of ten or twelve feet, and here and there, especially near the top, short stubs project, which, being detached and planted, will soon root and start out in life on their own account. This plant is an ornament of itself; but when, in June usually, it sends upward one or more tall stalks, three or four of them sometimes, thickly draped with large, pure white, bell-like flowers, what shall we say? It is then a beautiful object that one never tires of looking at, and its snowy plumes attract the eye from a long distance. But we have dealt with the esthetic part of our subject long enough; esthetic, yet not in this case useless, for one's home can not be made too attractive.

But it must have its creature comforts too; for we are of the earth "earthy." Not one of the least of these is the water supply. There are a few houses in Florida whose owners have provided large tanks on the roof, into which water is pumped from a lake or well by means of a windmill, pipes leading from the tank conducting water throughout the dwelling; and these convenient contrivances can, as we have seen, be had by people of moderate means. In a few localities only, well-water is not good, being hard from the underlying limestone rock; but all through the rolling pine lands the water obtained from the wells is soft and as pure as crystal; indeed, none better could be desired. During the summer months it is not as cool as the Northern taste could wish, bred up, as it is, with the idea that ice in the summer is a necessity. In fact, this lack of ice is at first one of the settler's greatest deprivations; but with this, as with all things, time effects a cure, and by and by the water seems to grow cooler, and rarely fails to quench the summer thirst. One could almost declare, after the first summer, that it actually has become cooler, so powerful is custom. It is possible, too, to make a decided change in the temperature of the water by keeping that intended for drinking in those large earthenware jars that are manufactured for the purpose, water-jars, they are called. The writer has seen them in use in South America, and they are equally useful in Florida; drawing the water over night and allowing it to stand out where the night air will blow over it is a good way to secure a cool morning drink. In the fall, winter, and spring months, the water is quite cool enough for any one, and often "makes one's teeth ache."

As to the depth at which water is met with, it all depends on location. If dug on a decided knoll, thirty or forty feet are not uncommon before the water-level is reached. On lesser knolls (it is very unusual to see a Florida home that is not built on a "rise") water is often found at from eight to twelve feet. Of course the water-level varies with the wet or dry season, and so it is always best to dig, if possible, when the lakelets round about have reached their minimum. If you can not do this, the well will have to be deepened as the surrounding lakes lower their waters. It costs from fifty to seventy-five cents per foot to have the well dug, and until clay is reached the 'sides must be curbed and the cost of planking must be added to the sum total. Usually the well for family use will not altogether cost more than eight to ten dollars. As a rule, the bucket, rope, and pulley are the means employed to obtain the water. Pumps are as yet a rarity, not quite so much as they were a few years ago, but still far more so than they should be, with a due regard for the patient workers on whom the burden of hauling up the heavy buckets from the depths of the well usually falls. There is quite work enough for the women of the family to do without this needless and heavy task being added.

So rare were pumps when we came to Florida, that ours was the first one for a circuit of some miles. So great a curiosity was our modest "Cucumber," that our humbler neighbors made many a pilgrimage to its shrine and opened their eyes in wonder at the ease with which "the waters drawed up." They had never seen, nor heard, nor dreamt of such a wonderful thing. Our colored washerwoman had to be taught how to pump water, and her shy and awkward attempts to work the handle were ludicrous in the extreme. It was the same with the plowmen coming in from the field hot and thirsty. They would look helplessly at "that 'ere queer post" guarding the well, and cautiously touch the handle and start back amazed at the ease with which it moved. Told to raise and lower it, they would lift it slowly a few inches and then as carefully drop it, looking bewildered when the spout, where they were told the water would appear, failed to deliver up its treasure. Then we would sally forth to the rescue, and a delighted grin would dawn upon their dusky faces as the clear, steady stream poured out. "Fore de Lawd, dat's powerful smart!" "Lawd's sake, hit is! After that we used to tremble for the life of our valves and piston as they rattled up and down to satisfy a strangely frequent thirst, so frequent that at last it compelled a remonstrance.

We repeat, every well should be topped by a pump, and every pump should be handy to the kitchen, if not actually inside its walls. Every housewife's work is hard enough without the unnecessary addition of hauling up heavy buckets of water. A sink under the spout to catch and carry away waste water, with a trough leading to a half-hogshead sunk in the ground, will be found of great advantage, not only in saving the carrying away of heavy pans of dish-water, but also in preserving the latter for use as a fertilizer. Let the reservoir be emptied every afternoon toward sunset, the best time always for watering trees. Dash the soapy water around the fruit trees within reach, not too close to the tree, for the true feeding rootlets are some distance from it, and you will be surprised to see how the trees thus treated will outstrip the others.

It is not a good plan to set out orange or lemon trees too near the house, yet we are all apt to make this mistake. The trees look so small when set out that it is hard to realize that in a few years' time they will be towering toward the house-top and their branches spreading wider and wider each year.

A case in point is that of a neighbor who, twelve years ago, in a country then unsettled, planted orange and lemon trees and built his house in the midst of them. For years past those trees have been crowding the house, so that it is entirely hidden save the roof, their branches rubbing against the walls, reaching through the open windows and so shutting out sunshine and air that now it has become imperative either to remove the too vigorous trees or build a new house further out in the one only direction left unoccupied by them, and the latter has been chosen as the lesser evil.

Forty feet is quite near enough to set an orange or lemon tree to one's house; nearer will surely be repented of sooner or later, and then the trees, bearing by that time, will have to be moved and all profit from them lost for several years to come, and only those who have tried it can tell the immense amount of courage required to move a bearing tree. In point of fact, we would advise setting no lemon or orange trees near the house at all, unless it were a few scattering ones of the Tangerine orange, which is particularly ornamental in shape and fruit.

We would inclose a half acre or so in a neat fence surrounding the home, and lay it all out in walks, a carriage-drive circling around the dwelling, and in Bermuda or other lawn-grass.

Then here and there we would have clumps of Texas China umbrella trees, mulberry trees, Russian preferred, Japanese persimmons, Japan plums or medlars, and a live oak or two.

One or two rustic summer-houses and a few stumps, some low, some tall, covered with cypress, thunbergias, yellow jessamines, coral honey suckles or Virginia creepers, would complete as beautiful, home-like a spot as one could find any where.

We would add, too, in one corner, a Scuppernong grape canopy, which would give a gloriously dense shade under which to swing one's hammock on a summer's day.

All these things are easily obtainable and cost very little money; but they are worth hundreds of dollars to the health and buoyancy of the home life. Natural beauties, like songs, go deep.

There are plenty of fruits that may be set in the house lot in addition to those we have mentioned.

Peach, loquat, Japanese persimmon, fig, and pear trees, guavas, limes, and bananas, these are the fruits to scatter around the house. These and flowers and shade trees and grass, surely they are quite enough without the larger growing trees, whose proper place is in the grove where they may spread and stretch their great and thorny arms without knocking down the house or breaking the windows.

Grape-vines, trained on canopy arbors, afford a pleasant shade, and it is ornamental as well as useful to run an arbor on each side of the walk leading from the house to the chicken-yard—an arbor with a top—and train grape and other vines over it.

The chicken-yard should not be too far from the house, and, unless it opens on a woodland where the fowls can range, it should be of ample dimensions, for they will not keep healthy unless they have plenty of room to range. The yard should be inclosed by a picket fence, high, if the common Florida chickens are to be kept in it; for they are veritable "gad-abouts," and are as quick to skim over a five-foot fence as to pick up a grain of corn.

Select the site for the chicken-yard with a view to convert it into a vegetable or fruit garden after the chickens have fertilized it for two or three years. It will be the richest part of your land.

Let the chicken-house be built of slats, placed about one inch apart; this will allow necessary ventilation and yet be tight enough to prevent the inroads of marauding skunks and 'possums, both of which are sufficiently bold and numerous to render precaution desirable. Balked of their prey by other means, they will even condescend to "grub" for it, and if bottom boards are not sunk a few inches in the ground, will dig below the slats and effect an entrance. But with the precautions named and a tight roof, not an open one as some of the old natives will contend for, you may snap your fingers at the four footed enemies of your feathered property; and, if there be any near neighbors of the "colored persuasion," whose love for chickens is proverbial, a padlock will put an effectual stop to their nocturnal depredations.

Fowls of all kinds, and almost all breeds, do well in Florida, and there is very little sickness among them. More on this subject anon.

Hawks make sad havoc sometimes among young broods that are allowed to have free range; but if kept in a small yard made for that purpose and with strings running across it here and there, high enough not to interfere with any one walking there, no hawk will make way with the young chicks. It is a singular fact that a hawk will not fly down below a string. In our own experience we lost dozens of our downy little pets until, learning of this device, we adopted it, and thenceforth not a single hawk swooped down into the chicken-yard. The chicks were kept there, protected by the strings, until about three months old, when they were turned out upon the world big enough and strong enough to take care of themselves.

And now for the present we are done rambling out of doors, and shall proceed to look around inside and discuss the question so perplexing to settlers, "Of what to bring, and what not to bring" for household and for personal use.

CHAPTER XI. "WHAT SHALL I NEED?"

Warm Clothing and Carpets Desirable. Cool Weather. "The Dark Days of January, 1886." Whether to Bring or Buy in Florida the Household Furniture. Hints for Shipping Goods.

This is a question that has doubtless perplexed every householder and prospective settler, when breaking up the old home and getting ready for the new:

"What shall I need there, what shall I take, what leave behind?"

It is a very curious thing to those who know Florida as it is, to learn how very wild and erroneous are the ideas floating about over the rest of the United States concerning their southernmost sister. Only a few days since, for instance, we read an editorial in a Northern paper, one too that should have known better, in which it was stated that all Florida houses outside of the cities were built on the edges of swamps, that there was not enough dry land in the State to permit them to be built any where else that snakes were every where under foot, and when the doors were opened in the morning the snakes would crawl into the houses. "The fools are not all dead yet;" but, for all that, we of Florida can well afford to laugh at these impotent attempts to injure a noble State that is well able to speak for herself by her works.

The tide of immigration that set in Floridaward ten years ago, and has constantly increased ever since, until to-day it is flowing wide and deep from every State in the Union, from England, Scotland, Sweden, is quite strong enough of itself to disprove all falsehoods and jealous misrepresentations.

Not less wide of the truth are some of the ideas taken up by intending settlers as to what articles of household furniture and clothing they will find use for after reaching their new home.

The idea of perpetual summer all the year round is one of these, and consequently all warm clothing is left behind, "packed up," or else reluctantly given away; and more often than not, when the mistake is made, the settler does not find it out until the very moment when the article left in the North is needed, and then he and his family suffer from cold.

"Suffer from cold in Florida!" we hear some of our readers exclaim. Even so; there are certain months of the year, as we have already noted, when it is quite possible to suffer from cold, if not properly protected from it; for it is certainly there to be felt.

It is not at all necessary that the thermometer should sink to the freezing point before the human frame becomes susceptible to a sense of chilliness; if that were so, then fires and warm clothing would be seldom needed in the more southern portions of this State. But, as it is, a temperature much below seventy degrees speedily chills the blood if one is sitting still, and there are many days of the Florida winter when the thermometer marks far below this. The winter temperature of Florida is much like that of the typical May and September of the Middle States—Pennsylvania, New Jersey, and thereabouts.

For over twenty years, in the latitude of Jacksonville, the thermometer during January, February, and March, averaged sixty-two degrees. At St. Augustine it was rather lower, fifty-nine degrees, the direct sea air counteracting the "southing" of this quaint old town as compared with Jacksonville. Further south and in the interior counties the average for winter is about sixty-eight, sometimes higher, less often lower; occasionally light films of ice may be seen early in the morning on water standing exposed.

We saw it twice in Sumter County during our first four Florida winters, and once it lasted in the shade an eighth of an inch thick until noon, the thermometer marking thirty-one—it had been twenty-nine at day-light; and that was the lowest we ever saw it until the winter of 1886. It was our first winter, and we felt as if we had met with a pretty cool reception in our new home, and wondered in rather a dazed, dumbfounded fashion if this was the way that Florida winters usually behaved. We felt rather disconsolate over it until assured by the old settlers of nine and ten years' standing that they had never seen such a cold storm before, and they told the truth too. For three days the wind blew and the rain fell, and the thermometer fell too, steadily going lower and lower until it reached the point we have named.

Florida houses, as a rule, are not built for cold weather; there is so little of it that many think it is not worth while to go to the expense of a tight building; still, on all ordinary occasions, there is no trouble in keeping warm and comfortable.

But this occasion we have referred to was not an ordinary one at all; such a storm, we are happy to say, was almost unprecedented. There was a small stove in the hall, quite enough to take the chill off the adjoining rooms during the usual "cool snaps," but now it proved totally inadequate; a high, damp, rain-laden wind, sifting in every where, which practically dropped the temperature many degrees lower than the thermometer marked, and could not be endured by mortal frames without suffering.

The dining-table was "toted" bodily into the kitchen, fortunately a large one; but the floor thereof, like those of most Florida houses, built as they are of unseasoned lumber, was decidedly open. Four pairs of feet, numbed and cold, led their desperately astonished owners to the attic, where a legion of comfortables, quilts, and blankets were hauled out from the resting-places where they had thought to remain in "inglorious ease," and were made to do duty as carpets in the kitchen, all of the *bona fide* carpets being down in their proper places in the deserted main house. That made the four pairs of feet more like themselves; but the four bodies hugged up close to the big kitchen stove, and the pine wood was kept freely burning.

Now this yellow pine, almost universally used by the "pinelanders" in Florida for cooking purposes, has a way sometimes of getting too much for one if due care is not exercised; there are certain pieces, easily recognized, that are very "fat," that is, they contain a larger proportion than usual of turpentine, and so ignite readily and burn fiercely. Being more used to anthracite coal than to pine wood, we did not realize this fact, neither did we notice that our supply of wood was of this fat description; so we piled it in the stove, and by-and-by the heat drove us further off; then, looking up, we saw the stove-pipe assuming a glowing hue close to the ceiling where it entered the brick flue; next we saw something more, to our horror, smoke and flames beginning to curl up from the ceiling around the pipe. Once a yellow-pine house takes fire there is no saving it, there are no hose carriages or fire engines to be summoned, and the wood burns fiercely and irresistibly. The sight of those creeping flames scared the chill blood away: one ran for a ladder to reach the trap that had been made in the ceiling to meet just such occasions as this, another scrambled like a cat up the partition, on a clothes-horse, plunged through the open trap, and dashed a pail of water around the blazing pipehole. Those below got a fine steam bath, and the one above came down looking like a chimney-sweep all over soot and cobwebs; but no one regarded appearances just then, the threatening calamity was averted, the fire was put out, and the immigrants were saved from being made homeless indeed. After that the flue was lined with a strip of sheet iron, through which the pipe was made to pass, and with reasonable care safety in the future was assured; and this is just what we earnestly urge every settler to do before he even kindles a fire in his house. It is an emphatic illustration of the old proverb, that "an ounce of prevention is worth a pound of cure."

We have already referred to the value of a copious water supply from a windmill and house-tank in just such cases as this.

But not every one will or can have a windmill; and it is well to provide such other "friends in need" as may be possible. There are hand-grenades designed for instant use, by means of which even a child can extinguish an incipient fire, simply by throwing one into its midst, and this result is accomplished "without injury to flesh or fabric."

These are made by the Hayward Hand Grenade Fire Extinguisher Company, of 407 Broadway, New York.

The "Babcock Fire Extinguisher" is another faithful servant in such emergencies; and even, as we write, the report comes in from a Florida town, half laid in ashes, which are yet smoldering: "Some have sneered at the little 'Babcock,' but they will sneer no more. But for its efficient work, our hotel must have gone with the rest; nothing but this saved it. "It is well to know, too, that a few bits of zinc thrown in the stove will extinguish at once any soot or fire in the chimney by dissolving the soot, a curious chemical result. This we know of our own experience. Sulphur is said to have the same effect.

In saying that Florida houses are not built for cold weather, we do not mean to assert that there are no houses in the State that are as weather-proof as a good class of Northern dwellings. There are some such with tight windows, tongued and grooved floor-boards, and plastered walls, just as cosy and comfortable in cold weather as any residence in the North; but these are the exceptions and not the rule. They are only found where the owner has a surplus of money, and usually it is the old settler become well-to-do from the profits of his grove who is the fortunate man; although of course among the incoming settlers are a few, here and there, who come for the climate and not to carve a fortune, who are able to build such a house as they choose, with every improvement and convenience.

Some prefer open fire-places, and certainly there is something cheerful about a great, roaring blaze, with the bright flames leaping and dancing up the broad chimney. But then in Florida such a big fire is very rarely needed, or even comfortable, and all the rest of the year one is confronted by either the blackened "hole in the wall" or by the screen that conceals it. To many it is an item to be considered that these great chimneys cost far more than the simple flues needed for stoves, the difference between fifty and five dollars being considerable. To our mind the small and ornamental stoves that are now in the market, costing from eight to ten dollars, with doors that slide back from the front, leaving a pretty little grate exposed to view, where the oak wood glows and sparkles, is far preferable to the old style of open fire-place; the heat can be regulated as desired, and when not needed, which is the case at least for eight months of the year, it can be removed from sight; it has all the cosy effect of the open fire-place with none of its disadvantages.

And now, before we turn from this subject of Florida winters, we will give our readers an insight into those few days of 1886, the counterpart of which neither they nor any present adult inhabitant of Florida is ever likely to see again; at least the chances are fifty to one that they will escape such a cool visit from Jack Frost.

The terrible "cold wave" that swept over the whole country in January, 1886, penetrating even so far as the Cuban shores, was a phenomenal one, and as such should be recorded as a period of unusual interest.

On the 7th and 8th of the month the Signal Service office at Jacksonville telegraphed all over the State that a very cold wind was approaching.

All day long, on Friday the 8th, there was a very heavy wind, and all through the night it blew and tore around our dwelling, beating the branches of the lime trees against the walls, ripping up the banana leaves into ribbons, and thrashing the roof with the branches of trailing vines.

A member of our family remarked that she "thought something was up," and we mildly suggested, as a big tin pan descended from its nail and rumbled over the piazza, bewailing its fate, that we "thought something was down."

The wind kept on its wild career during Saturday and Saturday night; but it was not until late in the afternoon that the first warning breath from Jack Frost's capacious lungs reached us and we began to realize that there would be full need for the huge wood-piles that hard work had placed *en cordon* around the bearing grove.

Before long, however, it became more than doubtful whether even the hottest fires could avail to save the fruit hanging upon the trees, the high wind carrying the warmed air away too rapidly to effect much, if any, change in the temperature of the air in the grove.

By seven o'clock in the evening the thermometer marked 35°, a thing not known here before, and it kept rapidly on in its downward course until, at seven o'clock Sunday morning, it stood at 23°! A hundred miles south of us, at the same time, it marked 19°.

That Sunday was any thing but a "day of rest" on our premises. All day long men and horses were at work feeding the fires and hauling more wood for the second night's campaign.

Over at the post-office, a group of blue-lipped, blue-skinned, blue-all-over neighbors were comparing notes—they were all on one key—F(roze) sharp; as to oranges, "Trees not hurt," so far.

We pulled an orange from one of our scattering trees, outside the fire protection, and it was a curiosity. A transverse cut showed particles of ice to its very center.

It was a joke we had never expected to see played on us in Florida (our joyous, genial Florida!) to try to pour water from our pitcher in the morning, two hours after the fire had been kindled in the stove, and find it literally "no go" because a thick covering of ice shut it in. But we don't blame Florida, it was all Jack Frost's fault. She did not like him any more than we did—pulled down a brown veil all over her face and went into a brown study; she was very absent-minded, particularly with regard to Jack, feeling she could cherish his memory more warmly if he were to absent himself. How can he expect to make warm friends when he treats them so frigidly?

When we stepped out of doors Sunday morning the first thing we saw called forth an exclamation—Jack Frost's card, in the shape of a long, thick icicle depending from the ice-coated stone filter that stands on our porch, and reaching from its point down into the bucket below, where it rested on a sea of ice, "more or less." In the provision closet, on the piazza, the butter was so solid that it had to be chopped; the beefsteaks were stiff as boards, and the potatoes, cooked the day before, were so solid that they actually bent the knife that foolishly essayed to cut them, and had to be put in the oven to thaw out before a second attack was made on them.

Didn't we wish we had a servant to take the brunt of getting breakfast that astonishing morning? No, we didn't. We had one once upon a time, and when the cold mornings came—just frosty and no more—our cook might always be found, at the time when breakfast should have been ready, with her feet in the oven, her hands spread over the stove-top, and her head sunk into her shoulders, patiently waiting for us to come and get her "some wittels."

No, we prefer having one less to wait on and more room for our own feet, which were cold enough to feel as if our teeth had somehow got into our shoes and were all aching together.

Hauling wood, feeding fires, shivering over the stoves, warm one side and freezing the other; so the day passed and another night came, and no one was sorry for the latter, except those unlucky knights whose duty kept them outdoors to battle with fire-brands against Jack Frost's assaults on our fruit. The rest of us were glad to creep between blankets, with a mountain of covers on top, and a hot water can inside. What a tale to tell of balmy Florida!

Monday, at seven in the morning, the thermometer marked 25°. The day was cloudy, and the wind died partially away. It was a noticeable fact, that whereas, ordinarily, a north wind alone brings us frosty weather, this unprecedented snap (even that of 1835 did not last so long) came from the west and southwest.

What a forlorn looking set of chickens were ours! They were astonished, depressed, especially their tails, which touched the ground as they sat around in groups with their heads sunk into their shoulders. Of course their water troughs were frozen over, and it was a comical sight to see these semi-tropical fowls striking their beaks again and again at the apparent water and then looking around in bewilderment at the result. It kept us busy pouring warm water into the troughs to give them an occasional drink.

Tuesday, at seven in the morning, the mark was 21°, the lowest of all; but toward nightfall the wind veered from the inexorable west to the north and the northeast, and there was a perceptible moderation of the sharpness in the air. The sun sank with the thermometer at 36°—higher than it had been since Saturday afternoon—and it was evident that the worst was over; indeed, the friendly Signal Office again notified us, this time, that Jack was going home.

It was full time, for the damage he did in those four days would with many take more than four years to repair. Not only frozen fruit, but in numerous places young trees were gone. In a few instances even large, bearing trees were killed to the ground. The extreme southern sections escaped but little better than the more northern portions, and the famous "frost line," that every body has been trying to locate these many years proved itself to be a grand fraud and non-existent.

It is a fact also to be noted that every where in the Great Lake regions, or wherever there was water protection, the damage done was less, because the temperature was perceptibly raised by the latent heat stored up in the great sheets of water over which the cold wave passed.

There were two or three decided flurries of snow during Tuesday; it was cloudy and moderating, and as some of us remarked, "If we were North, we should say, it was going to snow;" but we were just as astonished for all that. Snow in Florida was one thing we had never expected to see; nor ice that lay in the sun for three days without thawing, ice several inches thick, and not artificial ice either; nor ice that remained in our rooms all day long in spite of good, crackling fires; nor water, spilled within four feet of the stove, that froze as it touched the floor.

We are not likely to see another such visit from Jack Frost during our life-time, and we are perfectly sure no one wants to.

We have now said enough to show that it would not be wise to leave all warm clothing behind when bound for a Florida home; bring it all, on the contrary, no matter how old or shabby or condemned in the Northern home. That is one of Florida's good points, the ability to wear out one's clothes, even after the new shine is rubbed off; the fact is, we often think how we should pity the "old clothes man," if he should unhappily wander down to these regions; he would find no stock in trade, for every body wears the old clothes as long as they will hold together, keeping the best for Sunday-go-to-meeting occasions. He is wise who dresses according to his occupation, and rough work around farms is more suitably done in old clothes. For a year or more before we migrated from the North it was a standing joke, when articles of dress became too shabby to wear for our city home, yet were too good to give up entirely, to thrust them away into a trunk, with the laughing remark, "This will do in Florida." We hardly expected to see the Land of Flowers then, but we did, and every one of those cast-away articles came into use, saving something better. Go thou and do likewise, O future Floridian! It is a wise plan to follow, for it costs nothing and saves much. Old coats and pants, old dresses and sacks, old waterproofs, old shoes, good, but too shabby to wear in thickly settled communities; all these are treasure troves in the wild free life of Florida's new settlements, and do just as well and better to knock around in than newer and handsomer clothing, to whose welfare thought must be given. The heavier winter flannels that are worn in our Northern homes are worn by prudent people in Florida also during the months of November, December, January, and February. When the temperature rises, the change in dress is made from the outside; a chilly, bracing day requires woolen clothing in addition to the warm under-clothing; on milder days, and they predominate, wash-dresses for the women and alpaca coats for the men are in order; then, if there comes a sudden change, it is very easy to replace the heavy outer clothing. The wearing of flannel next to the skin is an important factor for the preservation of health, not alone in Florida, however; it guards the body against sudden changes of temperature as no other clothing can do, because it absorbs moisture from the skin, and so rapidly evaporates it that, when a cool breeze is blowing, even though one's outer clothing may be dripping with perspiration, it never clings damp and wet to the body, chilling it "to the bone," as the saying is. Gauze flannel in summer and heavy flannel in winter, these we would advise for Florida as much as for a more variable clime.

For summer weather one wears just the same as in the North, except that in the evenings a light jacket or other wrap of some kind is desirable, as also very often during the day if sitting out on the porch.

And now we are going to say something that will astonish most of our readers, yet we mean it, and it is true. It is cooler in the summer in Florida than it is in the Northern States, or in any other of the Southern; yes, though it is the most southerly of all.

The Swiss dresses, that ladies frequently find occasion to wear during the Northern summers, are rarely worn on the peninsula of Florida, because of the cool breezes that are constantly sweeping over it from gulf to ocean and from ocean to gulf. It is a breeze that is always at odds with the thermometer—always "giving it the lie" in the most reckless manner; for instance, one summer day our *mater familias* settled down on the porch to sew, but in a few minutes rose up and departed in-doors, with the remark that it "was too cool to be comfortable." It was mid-day in the middle of July, and, according to the Northern ideas and Northern practice at that hour, we should have been melting with fervid heat. We looked at the thermometer, and it marked 88°! The breeze and the thermometer were quarreling as usual, you see, and the breeze had the best of it; it really was too cool to sit out of doors, in the shade; and this was not a rare occasion either. Of course the sun is hot, so it is North, with no breeze three fourths of the time to temper its rays; and who does not dread the sweltering, breathless days and nights of intense heat that sandwich the cooler times all summer long? There is never a night in Florida when one can not sleep in comfort or is compelled to toss or wander about seeking a cool spot more often than not a blanket is needed before morning.

And now as to furniture. A great many Floridians live on bare floors all the year round; but that is not the way the better classes like to live, if they can help themselves.

We have heard of settlers who, before leaving their old homes, sold or gave away all of their household carpets. "What on earth should we do with carpets in Florida!" they exclaim. Do! why tread them under foot to be sure.

A Florida house has floors, surely; and they are the better for being covered, not only for their attractiveness, but for their owners' comfort. There is something utterly cheerless about bare floors that takes away all the home feeling from a room, no matter how well it may be furnished otherwise; the intrusive sound of every footstep, the scraping and thumping whenever a piece of furniture is moved, carries with it a sense of discomfort to the ear, as the bare boards do to the eye. As to the statement made by some, that "carpets bring fleas," it is simply humbug.

Matting is just the thing for summer use, and will do very well for the cooler months also, especially if rugs or strips of carpeting are laid by bed, bureau or washstand; these give comfort to the feet and relieve the otherwise chilly aspect of matting, especially if it be white. These rugs and strips too will relieve the dreariness of a bare floor, if such there must be. But for those who have carpets we would say, by all means bring them along and lay them on the floors, if not for all the year, at least for the winter months; you will be glad enough to feel them under your feet when the cool winds are whistling outside and the cozy fire is burning merrily inside.

Good lamps are important items in the comfort of a household; with a bright, clear, far-reaching light, the family circle of an evening is apt to be correspondingly sociable and cheerful; with a poor dim light, those nearest the lamp are the only ones satisfied, and the "outsiders" are more likely than not to go grumblingly to bed.

We found this so in our own experience: coming from a city of abundant gas-lights, such lamps as we were able procure were totally unsatisfying.

But we have solved this "light question" now entirely and fully, and that our readers may enjoy a clear, steady, brilliant light, without smoke or smell, or as much trouble to take care of as an ordinary lamp, we would advise them to do as we did—send to A. J. Weidener, 36 South Second Street, Philadelphia, Penn., for a Catalogue of the Champion Lamps, of the patent for which he is sole owner. The light is circular, has a patent extinguisher, and is absolutely safe. The lamps cost, according to the ornamentation and style, from three dollars upward.

Another thing that is more than "handy to have in the house" is one of the small soldering caskets that come on purpose for family use.

Every Florida household should be able to mend its own tinware, for not only is the tin-man frequently a thing of the future in new towns, but it is troublesome to send to him, even if within a few miles, to mend every little hole that you could do yourself.

We know all about it, and now we have read a declaration of independence, which was only delayed until we found out where to send for our soldering implements, these and rosin, with muriatic acid for greasy patients, are all one needs.

Housekeeping stores usually have the soldering caskets; but for those who do not know where to send, we will state that we got ours by mail, at a cost of sixty cents, from A. H. Pomeroy, 216-220 Asylum Street, Hartford, Conn.

In one year this little casket has saved at least ten times its cost, beside the convenience of being able to mend a leak without any delay or expense.

As to furniture: advice on this subject is more difficult to give, as a great deal depends on the point to which the settler is bound, especially if he has to buy new furniture. If it be near Jacksonville, Palatka, Leesburg, Sandford, Gainesville, Ocala, Orlando, or any of the larger towns, then it would be well to bring from the North only such few heir-loom articles of furniture as one is not willing to part with—carpets, matting, bedding, especially hair mattresses and feather pillows, pictures, brackets, books, and the little odds and ends that do not take up much room, yet go very far toward making a home cheerful and restful. It is all a question of expense, and where the requisite furniture can be bought on the spot it is usually found that the prices asked for them are little if any higher than the same things would cost if purchased North and brought here by the settler; the freight charges will make up the difference. At Jacksonville and Fernandina, household furniture, especially, is almost if not quite as cheap as in New York, the reason being that the merchants have very light freights to pay on these and other bulky articles, because they are usually brought by the lumber schooners as return freight. They carry freight to Florida cheaply, as they would otherwise have to come in ballast.

Householders near the seaports, Boston, New York, Philadelphia, Baltimore, who already possess the needful furniture and can make arrangements to ship it by schooner to Fernandina or Jacksonville, will save a great deal by doing so, and land their household goods on their new home site cheaper than they could purchase them. When it is desired to ship by schooner to the nearest point, and that point is south of Palatka, it is sometimes possible to find a vessel bound to the latter place. Always, when it is possible, the settler should ship his goods at least two weeks ahead of his own departure, if he wishes to find them awaiting him; three weeks are not too much if sent by schooner, and, in the latter case, it is usual to have the goods insured.

CHAPTER XII. "WHAT SHALL I EAT?"

Deprivations in New Neighborhoods. The Provision Closet. Conveniences and Food Supply Constantly Increasing.

Well, to be honest and true, as we always endeavor to be, we can only answer to this query, "Whatever you can get." And what that may be depends very much on circumstances: the depth of one's purse, the depth of one's lakelet, the "newness" of the neighborhood, the vicinity of a (comparatively) large town, and the transportation facilities. With a well-filled purse one may easily obtain a well-filled basket in the older-settled portions of the State, and in fact in many of the very new ones also, if there chances to be an enterprising, wide-awake merchant at hand, and modern people to appreciate his modern goods; for here, as elsewhere, the demand creates the supply.

And wherever this proves not to be the case it is sure to be only a temporary inconvenience, and one which, with a better hope for the near future, can be cheerfully borne. Certainly no settlers of ordinary intelligence can hope or expect to find in a new country, only partially reclaimed from the wilderness, all the innumerable comforts and luxuries of the countries whence they come—countries that have been for years upon years under the sway of advanced civilization. There they have at hand not only the productions of the soil of their own locality, but the accumulated necessaries and comforts and luxuries of all the countries of the world brought to their doors by steamships and railroads.

Take only the native fruits, the great orchards growing all around them. Were they there, with their apples and pears and peaches ready to be plucked and eaten when the first tree was felled, the first home laid out, in that part of the country? Rather was there only a vast "howling wilderness," with all the discomforts of a newly settled region; and, in addition, dangers from Indians, from wild beasts, and for more than half the year from cold and wind and storms also.

Ah! truly, the Northern and Western pioneers of civilization had a harder time by far than the Florida settlers of the present day! Deprivations there are, but no actual hardships, and not even severe deprivations. There are no Indians to fear; very few if any wild beasts, especially in those sections of the State now so rapidly filling up with emigrants; no terrible, freezing winters, with which a battle for life must be fought; no soil shut out from cultivation for five months of the year by snow, ice, and mud; no frightful storms, such as sweep the Western prairies and Texas plains, no terrible floods, destroying life and property in wholesale measure.

Taking all things into consideration, we can scarcely conceive of any settler, who is possessed of common sense (a most uncommon commodity, by the way) sufficient not to expect to see "figs grow on thistles and grapes on thorns," who yet will grumble at the few discomforts that may meet him in his new Florida home in the way of table-supplies. We use the masculine pronouns advisedly, because all the complaints on this score that we have ever read came from that lower half of humanity of whom it is said, "He carries his conscience on his palate, and his heart in his stomach;" an old Spanish proverb, and a very true one too.

But we do not mean to insinuate that "good things" for the table are not to be procured in Florida; no one need lack for plenty, if only he has energy, perseverance, and patience, a gun, a fish-hook, and a noose. We will explain the latter assertion presently, only premising that said noose is not intended for hanging purposes, humanly speaking.

When the writer settled near Leesburg there were only two stores in the then little town where groceries, provisions, and a "general assortment" of goods were kept; and the stock in these, though surprisingly large in quantity, was of the roughest in quality and of the most limited in variety.

It was a long while before we could get used to this state of things, coming, as we did, from the second city in the Union, with all the varied luxuries of the world as well as its mere comforts lying in profusion around us.

We would make up a list of articles needed for the household, and as a matter of fact not one in ten of those things that we had always considered as necessaries could be obtained, and some of them had "never been heard of."

"Have you any granulated sugar?" we would ask.

"No, nothing but Florida brown."

Now, we knew that Florida brown sugar, grown and manufactured on the spot, as it were, was in all probability a purer article than the perhaps adulterated white sugar we asked for; but, while it might answer for some purposes, it would not for all; still it "had to do," as we found that many other things "had to do" that once we would have looked down upon with scorn. We grew very meek and humble after a while, and came quickly to the conclusion that as "something was better than nothing," we would accept the former with gratitude. To continue our catechism of the storekeeper:

"Any farina?"

"No call for it, so don't keep it."

"Any corn starch, sago, tapioca?"

" No; the people have never even heard of them."

" Any cheese? any pickles?"

"Not enough sale for them, to pay to keep them."

"Then, in the name of all that is mysterious, what do you keep?"

"Coffee, Florida sugar, molasses, meat — "

"Ah! "How we brightened up. Meat! yes, we wanted meat; only too glad to get it.

Proudly the salesman brought out the meat; there was one thing at least they did have. He brought it forth and laid it on the counter—and our heart went down, down to China Meat! why it was pork—bacon; an immense thick slab of fat and lean, all crusted over with crystals of salt! and he looked so proud, and we felt so disgusted!

He looked at us, and we looked at the meat.

"Why, that is bacon!" we gasped.

"Yes, miss; it's very fine too, first-class meat ; how many pounds? " he said complacently.

"But we wanted meat!"

The salesman gazed at us meditatively; then a gleam of compassion stole over his features, a smile of pity for our ignorance or—insanity.

"Bacon is meat, and meat is bacon."

"Oh!" We felt subdued, reproved, sat upon, and meekly explained that, with us of the North, meat meant beef, mutton, any fresh meat from the butcher.

"Oh," he said, "you mean fresh! No, we don't keep fresh at all, except sometimes some one brings in venison to trade. Didn't know you meant fresh."

We bowed our head, and crept out of that store, wiser and meeker than we had entered it; to think we had been guilty of such benighted ignorance as to call "fresh," meat, and meat, bacon!

Then we picked up our courage, and wandered up to the counter once more, we had forgotten a part of our quest.

"Have you got any potatoes?"

The salesman's face expanded into a delighted smile.

"Yes, he had got some potatoes, very fine ones," and he brought them out to show. We gazed at them, at him, at the door; this thing was becoming monotonous. We had asked for potatoes, distinctly; we had not prefixed "sweet" to our query, yet he had brought us sweet potatoes.

"Not sweet potatoes, white potatoes!" we whispered faintly.

"You said potatoes, and these are potatoes. How could I know you meant Irish potatoes?" said he, with mild, reproachful indignation.

And then we learned another lesson, that while in the North we speak of Irish potatoes as simply "potatoes," and of sweet potatoes by their full title, the reverse is the case in the South; white potatoes are Irish potatoes, sweet potatoes are distinctively "potatoes."

Another time we wanted a one or two-gallon kerosene oil-can, and a one-gallon stone jug, but could only find a half-gallon kerosene can and a two-gallon jug. Again, a stove was wanted, and when found, there was no pipe nearer than two hundred and fifty miles. There was no sewing-silk, except black; no zephyrs, only inferior calicoes of antiquated patterns, and very little of other kinds of dry goods. There was no meat market, no "fresh" market, we should say, only we confess we are not properly educated even yet. Once in a while a cart was brought to one's house, in which reposed a whole or half a "beef," just killed by a neighbor, and shaded from the sun by palmetto leaves or pine boughs. And then the family, drawn forth en masse by so rare and exciting an arrival, would collect around the cart and watch the amateur butcher saw and cut, and slash and hack, in a manner painful to behold, to eyes accustomed to the neat, trim, carefully cut steaks and roasts of the Northern markets. The so-called steaks were nondescripts, and the roasting pieces "strangely and wonderfully made." They were a regular curiosity to the cook, and an absorbing study in anatomy to the carver, but what did we care? We had learned that beef was beef, no matter how it was cut, and were thankful to get any at all; we no longer turned up our noses at "fresh" meat unless, indeed, it was stale; rather paradoxical, that statement, is it not? but easily understood by those who dwell where ice is unknown, either in the rivers or refrigerators. We had occasion to turn up our noses a number of times during our first summer. We bought meat, and at the same time "bought experience," and the latter cost the most; the beef was six cents per pound, venison eight, but the experience was accumulative until we had purchased a goodly stock, and then it began to pay as a saving investment.

Used to ice and a refrigerator, where provisions might be stored all through the hot summer weather, it was a puzzle to us to know how to preserve any thing, especially meats, without their aid. We had a "slat closet," that is, a closet built much like a chicken-coop, except that the slats ran horizontally instead of perpendicularly. It was placed against the back wall of the house on the piazza that connected the main house with the kitchen buildings.

Where woven wire can be procured, it makes an excellent substitute for the slats, and is in fact better in every respect; for, unless one is willing to permit flies, bees, and other insects to feed at will on the daily provisions, the slats must have an insect-proof lining; mosquito netting or cheese-cloth, tacked on the inside of the closet, is the best in the absence of the wire net. This keeps insects at a respectful distance, and admits the air freely; for this latter is the whole aim and intent of the "open closet;" fresh air is the Florida refrigerator, and it is really wonderful how long fresh meats and other perishable provisions can be preserved in good order, simply by allowing a free circulation of air over and around them.

We bought our experience of this fact at the expense of our pocket and olfactories; the slatted closet did not keep insects away, we did not approve of their walking over our eatables, and the mosquito-net "dodge" had not yet dawned upon our benighted intellect. Beef, for instance, we put away after cooking in a covered dish, soups, gravies, potatoes also—and the result? The chickens, those universal household scavengers, fared royally. Their noses were not so well developed as ours, so they "did not mind;" but we cried aloud in despair, and those important promontories of the human facial landscape, the noses aforesaid, were in sore danger of taking a permanent upward turn.

It has been well said that the greatest discoveries have been made by accident. One day we forgot to cover up our beef, and it was one of the warmest days and nights of the summer, yet, to our astonishment, the beef was perfectly sweet the following day. That set us to thinking, and we left the covers off of our provisions next time of *malice prepense*, and thereafter the chickens fared worse and we fared better.

Moral: Put your eatables where the air can play over them, for Florida air is so pure and so dry that it acts as a preservative.

Another method of preserving beef or other fresh meat from one day to another, which was unknown to us in those early days, is to sprinkle a little powdered borax over it; it will then keep perfectly sweet, and a simple washing before cooking will remove all unpleasant taste.

Now that we have given some idea of how things used to be in the "old times" of a few years ago, let us see how they are now; and in what we may say as to improvements let us be understood as including every new-settled portion of the State, either in the present or in the near future; for a Florida town, once properly started, does not retrograde, it keeps on improving just as our own particular little town has done so that whenever a new-comer finds some accustomed comfort missing he may take refuge in the knowledge that it will soon turn up.

Ten years ago there was only one weekly boat that came steaming up the Ochlawaha from Jacksonville, and carried all the groceries and varied stock for the stores located all along the two hundred and fifty miles of its route; so you will readily see that no one town could hope to monopolize any great portion of the freight of a small boat on its weekly trip. That was one reason Leesburg was not better supplied at that time; in fact, the major part of its stock in trade was hauled in wagons for thirty-five miles over the sandy roads, Ocala being the main depot of supply. Another reason we have given, why should the stores keep what the people did not "call for?"

The large majority were of a class that had been used to "roughing it;" they had come either from the northern part of the State or else from other thinly settled portions of the South; a few families of culture and education were scattered here and there, the pioneers of the tide that flowed in swiftly behind them, but they were too few in number to make any change in the stores.

One year later, however, "coming events cast their shadows before," and instead of finding one in ten of the articles desired, we mounted to four in ten. It became possible to buy a spool of silk, to match skirt braid; to find currants, raisins, tapioca, Graham flour, buckwheat, cheese, and like classes of goods, that the town had never seen before. The weekly boat had become a tri-weekly in the orange and cotton season, and a semi-weekly all the year round. There were three mails a week, coming overland for sixty miles, instead of one; there was a telegraph line erected next, and then the St. John's and Lake Eustis Railroad opened a line of communication with Jacksonville via the St. John's River that shortened the two-and-a-half day's trip on the Ochlawaha boats to one day, or a little over. Then came a daily mail, and four or five boats a week in addition to the daily service by way of the St. John's and Lake Eustis Railroad. All these onward steps were not only the cause, but the direct result of the new class of settlers who were coming in—and are still, we may add—faster and faster.

Now, at this present writing, the change in this young city of Leesburg, fed by three railroads, is simply wonderful; and the rapid improvement here is but a type of the majority of the Florida towns as soon as a railroad reaches them.

There is almost nothing that can not be purchased in the larger and older towns. Many of them are tapped by more than one railroad or boat line; several have ice factories; many have large handsome stores, churches, banks, academies, every thing in fact that can minister to comfort, luxury, and refinement. All these things Leesburg now has.

In many localities, where the transportation lines have preceded him, the settler will find no difficulty in procuring all of the comforts and many of the luxuries of life.

The country is still new, but the days of deprivation are rapidly passing away. It does not pay for the settler to bring a lot of perishable provisions with him if he is bound for the near neighborhood of a town; the freight charges will "eat up" any difference in the price. For instance, a neighbor of our own brought from New York a barrel of flour; it proved not to be the quality desired, and a merchant "in town" offered to exchange it for a superior brand he had in stock, and a comparison of prices revealed the fact that the economical neighbor had paid more, including freight, than would have purchased a better article on the spot. And this is a type of many other things.

In sugars, lard, hams, flour, there is not much difference, as a rule, between Florida and Northern prices, though a good deal depends on the greed of the merchant and whether he has a monopoly; but in canned goods there is usually enough to pay the householder to send an order to the North, or, which is better, to Jacksonville, if that order be a large one, so that the saving shall counterbalance the freight. An order of sixty dollars, at Northern prices, would effect a saving of from twenty to thirty dollars, that is, the same goods at the ordinary Florida stores would cost that much more; at the same time canned goods are going out and fresh vegetables taking their place, as they should have done long ago.

So much for the question of "What Shall I Eat?" as regards the stores; but there are other and important sources of supply with which the merchants have nothing to do, and which make an energetic settler almost independent: these are the garden, the shot-gun, fish-hook, and noose, before referred to, not forgetting the poultry and "family friend," who furnishes the "cream of the joke," the cow. Of these more anon.

CHAPTER XIII. HOME SUPPLIES.

Fish, Flesh, and Fowl to be had for the Catching. The Gopher Tortoise.

We have now discussed the provisional question from the purchaser's point of view; but there yet remain other points of outlook to examine, not less important than the first, and to many of even more vital significance. Those who have means to purchase are in a measure independent; but the number is not small, of those who come to seek a home in Florida, who need to husband every dollar for necessary work, and to look at home as far as possible for food supplies.

There are many ways by which a thrifty, energetic settler can help to fill the larder without the expenditure of a single dollar, save, perhaps, as "invested capital," such as shot-guns, traps, and fishing-tackle, which draw a high rate of interest in the shape of game and fish. Besides these resources, there are the cows, chickens, vegetable garden, and fruits, both wild and cultivated.

Let us look into the game division of our subject first, and see what can be found for bullet, hook, and noose to capture for the family table, "without money and without price." Probably there is no country in the world where fish, flesh, and fowl, in the wild state, are more plentiful than they are in Florida all the year round.

All the year round, we repeat, and with emphasis, for it is no small item with the settler who wishes to depend in a great measure on the fruits of his gun and rod for his family provisions, that there is no time of the year when he is cut off from these important supplies. True, there are some seasons of the year when game is more abundant than at others; but there is never a time when it is not sufficiently plentiful to make an empty-handed hunt of a few hours' duration a thing of such rarity as to be practically unknown. There are few localities where deer are not still to be found within easy reach of the settler's rifle, although in the more settled regions they are becoming scarcer every year; for instance, four, yes, even two years ago, venison was frequently brought into our own growing little city for sale during the cooler months; but now it is more seldom seen, and has become one of the luxuries.

Yet, ever and anon, several graceful, dainty deer are seen trotting timidly across the clearings close to the newly erected dwelling-houses, and sometimes they, like more civilized animals, get into mischief, leaping fences and nipping off the young growth of the orange trees, or eating off corn fodder as it stands in the fields. These pilferings are usually carried on at night, and so the nimble marauders act with impunity until, their haunts being discovered, they meet leaden bullets flying around them.

One unhappy deer, not long since, was so torn and mutilated in leaping a barbed wire fence as to be unable to leap out of the inclosure, and the poor creature, thus self-entrapped, soon met its death at the hands of the owner of the trees it had helped to "nip in the bloom of their youth."

There is a little gray squirrel that is met with in both hammock and piney woods, darting like a light shadow over the ground, or leaping with wonderful rapidity from branch to branch and tree to tree. He is a good deal like the "wicked flea," one moment he is there, the next he isn't, and unless one's eyes are very sharp and quick he will vanish entirely while the gun is waving wildly in the air, striving for a "sight." This pretty, nimble little fellow is very good eating, and makes a first-class stew; but, as we have intimated, that celebrated adage of the cookbook, "first catch your hare," applies to him with a great deal of aptitude; a dog to "tree" him in a detached tree, whence there is no escape, affords almost the only chance of securing this tid-bit for one's table.

Rabbits are plentiful, and fat—ah! too fat sometimes, when they owe their fine condition to sundry raids on one's garden patch; if only they would make these visits in broad daylight, when they might be provided with a dessert of cold lead; but they are too cute for that. Under cover of the shield of night Mr. Rabbit sings thusly to his lady love:

> "Oh, come into the garden, Maud,
>   And when the day shall break,
> The settler'll find his 'green stuff' chawed,
>   And bless us for its sake."

The usual traps in use at the North for the capture of similar small game are useful here as well; but if they fail, and the garden is suffering from their raids, pieces of sweet potato, of which rabbits are very fond, with strychnine well rubbed into sundry slits cut in them, will solve the mooted question as to who is going to eat those vegetables, their owner or his uninvited guests. But it always seems a sad waste to call in this latter aid to the rabbits' destruction, so much good food is lost. But then, it is true, on a thrifty farm nothing is wasted, and so even the poisoned "varmints" can be buried in the garden they sought to rob, and thus made to contribute to its fertility, a woeful example of retributive justice.

Then there is that famous "critter," the 'possum. We of the North are apt to regard this nocturnal denizen of the woods as food fit only for the colored race of humanity; but the truth is that many a worse-flavored and tougher bit of meat finds its way to the table of the wealthy epicure than a nicely roasted 'possum. There is a prejudice abroad against it, and that prejudice is totally unfounded, and, where the Florida settler can capture and use to the benefit of his larder an opossum, we advise him not to throw away valuable food for no reason at all. A roasted opossum and a young, savory roasted pig could not be told one from the other, by the taste at least. We know, because once we overcame our own prejudice on this subject and did taste of the despised 'possum; we had helped to relegate that 'possum to the shades of the past, and we desired to assist at a decent burial also; if we had not seen that our meat was cut from a 'possum, we should have said it was a roast pig.

Every body knows that the opossums love chickens and eggs, and this is their most heinous crime; though why we should blame a dumb beast for what we account no sin in ourselves is one of the inconsistencies of human nature.

We too like chickens and eggs, and eat them whenever we can get them, yet in ourselves we find no sin. But then, perhaps it is not in the liking or the eating, but in the getting, and the manner thereof, that the sin lies; and in this view the 'possum does certainly deserve some moral lectures, for there is no worse chicken and egg thief to be found, except it may be that popular perfumer, the skunk; and for obvious reasons we prefer to have an opossum on the premises, if we must have either. It needs but a very little hole, or narrow slit, to be left in the hen-house for the opossum to obtain entrance to the coveted preserves, and then woe to the eggs in the nests under the setting hens, and woe to the chickens themselves. But, smart as the 'possum is, he gets sadly "taken in and done for" sometimes, as was the sad fate of the opossum we have referred to above.

We were about retiring to bed one clear, moonlight night, when our attention was attracted by a curious noise from the direction of the hen-house, some little distance away. It was a noise not to be explained in any ordinary way, and, after being satisfied as to its direction, one person with a pistol and another with a lantern sallied forth to find out the cause of the rumpus. Outside the hen-house we paused to listen; no chickens were screaming, only a low murmur of alarm could be heard among them; but clear and loud sounded the noise that had called us forth from our would-be slumbers, a decided, emphatic thumping and pounding against the inside wall of the hen- house, and what that sound meant, why it was, and what was causing that sharp hammer-like rapping, no one could imagine. Stealthily the door was opened, and then the light revealed what? A ludicrous sight, and no mistake! an opossum sitting erect on its hind legs in a nest, so intent on endeavoring to crack a China nest-egg, held in its forepaws, by pounding it on the wall, as not to heed our entrance! Fully a minute we stood watching its ill-spent efforts, then the light was flashed in its eyes, and it dropped the China egg, and rolled itself into a ball, lying there motionless at our feet. You have heard the phrase, "playing 'possum," and no one who has seen these cunning creatures "playing dead" will question the full justice of its application. The present possum we knew could only be dead through fear, and as our faith in its susceptibility to shocks was small, a bullet roused its dormant energies, and it started to run, when a second dose of lead converted its live feint into a dead faint.

"The way of the transgressor is hard," and it was signally true of this unfortunate robber; he came to eat and found too hard a nut to crack, and was eaten himself as the sole result of his venture.

Any man who has one or more persimmon trees on his lands, or near at hand, possesses just so many ready-made possum traps, for the animal is extravagantly fond of the wild persimmons that grow throughout Florida, so much so that its fondness for this fruit has become proverbial, and it will travel for miles, if necessary, for the happiness of hanging head down in a persimmon tree and using its forepaws as hands with which to fill its mouth with the coveted fruit.

An experienced possum hunter will always seek the neighborhood of these trees during their fruiting season, and, nine times out of ten, one or more of the creatures sought will be found among the branches, their exact position being revealed by blazing torches in the hands of their pursuers, when a few sure shots bring them tumbling to the ground.

Sometimes the "'possum hunts" are organized by negroes, who have only their dogs as guides and their hatchets and axes as weapons. In these cases the tree that shelters the 'possum is surrounded by an eager torch-bearing group, while two of their number with swift blows from their axes lay low the tree—it falls, and with it the unlucky 'possum to meet the eager hatchets aimed at its life.

Of all creatures, the opossum is one of the most easily trapped. Cunning as it is in some respects, it is exceedingly simple in others, and a rude trap that a rat or even a rabbit would shun is perfectly effectual for the opossum.

Leave open a straight and broad path for its escape, and fix a trap in a narrow, crooked corner of exit, and it will choose the latter, preferring the twisted by-ways of the world, just as do so many of its human compatriots.

Of birds that may be utilized for the table their name is legion, and any family that numbers among it a man or boy who can handle a gun effectually may count upon a full and constant supply at all times of the year. On the lakes and rivers are myriads of water-fowl, and in the woods abound splendid specimens of the wild turkey, fifteen to twenty pounds being no uncommon weight for these latter to reach—and they are "splendid eating," being fully equal to the much-vaunted domesticated turkey of the North. Of the smaller birds that are abundant in the piney woods as in the hammock, the partridge, or quail, comes first in the estimation of the epicure; and truly this fat, chubby little fellow, with his merry whistle and buoyant call of "Bob White! Bob White!" is as fine a tid-bit, broiled and served on toast, as one need ever wish to taste. But all the same, we always regret the killing of a partridge, partly because of that joyous whistle of his, and partly because he is so bold and saucy and fearless. You look out of your window in the early morning, and not infrequently the first thing you see is a "covey" of fat, brown little fellows, running about right under your hand, as it were, or sitting on the edge of your seed-boxes, or perhaps it is only a solitary couple who have left their nest close by in search of provender; you move, and they lift their dainty striped heads, cock their bright eyes at you, and run away a few yards, then stop and look back to see what you are going to do about it. If satisfied there is no malice in your heart, or yearnings in your stomach, they come running back again and resume their search for crumbs or seeds right under your eye, hunting about with the most intense business-like air imaginable.

And this is why we always feel sorry to see the fat little creatures lying limp and cold before us, the joyous whistle stilled forever, the brown head drooping, the busy feet stiff and nerveless. But they are good to eat, no doubt of that, and they are eagerly sought after with gun and traps; we have seen nine of the chubby fat tid-bits secured at one shot, and eight caught at one time in a trap baited with cow-peas; but usually the brown-bird collection is made more slowly.

Next in value as a food-supply comes the dove, a larger bird than the partridge and excellent for the table, but so wild and quick to take alarm that it requires a cautious gunner to creep near enough for a shot, and a quick and skillful one to secure any reliable aim. Doves are extremely plentiful during the fall and winter months, flying in large flocks of from fifty to a hundred, sitting close together on the ground, and rising at the same instant with a rush and whirr of wings that is startling to the unsuspecting pedestrian. Rarely indeed is the dove caught in a trap, for it is a wary bird, and not at all inquisitive as to what manner of forage may be lying under a certain tipped-up box; partridges will march in, a whole covey of them, to see what it may be, but the dove "never—well, hardly ever!"

The beautiful brown-coated, yellow-breasted, and black-cravated meadow lark, spite of its gay plumage and sweet little song, is lawful and frequent prey for the sportsman's gun. There is not so much of him, when cooked, as there is of the partridge and dove, but what there is very good and not to be despised.

Then there are snipe of various kinds, rice-birds, tiny little things, red-winged starlings, and a host of others, all more or less desirable for the table.

And then, if one wants beef and can't get it, there is at hand a first-rate substitute, either for a stew, or, better still, for soup-making: all one has to do is to go out in the piney woods and there, on a sloping hill-side, he will find the home of this subterranean beef-bearer—a small mound of sand thrown out, and slanting downward from it at a pretty sharp incline au excavation, flat at the bottom and arched on top like the typical entrance to a cave, only of course this is in miniature.

We see the entrance; but how far down into the bowels of the earth that tunnel extends no one can say without digging. It is the home of the "gopher;" and, by this, we do not mean the four-legged, fussy, prairie-dog creature of the West that is sometimes called "gopher." No; our Florida gopher has four legs, it is true, but of fur he has none, nor does he come out to his door like his namesake and sit up "on end" to see "the world and its brother" go by. Our gopher's legs are not pretty to look at; they are an ugly, dirty brownish-black, and his back is round, hard and arched, and covered by a rather disreputable coat, marked off in irregular checks; it is shabby, no doubt of that, but it wears well, and he needs never to go to his tailor for repairs; his head is flat and his nose pointed, and his neck long and scrawny. Altogether, we don't boast of our gopher on the score of beauty; we are afraid he would not take the first premium on that count; but just catch him, and make soup of him, and you will thereafter not speak slightingly of the lowly gopher, who is only a tortoise. How are you to catch him?

Well, we hinted at the means a while ago when we mentioned the noose as a food-provider. All through the spring and summer months, in fact almost through the whole year, except December and January, the gopher comes waddling out from its home every day, and usually between the hours of ten and two o'clock.

It travels slowly around, perhaps visiting its neighbors, or only taking a health promenade in search of roots, grasses, and cow-peas—it being very fond of the latter, greatly to their detriment. Sometimes, especially in the spring, there are eggs to be laid; and when this is the case this gopher seeks a place where the sand is dry and loose; here it scratches quite a large, shallow hole, and depositing some forty or fifty eggs therein, covers them and leaves them to hatch out at their pleasure; it has done its duty by them, and has no further concern in the rearing of the "large family of small children" those eggs may produce. When they creep out to view the world, they find it all before them to choose whither they will go, with no maternal whispers to check the downward course they at once enter upon even thus early in their young lives.

In other words, the little gopher makes for itself a little tunnel on the higher ground. It is never found in places subject to overflow; and, by the way, this quality makes the gopher a good indicator of the best lands for orange culture; wherever their holes are found, it is dry enough to set out a grove, no matter even if it be in the midst of the "dry season" that the selection is made. So, as we have said, the little gopher, issuing from the pigeon-like egg—pigeon-like in shape and size, but not in shell, since the gopher-egg is covered by a soft, tough membrane—makes unto itself a little cave with a tunnel-like tail to it, and as it slowly grows larger so does the cave lengthen out into a longer and deeper tunnel with an entrance at the surface that corresponds with the size of the inmate.

We have said that usually between the hours of ten and two the gopher comes forth for its daily promenade; if it were not for this habit, it would be an extremely difficult thing ever to capture one. As it is, if one chooses to saunter around among their dwellings during this period, keeping a sharp look-out, he will often be rewarded by picking up one or more without any trouble, except that of carrying them home, and that, as we know from sad experience, is sometimes a heavy task if one is not very Strong. Once we picked up a fifteen-pound gopher about fifteen minutes' walk from home, and by the time we got him there he weighed at least fifty pounds.

But if the settler does not care to hunt his tortoise in this manner, there is another way. Take a number of stout, short stakes, pointed at one end, and tie to each one a very strong, flexible cord, whose length must be regulated by the size of the hole where it is to be placed; make a slip-knot or running noose in the cord, drive down the stake in the solid ground to one side and back of the gopher's entrance, and then let your cord be of just such a length as shall allow a loose, open noose to be arranged across the mouth of the tunnel in such a way that the tortoise can not leave his hole without becoming entangled, and as he continues his unconscious onward waddle he is suddenly brought to the end of his tether by the drawing tight of the noose either around his neck or leg, as the case may be.

Back and forth he travels in a semi-circle, sometimes in a circle, until he winds himself up close to the stake, and then, disgusted with life, he draws back into, his shell and quietly awaits his fate. At other times, if the trapper is too long in visiting his nooses, he may find the cord worn away by attrition against the edges of the hole and the prisoner escaped; but usually, visiting the snares, which need to be marked by strips of white cloth tied to a stake near by, the gopher is found quiescent, and as far down in his tunnel as the cord will allow. Then you seize the cord and essay to draw him out; but, unless the former is very strong, you will only succeed in sitting down rather ungracefully with a broken cord in your hand, while the released prisoner scuttles away, rejoicing, to the very lowermost point of his subterranean castle. Therefore it is always well to visit the gopher traps armed with a spade and a basket, the first to dig out the captive and the second to carry him home. It is not often that the same hole shelters two gophers; but, that it is sometimes the case, we once proved in rather an amusing manner.

We sallied forth, as was our daily custom, to visit our snares, and on approaching one of them observed a round object projecting part way from the hole. Eagerly we pounced upon that unlucky gopher, wondering why it had not gone in as far as the cord would permit—when, lo! there was no cord attached to it at all! We dropped it in the basket and looked to see what had become of the cord. We saw it lying inside the hole; but it was quite heavily weighted. There was a captive to the noose after all; and this one, having retreated as far as it could, had blocked up the way for another following after it.

Deserted burrows are easily known by the pine-straw and trash that drift down into the hole, while one in use is smooth and the soil fresh and clear with distinct marks of shell and feet.

Gopher stew and gopher soup, especially, are highly esteemed, and so closely resemble beef in texture and taste that one may be easily deceived into believing it to be the latter.

There is another point in this snaring of the gopher turtle that should not be overlooked. It is an important object to the settler to rid his land of them, for they invariably choose the highest spots, just where crops are grown, to make their home; and hence the interests of the two are certain to clash.

The settler desires to raise cow-peas, for instance, and so does the gopher; but the latter spells his kind of "raising" cow-peas thus, "*razing*" and thoroughly he succeeds, for he is passionately fond of them. We have seen a quarter of an acre of cow-peas cut down to the ground by a few gophers in less than a week, and but for the prompt use of the noose aforesaid not a vine would have been left in the acre in less than a month.

Therefore, trap this ruthless destroyer wherever his doorway is seen. If the family do not care to use him as food, cook or chop the flesh and feed it to the chickens, who will rejoice over the windfall,

"Smite, slay, and spare not" the gopher, if you would possess your cow-peas or vegetables in peace. His shell, sand-papered, varnished and hung up by wires run through holes bored in the edges, makes an excellent hanging-basket for trailing vines.

"How much do gophers weigh?" do you ask. Sometimes as much as sixteen pounds; but they average eight pounds.

CHAPTER XIV. "OUT OF THE DEPTHS."

A Boat the first Requisite. Methods of Fishing for Trout or Bass. Salt-water Fish, Clams, and Oysters. Methods of Catching Fresh-water Turtle; Curious Quality of their Flesh.

Still upon the same subject, the household larder, you see. But then we feel that we are excusable, for there are few more important or more worthy the attention of the settler, whose bill of "ways and means" is apt to be limited ofttimes by a shattered pocket, and quite as often by the state of the local market.

Our schedule of home supplies is not exhausted, for we have not yet dived down beneath the surface of the numerous lakes, large and small, which are scattered broadcast over the State. We are ready for the plunge now, however, and have no fear but that we shall find much to bring up "out of the depths."

But first of all we must have a boat; for rarely, indeed, can a point be found where the water is deep enough for fishing close in shore with rod and line, except for "small fry." We have seen human "small fry" roll up their trousers as far as possible and wade out rod in hand; but this is not quite so comfortable or convenient a method of fishing as a boat would provide, and we very much incline to believe will never become popular, especially among ladies who "go a-fishing," as many do, to the benefit of their health and the increase of their enjoyments.

The most prevalent "water vehicle" among the old-time residents, and therefore presumably the most fashionable, is the "Florida batteau," in other words, a scow, pure and unadulterated—a roomy boat, and a safe one, guaranteed, if made after the usual broad pattern, not to upset; but still not so light nor easy to row or to guide as a "water-carriage" of a different build.

There is about as much diversity in row-boats as there is in wagons; and to secure a low-priced yet well-shaped, steady boat, is not so easy as it may appear to those who have not tried it. A cheap boat is apt to be poorly built—cheap both in materials and workmanship—of inferior woods and badly modeled. A really good, shapely boat can rarely be bought under fifty dollars as the minimum figure. Knowing this, we have gone to considerable trouble to seek out for the benefit of our settlers a reliable firm who will place in their hands a really good boat for a very low price.

This firm (R. J. Douglas & Co., of Waukegan, Illinois) we have already had occasion to refer to, as the manufacturers of the Champion windmill. The "Eureka" they claim, and honestly so, to be "the best boat ever put on the market for the money." Of a beautiful model, sharp-pointed at both ends (a rudder can be fitted if desired), with a ten-inch bottom board in place of the usual keel, it is at the same time swift, steady, and of light draught, just the very boat we need for ordinary row-boat purposes on our shallow-shored Florida lakes.

The cut on next page, for which we are indebted to the courtesy of the builders, coupled with their own description following, will give our readers a better idea of the natty little Eureka than any words of our own:

"Instead of keel, it has a 10-inch bottom board, 7/8 inch thick, which makes it perfectly flat on the bottom, and it has five strakes on a side. The frames, stems and wales, are of selected white oak in all grades; and in basswood boats the bottom and first two strakes are of pine or cedar and only the three upper strakes of basswood. The planking is 3/8 inch in clinkers and 1/2 inch in carvel boats. The row-locks are of our own design, and the sockets are fastened on with bolts so that they cannot pull off. Instead of wood knees, we use malleable iron brace from wales to seat, which is also fastened on with stove bolts. They are fitted with a good pair of ash oars and malleable iron row-locks, and are seated for three persons, and have three coats of paint on them. They make fine-looking, steady, strong and very serviceable boats for nearly all uses.

"Those made of basswood are cheapest: the thirteen-feet boat costing $20, and the fifteen-feet boat $5 more; the pine comes next, $25 to $30; and the cedar, which is the lightest in weight, is the highest in price, from $35 to $40, for the two sizes respectively."

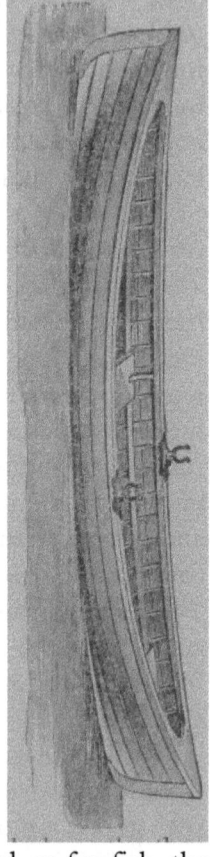

We are the proud owner of one of these latter, and, with one of the patent umbrella fixtures secured to the seat for shade, we ask nothing better in its line, either with or without the rudder; the latter, by the way, is an "extra" and costs $2. This cedar boat is so light hat it can be readily placed in a wagon and taken from lake to lake.

None of these boats weigh over one hundred and ten pounds, an item of no small importance when freight is to be considered, as the rate per hundred to Jacksonville from Waukegan is, at this present writing, only $5, and is likely to be less rather than more in the future. With such a boat as this, fishing and boating become a genuine pleasure; for who does not love the swift, easy flight over the water of a light, graceful batteau, that skims along with scarcely a touch of the oars?

And now we are ready to go a-fishing; and, as for fish, the settler need not go far to seek them; they are in every lake or lakelet all over the country, in every river, in every inlet or bay.

In the inland lakes and rivers, the principal fish is the trout, as it is here called — but in reality the true "black bass" of the North and West. This is a large fish of fine flavor, and a prime favorite with every one either for boiling or frying, the specimens caught weighing all the way from one pound to seventeen or twenty. Trolling is one way to capture them; and it is no despicable sport, as the boat is rowed along, to feel the sudden pull and subsequent jerks on the distant hooks that tell of a prisoner at the other end of the line—a victim of mistaken greed. What is there, we wonder, in that bright bit of whirling tin that spins around on the surface of the water that the swift trout should pursue and make fierce war upon it—to find itself, alas! "taken in and done for"? But, after all, why wonder at the foolishness of a fish, when we see the same thing every day enacted in the highest scale of creation?

Trolling is not the only method of capturing the trout: a good-sized hook, a strong line, and a small live fish at the end of the hook, will be very likely to bring its reward; for it is on these small fish, about three to five inches long, that the trout principally subsist, and if there are any in the vicinity of your "prisoner at large," it will not be long before it and the hook go down and your trout goes up.

If one wishes trout for breakfast and dinner, and has not time to go out on the lake and fish according to the old, approved method, there is another—a lazy way—of accomplishing the desired end.

Take as many bottles as you please—it depends a good deal on the size of your home lake—not small medicine bottles, but brandy or large wine bottles, cork them securely and tie around their necks lines of suitable length, to which trout-hooks are attached.

With hook and line or net, catch, close to shore, the small fry needed for bait, put them in a pail of water to keep them alive; then row out on the lake with them and the bottles; here and there, as you go, bait a bottle-hook with a live fish and drop it overboard; then go back home, and once in a while take a look at the surface of the water; if you have a spy or opera-glass, so much the better. It is surprising how far off the floating bottles can be seen, and if a trout has seized upon the bait, that fact is easily noted by the erratic movements of the bottle and the agitation of the water around it; and then one has only to row out and haul in the captive.

Another way of using the bottles is to cast them out over the lake, and then row slowly about among them, keeping watch upon them all. The time occupied is just the same as if fishing from the boat with one hook; but the chances of a successful result are enhanced just as many times as there are bottle-hooks floating around.

There is something interesting, and exciting too, in this novel way of fishing with "a dozen irons in the fire"—a dozen hooks in the water at once. The eager eyes travel here and there, watching each movement or suspicious bob of the bottle-buoy, until doubt becomes certainty, and then how the oars rattle in the row-locks! Then is the time when, if one is in a "Florida batteau," a scow, in other words, he would give much to be in a "Eureka," or other light skiff, so as to skim the faster over the waters. That bobbing, dancing bottle—now laying flat on its side, now standing on end, now disappearing, now popping up to the surface again, several yards from where it went down—is so very tantalizing that one is tempted to sing as a dirge:

" Thou art so near, and yet so far."

The captive trout, though at the end of the line, five to eight feet below the surface, seems always to know and recognize the approach of an enemy as the boat nears the float, and the bobbings and disappearances redouble in frequency, until it often becomes a regular game of "will-o'-the-wisp," to catch the bottle; like the wicked flea, you put your finger on it, and it is not there. If the fish is large and strong, say a ten-pounder or thereabouts, the bottle is very likely to give the boat a little exercise in the way of chasing, and the enemy being rather erratic and prone to a change of direction at any and all times, without reason or rhyme, the sport becomes lively.

But then, when at last a hold of the fleeing bottle is secured (look out for impromptu baths or capsize, though), and a large, fine trout lies flopping at one's feet, causing visions of an epicurean meal in the near future to rise before the palate's eye, as it were, then one forgives the poor fish for the struggle it has so bravely made for its life. Should two or three of these novel fish-floats be seen bobbing around at the same time, the rule of "one at a time" becomes tantalizing, especially if the first captive prove to be a refractory soft-shell turtle, as sometimes happens.

We have spoken of the bottles being used in this novel method of fishing; but, in our own experience, we prefer floats made of small pieces of board twice as long as wide, the line being secured at one end and a slanting hole bored near the other, into which is driven a slender stick bearing a white or scarlet flag. This flag, owing to its sloping position, almost touches the water until the float is pulled down at the other end by the fish, and then it rises almost upright, forming at all times a much plainer guide to the whereabouts of the float than does the bottle, and for this reason it is to be preferred; a stout piece of wire will answer for a flag-staff for the bottles.

The bream is another excellent fish, not nearly of so large a growth as the trout, but still just the right size for a pan-fish, full-grown specimens weighing from one to two pounds. These, too, are caught with hook and line, with minnows, earth-worms, or sawyers, as bait. Minnows are easily caught, close in shore, with a fine hand net; as to earth-worms, we doubt if there is a country in the world so destitute of these familiar denizens of the Northern subterranean barn-yard as the piney-woods region of Florida.

In the clay hammocks there are plenty of them, also in the muck-beds along the lakes or rivers; but in the sands of the pine lands they are indeed of the genus *rara avis*; in all our own diggings and grubbings we have met with but two specimens of the genuine red earth-worms, and cannot account for the finding of those. So the earthworm, as bait for fish, is a fraud for the pine-lander, and he has to fall back upon the fat, white, chubby "sawyer," whose busy chip! chip! can be heard beneath the bark of the pine trees all day and all night. Sawyer is the name given it, but its true name is *Scolytus destructor*, which is the scientific designation of a small wood-boring beetle; and that which the Floridian terms the sawyer is the larvæ of this insect, which, starting from the inner part of the tree, where the mother has laid her eggs, works its way outward, growing larger and fatter as it progresses, until, when the searching angler finds it between the bark and the wood, nearly ready to develop into the full-grown state, it is a tempting tid-bit for bream and perch and for all the smaller fish of lake or stream. It is quite true that the sawyer's head is rather tough and its cutting tools hard and sharp; but the rest of it is so fat and toothsome in their eyes, that the eager fish heed not these disadvantages, but rush open-mouthed at the delicious *Scolytus destructor* whenever the opportunity offers.

A tree that has been felled or uprooted while in full vigor will in a few months be found riddled with small round holes, and with larger ones, where the beetle has entered to lay its eggs, and where the larvæ has finally emerged; and then, if with a sharp hatchet a broad ring of bark is removed, fine, plump sawyers will be uncovered. Any prostrate tree, if it has not lain on the ground for more than a year, will furnish the angler with an abundance of bait.

Along the coasts, and in the salt-water bays and inlets, fish are extremely abundant, of fine quality and of all sizes, from one pound to over two hundred pounds. As for oysters, those famous shell-fish of the Northern markets, the sea-coasts and inlets furnish them *ad libitum*, and no "second-class articles" either are the Florida bivalves, as those settlers who are so fortunate as to be near the source of supply, or who dwell along the numerous lines of railroad now reaching out all over the State, can certify.

No less toothsome also are the clams which are abundant along the coasts, while the salt-water mullet, a fish somewhat resembling the mackerel in taste, when similarly cured, is a splendid fish also, when fried, fresh from the water.

The inland lakes, both large and small, are not only the homes of many kinds of fish other than the trout or bass, such as bream, perch, pike, cat-fish, gar-fish, but of two species of turtle, which are less easily caught than the gopher, it is true, but still well worth the trouble of capture. One of these is a soft-shell, and an ugly fellow he is both to look at and to handle. He weighs anywhere from two pounds to twenty, has a hard, round, black center-piece on his back, a veritable shield, and around its edges a wide margin of leathery-like substance, soft, but extremely tough; from beneath this attractive attire protrude four long, scrawny, black legs, a short, pointed tail and a long, thin neck with a slender head, terminating in a round, projecting snout, anything but handsome to look at, and anything but comforting to feel! For this soft-shell turtle is by no means the meek, unresisting creature that the gopher is, and when captured has a way of expressing his opinion that is very apt to prove painful and lacerating to one's feelings.

In this respect our Florida soft-shell is quite the equal of his cultivated Northern brother, the "snapper," and it behooves his captors to watch sharply that their respective positions are not reversed; for the soft-shell not only snaps with his horny, vise-like snout at anything that comes within reaching distance, but he stretches out his scrawny neck, fixes his glittering little eyes upon you, and then, bracing his hind legs, actually springs toward you, lunging again and again with a determination worthy of a higher scale in creation; and when he has given this little game up as a "bad job," and has settled down resignedly, it only needs a stick poked at him to rouse him up once more to a series of leaps and springs rather astonishing in a turtle.

"Once upon a time," before we were so well versed in the tortuous ways of this ungainly denizen of the lakes, we picked up a small (two-pound) specimen that was waddling along over plowed ground, seeking a place wherein to deposit its eggs.

We were delighted with our prize, the first of its kind, and holding it out in front of us, a hand on either side, hastened homeward. We hastened—yes, and a few steps further we concluded, quite suddenly, to lay down our prize. There was no hesitation about our movements; our resolution was quick but unfaltering, and in point of time coincided with a vicious dart of the horny snout in the direction of our fingers. We were not anxious to see what the bones that underlaid our "too tender flesh" looked like, so we called aloud for a shovel and a basket, and while they were on the way admonished our frisky turtle with a stick, assuring him that his angry plunges were futile; then we shoveled him into the basket and the next day he appeared in a harmless character on our table, and a very good stew he made—what there was of him.

We have outlined above one way of catching these softshells. In the spring of the year, from February or March, until late in the summer, they leave their watery homes and waddle slowly along on dry land to lay their eggs. Finding a spot that suits them, they scratch a deep hole in the sand, deposit a long string of small soft-shell eggs in it, cover them up and leave them for the hot sun to hatch, knowing, as we must suppose, that their young, as soon as they emerge from the egg, will follow their instinct, which leads them at once to the nearest water.

It is a curious fact, that if there be a fence near the lake from which the turtle emerges, it will follow the line for a long distance, and if an angle is met with there it will halt, too stupid to turn and retrace its steps or to follow the fence line in its new direction. On our own premises there is just such a "corner," which we may well term "a corner in turtle." Following a fence which runs close to the lakelet in which they live, the soft-shells stop short on reaching a sharp angle not far from the house, and, after vainly butting and scratching the pickets, draw their heads into their shells and disdainfully await the upshot of their adventure—which is the stew-pan.

So marked is this predilection for the fence, that all through the turtle season a sharp watch is kept on it, and especially on the "corner," which was originally our nursery, but had to be abandoned after the turtle selected it for the scene of their antics, as they were like the famous " bull in a China-shop."

The "soft-shells" are frequently caught by the hook and line, and for this purpose a large, strong hook and a stout line are needful, the former baited with raw meat or, which is quite as good if not better, bits of red flannel. Sometimes they are caught when the hook is dropped deep, but more frequently when it is shallow, that is, very near the surface of the water, if not actually on the surface.

Where one's lake is near the house, so as to be easily watched, it is a good plan to drive down a stake in as deep water as can be conveniently done and then stretch a rope from this stake to another nearer the shore. This rope should be a foot or more above the water, and at intervals of about three feet large hooks should be hung from it, some on short, some on longer lines. Keep these hooks permanently baited with meat or red flannel and look at the rope now and then to see if anything is jerking at the lines. If there is, jump in your skiff or scow, take a sharp hatchet along, and in a moment more you can haul your prize on board before it has time to say "Jack Robinson," or to practice "I'll bite you." Clip its head off with one quick blow, but remember that the latter is dangerous for several minutes after becoming independent of its late boon companion, the body! The jaws have considerable muscular vitality left in them, and need but a touch to close with unpleasant vigor on finger or toe.

Sometimes the soft-shell gets caught in a manner as unexpected to its captor as to itself, by snapping at an innocent-looking little fish that has been prepared as bait for trout; and when this happens the result is very likely to be "an elephant" on the hands of the angler; for, when one sallies forth to catch a peaceable fish, one is not often armed to do battle with a ferocious enemy in the shape of a turtle.

Not long ago a lady friend of the writer's set out alone to row quite a distance to reach a certain fishing-ground, and on reaching it, hot and tired, her first capture—quite a superfluous one too she considered it—was a fifteen-pound "soft-shell." What to do with it? was the question, and one not to be pushed aside for future settlement. It could have been met by cutting the line and allowing the angry leviathan of the deep to take itself and the hook to the great unknown below.

But our friend was plucky and hooks were scarce, and so were such monster turtles as this. To cut the line was out of the question; yet here was the ugly creature ready for a snap, and nothing but a little pocket-knife at hand to amputate the threatening jaws—no hatchet nearer than a mile across the water. And the fish, large trout, were leaping all around, and this uninvited guest had monopolized the only hook! It was a hard case. But our friend met it by tying the line short to a thwart at a safe distance from her feet, taking up the oars and rowing home with her captive, who took the place of the anticipated trout-dinner. But now, when she goes a-fishing, several hooks and lines and a hatchet go to make up her outfit.

If only one can forget how very uninviting the soft-shell appears when alive, and look at it only as it is on the table—carefully stewed and seasoned and, if preferred, a little wine added—no complaint will be made as to the quality of the meat; and it is besides very nutritious.

There is yet another turtle found in all lakes, large or small. But this one is neither snappish nor homely in aspect; on the contrary, its appearance is rather attractive, and its manners of the gentlest. Its shell is hard, decidedly arched, and well covered with clearly defined black and orange blocks; it is rarely caught with the hook; and almost the only chance of capture is to watch the neighborhood of the lakes in the spring-time on sunshiny days, as then, like the soft-shell, it leaves the water and travels up to the soft sand to lay its eggs.

This turtle, as usually found, weighs from six to ten pounds, and while not quite as rich in flavor as its homelier brother is still an excellent article of food.

It is no uncommon thing, when plowing or walking in a field in the late spring, to turn up a queer little yellow and black object, no bigger than a silver quarter or half-dollar, which is a young hard-shell turtle, recently hatched; they are pretty creatures, and their markings as clearly defined as those of the adults. They are readily domesticated, so that they will eat from the hand without fear.

Six years ago the writer packed one of these tiny turtles in a tin box with damp moss and sent it North, where it still flourishes in a New Jersey aquarium, very little larger than when it was picked up in the Florida sands, the growth of a turtle being very slow. Water turtle should be killed at once, unless there is water to keep them in, as they cannot live more than a day or two out of their native element. In this they are unlike the gopher tortoise, which is all the better for being kept three or four days in a box or barrel.

There is one very odd quality possessed by the flesh of these several kinds of turtle (including the gopher) in common with the great sea-turtle that are so abundant all along the twelve hundred miles of Florida's sea-coast.

This curious quality was thus described in the year 1682 by one "T. A., Clerk on board His Majesty's ship, the Richmond":

"This I am assured of," says he, "that after it is cut to pieces, it retains a sensation of life three times longer than any known creature of the creation. Completely, six hours after the butcher has cut them up and into pieces, their mangled bodies, I have seen the callope (*callipee*, a part of the flesh), when going to be seasoned, with pieces of their flesh ready to cut into steaks, vehemently contract with great reluctancy, rise against the knife, and sometimes the whole mass of flesh in a visible tremulation and concussion. To him who first sees, it seems strange and admirable."

This same old-time writer records of the turtle, that "it has three hearts"; and to this superabundance of the vital organs he ascribes its wonderful "tenacity of life."

It is really true that hours after the turtle has been cut up the flesh will, when salt is sprinkled upon it, contract violently, and jerk and quiver in a manner that looks, to say the least of it, rather uncanny.

The true explanation is, not actual vitality, but some peculiar quality of the muscles and nerves by which galvanic or electric action is generated by the action of salt, or, as we have sometimes seen it, by hot water. The violent twitching is not pleasant to look at; but is not as "Ye Ancient Mariner," "T. A.," would have us believe, "a sensation of life."

CHAPTER XV. THE DAIRY QUESTION — OLD STYLE.

The Native Florida Cow. Methods of Milking. How to Make a Cowpen. Best Plan for best results in Fertilizing the Soil by Cowpenning. Treatment of the Florida Cow.

And now we arrive at the dairy question, and a very important one it is too, as every housekeeper knows.

"A curous kind of a critter is a Florida keow, anyway you take her; curous, mighty curous."

So pronounced a tall, raw-boned New-Englander, as he stood on the deck of the staunch steamer that was bearing the writer to a new Florida home.

"Why 'curious'?" we pondered, thinking over this cow question; but we did not like to betray our ignorance by asking questions; so we waited patiently until time and experience had solved the mystery.

And now we have come to the conclusion that our New Englander was right. Viewing the native Florida cow, as usually treated, with the eyes of a thrifty Northern farmer or dairyman, it is indeed a "curous critter," and its mode of treatment more "curous" still.

To the great mass of the people in the North, the term "cow-penning," as regards land, is an unknown quantity, and very few can give an intelligent reply to the question, "What does it mean?"

What its true significance is, we shall see presently; just now, to begin at the beginning, we will turn our attention to the "curous critter" itself.

For many years past immense herds of cattle have been roaming all over the noble State of Florida, and luxuriating in her genial climate; but of late these herds have been scattered, and driven back further and further south, until now, in the northern, middle, and eastern counties, we find their representatives comparatively "few and far between," and all in a state of captivity, and prisoners at large.

Where did they come from originally? Well, to answer that question, we must go back to the first settlements of Florida, those of Spain and France, which we have elsewhere referred to.

The early settlers of these rival nations imported from their home-countries numbers of the finest cattle, and here they flourished until, in the frequent and bloody quarrels between the two sets of pioneers, French and Spanish, settlers and settlements were alike swept out of existence, and such cattle as were not killed on the spot escaped to the forests and became the progenitors of the present race of Florida cows, and a degenerate race they are, we must confess; in other words, they have passed from a state of civilization, as it were, back to a state of nature.

For every one knows that the splendid milkers of the modern dairy are the outcome of generation after generation of careful selection, breeding and cross-breeding, of nutritious food and plenty of it, of good shelter and gentle treatment.

A copious flow of milk is never met with in wild cattle, and practically Florida cattle are wild, inasmuch as neglect, unkind and injudicious treatment have set them far along on the backward track toward that natural state wherein little if any more milk is secreted than is needed by the calf.

Dame Nature, you see, is not like man; she never wastes her materials or energies, but treasures up all her powers, and as soon as their exercise is not needed at one point directs them to another.

For the first few weeks of its life a calf needs milk, needs not much in quantity but richness in quality, and thus nature provides it: the irregular milking, varying in quantity and time, conduces directly to the drying up of the lacteal organs, which is just what she intends it shall do.

And, as we have said, this plan of hers can only be overcome by patient years of care and attention directed to the one object of producing heavy milkers.

The progenitors of the present much-maligned Florida cows were of the finest breeds then known to Europe; it would not have paid the early settlers to bring inferior stock across the ocean, and their degeneration is due solely to causes that would and do affect the human race under the same circumstances.

Take the members of the noblest, bluest-blooded family in the world, and turn them "out to graze," as it were, and to shift for themselves, where, a few generations later, would be their culture, their signs of nobility?

Then don't ridicule our Florida cow for being what neglect and ill-treatment has made it, a small producer of milk; rather let us give it the needed capital to invest in the manufacture, and not only its owner but the scoffing outside world will stand aside astonished to see what this slandered animal can do when it has a fair chance.

And now, having spoken a good word in advance in behalf of our native cow, let us go more into details.

Every settler who comes into this State, unless indeed he takes up his abode in one of the few cities, and sometimes even then, must make up his mind either to use no milk, or condensed milk, or to invest in several Florida cows, or one thoroughbred at least. We say "several" advisedly, as will be seen directly.

Very few are willing to do without this every-day article of civilized life, or to be content with condensed milk, which, excellent so far it goes, does not go far enough to meet all culinary demands.

So the purchase of cows is soon decided upon and the next step is to prepare a pen for their reception. A barn or barnyard or even a shed is not necessary in Florida for the protection of stock, unless they are to be kept confined, and this is rarely done with common stock.

The first step is to clean the ground where the pen is to be made, bearing in mind always that this spot will be the future vegetable garden, especially on pine land, and it will be enriched by the nightly penning of the cows.

Many simply girdle the pine trees and leave them standing, to litter the ground with falling bark and boughs for years to come, until they fall to the ground bodily, crushing the fence or any valuable trees that may be near. This is a slovenly mode of procedure, unworthy of a thrifty farmer.

It is a grand old axiom that "Whatever is worth doing is worth doing well," and we commend it to the attention of nine tenths of our Florida farmers.

In preparing the place for a cow-pen, "do it well;" that is, take every stump out of the ground, don't leave a single one to be a perpetual eye-sore and a perpetual depository for weeds and ants, which will surely take up their abode around the stump where the plow cannot reach them. Let the ground be made clear of stumps and trash, and then plow it thoroughly, two or three times if possible before putting up the fence, which latter is usually made of rails laid in the " Virginia style," the "worm fence" of the North.

The size of the pen varies with the number of cows to be penned, and this is a matter of which the settler must judge for himself; but it is always about twice as long as it is wide, and should be so situated, if possible, that one end abuts on the open woods and the other upon an inclosed field or woodland, where the calves may have a range. It is a cruel thing to shut them up all day long in the pen without food or shelter; and yet this is, we are sorry to say, the common practice all over the State.

The pen must have two entrances from the outside, one into the pen, the other into the field; and these are made by arranging one panel of the fence so that the rails may be easily slipped back and one end dropped to the ground.

Across or near the center of the inclosure another fence is run to divide it into two pens, for without this precaution there would be "no end" of confusion during the milking process; this too must have a panel arranged in the center with drop rails, thus affording an easy access from one division to the other.

And now every thing is ready for the reception of the expected guests, and the more there are of these the better, not only that the family may have a good supply of milk, but that the future garden-spot may be the richer.

We have already intimated pretty plainly that Florida cows are not remarkable for the large quantity of milk they yield. One that will give two quarts and a pint at a milking, the calf taking a liberal share of the same, is regarded as a better cow than the average, and yet what Northern farmer would give shelter to this "better cow?" Not one, for he could not afford it; but in our genial climate the question of expense for shelter and food is not considered, for they are not required. In the first place, cows are cheap; an "extra good one" can be bought for $20, and the average kinds, $12 to $15, always, be it understood, with a young calf; for, as the Chinaman says, "no calfee, no milkee!" In the second place, the value of land that has been cow-penned is greatly enhanced, so highly (and justly so) is it valued, that many Floridians purchase herds of cattle for the sole purpose of penning them up at night.

The vast pine forests are filled with the far-famed wiregrass, a long wire-like grass growing in tufts, said to be very nutritious, and upon which the cattle certainly do grow fat. In the hammocks are other luxuriant grasses and shrubs, and an abundance of the long, gray moss, so widely known as "Florida moss." These forests, both pine and hammock, afford free pasturage to all, and the cows being turned out all the day long feed themselves without expense to their owners both winter and summer.

The calves are kept at home during the milking season, not only to prevent them from getting more than their share of the milk, but also as a hostage to secure their mothers' return at night, and as a rule their detention has the desired effect. The cow, turned out in the morning, comes back to the pen toward evening with curious regularity. We have often wondered how they manage it; for sometimes they wander much farther afield than at others, yet almost invariably they may be seen at the same hour solemnly marching into the pen where their eager little ones are anxiously waiting their advent; for they too know the hour for their supper-time, and may be found gazing wistfully through the bars at their sedate-looking parents, murmuring in *low*-ered accents the mournful refrain,

"Thou art so near, and yet so far."

The whole process of milking a Florida cow by what we may term the "native method," is full of novelty and amusement to a stranger. The milker drops the sliding bars of the dividing fence, and one of the patiently-waiting cows steps through into the calves' pen to be met ere fairly clear of the rails by an instant bombardment from its loving, most disinterested child; and it behooves the milker, if he wants to secure any portion of the lacteal fluid, to be very quick in putting up the bars again and gaining the side of the cow just admitted.

While the calf is very young it is allowed full control of three of the teats; when it is two months old, if strong and healthy, two teats are enough; as it grows still older, one teat only is given up to it; and at last, when the calf is five or six months old and has become as expert a grazer as its mother, it has no need of any milk at all.

But woe be to him who should seek to separate it from its mother, hoping to get all the milk himself! The result would be disastrous.

We have already seen how nearly the native Florida cow has gone back to its natural or wild state, and in this state the milk never "comes" until the teats are pulled upon by the calf; hence the cow persistently holds back her milk till her offspring draws it down, and it is very rarely that she can be induced to do otherwise, So long as the milking continues, the calf must be allowed to pull for a few moments on one teat at least, even if it should be a year or more old, as often happens.

Of course this makes the process of milking rather an arduous one, for the older and stronger the older and stronger the calf becomes, the more impatient is it of any restriction placed upon its raid on the milk-bag; the moment the calf ranges alongside of its mother, the milker must be ready to grasp the teats not intended for its use, and to hold them until the milk is fairly down. Very often it comes slowly, and then terrific is the bombardment the impatient offspring administers to its usually gentle mother; its violence and frequency is apt to repeatedly jerk the reserved teats away from the milker's hand, and, if not recovered on the instant, "presto! change!" instead of a full teat there is an empty one!

Not only so, but unless the milker is wise enough to go down on one knee and make a brace for the cow either with his head, or by placing his hand on her side and his elbow on his own knee, she will very likely be upset or so "hustled" against him as to lay him on his back.

Usually the cow does not seem to object to this energetic attack, but patiently stands as still as she can, chewing the cud and sleepily nodding, though she does sometimes protest against it by moving forward a step or two after each thump, and every such action must be followed up by the milker instantaneously or he will lose his share; for the calf, like its mother, is "a curous critter," and ever on the watch for an opportunity to take possession of the coveted reserve.

The milker holds the teats, one, two, or three, as it may chance, until he feels them swelling out, then the milk has "come;" a moment or two longer he waits "to make assurance doubly sure," and then, if he is alone in the pen, he springs like a madman to the sliding panel, drops the bars, rushes back and drags the calf forcibly from its mother's side, giving the latter the command to "go!"

It is curious how soon both the cow and calf learn the meaning of this summary injunction: the one steps back into the pen with the other cows and the other watches its retreat mournfully, licking its foam-flecked lips the while, but seldom making any attempt to follow its dam.

Then the milker puts up the bars and proceeds to milk the cow; no generous pail has he into which the copious white streams go churning and foaming; his pail stands in a safe corner by the fence or is hung on a hook, and in his hand he holds a two-quart milking-cup—for the Florida milker can use only one hand in the process, the other must hold the cup that receives the milk. He must be ever on the *qui vive* for unexpected movements, for the cows are not the steady, well-trained animals of the northern dairies. There is a difference in them, it is true; with the steady "old stagers" he may kneel on one knee and milk in comparative comfort; but if he has to deal with a half-trained cow he will have to stand stooping just low enough to grasp the teats, and so be ready to follow or avoid any eccentric movement of body or leg, the latter having sometimes a tendency to fly upward on small or no provocation.

More often than not a return of the calf and a second separation and milking are necessary, because the cow does not "give down" all her milk at the first invitation; when the milker is satisfied that he has all he can get, or needs, the cow is returned to the calf and the latter is left to finish up at leisure, while the same tedious process is being gone through with the other cows.

This mode of milking is only one of several methods of dealing with the cow and calf, and is adopted by those who are too dainty to be "bothered" by allowing the calf to pull upon one or two teats while they are milking the others. This latter is really the best way as well as the most expeditious, for the milk comes down steadily without intermission until the supply is exhausted, and then the calf is allowed to clean up the remnants, while. the milker calls out "Next."

It has the disadvantage, however, of proceeding in the face of a vigorous bombardment that ever and anon jerks the teats away, and of requiring an occasional wiping of foam from finger and teats; but one gets used to these trifles by and by.

Another way when the milker has an assistant (as should always be the case), is for the latter to place a stout rope or broad leather collar around the calf's neck, and then, when the milk has "come," to pull it away till the milker gets through or desires its return to "draw" any milk that may be left. This method is quicker than the first, and neater than the second.

Frequently, however, the second mode of milking is the only one practicable, because it is not every Florida cow that will permit herself to be milked, unless the calf is actually milking her at the same time.

Three pints of milk to each cow at a milking is a fair yield, and where there are five or six at least, as is usually the case, even this counts up and adds no little to the comfort and economy of the household, giving an abundant supply of milk and cream, "cottage cheese," and butter.

No doubt it seems very much like "much ado about nothing" to the Northern farmer, with his fifteen and twenty-quart cows; but it must be considered that these Florida cows cost their owners nothing to keep them, little to buy, and that while they give him milk and butter they are at the same time doing what is more important, enriching the land by their droppings when shut in for the night.

Many Floridians, as we have said, keep cattle for this purpose alone, and were this their only value they would be a good investment as commercial fertilizers.

The high pine lands of Florida are not, as a rule, very rich lands; but they are what is better, healthy. The low hammock lauds are rich, but they are unhealthy as a rule, and their life-long denizens will usually be found putty-colored of face and languid of manner, caring little for progress and still less for personal exertion, because all the spirit and energy are sapped out of them by the subtle malaria that haunts the beautiful hammocks and renders repulsive what else would be most charming. Understand, however, that this does not apply to the less frequent high hammocks.

Perhaps it is just as well that this is so, too, because human nature is apt to be unreasonable and pugnacious.

Hammock lands are limited in area, and if they were very desirable in all respects as places of residence every one would want them, and, as a matter of course, every one could not get them; and then would Florida be turned topsy-turvey, and the case of the celebrated "Kilkenny cats" would become a case of "Florida Crackers."

As it is, however, the bulk of the populace are wise enough to prefer the poorer pine lands with health to the rich low-hammock lands with disease; the former can be fertilized and made sufficiently rich, the latter can not be made healthy.

And one of the cheapest and most popular means of enriching the land is that of cow-penning it. It is, as it were, "killing two birds with one stone." Milk, butter, fertilizer, all in one; who could ask for more?

The more cow-penned land one has the more valuable is his property; for this is not an evanescent enriching; once fertilized in this manner, the land continues to produce good crops of fruit or vegetables, as the case may be, for many years thereafter, and no grove is more healthy or prolific than one that is set out on cow-penned land.

"How long does it take to thus enrich the land?" you ask.

That depends entirely on the number of animals penned and the space inclosed. The rule is to have the ground well covered with "droppings" before starting a new pen.

When this is accomplished, be it sooner or later, it is time to move on, if the raising of sweet potatoes is the object in view; if other vegetables requiring a richer soil are desired, then it is advisable to plow the ground at this stage, and begin the cow-penning again on the same space.

From March till November the cattle night after night are shut in their inclosure, and where one owns twenty head or more, it is surprising how much poor land will be transformed into rich land in the course of a single season before it is time to "turn the cows out."

And now as to the cow-pen itself. We have already seen how important a matter the enriching of the land by means of the nightly penning of the cows is to the Florida farmer. But it might easily be made the source of much greater riches than it is.

The usual mode, as we have said, is to plow the land before penning the cows, and, after the ground is well covered with droppings, to plow and inclose another space, using the first as a garden or sweet potato patch.

By this primitive method the most valuable portions of the manure are totally lost; and yet the average farmer who follows it thinks he is doing the best he can.

The droppings are left for weeks or months on the surface of the ground, leached by sun, rain, and air, the ammonia, that most valuable plant-food, escaping into the air as fast as the manure is deposited, while the liquid portion evaporates so as to be a complete loss, and, as every one knows, this is the most valuable of all manures.

Now matters might easily be managed much better than this. We would suggest that the cow-pen, instead of being made movable, be a permanent one.

Make it a barn-yard instead of a pen, and then there could be a roomy shed placed in one corner of the calves' division, into which the cows might enter from the one side and the calves from the other; so that the milker would not only be protected from sun and rain while milking (and the latter is a very frequent accompaniment to the dainty pleasures of the cow-pen, especially in June, July, August, and September), but would also be saved from kneeling down in the midst of the uncleanliness attendant upon the usual method.

But this would be only an incidental gain, as it were; the greatest gain of all, apart from the comfort of the milker, would be found in the increased amount and vastly improved quality of the fertilizing substances accumulating in the yard under the new *regime*.

Before and during the cows' home season, haul into the yard a thick layer of muck, then another of leaves, surface mold, or grass; next, more muck, and over all pine needles and leaves and grass, or any other of the odds and ends of rottable matter that may be had for the gathering around every Florida home.

The more and the deeper the amount of trash collected the better; the latter will absorb and retain the liquid manure, and the solid will be trampled down into the mass and their value preserved intact, especially if an occasional sprinkling of land-plaster, just enough to whiten the surface, is given.

Keep adding to the pile, preserving its level surface all the season, or, if preferred, remove the first installment at the end of three or four months and commence afresh.

The result will be a fertilizer especially adapted to orange trees, or in fact to any other species of vegetation—rich enough to produce splendid results, yet not rich enough to scald seeds or roots.

By adopting this method not only will additional comfort be provided for the milker, but the same number of cows will furnish five-fold the amount of a far more valuable fertilizer than that obtained by the slovenly method now almost invariably practiced.

Another shed, made of the "rough edge" boards, sold so cheaply by our saw-mills, would add not a little to the comfort of the cows, not only as affording shelter during the heavy night rains, so common in the summer and early fall, but as a feeding place. Under this shed, built in the cow's division, should be placed boxes containing salt, so arranged that the cows may have free access to them. It is a great mistake to suppose that Florida cows do not need salt; they do need it just as much as any other cows, only they are not, as a rule, educated to eating it; give them a chance to find out what it is, and they will seek it as eagerly as any Northern cow.

It is necessary to the preservation of their health, and is in fact one of the most powerful of those preventives an ounce of which is "worth more than a pound of cure."

Equal quantities of salt and oak-wood ashes mixed together in water and then dried in large lumps will, it is said, draw homeward the most refractory cows, so extremely fond of it are they. Try it and see.

All through the summer, from spring until fall, the wiregrass and shrubs of the piney woods furnish ample sustenance to the cattle that roam at large far and wide. But, as winter draws near, the grass ceases to grow and becomes tough and dry, while the shrubs drop their leaves, and the saw-palmetto, on which also they feed, loses the crispness that seems to be its chief attraction.

Then the cows begin to come home later and later, even those that have hitherto been in the habit of coming in early, and the milking has to be done by the light of a fire built in the pen, or by that of a lantern; the latter is much more convenient, and its rays are quite sufficient to guide both the milker and the cows.

This coming home late to their calves, all through the season, is a fault of which not a few Florida cows are guilty; but who can blame them, seeing how entirely their education has been neglected and how very badly they have been brought up! In fact, like the celebrated Topsy, they have had no bringing up, they have "just growed."

This vexatious fault that we have mentioned is one that may, however, be easily corrected. All that is necessary to bring the cows home regularly at or before dusk is a few stalks of corn-fodder, a handful of cow-pea vines, or some such little tid-bit, fed to them after the evening milking is over.

Let every settler who is annoyed by his cows keeping late hours try this plan, and emphasize it by placing here and there in the pen small boxes containing coarse or rock salt, and he will have no further occasion to complain of his cows; we have tried it, and know whereof we write.

It is really wonderful how marked is the effect of such a simple mode of treatment. We have known two neighbors living side by side, the one never fed his cows at all, and each afternoon toward dusk was obliged to mount his horse and search the woods for several miles around, uttering the while the peculiar "cow-call," which each man varies to suit himself, the several herds soon learning the particular call to which they owe fealty. This our neighbor had to do each afternoon, no matter how inconvenient it might be—either this, or else to wait the voluntary return of his cows, and be prepared to milk them at any hour they might choose between early evening and dawn. The other neighbor fed his cows after the evening milking was over, only a mere handful of green or cured fodder, and this was enough to bring them home regularly before dark; never once was he obliged to seek them; not only so, but this extra feed, meager as it was, made a marked difference in the yield of milk.

Moral: It pays well to feed one's cows at night, be it ever so little.

It is curious how these same uneducated Florida cows show their knowledge as to the proper time for them to be turned out into the hammock-world with their offspring at their side; whether it be the diminishing supply of tender grass, the shortening days, the cooler weather, or some mysterious internal instinct, certain it is that they do know, and if their calves are not in due time set at liberty to wander forth with their dams to the luxuriant hammock, the latter will, sooner or later, betake themselves to their usual winter haunts minus their offspring.

And then, when this happens, their owner has a perplexing problem before him; whether to turn the little ones out (first marking and branding them) to shift for themselves, or to feed them at home all winter. In nine cases out of ten the latter is simply impossible; so out they must go, alone—in all likelihood never more to be seen by their owners.

From the first to the middle of November is the usual time of turning out the cows, and it is not wise to defer it later, as both cows and calves are apt to suffer from a short supply of food.

All through the mild Florida winter the open hammock lands, scattered all over the country, are alive with the cattle thus set adrift by their owners, each of whom has his own particular brand and ear-mark by which to identify his property.

Numerous natural grasses and shrubs grow all winter long under the dense shelter of the grand old oaks of the Florida hammocks, and the long gray moss which lends so weird a charm to the scene affords also no despicable source of nourishment to the cattle who take up their temporary residence in its midst.

"Once upon a time," when we were unversed in the "curous" ways of this "curous critter," we used to wonder why there was so little moss hanging low down from the oak trees. Now we wonder no more; we know. The cows confiscate all that comes within their reach, and that is why the human moss-robbers must literally "look aloft" for their share of the booty, upon which, doubtless, many a hungry cow has looked with wistful eye.

As a rule the cows which are hammock-fed during the winter season, that is from November to the end of February, come back to the pens plump and in good condition, when they come at all.

For it is not to be supposed that this promiscuous "turning-out" year after year is going to continue without occasional losses. It not unfrequently happens that cows disappear from their owners' ken, in spite of all searching for them far and wide. Sometimes they die; sometimes they are killed and eaten by unscrupulous parties, usually of the colored persuasion; sometimes they stray away of themselves, having quarreled perhaps with the companions of their accustomed haunts; but all that their owners know of a certainty is that they "are gone, but not forgotten."

As to the calves of the previous season, no surprise is felt if they are missing; in fact, if a calf born one winter or spring lives to be turned out with its dam in the fall, the surprise comes in just there, and no after performance of that calf need excite the least astonishment.

For, be it known, that it is a comparatively rare thing for a Florida calf to survive its first summer; seldom does it pass its sixth month. It is a more common thing than otherwise for the cattle owner to lose eight out of ten calves before the season is over.

The reason for this great mortality is not far to seek. In the first place generations of exposure, neglect, and ill treatment, combined with a constant "breeding in and in," have weakened the Florida native stock, and, as a natural consequence, the calves have but little *stamina*, and the modicum they do possess is destroyed by the treatment they receive, in nine cases out of ten, from the day of their arrival in the cow-pen. This latter is the true cause of the enormous mortality among Florida calves, and it is full time that our people were wakened up to that fact.

What Northern farmer would dream of shutting up his calves in a small inclosure, devoid of tree or grass, keeping them all through the long summer months without shade or water, and without food as well, except a scanty supply of milk morning and evening?

Yet this is what nearly all the old-style Florida population do! The older "Cracker" portion, because their fathers did it before them; and the less intelligent of the new-comers, because "it is the custom of the country ; " and so they suppose it to be all right, until they find their calves dying off and their cows—who persistently hold back their milk until coaxed by the gentle lips of their offspring—"drying up," as a consequence of the cruel, short-sighted policy pursued toward the latter.

The wonder is that a single calf survives such an ordeal. We have often looked into pens on a hot summer's day and felt our blood rise to boiling heat, not from the rays of the sun, but with a fierce accession of wrath at beholding the helpless, patient little calves lying close to the rail fence, seeking what scant shade might be found, their sides panting, their tongues hanging out, not a particle of food or shelter or water within their reach from the rising to the setting of the sun!

Give the Florida calf a good pasture lot; fence in a portion of your piney woodland, if you can do no better; keep water and salt within reach; give an occasional bucket of mixed bran and meal, some chopped-up sweet potatoes, raw, and an occasional feed of hay or fodder; put up a rough shed that will turn water, surround it by a light railing, so that the calves may be shut in there and prevented from lying on the wet ground on rainy or cold nights, which are sure to come, especially toward fall, and rest assured that the Florida calf thus treated will astonish its owner by declining to die, or to do any thing else but grow up fat and healthy.

Just try it and see, you who have hitherto been content to follow in the worn-out grooves of the old-time settlers.

An important step toward the attainment of this much-to-be-desired result—namely, the regeneration of the native stock—is, first of all, more gentle treatment than is usually given them.

Many a time has our righteous indignation boiled and seethed and finally overflowed in a torrent, because of the brutal manner in which cows and calves are treated by the ignorant classes who, apart from questions of common humanity, do not know enough to recognize the fact that they are despoiling and depreciating their own property.

And it is not only these ("the poor white trash"), of whom happily there are few in our beautiful State, or the naturally cruel negro, who thus wantonly ill-treat animals. It is often done, or allowed to be done by dependents, from sheer carelessness. Many a cow and calf are beaten and driven and kicked, not once in a while only, but every night and morning, by those who are intrusted by the owner with their care. Perhaps, as the pens are usually at some little distance from the house, he may not know of the cruelty with which his cattle are treated, or he may suspect that "the darkies are a little rough," but does not take the trouble to verify his suspicions or make himself conversant with the amount of damage this "little roughness" is doing to his property, to say nothing of the humanitarian aspect of the case.

In either event—that of ignorance or mere suspicion—we can not hold the owner guiltless of wanton cruelty, for it is the clear duty of every stock-owner to see that his animals are well and kindly treated, and not left to the "tender mercies" of a race proverbially cruel to animals, and even to each other.

We have elsewhere alluded to the necessity that often exists of riding out on horseback toward nightfall to hunt up the cows that are apt to be dilatory in returning in due time to the pen.

Just here begins the opportunity for the cruelty we have referred to; in nine cases out of ten, unless it is the owner himself who goes forth to seek the " bunch" (as a herd of cattle keeping together are called), the cows are driven home, not at the quiet, easy walk that is so necessary to the preservation of their milking qualities, but with a horse trotting fast behind them, a dog oftentimes barking and biting at their heels, a voice shouting at its utmost, and a long-lashed whip cutting and slashing across the backs of any that may drop behind the frightened, flurried, galloping herd.

Thus they come rushing into the pen, heated, panting, their heads drooping, their eyes staring with affright, the foam dripping from their mouths—altogether as dejected and weary a lot of cows as the most cruel heart could desire to see.

And then comes the milking and further opportunities for brutality, and this time the calf is a victim as well as the cow. If the two are separated, by the cow being driven back to the outer pen after the milk has been drawn down, the process is accompanied by kicks and blows to hurry the cow and keep back the calf.

If it is considered, as it usually is, too much trouble to separate them, then, after the milk has come down, the milker being provided with a stick, reaches under the cow, and if the hungry calf, that sees itself being deprived of its supper, ventures to come within reach it is saluted with heavy blows across its head and legs, till bruised, and ofttimes bleeding, it limps away.

Then if the cow, stung by a fly, dares to use the weapon the Creator has given it to protect itself against its insect enemies—its tail—and the latter interferes in the least with the milker's comfort, it is greeted with a blow or kick; or if—because a sore teat is rough handled, or a fly bites, or a sudden movement or shout startles its already overstrung nerves—it lifts its leg to free itself from its tormentor, anther kick or blow, often on the sensitive bone of the leg, is the result.

Again, when a young cow fresh from two or three years freedom in the open range is to be "broken" for milking, how is it done, only too often? Not by kindly treatment and gentle persistence. No, but by driving it into a corner of the pen, lassoing its head and unmercifully lashing it with the cruel "cow-whip" until it is exhausted and stands or lies down in helpless misery.

We have watched closely, and regret to say that there is all too much of this sort of cruelty being practiced, even where it is unsuspected by the owners of the unfortunate cattle, whose interest and duty should combine to render such an abuse of his property impossible.

How can such things be? Why, certainly, only by criminal negligence on the part of those who leave their stock at the mercy of dependents.

If the owner is not able to attend to the wants of his cattle in person, let at least his presence at odd times and seasons in the pen or field act as a check, and let it be understood that the man, woman or child, who is proven to have ill-used the animals under their care will be discharged on the spot.

Not till the present usual manner of treating the Florida cow is totally changed can there be any decided improvement in the race. It is this loud shouting, driving and beating that makes them, as they often are, half wild and intractable.

Wherever it is possible the owner should overlook in person all work wherein the comfort of his cattle is concerned, and if those who are now resting in the self-satisfied belief that their own individual herds are receiving proper treatment will but take the trouble to "make assurance doubly sure," they will, in the majority of cases, be surprised at the revelations awaiting them.

Among our own cows is one that, when purchased, we were told we could not milk, because the wife of the seller, though used to cows all her life, was afraid to do so unless her husband stood by with a whip in his hand, ready to punish the cow for kicking. But we liked the looks of the animal, a young one with her second calf, and had some confidence in our newly acquired milking accomplishments, chief among which we counted the banishment of clubs, whips, and loud voices.

Well, that cow kicked us pretty regularly for the first few days, and we did not kick back; we bewildered her by patting her, speaking gently, and quietly persevering in our intention to milk her. After the first five days she thought better of the kicking business and decided to resign in favor of her less kindly treated relatives. She never kicked again.

In one week she allowed us to stroke her head, and in another she ate from our hand and gradually permitted us to "come up to the scratch," behind her ears.

Then we invited the former owner into the pen, and the cow shrank into a corner the moment she saw him. He retired further off, and she then allowed herself to be milked as usual, never lifting her once too "jerky" leg, although her calf nearly butted her off her balance.

The latter too, wild and nervous when it first came into our pen, soon became so familiar as to pick our pockets of any thing that might be fluttering therefrom, to take our straw hat off our head and a piece out of the brim if we were not on the alert, to chew up our jacket, to twist its tongue around our hair, and to take whatever advantage it could of our defenseless condition in the milking pen, when it was disengaged and we were not.

Now this has been our own experience in two other cases, and therefore we speak whereof we know; gentleness in handling cow and calf will insure gentle animals and increase the yield of milk in the former; few persons are aware how directly the latter is affected by rough treatment, "running the cows home," striking and exciting them.

We have been thus particular in describing the old-style methods of milking and cow-penning, because it is a question of but a few years more before they will be, save in isolated localities, things of the past, to be remembered with wonder and amazement, but practiced no more.

The old style still prevails, however, over the greater part of the State where the means and opportunity of improvement are yet in the near future.

CHAPTER XVI. THE DAIRY QUESTION — THE COMING STYLE.

Native Stock to be Improved by Crossing with Thoroughbreds and Proper Treatment. Acclimated Thoroughbreds should be Bought of Florida Breeders

One of the most important questions that Florida has to face in the near future is how to improve her cattle.

The time when this was a matter of little importance has gone by, and the new and more intelligent class of settlers who are steadily flowing into the State, coming from older lands where they have been used to better things in the dairy line than they have found awaiting them in their new homes, will never be satisfied until they have tested what can be done in the way of improvement.

We hear some of the old time fogies say, "Nothing."

We beg leave to differ and say, Every thing.

There is no reason in the world why Florida should not in due time stand forth as fine a cattle-raising State as one need desire.

But to accomplish this end there is much to be done; and time, care, patience, and systematic perseverance are requisite to succeed.

It is the common opinion in the North, among those who are not well informed, that grass can not be raised in Florida; and even in this very State itself we sometimes hear the same assertion.

But never was a greater mistake made.

Because all kinds of grass will not grow equally well on all soils, and endure the vicissitudes of all climates, there is no reason to assert that no kinds of grasses can be found that will flourish on Florida soil and beneath the Florida sun. On the contrary, already the merits of many grasses have been tested, and with perfect satisfaction, not only in cultivated fields for cured fodder, but also in the meadow as permanent pasture; and the number of these food-suppliers is constantly on the increase.

Those who make the above sweeping assertions are either woefully ignorant or maliciously slanderous toward a great State.

No family who owns an acre or two of moderately-good land has any excuse for not having an abundance of milk and butter even in much maligned Florida, as we shall see by and by.

A well-fed cow is one of the best friends a housekeeper can have, and no better investment could be found for the amount of money that will buy and keep one of these valuable animals, for whose product there is a demand every hour of the day. Especially is this the case in the new Florida home, where more often than not only the plainest and most simple kinds of food can be procured, and where the milk, butter, and cheese furnished by the humble cow are a mine of wealth to the perplexed wife and mother, in whose ears the daily cry of "What shall we eat?" is ever ringing.

Now, as we have seen, the native Florida cow gives but little milk when, as is usually the case, she is turned out during the day to pick up her own living as best she may.

And so the lack in individuals is made up in numbers, and thus from four or five cows enough milk is procured to yield the family an ample supply.

If we stop to think about it we will see a reason sufficient in itself to account for the small yield of milk from each cow, even apart from its degenerate state and the comparatively small amount of food it obtains; and this is the excessive amount of exercise it is compelled to take all day, and every day, to get even this modicum of "greens."

Whence came the popular phrase, "fat as an alderman," except from the well-known fact that sitting still all the day long and eating and drinking at pleasure, is very apt to make a man fat?

It is not often that a person who is in the habit of taking constant exercise accumulates flesh; he will become muscular but not stout.

And it is just the same with animals. The Florida hog, roaming the wild woods for its living, is thin and scrawny; the cow is not thin, but neither is she fat, like her more fortunate Northern sisters who have only to stand or lie still at pleasure, and eat, eat, eat, drink, drink, drink, day in and day out.

In the one case the milk factory has to hunt up the material to manufacture, and meanwhile the works are running on half time and power; in the other an abundance of material is supplied and the engines in the milk factory have only to use up the raw material fed to them in sufficient quantities to keep them running at full speed.

In the one instance there is a constant waste of time, power, and material, in the other they are all utilized to their fullest extent.

In an agricultural paper not long ago we saw this very question ably discussed, and figures given to show the amount of food that went to make up the loss in bones and muscle, when cows were obliged to wander for miles after their daily food, as compared with cows well fed and kept in a stall or home pasture, and the difference was startling.

We have always believed that one great reason for the paucity of milk yielded by the native Florida cow is the amount of exercise she is compelled to take each day, in the search for provender, and lately we have seen it proved that such is really the case.

A neighbor took a common native cow and calf off "the range" when she was giving only one pint of milk (in addition to one pint allowed the calf), and her yield of milk increased six-fold within two weeks, simply from being fed a mess of bran and corn-meal twice a day, with an armload of fodder now and then, and not being compelled to wander for miles in search of food.

Who will say that this small amount of food was not a good investment?

And, moreover, it shows that a great deal can be done with our common native stock even in their present degenerate condition. In fact it is to this stock, already acclimated and used to "roughing" it, that Florida must look for the basis of future improvement in the dairy.

All Florida wants is to have her native stock brought back to where it was when the earliest settlers imported it from Europe; and to attain this end each neighborhood needs only to secure a few pure Jersey, Guinea, Durham, and Ayreshire bulls.

Then, in a few years, when the female descendants came to be milkers, a vast difference would be at once perceptible. Kill off the males of the old stock, import those named above, as they have been proven to be especially adapted to Southern climates, provide food and pasture, and the dairy question is solved completely and satisfactorily.

There is more merit in the common cows of Florida than they get credit for; they respond very quickly to a more generous supply of food than they usually receive; and if this were steadily given and the improving elements above alluded to introduced among them, her people would be content and with reason.

It is not to be denied, however, that it is not every one of these "curous critters," as at present constituted, that will permit itself to be well treated. Many Florida cows refuse to eat any thing whatever except the wild grasses on which they have grown up, and no amount of coaxing or imprisonment with such dainty food set before them as would delight the heart and fill the stomach of a properly educated cow will induce them to eat or drink.

We know of one instance (among several) where a cow was penned up, and an abundance of corn-fodder, cow-pea vines, bran, corn-meal, turnips, potatoes, kitchen-slops—in short, every thing that could be thought of to tempt her—were laid at her feet, all in vain; not a morsel would she touch, not a mouthful of water would she drink.

"Greek met Greek;" the owner resolved to starve the cow into eating; and the cow resolved to show that she had a mind of her own. So for five days the struggle went on; and just as the owner, alarmed at the rapidly departing flesh of his mulish animal, concluded to own himself vanquished, the cow settled the disputed question in a very emphatic manner. She leaped the fence, an unusually high one, and was never more seen by her owner.

But then again there are many Florida cows that eat as readily as their Northern sisters, and these are the ones to experiment upon; the younger the cow, the more tractable she will prove to be in this respect. The old cows are like old people, they do not take kindly to new habits or ideas.

Another point to be gained in the treatment of Florida cows is to teach them to yield their milk without the intervention of their calves.

This will be a difficult matter for obvious reasons. While perseverance on the one side and obstinacy on the other are in progress, the cow may "go dry," as holding back the milk, even for a few milkings, tends directly to this result.

But when this catastrophe threatens, the calf should be hurried to the rescue, and, after milking its refractory parent, be again removed from sight.

The disposition to hold up the milk may, in most cases, be overcome by patience and gentleness, and feeding the cow while milking; bathing the teats and udder with lukewarm water and gently handling them, will almost always induce her to "give down" her milk, and once the habit is fixed it will never be forgotten.

As to the calf, it should of course be allowed to be with its mother for the first twenty-four hours, as it is necessary to its welfare to draw the first milk; but, after this period, it should be taken entirely out of sight and hearing of its mother.

Of course success in this direction will not always be attainable; but if a young cow be made the subject of the experiment, and especially if she is being fed so as to increase her flow of milk and render its retention beyond one day incompatible with her comfort, it will seldom fail; and once this step is gained, the calf can be taught to drink milk from a pail for the first two weeks and then be fed on slops, potatoes, bran, corn-meal, or from two to four ounces (no more) of cotton-seed meal a day, mixed with the bran, until able to graze, and then the owner will no longer be obliged to share the milk, or be dependent on the life of the calf for any yield at all from its mother.

The introduction of "blue blood" among the ill-used, degenerate Florida cows, is a far better method of improving the stock than by the general importation of pureblood cows.

Again and again has this been tried, and with disaster in almost every instance. Sometimes out of a dozen or more fine stock, imported from Northern or Western States, not one has survived the change; Jerseys, Devons, Ayreshires, Durhams, Holsteins, all have gone the same road.

And yet, in spite of this ill-fortune, some of the younger stock was left, enough to form the nucleus of the homebred pure-bloods that we find scattered here and there over the State, a delight to their owners, and a boon to the enterprising settler who is wide awake enough to realize the advantage of procuring good stock already acclimated.

Never go outside the State to purchase stock if you can possibly obtain it nearer home.

The acclimation of animals is a more serious thing than most people are aware of. If a domestic animal is taken from a cold to a warm climate, or vice versa, it will almost invariably lose its appetite and its health, and literally pine to death. If it survives this ordeal, however, and regains its usual health, it is henceforth acclimated and has "crossed the Rubicon" so far as change of climate is concerned.

One of the most noticeable immediate effects of the removal of cattle to a warmer climate than that they have been accustomed to is an accelerated pulse, a gain of from fifteen to thirty beats a minute; in other words, fever sets in, and always more seriously with adults than with young or half-grown cattle; sometimes the latter are very slightly affected;

occasionally, where proper treatment from the start has been given, they escape it entirely.

"What is proper treatment?" you ask.

Provide sufficient and effective shelter from the sun; do not allow the cattle to be excited, or driven, except at a walk—and not even this when it can be prevented.

Do not feed them Indian corn, or any other heat-producing food. Do not turn them out in the open woods to graze: they can not bear the same treatment that is given to the inured native stock. Keep them under shelter, except perhaps in the early morning, or for an hour or two toward sundown. Horseflies and ticks are sorely trying to the patience and flesh of even the native cattle. Have a Stall for your thoroughbreds, with wire netting in the doors and windows. Never mind if you are laughed a : your poor cattle will bless and reward you.

Remember that the native grasses of Florida and other plant foods are different from those they have been accustomed to, and that they have this change to meet in addition to that of the climate.

Feed hay *ad libitum*; you can make it yourself from crab-grass, Bermuda, or other similar grasses; cured fodder of any sort can also be used, if sweet and good; bran also is good—any thing in fact that is not heat-producing.

But still, even with constant care, the investment in imported stock is apt to be a great risk. A breeder of many years' experience assures us that, "The most that can be hoped for, when animals are subjected to great climatic changes, is to keep them in sufficient health to bear offspring, from which stock may finally be obtained, not only acclimated but naturalized."

There are many who assert, and apparently with reason, that the chief trouble and risk in bringing cattle into this State from the West or North is, after all, not so much the simple question of acclimatization, since the Florida climate is, during a large part of the year, quite cool enough to be bracing, and during the remainder scarcely as warm as the animals have been used to in the summer season in their old homes.

These observers assign another cause for the trouble.

It is a well-known fact that in Texas, and other Gulf coast States, the cattle are subject to a fever, popularly known as the "Texas fever," and Florida is one of these States. The fever very rarely, we might say never, attacks an animal "to the manor born;" but bring in a stranger, and it is at once seized upon. The older ones, as we have noted, do not often survive the ordeal, but the younger take it more lightly; like the measles or mumps, it is severe on the old folks, but smites gently the young.

And, looking the matter carefully over, it seems to us that the change of climate, pure and simple, may indeed exert a less active influence than the germs of the famous "Texas fever," which lies waiting to seize the stranger, but passes by the native born in silent contempt. We see this action constantly occurring as concerns human beings, why not, then, with the four-footed animals also?

This being so, it becomes doubly wise to obtain our improved stock within our own borders; and it is, besides, simple justice to those who have had the nerve and perseverance to invest in blooded cattle, bring them to a new country, and take the consequent losses and risks, in order to make the necessary start on the upward road of improvement.

It is only right that these men, the pioneers of the acclimated, naturalized Jerseys and other full-blooded cattle, should reap the reward of their pluck and foresight, and be given the preference in the purchase of such stock by the Florida settler.

As yet they are few and scattered, and so little known as breeders that we have been compelled to make inquiries far and wide all over the State in order to obtain the addresses given at the end of this chapter for the convenience of our readers.

But we have as yet said nothing regarding a breed of cattle which as yet is but little known, save in those localities where it first came into notice, the southern parts of Georgia.

No one knows where the little "Guinea" cow came from originally, only that Colonel Stapler, of Lowndes County, Georgia, owned the first of them.

We saw it stated once, by whose authority we do not know, that the Guinea cattle were found early in the present century roaming wild on one of the numerous islands that fringe the Georgia and Carolina coasts, having escaped from a foreign vessel that was wrecked there. It is conceded that the Guinea more nearly resembles the famous little Brittany cow than any other known breed, and it is not a wild assumption to suppose that the aforesaid "foreign vessel" hailed from those parts.

How true this may be "deponent sayeth not." We are satisfied to know that the Guinea cattle (so named by the original owner, Colonel Stapler), are splendidly adapted to Florida in every respect—except, indeed, as beef cattle.

Many consider them superior to all others. They are too small to find much favor with the butcher, even if their value and scarcity did not keep them out of his hands.

The Guinea cow is a living illustration of the old adage, "The most valuable articles are done up in small packages." Coming from a section of country so nearly allied to Florida that the change in climate and food is so slight as not to affect their health in the least, the little Guineas are the *ne plus ultra* of family cows for this State—"the poor man's cow."

The Guinea asks for but little food in addition to the supply of grass it can pick up on the range, for in its Georgia home it has been accustomed to forage for itself, just as do the common Florida cows.

Some one describes the Guinea cow as "a yard high, a yard and a half long, and about a yard wide."

Another "some one" writes of her thus, in more technical terms: "She is broad on the back, slim neck, small and delicate legs and feet, well filled up in fore and hind quarters, long for her height, which is just thirty-nine inches, and has an eye in which meekness and content, with gentleness, shines. She keeps fat where a common Florida cow would starve, and gives about two gallons of milk of a high grade twice a day. This little cow might butcher about four hundred pounds net, and is undoubtedly the most contented and gentle animal in Florida." Another writer says: "Their bodies are scarcely a foot from the ground, and the udder is enormous. They are hardy and gentle, active browsers, and eat about half what is needed for an ordinary cow." And yet another says: "They are usually of a deep red color, always fat and gentle, with crumpled horns and broad escutcheon. They require less food and give more milk than the ordinary cow, and are much hardier and more intelligent."

After these verdicts from those who have had experience with the " little cow," it is scarcely necessary for us to add more in her favor.

Little as the Guinea is yet known outside of certain limits, the demand is larger than the supply, a defect that it will take time to remedy. There is a good deal of diversity too among these Lilliputian cattle; they vary in size and in color, and also in the shape of their horns; some of the latter are slim and delicate, others are crumpled, while others are entirely missing. In color some individuals are red, some brown, some spotted. The prices asked for Guinea cows vary from forty to one hundred dollars, but the males are held at much lower figures. At the same time, valuable and desirable as the little Guinea is for family use, where the means for ample feeding can not be afforded, the Jersey, pure or graded, will still continue the most popular cow with those who are able to care for it properly, because the yield of milk and butter is greater, and where crossed with the common stock a larger animal for butchering is obtained.

Stepping for a moment beyond the purely home-life view of Florida cattle, let us take a brief glance at an industry which is destined to be more to Florida in the near future than it is now to Texas, "the great cattle State." In South Florida there are thousands of acres of the finest stock ranges, lands fit for little if any thing else, and certainly for nothing as profitable; grazing lands well and always supplied with an abundance of water, ranges over which the western stock-raisers go into ecstasies.

Few persons are aware that in the wild southern counties of Florida there are "cattle kings" whose wealth can scarcely be counted, most certainly not by themselves.

An amusing incident in this connection occurred recently. Two gentlemen, settlers in Sumter County, believing that they could purchase cows to better advantage in Brevard County than nearer home, went thither on horseback. Reaching their destination they began to look around for the desired cows; in the course of their search they came upon a tumble-down hut where they were greeted by its master, the most ragged, unshaven, unshorn, and uncouth specimen of humanity they had ever encountered.

"Want to buy cattle, does ye?" he said. "Well, how many now? I've got a little bunch I might sell."

Our friends looked doubtful; surely this ragged individual could not own as many as they wanted, and they did not care to purchase in driblets.

"We want twenty good milch cows," they replied.

"Hoot! Is that all? I'd sold ye a hundred or two, but I don't never trade for no less than that."

And, as he persisted, our friends rode on, wrathfully muttering, "Such airs for a ragged wretch like that!"

Subsequent inquiry, however, revealed the fact that the "ragged wretch" was the owner of at least fifty thousand head of cattle. "And all he knows what to do with his money is to buy bacon and corn-meal," exclaimed their informant. "Talk about the foreign missions, let the churches look to the heathen at home first. We want missionaries here if any where on earth."

No expensive shelter is needed for the stock. There are no losses from cold or starvation as there are every where else, and while the Western stockman feels elated if he loses no more than one third from severe weather alone, the Florida stockman, even with the prevailing crude methods, or, more correctly, no methods at all, seldom loses twenty per cent from all causes combined. And yet, in the far West, with all the disadvantages of cold, short feed, bitter storms, and frequent drouths to meet, the cattle men coin fortunes that count by the million of dollars.

What then, should the Florida raiser, with none of these drawbacks to meet, not be able to do? Already several large ranches are preparing to answer that question.

And it is not in South Florida alone that a large revenue is destined to flow into the State through her cattle ranches, her horses, sheep, and hogs. Northern and Middle Florida, the whole State in fact, is a great natural stock country. Middle Florida, especially, presents the finest possibilities for the raising of stock, and it only needs the introduction of improved methods to make the entire northern section of Florida the rival of any section of the United States in the character of its stock.

Already some of the middle counties are supplying Jacksonville with butter of excellent quality, and near Tallahassee, Leon County, the dairy interests have assumed such proportions that a creamery for the more satisfactory manufacture of butter is about to be started. Seventy-five per cent of all the Leon County cattle are grades of thoroughbred stock.

And now, before we turn from the subject of the coming style of the Florida cows, a few words with regard to how to treat them.

Bear in mind that the yield of a milker does not lie altogether in the breed, no matter how excellent the stock may be, nor how good the care and management it may receive; unless properly handled at milking, all these will not avail for best results.

A kind manner, a gentle voice, quiet, steady movements, a caressing hand, regular times for milking and feeding, will go far toward making even a common "scrub" cow a fairly good milker, and the pure bloods are even more susceptible.

We have already referred to the importance and wisdom of procuring Florida-bred blooded cattle, so far as is possible.

That this may be done to a greater extent than is generally supposed, the following list of reliable breeders of pure bred stock, principally in Leon County, will prove, and we trust it may be a medium by which our readers will profit.

For these addresses; we acknowledge our indebtedness to Mr. R. C. Long, of Tallahassee, one of Leon County's oldest and most respected citizens, now acting as a real estate agent for that section.

Shrader Brothers, Waverly Stock Farm, three miles from Tallahassee; herd of about forty Jerseys. Five years in business.

C. J. F. Allen, Ethel Meadows Farm; herd of sixty Jerseys. Three years in business.

W. J. Vaison, Mount Airy Farm; herd of thirty Jerseys. Six years in business.

Col. John Bradford, Bradfordville; herd of eighty Jerseys. This stock was first introduced from the Channel Islands in 1857, and has been carefully bred up to the standard ever since.

Robert F. Bradford, Bradfordville; herd of twenty-five Jerseys, originally from above herd ; in present hands ten years.

N. W. Eppse, Pine Hill Farm; herds of Jerseys and Durhams, about ten of each. In business ten years.

Thomas J. Roberts, Roberts' Farm; herd of one hundred Durhams. Twenty years in business. This is the finest herd of Durhams south of Lexington, Kentucky.

Capt. Patrick Houston, Lakeland Stock Farm; Durhams, Jerseys and Guernsies, two hundred and fifty in the herds. In business fifteen years.

CHAPTER XVII. PASTURAGE.
Bermuda, Johnson and Para Grass. Beggar's Weed or Indian Clover

While it is not within the province of this present work to enter exhaustively into the question of a fodder-supply for the "family friend," whose value we have been considering, we know that the new settler will need at once a few items of information in this direction; hence the subject of pasturage. A permanent "meadow-land" will not come amiss, as its preparation should be one of the first things attended to.

The subject of pasture grasses for Florida is one that is just now exciting much attention, as its vast importance is coming to be understood and appreciated.

Bermuda grass has probably been better proven in Florida, at the present time, than any other, because it was literally one of the first in the field. This name of "Bermuda" is not to be understood as signifying that the grass originally, or indeed ever, came from the island of Bermuda. It is simply a corruption, and a very natural one too, of the name of its introducer into the United States. Some years ago a Captain Permudy sailed into the port of (we think) Charleston, hailing from Africa. Among other plants and seeds, he brought a few roots of the grass, which at first was known by his name; but soon, as we have seen, was credited with that of "Bermuda."

Now, Bermuda grass never matures seed north of Florida, and not abundantly even here, and consequently is propagated altogether by roots. "Pick up a sprig, throw it down, and in five years it will be all over your place, even if it falls on a rock," is what some people will say to the "anxious inquirer" as to how to plant Bermuda grass.

We heard lately of a gentleman who followed this unique plan, only that he threw down his sprigs on the ground, instead of a rock, and made a little pen around the precious morsels to protect them from live-stock marauders till they should get a fair start. But the roots seemed in no hurry at all. They sauntered very slowly and deliberately across their little inclosure; and finally, after two years of patient waiting, the outraged owner gathered in his crop of Bermuda grass, roots and tops, just filling a bushel basket. But he was one of the persevering kind that are sure to succeed sooner or later. He had, moreover, less faith in himself than he had in the grass. The first trial had been made on high, dry land. Now he set out his roots on the sides and bottom of a deep gully and on low, moist land. There, to his joy and somewhat to his surprise, the grass made more growth in two months than it had done in the two years before.

The next season he set out a five-acre field with Bermuda, putting down the sprigs, their joints well covered, two or three feet apart. In three years those detached patches had joined into one beautiful green meadow, where sheep, cows, and calves, were made happy and fat.

And just here we have one of the great points of excellence of this valuable grass, namely, its adaptability to low, moist land, where most grasses will not thrive at all. So thoroughly at home, in fact, is the Bermuda in damp situations, that it does not mind getting into the water any more than a duck. It may be placed in hollows subject to occasional overflow, without suffering the least detriment, after weeks or even months of enforced retirement beneath the waters.

It grows well on "white-sand land," or the poorest clay, and is an incalculable boon to the owner of worn-out or washed-out lands. It will enrich them by its decaying roots and leaf-blades much faster than can be done by turning under cow-peas or other green stuff, and at the same time yield abundance of forage or pasture for stock.

"It is just impossible to get rid of it," say some of the never-to-be-satisfied individuals, of whom the world is full. Well, who wants to get rid of it? Certainly not he who owns a cow or horse, or who desires a beautiful green lawn before his house.

It is difficult to kill out once it has a fair start; no doubt of that; and therein lies one of its greatest claims to excellence rather than the opposite. Its very persistence is so much the more in its favor, since it is to this quality that its exceeding value as a meadow-grass is due. Year after year it may be cropped by cattle and yet not suffer, while the majority of pastures are ruined by successive croppings.

All that a Bermuda-grass hay-field asks for is an occasional top-dressing of stable manure, land-plaster, or commercial fertilizer; and these it must have, since a grass of such vigorous growth, constantly cut and removed, will necessarily use up all the available plant-food within reach, and then, if more is not supplied, it can but suffer from starvation, just as a human being would do in like circumstances. This, as we have said, is where the grass is cut as hay and taken off the field. But where cattle are turned upon it the case is different. A considerable amount of fertilizing material is deposited, and a great deal of the grass is left to die down and rot. All the attention that a Bermuda-grass pasture needs (unless set on very poor land, and then it will require a top-dressing every two or three years) is to plow it once in about four years, to loosen up the mass of roots and prevent it from becoming sod-bound. Tall-growing weeds should be carefully cut down for the first year or two before going to seed in fields of Bermuda designed for hay-making. After that the grass will root out all weeds for itself. In pastures there are few weeds that the cattle may not be left to take care of.

Bermuda grass will grow six to thirty inches high, according to the quality of the soil; a well-filled tract, about twelve inches high, will yield over one ton of cured hay at each cutting per acre, and it can be cut two or three times a year. Which it may be—twice or three times a year—depends not only on the amount of food this vigorous grass can obtain, but also on the humidity or dryness of the season, for Bermuda is, as we have said, a great lover of water and can not long resist drouth; here in truth is its one fault; but happily, so remarkable is the facility of our Florida soil for retaining moisture during the dryest seasons, that her pastures rarely indeed suffer from the effects of drouth; but when they do, it is the Bermuda that shows its effects most quickly, though it recuperates as soon as the rains begin again.

Bermuda grass, intended for hay, should be cut at the very first indication of the stems turning yellow and dead-looking at the base. If not cured at this period the next cutting will be injured, and, moreover, so far delayed that it may be lost entirely ; and, besides this, if the grass is allowed to become too old it becomes very tough, and is not only hard to cut but is less nutritious. It is very easily cured, and this is a great point in its favor. A few hours after cutting it may be raked up into windrows and then, a few hours later, placed in small cocks to complete the curing. The latter is not, of course, imperative; the grass may be left in the windrows as one chooses, but if a rain comes on during the day and a half of curing, it will be less injured in the cock than in the windrows.

We have often heard the inquiry, "How can we kill out coco or nut-grass from our fields ?"

We reply, Plant Bermuda grass.

There is no other kind of grass known that Bermuda will not kill out, excepting only broom-sedge, and that, we confess, gets the better of the more tender Bermuda roots; but to eradicate any other objectionable tenant of the field, all one has to do is to plow said field, then chop up, pretty fine, sprigs of Bermuda roots and scatter them broadcast over the rough ground; then run a harrow or cultivator to level it off—first one way then the other. Do this just after a good soaking rain, and then you can fold your hands and leave the Bermuda grass to "root out" your enemy, as it will surely do in time, leaving in its place as glorious a green pasture as one would need wish to see.

We have elsewhere alluded to the one fault that some people find with Bermuda grass—that "it can not be got rid of." Now, if any one is so foolish as to wish to get rid of such a treasure, it can be done. There are two ways of killing it; the one to plant among it, in close drills, those varieties of cow-peas which make the most foliage; plow through these several times during the season, so as to tear up the grass and throw its roots under the pea-vines. All grasses love sunshine, and none more than

Bermuda; cast into the shade for any protracted length of time it will languish and die. Plowing it in September, and running a harrow or cultivator over it two or three times during the winter mouths, will also destroy it. But when we hear any one talking about getting rid of Bermuda grass, be it where it may—whether in orange grove or field—we always think of those significant words regarding the folly of "casting pearls before swine."

We are proud, ourself, of a beautiful lawn of Bermuda in front of and on every side of our dwelling. Pleasant to the eyes, pleasant to the feet, pleasant to horses to crop, to the cows and calves to eat as fodder, and we do not want to get rid of it, though it is creeping lovingly around the roots of our pet orange trees.

And this is what we have seen—we and others who have tried it—that wherever the Bermuda grass is thus allowed to play among the trees, the ground, in a year or two, assumes the rich dark tint given it by humus or decayed vegetable matter, and the trees make a correspondingly improved growth. It is as though a rich leaf-mold had been conveyed to such spots.

So we say, long may the Bermuda flourish among our orange and lemon trees. The more of it, the better. We do not believe in "killing the goose that lays the golden egg."

There has come (literally) into the field, of late, another grass that promises to win its way into public favor, and to stay there.

This is the Means or Johnson grass, named, like the corrupted Bermuda, from its introducers. In Georgia it is the "Means" grass, because Mr. Means first brought it prominently before the people; in Alabama it is the "Johnson" grass, for a similar reason; and, after all, it is hardly a grass either, but a species of sorghum.

Now, when any of this much and justly prized family appear in the world, they have a strong resemblance to their next of kin, corn—so much so that it is difficult to tell the one from the other.

We heard of a case in point the other day, amusing to an outsider; but the reverse, we suspect, to the unfortunate victim.

A gentleman, owning a large field of Means or Johnson grass, decided to vary the programme, and had the grass plowed under and corn planted in its place. He raised a good crop, and the repeated plowings nearly destroyed the grass, which was part of his object. He planted corn the second time, and sent out his field hands, in due time, to hoe and thin out the corn to a stand. They worked industriously for several days before he went to view the result of their labor; when lo! he beheld his young corn almost entirely cut down and the Johnson grass—"its double"—flourishing in long, thrifty rows!

Moral: Don't plant corn in Johnson grass (or sorghum) fields, or if you do, thin the corn out yourself.

This grass matures seed readily, in this respect differing from the Bermuda, while, like the latter, it can also be propagated by roots. The ground should be prepared for its reception just as for any other grass, plowed thoroughly, pulverized by harrow or cultivator, and bushes and tall weeds kept down for a year or two.

The seed should be sown broadcast, one bushel—weighing twenty-eight pounds—to the acre, the land being harrowed after the seed has been scattered. Early in the spring or late in the fall is the proper time to sow it, the latter having the preference.

Johnson grass is a great grower, yet it impoverishes the land very little if any, deriving a large proportion of its sustenance from air and water. Of course its growth depends very much on the quality of the land; on rich soil it can be cut oftener than on poor, as it springs up more rapidly; if the soil is deep, so much the better, for the roots penetrate to a depth of eighteen inches and are as famous foragers as the "bummers" of an army.

Johnson grass can be cut four or five times in a season, if the latter is favorable, for it, like the Bermuda, likes moisture, but not to the same extent; it does not yield as much per acre as the Bermuda, but if the land is moderately good and the stand of grass what it should be, nearly a ton of cured hay at a cutting will be the result. It grows from three to ten feet high, according to the quality of the land or amount of food given it, but should not be allowed to reach a greater height than the former, as then it is about going to head, and the leaves are tender and numerous. If left too long, both stem and leaf become fibrous and tough, and in this state the grass is not only difficult to cure, but stock decline to eat it, and thereby show their wisdom.

The growth of this valuable grass is remarkably rapid, and in moist, warm weather, or on damp ground, it often makes a leap of fully an inch in one day. The seed, however, is rather slow in maturing, requiring more than two months, sometimes nearly three, from the time the grass starts to grow. It is a heavy black seed, and unless allowed to ripen fully it is useless to plant it, as it wall not germinate; hence the necessity of procuring the seed of Johnson grass from a reliable source.

It is not as good a pasture grass as the Bermuda. It will not bear constant cropping or the trampling of stock.

Carelessness in this respect will cause it, in the course of three or four years, to disappear entirely; but, even then, plow the ground, wait a month or two, and lo! there is the grass again as thrifty and thick as ever!

The roots of the Johnson grass do not spread much, and hence, unlike its rival, the Bermuda, it is easily kept within its allotted limits, providing, of course, it is cut at the proper time, which is a month before the seeds mature.

Frequent cuttings during the summer and several plowings during the winter will effectually destroy a meadow of Johnson grass. This plowing, too, is not as hard a thing to do as might be supposed, because of a peculiar habit the roots have of swelling out twice as large during the growing season as they are during the winter. This expansion has the effect of loosening the soil, so that the roots offer very little resistance to the plow.

A field of Johnson grass needs to be re-seeded once in every five or six years, and this can easily be done by allowing small patches of the grass scattered over the meadow to go to seed.

The latter, when fully ripe, may be either gathered and sowed broadcast, or left to drop where it may.

It is a good plan for a pasture, to sow both Johnson and Bermuda together. The former will be thicker and finer, and the latter will grow faster than if set alone; but, after a year or two, the pushing roots of the Bermuda will get the better of the others, and finally the Johnson (or Means) grass will retire from the field of battle until the war-cry of the plowshare, and the clash of the trace-chain shall summon it to the front again.

The amount of nutrition in Johnson grass, properly cured, is almost but not quite on a par with that of Timothy or Bermuda, and all kinds of hay-eating stock are extremely fond of it.

It is cured in the same manner as Bermuda, with the advantage of drying better in the windrows than the latter, as it does not lie so close, exposing the grass to the air as much as possible and as little to the sun as may be.

These are the main objects to be attained in curing hay. Too much sun is as hurtful as too little drying.

When we add that this grass, unlike the Bermuda, will not endure being occasionally overflowed, much as it likes a reasonable degree of moisture, we have said all that is necessary regarding this particular grass, which is destined to take a significant part in the future welfare of Florida. Another most valuable grass, either for pasture or haymaking, is the Para grass, which, as the name implies, comes to us from Brazil.

The seed of this grass does not mature in this climate, and therefore it is propagated by rootlets only. The rows should, on rich land, be not nearer than six feet apart, and the cuttings be set from three to four feet in the rows.

Para grass is a splendid hay-producer, and even on poor land is very quick to cover the ground. It is extremely nutritious, and all kinds of stock are very fond of it.

It can be made into a pasture, or lawn, simply by planting broadcast, and, as in the former case, turning cattle in upon it. On the lawn, however, the scythe and mower must needs take the place of these animated clipping machines.

The best time for cutting is just as it manifests an inclination to go to seed, which attempt, as we have seen, will only prove "love's labor lost." Para grass in Florida is never "seedy," though it always "goes to grass."

"Sweet Beggar's-Lice," or Indian clover (and we prefer the latter name as being less unpleasantly suggestive) is a plant of great value to the Southern farmer, and one that deserves to be better known than it is.

For pasture, for forage, and for turning under as a fertilizer, it has no superior, if in truth it has an equal.

Botanically the plant is termed *Desmodium canesceris*. It is leguminous, and yields a large amount of rather flat seeds of an oval-triangular shape, very oily, and tasting like that of the pea, whose leaves, by the way, those of this plant resemble.

And just here we will caution our readers not to mistake for Indian clover that obnoxious weed, bearing a burr-like fruit or nut with hooked prickers, which in the North is usually known as "Beggar's Lice." We have met the latter ourself many a time, and have retired from the field routed and blessing the weed for its numerous sharp-pointed remarks, whose sting often abided with us for hours afterward. The "Beggar's Lice" of Florida is of a far different character. It is tender and useful, not tough and noxious, and its seeds, though they do cling to one's clothing, cling lovingly, and do not wound one's feelings by stinging, pointed thrusts of a personal nature. Our "Beggar's Lice" is a much more peaceful and reputable character than its Northern brother.

It should be sown in drills, the seeds dropped quite close together, the rows just far enough apart (three feet) to admit of the plow and cultivator; if allowed to go to seed, it will come up the next season strong and thrifty, and, in fact, even if not so allowed, the roots, if left undisturbed, will send up a yearly growth. So it will be seen that Indian clover, once planted, will go on reproducing itself if given the opportunity, without any further trouble on the part of its owner. It should be cut just as it is blooming, to seed; cured at this time, the hay is sweet, aromatic, bright, juicy, and very nutritious, the stems tender and succulent. In good soils Indian clover will grow to a height of eight or ten feet, throwing out long lateral branches; but it will do well on very poor soils also, as it, like the cow-pea, draws largely for sustenance on the air, requiring but little food from the soil. Its analysis shows sixteen and a-half per cent, of albuminoids, and a large proportion of saccharine matter. All kinds of stock are extravagantly fond of this precious forage plant, whether fed to them green or cured, in pasture or in stall, and will turn to it in preference to oats, hay, corn, or pea-vines.

Not long ago it was thought that Indian clover could only be used in a green state; but this idea arose merely because the process of curing it was not understood, experience having proved that it is really more easily cured and handled than pea-vines, or many kinds of grasses. It should be cut as early in the morning as possible and left spread on the ground for eight or ten hours only, then carried to the barn and stored, but never in large bulk; if left too long in the sun the leaves will shatter and fall.

Should the plants be large and heavy when cut, they will be the better for turning over at least once during the ten hours' exposure to the sun.

Indian clover makes a splendid pasture, growing up as fast as eaten off by stock, and as food for a milch cow it has no superior—not only greatly increasing the quantity of milk, but also its richness.

In many sections of Florida this valuable plant is indigenous and regarded as a weed! We only wish the world was full of such "weeds." How little care and poverty there would be left in it!

CHAPTER XVIII. FLORIDA POULTRY.

Nearly all Varieties do Well. How to Treat them Successfully

Just as all kinds of poultry will not do well in all localities North, just so they will not all do equally well in Florida, though nearly every variety tried faithfully thus far has met with more or less success.

On first settling in our present Florida home, we transported hither a portion of our "old home" stock—Houdans, Light Brahmas, Partridge Cochins.

Of these the Cochins, who, as every one knows, have a bad habit of "running to fat" on small provocation, soon grew disgusted with the climate, or soil, or something—they never told which. Most likely it was the climate, for as a rule stout people don't like warm weather; but, however it was, the Cochins first refused to lay eggs, then grew melancholy, and then decided to lay—themselves down to die.

That ended the Partridge Cochin era. And we have heard the same report from so many quarters that we must consider it a settled fact that their family do not approve of Florida as a residence; most certainly we do not approve of their conduct while here, so the disgust is mutual.

Of the Houdans, we brought a trio; as fine and proud a crested knight as ever challenged another to a chickenhearted combat, and two beautiful dames, with nodding plumes upon their dainty heads. We were proud of our Houdans, their black and white suits were so handsome and glossy, their eggs so large and white, and their flesh so firm and tender for the table. They were very graceful in their movements, so long as they confined themselves to a walk; but alas! when their greediness overcame their dignity and they started at a "two-forty" rate for the hen commissary department, "great was the fall thereof."

Did you ever see Houdans in a full trot? If so, you have laughed; that long fifth toe of theirs, not so useful as the fifth wheel to a coach, is death to all grace and smoothness when in rapid motion; one moment it catches in a wisp of grass, the next one toe overlaps the other, then both together clasp a twig, and so their unlucky owners' "rapid transit" is effected by a series of leaps into the air to avoid summersaults which can not always be avoided.

We have often felt sorry for our Houdan pets when we have seen them standing disconsolately alone, or else hopping about at a sore disadvantage because of a wrapping of string or moss, or tough grass, that had somehow got around those projecting toes and tied the two legs together. We have seen the toe almost cut off by the pressure of a piece of string, or the leg sore and bleeding from the same cause.

Once upon a time (not in Florida) we had a large quantity of young chicks, many of them Houdans. During a long, wet spell, they were kept housed in a large barn with a clay floor. After a few days we noticed that every Houdan chick seemed to be afflicted with St. Vitus's dance—the way they staggered, waddled, rolled, tumbled, and kicked, was marvelous.

An examination showed that the little fifth toe, just touching the damp clay as they walked, had collected, little by little, a large, hard lump of the latter, in some cases enveloping the entire foot, in others only the offending toe itself, but in all seriously affecting the well-being of the helpless little sufferers. The other chicks, with the regulation four toes, experienced no inconvenience at all from the clay. And so we can not but regard the fifth toe, which is one of the distinguishing marks of the Houdan family, as sometimes a serious detriment to these valuable fowls.

If it were an evil beyond remedy we would pass it over, just as we all are compelled to do with insurmountable obstacles as we trudge along life's pathway; but it is not.

The objectionable toe may be cut off with scarcely any pain to the bird while it is very small, and if an antiseptic be employed, and the chick be kept in a perfectly clean coop for four or five days, the cut will heal without trouble and the patient be saved from many a "scrape" into which the fifth toe would be sure to lead it.

From our trio of Houdans we set several nests (they themselves never set, as every one knows), and hatched out fifty or more fine, healthy chicks. These, and as many Brahmas, were as pretty a sight for a primitive Florida poultry-yard as one would wish to look upon.

But—there was a but, you see!—we had just settled; were unable at once to fence in all our outlying woods, so that the picketed chicken-yard abutted on the open range which was haunted by a "bunch" of Florida's worst curse, razor-backs, which ever "go about seeking what they can devour," of most positive and serious detriment to ninety- nine people, of very little value to the hundredth, their owner. Thank Heaven! their days are swiftly passing by; and good thoroughbred hogs are taking their place.

Well, these free rangers haunted the line of our chickenyard fence, where our valuable chicks, with the well-known perversity of chicken nature (which, by the way, is wonderfully human), would push their way through to the uninviting, unknown country beyond. The result was that we noticed that our chicks were fast diminishing in number; but some time elapsed before, not being versed in the lawless ways of the freest and most perfectly protected of all Florida's citizens, we laid the disappearance to the true cause—and not then, until with our own eyes we saw a sow and four of her young ones calmly devouring at one time the same number of our chickens, which had strayed a few inches outside the fence.

But what could we do? We dared not kill the marauders; they were of the most powerful family in the State. The laws were made for them, not for us. If we could not afford to have a fence built large enough to inclose several acres outside the chicken-yard fence proper, so as to insure our tender young pets from straying within the circle of their ugly jaws, then we must not keep chickens at all, but must do without their eggs, flesh, and guano, because a neighbor chose to own pigs. He did not keep them, be it observed; the neighborhood did that; he only killed and ate them, after other people's chickens, potatoes, corn, cabbage, etc., had fattened them for him.

So we were compelled to set aside other needed improvements and expend a considerable sum to erect a fence to shut out the most free citizen of Florida from devouring our own property on our own land; we dare not touch a hair of its long, lank body—that was sacred.

But before that fence could be put up, and before all vulnerable points in it could be repaired, eighty out of our hundred chicks were gone—gone without redress. Every one of the little Houdans was among the missing, lost in a general massacre of the innocents; but we knew where each little body was buried.

More Houdan eggs were set, and, while they were in process of hatching, one of the two hens flew over the fence and fell a victim to the rage of the baffled slaughterer of the innocents. Then the other hen and the cock drooped and died without apparent cause, "At least," we thought, "there are the two nests of Houdans to come, poor little orphlings!"

But alas! for human anticipations! Just as the cheerful little "peet, peet," began to be heard beneath the pure white shells, a neighbor's dog raided the hatching-house, and of the 'last of their race" not one remained to tell the sad tale.

But, for all that, we have since had ample opportunities to prove that Houdans are admirably adapted to Florida, and we rejoice to know this too, for among all the various breeds of poultry there is not one superior to the Houdan; and in this judgment, based upon our own experience, we are fully corroborated by the National Poultry Company, a great English institution, who claim that the Houdan surpasses all the other varieties with which they have experimented.

It is of French origin, and sprung from a cross between the Dorking and White Poland strains. It is from the Dorking side of the family that it gains the fifth toe, and, characteristic with it, it also gains the deep, compact body, short legs, and small bones of the latter, with the improvement of much less waste or offal in proportion to its weight. This latter is greater than that of any other French breed, the hens sometimes weighing ten pounds, though this is not very common; from seven to eight pounds is the average. Its plumage is black and white, its head is surmounted by a fine Polish crest of feathers, and the wattles are pendent and well formed; as to the comb, possessed by both cock and hen, but in a far greater degree by the former, it is the oddest of all varieties, resembling more than any thing else the two leaves of a book opened, with a long, slender strawberry in the center; this comb in the hen is distinct but small.

Some of the good points of the Houdan have already been referred to—the deep, compact body, short legs, and small wastage when prepared for the table; these qualities it inherits from its ancestors, the Dorking, but it matures earlier than the latter; its flesh is even finer, which is saying a great deal, and it is more hardy. Another point of improvement over the Dorking, and a very important one, as all poultry fanciers know, is that Houdan eggs almost invariably hatch, and hatch strong, healthy chicks too.

The chickens feather very rapidly and early, yet are not weakened by this rapid progress, and are more hardy than any other chicks except the Bramahs.

They mature very early too, it not unfrequently happening that the young pullet lays her first egg when only five or six months old—and what a time not only she but her whole family make over the happy event; never was egg so beautiful as this laid so proudly in the nest by the young aspirant.

And certainly the Houdan eggs are beauties, as eggs go; so large and heavy and white; eight to the pound is the rule given for the eggs of this aristocratic family, but, like other aristocrats, they frequently scorn all rules; not once or twice, but many times in our Northern poultry-yard did we gather Houdan eggs, of which six, five, or even four only, were required to make a pound in weight.

These giant eggs are fine to eat, but bad to sell by the dozen as ordinary eggs, and very, very bad to set; they will never hatch, and he who tries it will find it "love's labor lost."

The Houdan hen lays one hundred and fifty eggs per annum, a larger showing than any other varieties except Leghorns and Hamburgs, and even there the difference is more nominal than real, since the eggs of the two latter are lighter in weight.

"Them dratted hens!" we once heard an irate countrywoman exclaim, "they're wearin' my life out with breakin' 'em of settin'; soon as I break up one, another is took with the settin' fever, and they keep me busy catchin' 'em, and puttin' 'em in coops; I shut 'em up for a week, and then let 'em out, and they just go like a streak for the nest I took 'em from! I put 'em under the pump, tie 'em to trees, talk to 'em, whip 'em; it's all no use; set they want to, and set they will, if it's on china eggs or stones, or nothin'; drat the critters!" There was a good deal of truth in the good woman's lament too, as every one knows who has had dealings with the poultry-yard.

Setting hens, determined creatures that they are, are all very well when wanted, but very often one prefers more eggs laid and less time spent on the nest, especially if one has an incubator; and this is one of the great advantages of having the bulk of one's flock composed of non-setters, among whom the Houdan ranks first.

Another point in favor of the Houdan is the fact that they are much smaller eaters than any other breeds, according to their size. Later on we will give results of an experiment made to ascertain the greatest profit on the same number of fowls of different breeds, which proves the Houdan to rank first, very decidedly.

Altogether, we do not fear making a mistake in recommending the Houdan to the special attention of the Florida farmer, since it will bear the climate well, and is certainly the most profitable breed for the farm in all respects.

With us, and wherever we have heard of them in Florida, the verdict has also been uniformly in favor of the Bramahs. So far as appearances and actions went, our Bramahs, "transported for life" though they were, did not see any difference between their old home and their new.

They strutted, cackled, crowed, laid eggs, hatched chickens, and brought the latter up in the way they should not go, just as they had always done, and so have they continued to do up to the present day.

In fact, so well have our Bramahs flourished in health, size, and "hen-fruit," that we can ask nothing better of them, considering that, as well as they behaved in their old home, they have behaved better in their new, especially in point of health.

Too much can not be said in favor of the race of Bramahs, both "Light" and "Dark." Certain it is that, ever since this magnificent breed was introduced into the general poultryyard, it has become more and more a favorite, and now is regarded every where as a settled stand-by, just as regular a thing in the "yard" as bread is upon our tables.

We do not need to describe the Bramahs here. Every one knows them by sight.

As to their special points of excellence, however, we have somewhat to say.

The chicks are hardy, and grow rapidly; but there is one period of their existence—when they are casting off the beautiful fluffy coat in which they come into the world, and assuming instead the feathered garb of maturity—at this period of their existence, we say, they are very ridiculous-looking objects, and have provoked many a laugh at the expense of their long, bare necks, skinny bodies, and featherless tails and wings.

But wait a little, and you will see what a proud, shapely swan will be evolved from our "ugly duck;" and a most beautiful swan it is too, according to the saying that "handsome is as handsome does."

The pullets, as a rule, commence their life-work of laying eggs at the "early age" of six months. Lewis Wright, the celebrated English fancier, tells us, in his "Practical Poultry Keeper," that "they lay from thirty to forty eggs before they seek to hatch." Now this may be very true, but our hens never did that way; their setting propensities are rather obstreperous at times, and our good old countrywoman's outburst of righteous indignation against "them dratted critters," comes often to mind.

As simple producers of eggs the Bramahs have several superiors; the eggs are large and fine, seven to the pound is the average, but they only lay from eighty to one hundred per annum, the number varying according to the shelter and food given ; this of the Light Bramahs, the Dark rarely lays over seventy eggs each year.

It is in hardiness, size, and quality of flesh, that the Bramahs take such high rank. They mature early, and at two months old are frequently large enough to figure upon the table as that delicious morsel, a "spread eagle," weighing at that period of their young lives from one and a half to two pounds. The full-grown cock should weigh from twelve to thirteen pounds, and the hen eight to nine pounds; at six months old the cockerels should not weigh less than eight, nor the pullets less than six pounds.

The Dark Bramahs are even heavier than the Light; they are in fact, so Lewis Wright tells us, the heaviest of any known breed; for the full-grown cock, fourteen to fifteen pounds is not uncommon, and there is one cock on record, shown at an English poultry show, that weighed no less than eighteen pounds!

This is true of the perfectly pure strain only, and the hens are as excellent as the cocks; as winter layers no breed equals them, and they usually lay thirty eggs before desiring to set, and then what splendid mothers they make. The Light Bramah is very good, but the Dark is better still, in this respect. Did you ever see a proud, strutting hen marching along with her dear little fluffy family twittering and chattering all around her, but, mayhap, some stopping or straying aside when they "had n't orter?"

Did you ever see the proud mother, in that case, stop and turn back to collect the little runaways?

No, you never did, unless they cried out in some real or fancied distress, that is, not unless the hen has chanced to be a Dark Bramah; for this best of all chicken mothers is the only one of her race who turns her head to look behind her as she promenades with her little ones; no straggling does she allow to go unnoticed, however quiet the prodigals may be about it, nor however slyly they may get exactly behind their "dear mamma," she has eyes in the back of her head, and they soon find out there is no hoodwinking her; neither does a poor little wight get entangled in the weeds or grass, but that with beak and foot she manages to extricate it; if they are attacked by a foe, hawk, pig, dog, or cat, she is bound to have her part in the fray, and generally comes off victorious; nor, like the majority of good mothers in chickendom, does she persecute the fluffy ones of other mothers; on the contrary, we have frequently known Bramah mothers, both Dark and Light, to adopt as their own chicks that had been deserted by their rightful mothers, knowing or making no difference between the strangers and their original brood.

An amusing instance of this strong instinct of motherhood in a Light Bramah hen came under our notice a few months ago.

A hen determined to set—they always are very determined, you know—had been shut up in a coop by herself to compel her to a change of ideas.

She was very indignant, as we all are when forced to give up our own will, and after scolding and pouting she put her head to one side, and looking out through her prison bars—the said prison standing in the nursery-yard—she gazed upon the multitude of young chickens around her, and thought a thought original with herself: "They won't let me set; very well then, I'll have a family without setting so much the better for me!"

So she clucked and clucked, and coaxed, until she had gathered around her, inside the coop, as many chickens as it would hold, from the downy balls on legs, recently hatched, to the largest that could squeeze through the bars to reach her.

That was amusing enough; but at night when we went to close up the coop from nocturnal enemies, it was still more comical to see five coops each occupied by an angry, ruffled hen, not a single chicken of their respective broods having remained faithful to them, but all having deserted to the stranger-mother who had literally "taken them in!"

Her coop! the floor of it could not be seen for the number of squatting, contented chickens of all sizes that had been unable to push beneath the abductor of the innocents, whose broad white wings were spread out upon each side almost horizontal with her back; little feet and little heads with bright, inquiring eyes, peeped out from beneath her soft white feathers, and two wee ones had clambered upon her back, and cuddled down among the feathers of her neck.

It was one of the most touching and most curious sights we ever saw, all the more so that we knew, though she did not, that this motherly hen, forbidden a family of her own, had been condemned to death.

Unwittingly she had saved her own life. The will to sacrifice her was gone; instead, she was set at liberty, and offered a nest of eggs, which she scornfully refused. Why indeed, should she set patiently for three weeks in one spot, when she could, by simply clucking, gather around her "a large and interesting family of small children?" For that nondescript family, from the largest to the smallest, was not a temporary case of adoption on either side. The chicks declined to return to their original mothers; and so at last these much injured and wrathful individuals were removed to the main quarters to console themselves as best they might for the unnatural conduct of their children.

And now, about Leghorns, of whose adaptability to Florida we can speak very favorably. The Leghorns, both white, brown, Dominique, and black, are excellent chickens, especially if the chief object desired is the greatest quantity of fair-sized eggs.

The white Leghorns, especially, are great layers, from one hundred and fifty to two hundred eggs per annum being their allotted number, nine being required to make a pound.

The Leghorns mature early, usually in from four to five months; not having so far to go in size and weight, as the Bramahs or Houdans, they naturally finish their growing journey a little earlier.

Hamburgs, Polish, and Black Spanish are good layers; but the chicks are delicate, and their points of excellence are so fully equaled by the other breeds named, that have likewise superior hardiness and size, that it does not pay to raise them for profit.

A great deal has been said during the last few years of the comparatively new breed, Plymouth Rock, which is a cross between the old-fashioned Dominique and the Black Java, a breed now almost extinct in the United States; it has the gray color of the Dominique with the single comb and yellow legs of the Java.

The good points of the Plymouth Rocks are these: they are hardy, they are of good size, the cocks weighing from eight to nine pounds, the hens from five to eight pounds ; their flesh is short-grained, juicy, and tender.

The hens are good setters, albeit happily they do not "take a notion" to set so frequently as many other breeds; good mothers are they also, but not equal to the Bramahs; of eggs they lay from one hundred to one hundred and twenty per annum, eight to the pound. They are moderate eaters in proportion to their size, and are accomplished foragers; yet, where it is necessary to confine them in close quarters they are contented and do well.

In point of attaining maturity, however, they have several superiors, and, taking the Plymouth Rock altogether, while it is undoubtedly a valuable bird for the poultryyard, we do not consider it as the very best breed for all purposes, nor do we believe that it will long hold its present place, which, by the way, is not so high as it was a few years ago.

The Langshan is going to displace the Plymouth Rock as the fowl *par excellence* for all purposes, and justly so, as we will see.

The Langshan, not having been very long a candidate for public favor, merits a "pen-picture" at our hands that it may be properly introduced to its future friends, the Florida farmers, to whose climate it is particularly adapted.

Its plumage, then, is black, with a greenish luster, the comb is straight and of moderate size, the legs are slate or gray and well feathered ; both cocks and hens are proud and stately in walk and mien, as well they may be; in size they closely resemble their kindred, the Bramahs.

The Langshan lays early, feathers very rapidly, and is a strong, healthy bird.

The hens are wonderful layers, especially in winter; those hatched in June will begin to lay in the latter part of December and will not cease until spring, when they desire to set, and their eggs are large and fine.

But most remarkable of all is their value for the market or table.

Take several broods of different varieties of chicks, among them the Plymouth Rocks, and the latter will excel almost all of them in rapidity of growth, plumpness and shape. But place a brood of Plymouths in competition with the Langshans, and they are—to use a phrase more expressive than elegant—"nowhere!"

Two rivals, one claiming superiority for the Plymouths, the other for the Langshan chicks, not long ago decided to settle the matter by placing a brood of each kind together under precisely the same treatment.

In three weeks the Plymouth Rock man gathered up his chickens under his wing and departed, saying, "Suppose we don't play any more!"

The Langshans had been hatched on May the 23d, and on July 3d, at six weeks old, they weighed two pounds, which was little less than marvelous. No wonder the Plymouth Rock man fled in dismay!

Langshans are not. as some suppose, identical with Black Cochins. Their plumage is similar, but that is all. The atter are poor layers, the chicks delicate, long-legged, and slow of growth.

Very often a "cross" between two good breeds will produce a better bird for general purposes than any one pure breed. For instance, the progeny of Houdan and Bramah is a splendid bird, hardy, of quick growth, the hens fine layers, and setting occasionally.

The Houdan and Langshan, the Leghorn and Bramah, or Plymouth Rock, the Langshan and Bramah, or the Leghorn and Langshan, all these produce most valuable additions to the poultry-yard.

Some time ago a well-known fancier took ten pullets, six months old, of each of the breeds mentioned below, and, confining them, kept an exact account of the amount of feed they consumed, the eggs laid, and value of flesh produced, for a given time, and here is the result:

Bramahs — cost of feed $9.22, value of eggs $12.10, meat $14,00. Total value $26.00. Total profit $18.28.

Cochins — cost of feed $10.15, value of eggs $11.80, meat $11.90. Total value $22.38. Total profit $14.38.

Houdaus — cost of feed $7.35, value of eggs $15.66, meat $9.10. Total value $24.76. Total profit $19.81.

Leghorns — cost of feed $5.77, value of eggs $16.14, meat $7.30. Total value $23.44. Total profit $17.97.

Thus we see that the greatest profit on the investment is in favor of the Houdans, with the Leghorns next. Unfortunately Langshans were not tested. Wyandottes are also most excellent fowls, and should be in every Florida poultry-yard.

It takes all kinds of people to make up the world, and so does it take all kinds of fowl to make up a genuine poultry-yard.

"Variety is the spice of life," and we want it in the Florida poultry-yard; turkeys, ducks, geese, let us have them all; for "that way "profit" lies."

Turkeys, as a rule, are not regarded as being very profitable, the enormous percentage of mortality among the young chicks eating up all the possible gains; this, as we say, is the general rule, but there are enough exceptions to it in the few who succeed in raising almost every chick to prove that it need not be so with proper care.

In our fair land of Florida, with its gloriously mild winters, the delicate turkey finds a congenial home, and will thrive with far less care and expense than in a more vigorous climate.

All who attempt to raise turkeys should bear in mind that during the first six weeks or two months of their lives the little "turks" are excessively delicate, and that the least wetting even from a slight shower is enough to damp the ardor of fully half the brood that may be exposed to it, and causes them to seek shelter beneath the sod.

But if one can manage to detain the young "turks" under cover in the early morning, or during wet weather, until the red protuberances (which begin to appear when they are two months old) are fairly developed, and the chick has become a poult, the delicate period will be safely tided over, and henceforth the poultry-yard can boast no fowl so hardy as the turkey.

This matter of keeping them sheltered from dampness until at least two mouths old is one of the two great secrets of success in rearing these valuable birds; without it, there is no profit in them; with it, there is much.

The rearing of turkeys on a large scale to supply the Northern markets would prove a very profitable business in

Florida, since here the only shelter needed would be a tight roof and four walls just high enough to prevent exit, with netted openings; no boarded floors or glazed sashwindows to keep out the cold and dampness, as at the North, but with only so simple a shelter as this, not a chick need be lost from exposure.

The "Old Turk" should be allowed a harem of twelve hens; the cocks at three years, and the hens at two, are in their prime and, unlike chickens, continue so for three or four years later, their offspring being fine, healthy chicks; and, with regard to the latter, it should be borne in mind that the size of the hen is of more importance than that of the cock; if he be of moderate size, strength, and spirit, that is enough to ask of him, except that he behave himself.

And, do you know that he don't generally behave at all like a loving husband or father?

No, he is a grand old rascal, a regular dog-in-the-manger— a Tartar, a Turk. When he and his wives are roving the woods in a wild state, he makes it the business of his life to hunt out their nests and destroy both the eggs and chicks; and thus the poor hens are driven to sedulously conceal their eggs, and later on their "large and interesting family of small children" from the wanton cruelty of their cannibal father.

So you see there is naturally a good deal of the savage in the old turk, and the worst of it is that he does not always lose it by domestication, and, for that reason, it is as desirable to know the precise character borne by a cock before purchasing it as it is to inquire into the past of a new inmate in one's household. If he is of a peaceable disposition, kind to the chicks and setting hens, you are all right, but if the reverse, then "look out for squalls!"

The old turk's wife is very prudish and bashful when setting, and only those persons with whom she has become familiar should ever go near her at such times, since, in her agitation, she is more than likely to break some of the eggs; she is a very faithful setter, so much so that, unless she is daily removed from the nest, she will continue on it until she literally starves to death. Such a catastrophe is not uncommon where her peculiarity in this respect is not known or heeded.

Certainly, both Mr. and Mrs. Turk have their "queerities;" while, as we have just said, the latter will rarely leave the nest voluntarily, she frequently makes up her perverse mind that those who removed her may take her back again, if they wish her to go at all, for go she won't of her own accord; consequently, her offended ladyship must be watched and, if needs be, forcibly invited to return to her maternal duties after a recess of not more than twenty minutes.

Two days before the little ones are due—in from twentysix to twenty-nine days, not thirty-one, as often alleged—the hen should be bountifully fed, and the nest carefully cleaned during her absence, powdered lime sifted in the bottom, or insect powder among the straw; then, seeing that the hen returns in good time to her post, place an ample supply of food and water well within her reach from the nest, for she must on no account be disturbed again till all the chicks are out.

For ten days before the latter are due the eggs should be sprinkled daily; following these simple precautions, there will seldom fail to be a good hatching.

The empty shells should be cleared away as fast as the chicks come out, but the latter must never be taken away from the mother, and never be forced to eat, as too many amateur turkey-raisers seem to think must be done, for it is not to be denied that the little turks are very stupid, so stupid as not to know how to eat, or to peck at the food offered them.

A couple of chicken's eggs, put into the nest five or six days after Mrs. Turk begins to set, will solve the difficulty, for the little turks will speedily learn to imitate the pecking of the little chicks.

Most turkey-raisers feed the young ones on oatmeal and bread-crumbs mixed with boiled nettles. This is a fatal mistake, and the second reason for the usual difficulty in rearing them. The little turks are for the first few weeks of their lives predisposed to diarrhea, and this tendency is encouraged by the oatmeal diet, hence disease and frequent deaths.

For ten days feed nothing but hard-boiled eggs—thoroughly hard—chopped fine, mixed only with minced dandelions or nettles, if they can be obtained; at the end of the ten days add bread-crumbs and barley-meal to the egg, gradually reducing the quantity of the latter until, at the end of three weeks, it may be discontinued altogether and boiled potatoes and small grain be substituted. Curds are also excellent feed, if squeezed very dry, not without; water, pure, and plenty of it, should be placed within easy reach in shallow dishes, so arranged as to insure the little ones from getting wet. At least twice a week add Douglass' Mixture to the water, about a teaspoonful to a pint of water.

A close adherence to the easy rules here laid down will make the breeding of turkeys one of the safest as well as most profitable of the Florida farmer's many resources, bearing in mind this maxim, which applies, indeed, to all kinds of "live stock":

"To attain great size, animal food and good feeding generally must be supplied from the first."

"A cross with the American wild birds," says an eminent authority, "improves the stamina of the young turkeys, and, whenever possible, should be employed."

Moral : First catch your wild turkey, then tame it and place it in your poultry-yard, and then " make a note on't."

There are many who advocate the keeping of the Guinea fowl, alleging that it does an immense amount of good as an insect-destroyer, if given the free range of a garden or orchard. Well, doubtless that is true; but how about this same quarrelsome individual as a nipper of "fruit in the bud"?

We notice that its most enthusiastic supporters do not care to have this question asked of them, after the blossoms of their vegetables, melons, and low-hanging fruits have appeared on the scene—and vanished from it; usually the marauder vanishes also about the same time. The remedy for this is easy: Keep them out of the garden until the plants are done blooming, then they will do good service.

Guineas mate in pairs, and the hen lays about one hundred and thirty eggs per annum. They are very fine birds for the table. Moreover, the guinea-hen lays but three months in the year, and the majority of her eggs are lost, because she sedulously conceals her nest, and as often as it is found, and the eggs disturbed, will seek another.

The young guineas are very delicate; must be carefully and frequently fed, and kept out of showers and wet grass.

But ducks! We would have every one who has a river or lake near by, or even those who have not, to keep on hand a goodly supply of these fat, comfortable-looking birds, whose great value as garden assistants not every one knows, very few in fact.

Give them a chance to help themselves to the slugs and worms that are the farmers' greatest foes, and see how quickly these pests will disappear; but look out for your strawberries! Dearly do ducks love these delicious berries, and where they are the latter soon cease to be; other fruits hang too high to be in much danger, and ducks do not scratch or do other damage to plants.

Around our Florida lakelets, where tiny frogs and fish and water plants abound, ducks enjoy themselves to their utmost, and cost their owners very little, if any thing, for feed, since scraps that the more dainty chickens refuse they will eat almost invariably.

When put up for fattening they should be allowed only a trough of water, and be fed on barley-meal, if it can be had, if not, on corn-meal. If celery or "celery salt" can be obtained, it will impart a delicious flavor to the flesh, mixed with the feed.

The drake does not approve of a large harem; three wives, or even two, are quite enough for him; and these wives, being rather eccentric in the matter of the "how, when, and where "of laying their eggs, should be detained in the hen-house each morning until they have left their eggs there, being otherwise quite as likely as not to drop them in the water while swimming. They will soon learn to connect the detention and the eggs together, and thenceforth will waste do unnecessary time before giving "straw bail " for good behavior.

Ducklings must not be permitted to get in the water, not even in their drinking - dishes, until two weeks old, and then not for over half an hour at a time, unless their feathers are well grown, otherwise they will die of cramp.

The best breeds for profit are the Aylesbury, Rouen, Pekin, Muscovy, and the common duck.

There is no reason why the goose should not do well in Florida, and yield a handsome profit, both as regards feathers and flesh.

Three geese to one gander is the rule, if sturdy goslings are desired. Nests should be prepared especially for them, two feet six inches square, and one for each bird, since where a goose lays her first egg there will she continue to lay them thenceforth.

The eggs should be set so as to hatch in cool weather, for warm weather does not agree with goslings at all; from thirty to thirty-four days are required for the hatching. The goose, like the turkey, is a very steady setter, but should be made to leave the nest each day and take a bath. Be careful, too, to see that at all times a good supply of food and water is in reach, for, if neglected, the goose (who is no "goose" after all), will take care of herself by eating her eggs one by one.

The gander is not at all like the wicked old turk whose unfatherly conduct we have just noticed ; he is a very different sort of fellow, and while his wives are on nest duty he need not be deprived of their society; on the contrary, they seem to delight in his presence, and he sits contentedly for hours by the nests, evidently taking a deep interest in the future hopes hidden away beneath their downy bosoms, and sometimes steps into the nest and carefully covers the eggs while its proper occupant is feeding.

Do not disturb the goslings while hatching, and for two - weeks keep them under shelter, feeding them on boiled oatmeal and rice, with water from a pond, if possible, placed in a shallow dish, too shallow for them to swim in.

After they are fully fledged they may be left to shift for themselves, if they have a good range, only needing two small feeds of grain a day besides what they can pick up.

Bantam chickens are so well known, the world over, that we need only call attention to their fine qualities as insect exterminators; in the garden and orchard they are invaluable, and what little damage they may do is out of all proportion to the good they accomplish.

We have previously noted the wisdom of procuring Florida-bred cattle, and those remarks apply also to poultry—it is better to deal with home-breeders, wisely, as well as being more just, to encourage "home industries."

There are already several reliable establishments of purebred fowls in Florida.

W. W. Fendrich, Post-office Box, 381, Jacksonville, has a large variety of feathered stock to offer the Florida settler — acclimated birds every one of them. Here are their names: no despicable collection, you see, for a new country poultry-yard:

"White Leghorns, Light Brahmas, Brown Leghorns, Wyundottes, Langshans, Bronze Turkeys, Imperial Pekin Ducks, Plymouth Rocks, White Guineas.

Then down on the Manatee River we have another reliable breeder in A. J. Adams, of Manatee. He has in stock almost every breed of poultry that can be named, of chickens, turkeys, and ducks; also "Booted White Cuban Carrier Pigeons," and several breeds of hunting dogs.

Another breeder, "honest and true," is E. W. Amsden, of Ormond, Volusia County. He makes a specialty of White, Silver, and Gold Wyandottes, White Leghorns, and Pekin Ducks.

Other reliable breeders there are; but of these we have personal knowledge, and while we name them here, "unbeknownst" to themselves, we feel that we shall be forgiven.

CHAPTER XIX. THE POULTRY YARD.

Shade, Grass, and Pure Water Requisite. The Nursery. How to guard against Hawks. Movable Coops and Fences.

The possession of poultry necessitates a place to keep them in, unless indeed one chooses to allow them the run of the flower-beds and the house, and if so, then good-bye to neatness, beauty, and the refinements that should make the surroundings of a true home—farewell to flowers, and to all low-hanging fruits; for, while they agree only too well with chickens, the latter do not agree with them, to judge by results, for they "wage war to the death" upon them. And so we hold that no refined and sensible person will voluntarily allow poultry the free run of the house inclosure; let them have their own premises, it will be better, far better, for both parties.

Let us look first into the best plan for a permanent poultryyard and house, and afterward we will examine that other matter of portable fences and poultry-houses, which is attracting a good deal of attention in the "chickenhearted world" just now.

Where merely a home supply of flesh and eggs is desired, with the opportunity for a small surplusage for sale, one yard only is needed; for in this case all the adult chickens may be allowed to roam together.

For a flock of fifty to sixty, a space of about one hundred feet square will be enough, though it is always best to have the poultry-yard as roomy as possible, unless the truck garden, house inclosure, and all forbidden grounds are closely fenced; in this case, the poultry-yard may be dispensed with entirely, since the chickens and their kindred may be allowed to roam in the open without risk of damage to vegetation.

But if there be a poultry-yard, it should inclose, if possible, at least one corner of a lakelet where water will be always accessible to its denizens. This will not only save the labor of carrying water to the yard, no light task, especially in warm weather; but the abundance of "small fry" to be found in the margin of the water, such as insects, small frogs, and fish, will make the chickens and other poultry happy and fat.

Mulberry trees should be set here and there in every poultry-yard, not only because of the dense shade they furnish, a very important item though, but also because of the liberal supply of food they furnish without labor or expense on the part of the owner. The very best mulberry for this purpose, though all are good, is the Hicks, which is described by P. J. Berkmans, our celebrated Southern nurseryman, of the Fruitland Nurseries at Augusta, Georgia, as "wonderfully prolific, fruit sweet, insipid, excellent for poultry and hogs, fruit produced during four months of the year."

Try planting a few of these valuable trees in the poultry-yard, grouping two or three on the south and west sides of the hen-house, to shade the latter, and it will do you good to see the amount of enjoyment your feathered pets will obtain during those four months, when the plump, ripe berries, so cooling and healthful, are dropping at their feet, to be had for the picking; they will need very little other feeding during these happy mulberry months.

Whenever it is possible Bermuda, or some other turfgrass, should be started in the poultry-yard before it is inhabited ; grass will have no chance to take hold otherwise, and if the poultry range is divided into one or two sections, so that rye, oats, cow-peas, rice, or some other grain crop, may be grown there, and the chickens admitted or kept out at will, an immense amount of good will accrue to all interested. The pickets, or wires, should be set closely together, that the half-grown birds may not push their way through.

As to the young chicks, from the day they are hatched until they are fully two months old, and in some cases yet longer, they should be kept in a separate yard set apart especially for them and their mothers.

Let the fence of the "nursery" be eight-foot pickets set on top of two ten-inch boards laid on edge horizontally, one above the other, half of the lower board being sunk into the ground; either this, or else ten-foot pickets without the boards at the base, but with, instead, a strip of wire netting, two feet wide, nailed on at the bottom, its edge sunk a little below the surface of the ground.

This bottom protection is very important, both to keep the little ones in and their four-footed foes out; for in Florida, as in all newly-settled countries, skunks and opossums go about literally "seeking what they may devour," and sometimes foxes too come prowling around, for dearly do they love chickens, young or old.

A fence of this description will do more than merely protect the chicks from their four-footed foes, it will save them from their most deadly enemy, the hawk, whose fell swoop is made not at night only, when it could be guarded against, but at all hours of the day, from sunrise to sunset; and within this close fence, that will prevent the chicks from straggling outside, they can be protected effectually.

When we first settled in our- Florida home, our young poultry shared the fate of those belonging to our neighbors; they "soared heavenward on the wings of a" —hawk, whole broods often vanishing, one by one, till no more were left to appease the *fowl* appetite of the marauder.

We had a small yard apart from the main one especially for the little chicks, to preserve them in the daily rush for food (when chickens show strong human tendencies!); and one day, after seeing a hawk pounce down before our very face into this little yard, carry off number thirty to our knowledge (and it might have been more), one day—we repeat, after having had our feathers ruffled in this manner we bethought us of having read somewhere that birds, and especially hawks, would never descend below a line stretched across their downward path; so we straightway put the idea into practice, running a few lines of ordinary twine back and forth over the nursery, just high enough to escape striking our head.

We had not much faith in the remedy, for the disease was desperate; but it is a remarkable fact that from that day, six years ago, to the present, we have never lost a single chick by hawks, except such as managed to stray outside their fortress, which was not properly closed at the base of the fencing.

With an inclosure such as we have described, and wire or tarred twine, tarred to make it durable, drawn across it from the top of eight- or ten-foot poles, no chicks will be lost by hawks, skunks, opossums, or any other foes of poultrydom.

A roomy shed, or shelter, placed in the center of the nursery, will afford shade and protection from rain, and here the coops should be placed, unless there are large trees here and there, or a Scuppernong grape canopy, to take the place of the less sightly shed. Place the coops near the outer edge of the latter, facing inward, a wide board being placed before each coop, with a narrow ledge running around it, like a shallow dish; place the feed for the household on this, and there will be no dirt mixed with it, and none lost on the ground, for the ledge will prevent its being scattered off the board. Keep here also, at all times, a supply of cracked oyster-shells and bones; it is as necessary for little chicks as for adult fowls, though few are apparently aware of this fact.

If you choose, you can supply your own cracked bones and oyster-shells, at very little if any expense, and, what is also an important item, have them always at hand.

After the bones left from the table have been thrown out for the poultry to pick clean—and you may trust them to do their work well—gather them up and keep them where they will be dry.

For our own use we prefer putting the bones in a dripping-pan and setting them in the oven till they are a light brown, not that it is necessary, but we believe that bones partially burned serve a double purpose—the poultry obtain the bone ingredients, and also a slight dose of animal charcoal, which is a splendid digestive medicine.

When the bones are "done brown," we drop them into a little hand-mill that is a famous devourer of bones, dry or green, corn, oats, oyster-shells, cotton-seed, or, in fact, of any thing else that may need grinding, either fine, like meal, or coarse.

Possessing one of these wonderful little workers, which cost but $5, or, with iron legs, $7, a family may provide its poultry with an abundance of the cracked bone and oyster-shells, so important, as every one knows, to their well-being. This, where so many of us live remote from commercial centers, is of itself a great thing. Besides, when cracked corn is wanted for little chickens, all one has to do is to drop the whole corn into the jaws of the Little Giant, a few turns of the wheel, and lo! it disgorges the grain, digested and in just the right shape for the hungry little ones. Is cotton-seed wanted for stock food or fertilizers? drop in the seed and out it comes as fine a meal as you choose. Is corn-meal wanted for the table ? you have it at a few turns of the wrist. Crackers may be made into dust, stale bits of bread made ready for puddings; in fact it soon becomes indispensable in the household.

Not the least important of its work is in the grinding of bones for fertilizing purposes. Every scrap of bone not needed for the chickens should be added to the compost heap, and the Little Giant will "chaw" them up to order, fine or coarse. The truth is that the value of this little mill can hardly be overestimated, as every one who takes our advice and purchases one will at once acknowledge. There is a larger size, which is stronger, and grinds bones with still greater ease and rapidity; this costs $12, on iron legs $16.

We have two of them ourself, one, the larger size, that is used for the poultry and stock, and the other for household purposes, grinding coffee, rice, converting coarse sugar into pulverized, and a host of other things.

We should feel utterly at sea without the hand-mill of Wilson Brothers, 43-45 Delaware Street, Easton, Pennsylvania.

Best of all coops is a triangular one, resting on, but not fastened to, a board bottom, projecting a little in front beyond the coop, but allowing the coop to fit down over it at the sides and back, that heavy rains may be shed on the ground and not run inside. In the usual upright-wall coops the chicks are often trampled on by the hen; but the triangular or peaked-roof style permits them to get away under the eaves in safety; we have never lost one by trampling in a coop of this shape.

And now, to go back to the main poultry-yard: we have seen how this should be inclosed; first, as to the house. This, in Florida, is by no means the elaborate or expensive building it should and must be in more rigorous climates; here are no ice or snow, or high, piercing winds to guard against.

A plain building, suited in size to the number of fowls to be sheltered (twelve by twenty feet is ample for one hundred and fifty), is all that is needed; let the sides be made of pieces one inch by three, nailed on horizontally, a space of one or two inches being left between them, except half way up from the bottom on the north and west sides; here let there be room to fit in temporarily, during the winter, the three-inch wide slats, " battens," so as to make the sides in these places solid, and shut out the winter winds.

This will give ample ventilation, and yet keep all foes at bay, if the base-boards are close and the lower one sunk below the surface.

A good many of the old Florida settlers say to newcomers, "Don't put a tight roof on your hen-house; let the rain come through on the chickens when on the roosts, it will kill the lice."

Pay no attention to such advice; it is bad from beginning to end, and fatal to the health of the poor, helpless chickens, who are thus compelled to sleep (if sleep they can) with a heavy drip, drip, drip, of water on their heads, gradually soaking and chilling them, just when their systems are most relaxed and they should be most carefully protected from wet and wind. No, no! put a good, tight roof on your hen-house, and let it run well over the sides too, so that the heavy rains we are subject to in Florida can not drive far inside; and as to that idea of "killing the lice," in the first place, they "hadn't oughter" be there, and will not be, if proper care is taken ; and, in the second place, only boiling water will kill them; and, even in this semi-tropical climate, it is very semi-occasionally that the rain comes down at this temperature; and, meantime, the ordinary rain-water will kill chickens in long-continued doses.

The house should be considerably longer than wide, and the perches run lengthwise in the center, both for convenience in passing around them, and to insure dryness to the fowls; the middle perch should be the highest, and the others be so graduated that the little ones can reach them when they first begin to roost.

Under these perches a sloping platform should be placed to catch the droppings, an important item, both for cleanliness and economy, since in this way all the valuable guano is saved. The platform should be scraped clean every day or two, and if each time a light sprinkling of land plaster be scattered over it, so much the better, it prevents the escape of the ammonia, and thus corrects the "chickeny smell," that is often more decided than pleasant.

A door for entrance, and one or more traps, with dropdoors for the chicks to pass in and out, one into each division of the yard, if the yard be divided into "grazing sections," and then the house is complete, except the nests.

These should be set on the floor, facing the wall in rows, two or three nests in one connected piece, with breaks left here and there in the rows for the hens to pass back and forth; there need be only a narrow strip left between the nests and the wall, since, by making the tops movable on hinges, they can be raised from the outer side and free access to the nests obtained.

Hens dearly love retirement and partial darkness, either when laying or setting, and if the nests are faced outward, or set on the floor without tops, like open boxes, they will scornfully turn their backs upon them and hunt out some quiet corner for themselves somewhere else.

So much for the permanent yard and buildings. The nursery, by the way, should always be of this character.

Movable fences are often very desirable to have, and form a splendid medium for fertilizing any particular spot or tree, without giving up a whole field or grove to the roving and meddlesome propensities of the flock. Movable fences and movable houses for poultry are great things for our Florida groves, and we would strongly advocate their use; the more of them the better. A temporary poultry-yard, confining twenty or thirty chickens for one or two months in the year around an orange tree, would make a marked difference in its growth and vigor; try it, and see.

It is easy enough to make the fence—when you know how—as easy as Columbus found it to stand an egg on end,—and here is one way to do it: we shall speak of others further on:

Procure pickets two inches wide, by half an inch thick, and six feet long; nail them to two rails, three inches square and twelve feet long; at each end of every rail, U-shaped pieces of stout hoop-iron (hogshead iron is best) are fastened by screws, so as to form staples, through which posts seven feet long and two and a half inches in diameter, pointed at both ends, are thrust and set firmly in the ground.

The rails in the alternate sections are at such distances apart, that while the tops of the pickets are in line, the staples at the ends—the U-shaped pieces of hoop—may not interfere with those of adjoining sections.

Each post, when in position, has a brace upon the outside, made by sawing in half one of the rails, beveling both ends of the two braces thus obtained, and fastening upon them at an obtuse angle staples like those on the rail; set one of these braces up against one of the posts it is to strengthen, and you will see at once just how the staples should incline; one of them is to be slipped over the top of the post, and the other to rest on the ground with a peg driven through it, the top of the latter inclining away from the fence. Braces thus arranged will, as it is easy to see, hold the fence in position, no matter how the wind may blow, if only the peg is stout and well driven into the ground, the staple-loop over the post holding equally in any direction.

Gates are made in the same way, only that they are hinged to stout posts, which are set up and braced in a similar manner.

For movable poultry-houses there are several plans, and if none of these happen to suit in all respects, it is not a difficult thing for an intelligent mind to suggest, or an intelligent hand to execute any necessary modifications. The main point is to have as light a structure as is consistent with strength and durability; large size is not requisite when the object is only to provide safe shelter during the night and nests for the layers, and, in our genial Florida climate, this is all that need be thought of.

We have spoken elsewhere of triangular coops for little chickens in the nursery. Now, this triangular shape is a good one also for a movable poultry-house in its simplest form.

Of course, for this purpose it must be considerably larger than if designed merely for a hen and brood; there is no need that it should stand higher, but its length should be proportionate to' the number of fowls to be housed.

All of the material used should be as light as possible, without sacrificing strength. Quarter-inch boards, nailed to end-laths, three feet long and overlapping like weatherboarding, are best for the roof, which, of course, is in two pieces or sides. When these are put together by means of hooks or screws (the latter being preferred) one side should project at the top above the other to shed rain.

It does not matter much at what angle the sides are joined to form the pitch-roof, so that height enough is left for the perches, which run from end to end, lengthwise, the nests being set on the ground against the ends.

The triangular ends of this simple poultry-house are made either of battens nailed across, close enough to keep out skunks and opossums, or else of wire-cloth; trap-doors, one at each end, that are closed at night, complete this little poultry-house, in which are combined lightness and strength, safety and ventilation,

A portion of the end-pieces should be solid, so that a couple of perch-poles, with ends projecting so as to be used as handles in moving the house, may be passed through holes made for the purpose.

Access to the nests is gained by hinging the lower endboard so that it can be raised and the arm thrust inside.

The house should always rest on a sound board bottom, as a guard against nocturnal enemies who otherwise would find no trouble in effecting a subterranean entrance.

When there are two persons to handle such a house as this, one at each end, there will be no necessity for making it in sections; it will be light enough to handle in one piece.

Another form of portable poultry-house, much favored in England, is set upon wheels—small wheels, with broad tires—and moved by horse-power.

This is an excellent plan, too, since the house may thus be made much larger and stronger, yet be transported with ease from point to point, together with its feathered occupants; hinged shafts may be used for this purpose or merely staples, to which ordinary plow-chains may be hooked.

This "house on wheels" should be made strongly, but not of needlessly heavy materials; a low frame-work with wire-cloth stretched over it to form the sides and ends, and broad, overlapping eaves, with perches well up toward the roof, to avoid all driving rains, would serve the purpose admirably in our mild Florida climate, with the proviso that one side, which should always face toward the northwest in winter and the southwest in summer, be lined with some sun-proof and wind-proof material, the former in summer, the latter in winter. Quarter-inch boards, set sloping against the side, are good for this purpose, and also afford outside shelter during the day.

Where several movable poultry-houses of this sort are desired, it is not necessary that each one should have its own set of wheels; one set will do the work, if placed on a platform, or truck, large enough to carry the poultry-house, which, in this case, must be provided with a sound board floor of its own ; the truck being low, it will not be difficult to slide the house on or off.

Another kind of movable poultry-house is made of slatted or wire-cloth sides, joined by the same method employed for the movable fence already described (the post and staple ends), the roof being like that of the triangular house.

It is not our province here to enter in detail upon the proper care of poultry as regards food, cleanliness, and their sequence, health, or otherwise. We shall touch only briefly upon these points, leaving it to the numerous works devoted especially to this object to enlighten those who desire further information.

One of the most important adjuncts to successful chicken-raising is pure water. Very few realize the extent of the mischief done their fowls by allowing them to drink warm, dirty, or impure water; their drinking trough should be always in the shade and so arranged that they can only gain access to it for its legitimate purpose, not jump into it, or scratch dirt into its midst.

This object is easily attained by using a low, triangular trough, having a sloping roof over it, and wire-netting with meshes wide enough to admit a chicken's head, but no more, closing in the front and sides; let this trough stand on a grassy spot, or a clean board floor, then the fowls will always have clean, cool water; wash the trough out every two or three days, and, if lined with zinc, it will be so much the easier to keep clean and pure.

For the nursery a cheap and effective drinking-fountain may be made thus: Take a tomato, or similar can, from which the top, in emptying, has not been entirely cut out, but only bent in; straighten out the ragged edges so as partially to close the can again, then cut a hole about the size of a lead pencil, a quarter of an inch from the jagged top; fill the can with water, put a saucer on it, upside down, then quickly invert can and saucer together; the water will come out in the saucer until it reaches the level of the hole, and will always remain at this point until the can is emptied by the chickens drinking the water, which, thus protected, will keep pure and clean.

When the mother hen begins to show a disposition to desert her little ones, let her coop be lifted into the main hen-house and placed against the wall, then, when she does leave them and goes upon the roosts, they will follow, and thus be easily and naturally taught to seek the perches at night; if they don't, take their coop away. This is a more important matter than is generally realized, although every one who has raised chickens knows how much trouble and annoyance is caused by this desertion of a brood.

The poor little chicks, worried by the absence of their one-time careful mother, and crying pitifully and vainly for her return, huddle together in a corner of their late happy home, shivering from the unaccustomed night exposure, pushing, crowding, crushing each other, one and all seeking the shelter of the center of the restless mass of lamenting chickendom; and so they suffer until darkness and sleep overtake them, and thus they continue, if allowed, until the coop becomes too small for their rapidly growing bodies, until at last the slow instinct of their race bids them finally abandon the coop and seek a higher place.

But, meantime, they have been crowding and sleeping in close quarters, insufficiently ventilated, until most likely some of them have died, some contracted weakness, and some become stunted in growth.

All this can be avoided by the simple plan we have suggested. In every hen-house there should be some low, flat perches that the little ones can reach and roost upon without injury. And right here it is well to remark that narrow, or small round perches are very injurious to chickens of all ages, being apt to produce curved breast-bones, to say nothing of the nightly discomfort to the birds themselves. Perches for adult chickens should be two inches wide by one inch thick, the edges beveled, and the perch set with a very slight slope forward.

The eggs in the nest of a setting hen should be sprinkled daily for eight days before the chicks are due; if this is neglected, the membrane or lining of the shell is apt to be dry and tough, and then when the chick's "little bill," coming due, is presented, it meets with a protest, and the frail life goes at once into the court of bankruptcy, whence it issues nevermore.

Keep the eggs moist by this method and the chicks will easily make their way out into the world, but never try to "help them out" by breaking away bits of the shell and membrane ; leave Nature alone, unless the membrane seems inclined to stick to the little body, after the shell is peeled off, then moisten the stiff parts, but do not pull it away; a drop of blood drawn is weakness or death to the chick.

It is advisable to place the nests of setting liens (without board bottoms) on the ground; but if this can not well be done, the nests should be made extra deep and well filled in with earth, packed to a concave shape and lined with short straw, occasionally dampened.

Place the nests in rows and make the divisions between, not of solid boards as is usually done, but of wire-netting, open enough for the adjoining hens to make each other's acquaintance during the long period of incubation, and yet not so large as to allow them to interfere with each other's eggs.

By pursuing this plan, and setting two adjoining hens at the same time, the broods will come off together, and the hens can be placed in one coop, where they will agree perfectly; and thus their owner saves time, trouble, and space, by being able to attend to two broods together.

CHAPTER XX. POULTRY PATIENTS.

How to Treat the Few Diseases Florida Poultry are subject to

Florida's mild climate is especially adapted to the raising of fowls on a large scale with a view to profit both in eggs and flesh.

The terrible diseases that so frequently rush rampant through so many Northern poultry-yards, dealing wholesale death and destruction, are very rarely if ever met with on Florida soil. Nine tenths of these disorders are caused by exposure to inclement weather. Hence, there is no other State in our great Union so especially adapted to successful poultry-raising, since here the primary cause of numerous failures is totally unknown; and that Florida will yet become the leading poultry-yard of the United States we do firmly believe.

Florida chickens are subject to very few diseases; and these, if proper care is taken, may almost invariably be avoided, or at least cured. The most prevalent and most fatal trouble that Florida chicken-"flesh is heir to," is here termed "sore-head," or "warts," though neither of these names is proper or distinctive. The fact is that the name "sore-head," or " warts," is no more the name of a disease than "sore toe," or "sore finger." And the disease they are intended to designate is, in Florida at all events, not one disease but several distinct ones. Thus, sore-head may mean that a chicken has distemper, catarrh, ulceration, or canker, which, in its worst stage, becomes that fatal disease, roup.

These several diseases are twin sisters. The one following the other as natural, progressive steps, and all proceeding from that most simple but fruitful source of disease in the human subject as well, "a common cold," only in the latter the various ramifications and consequences that proceed from it are known and recognized, while in the poor, helpless fowl they are all classed (hereabouts) under one name, usually "sore-head," from beginning to end. The first stage of the trouble is properly termed distemper, or catarrh. It is a disease that chickens are heir to all over the world; it is hard to tell always the why and wherefore of its appearance; all we know is that it will come sometimes, and that too in spite of every care and attention.

The distemper usually seizes upon young chickens when they are shedding their "second chicken feathers," in their second or third month. As soon as one of the flock is seen to be quiet and listless, and disposed to remain on the perch in the day-time, its face and comb red, and a fullness or puff under its eye, look to it, and at once! Do not lose an hour before shutting it up in the hospital, that should be an adjunct to the poultry-yard, and commencing active treatment; for while distemper is a disease that is light in itself, if left to take its own course it will usually result fatally.

Listlessness and loss of appetite are the first symptoms; the second day a slight froth appears in the corners of the eyes. When treatment is delayed until this froth appears the race with the destroyer is a close one; and even, if the chicken eventually recovers, it is usually with the loss of one or both eyes; in the latter case it must be killed or it will die of starvation. Watch closely, therefore, for the first symptoms we have noted, and as soon as discovered place the patient under the following

TREATMENT FOR DISTEMPER.

If taken before the froth in the eyes appears, wash the head and beak clean, and blow down through the nose into the throat, either with the mouth or a rubber nipple; this cleans the tear-tube. Then bathe the head and wash the throat inside (the latter with a feather stripped to near the point) with a solution of one part of carbolic acid to ten of water. Keep the bird in a quiet place, and give it nothing but water, no food. The third day give a little potato, bread-crumbs, or hard-boiled egg. The fourth day it should be in condition to be turned out into the yard again.

When the froth has shown itself, or the head is much swollen, use the same treatment as above, with this addition: thoroughly steam the head and throat, by using a large sponge and hot water, and give a dessertspoonful of castor oil; use the carbolic wash at short intervals.

CATARRH.

This disease differs from distemper, inasmuch as a slight cold differs from a severe one. Its symptoms are a discharge from both eyes and nostrils, accompanied by a hiccough or sneeze.

Place the bird by itself in a sheltered place out of the sun and draughts; feed it only on soft, well-cooked food, seasoned heavily with red pepper and ginger, or licorice and black pepper, and put three drops of the *mother* tincture of aconite to half a pint of the drinking-water; renew the latter each day.

This treatment, if the case is only catarrh, will be all that is necessary; but if it is severe, then it is no longer catarrh, but

CANKER OR ULCERATION.

The first symptom of this trouble is a watery discharge from the eyes; later the discharge assumes a firmer character and emits an offensive odor; the throat and tongue become studded with ulcers, and unless the disease is speedily conquered the bird dies of suffocation. Use McDougall's Fluid Carbolate to wash the head and eyes, four parts of water to one of the carbolate; swab the throat with the undiluted carbolate three or four times a day; give soft food, with flour of sulphur mixed with it, and put a little of the latter with the drinking-water.

McDougall's Fluid Carbolate should be kept by every drug or general merchandise store; it is a most valuable remedy, being a neutral solution of carbolate of lime and sulphate of magnesia, and entirely free from corrosive or irritating effects, yet combining all the most valuable properties of both carbolic and sulphurous acids.

If, however, this carbolate can not be obtained, there are other remedies to take its place.

An ounce of chlorate of potash and an ounce of crushed sugar to a half pint of water should always be kept ready for use in every poultry-yard. The water only dissolves a certain proportion, and no more, of the salt, and it should always be made as strong as possible; in other words, a "saturated solution." The sugar serves the double purpose of loosening the phlegm in the throat of the bird, and by disguising the saline taste of the chlorate makes it more easy to administer.

Chlorate of potash, in the above proportions, is a splendid remedy for the human throat as well as that of poultry; it removes canker and ulceration in the mouth and throat, cools and allays fever, and by its inward action destroys all traces of canker in the system, and thus renders the cure a permanent one, in this being unlike merely local remedies. As long as any chlorate remains undissolved in the bottle more water may be added, taking care that the proper proportion of sugar is kept up.

To adult fowls give a teaspoonful of the solution three times a day, or oftener, if the case is severe, also swabbing the throat and mouth thoroughly with the same an equal number of times; and here it is well to observe, in swabbing the mouth always take care to run the feather into the slit in the roof. An ounce of this solution to a pint of water makes an excellent remedy for common colds or distemper in young chicks.

Yet another remedy, claimed to be infallible, not only for canker, but for its most virulent form—roup—is to place the affected birds in a close room, then take a shovelful of red-hot cinders and sprinkle on them a teaspoonful of flour of sulphur; let the bird breathe the sulphurous acid gas thus evolved for ten minutes. It will cause it to sneeze, and if the case is far advanced a great quantity of matter will be thrown up through the throat and nostrils, and an almost immediate cure will result.

This remedy is also successfully employed for catarrh in human beings, and for epizooty in horses, never failing of a cure after four or five applications.

All of these diseases we have named proceed directly from exposure to cold, to rain, wind, and draughts; and, knowing this, that "ounce of prevention" which "is worth a pound of cure" is easily obtained, as we have already pointed out, in the arrangement of our hen-houses.

As we have said, all these diseases are often carelessly classed, by those who are unobservant, as "sore-head;" nine times out of ten, if you ask a Florida-raised neighbor who has sick chickens, "What is the matter with them?" he will answer, "Oh, sore-head, of course!"

There is one distinct disease that deserves the name, since a sore head is its outward effect. But this trouble, popularly called in the South sore-head, or warts, is really nothing more nor less than genuine

ERYSIPELAS.

It is not often seen in the poultry-yards of the North, though when it does appear it is almost invariably toward the close of summer, and it is more prevalent in the extreme South because the warm season is there longer continued; in other words, the superinducing cause of this disease is exposure—not to cold, but to heat. It rarely if ever attacks chickens over a year old, but prefers the young ones of one to three months old, who are "always on the go" out in the sun, and whose little frames have not yet become inured to exposure. It never attacks them in cold weather, and usually only during the summer, though sometimes in early spring or fall, if the season is very warm.

The first symptoms of "sore-head," or erysipelas, as it should be termed to avoid confusion, since erysipelas it is, and nothing else, is dullness and the appearance of small pimples about the head and face; these increase and become pustules, which exude a serous fluid; the head and eyes swell, the mouth, tongue and comb become covered with pustules, discharging an offensive matter.

Now erysipelas, as every one knows, is an ugly disease, especially when it attacks the head; if taken in time, however, it can be usually conquered. Place the bird at once in a clean, sheltered coop, in as cool a place as possible; administer a tablespoonful of castor oil each day until it begins to improve; give green and soft food, mixing a teaspoonful of flour of sulphur with the latter, daily, for a week or ten days, and let its drink be one part of Douglass' Mixture to two of water. Keep the sores moist with lard and sulphur, well rubbed in. If the sulphur seems to irritate, stop using it and substitute a neutral solution of carbolate of lime and sulphate of magnesia.

To the discovery of the true name, cause, and remedy of the so-called "sore-head," or "warts," the writer has devoted much time, study, and observation, and now, for the first time, throws open to the Florida public the result of several years of careful experiment.

When we first settled in our adopted State, bringing with, or rather sending ahead of us a fine collection of Houdans and Light Bramahs, from a yard perfectly free from disease, we were considerably puzzled by the appearance in a few months of "sore-head." It was then August, and the flock had passed through the heat of May, June, and July in their new quarters, and it was among those hatched in May and June that the disease appeared.

They had a roomy chicken-house, but the roof was not tight, we having, under protest, taken the advice of "old residenters" on that point. They had an ample run; but our new home was being carved out of the wilderness, pine trees were being felled, and shade was lacking; the fowls ranged all day in the hot sun, then at night there frequently came heavy rains, and, owing to the open roof, the water poured down on the backs of the poor, sleepy birds, drenching them to the skin. The rains, too, were more often than not accompanied by high, cool winds that blew across the unfortunate victims of a mistaken system.

Do you see the *causus belli?*

An overheating of the blood during the day, a sudden chilling at night—here surely is as plain and prolific a source of erysipelas as could be invented! We do not need to look further for the as yet but little understood cause of the dreaded "sore-head."

Here then, as we believe, is the source. The remedy is easy: Provide plenty of shade for your poultry; make shelters until trees have time to grow; let the roofs of your hen-houses be water-tight, and so place the perches that the wind can not blow on the sleep-relaxed frames of the poor birds that are dependent on you for all their health and comfort.

For two seasons "sore-head," or erysipelas, decimated our poultry-yard, and then, suspecting at last the true reason of the trouble, we protected the birds from dampness by a tight roof, a dense covering of clinging vines served to shut out a direct draught, and we made shelters of boards and tree-tops where the trees were not sufficiently grown to afford shade.

Since that time we have not had a single case of "sorehead," and very few, almost .none, even of a slight distemper; yet our flock is large, and there has been no other change in their treatment, except, indeed, that they are no longer fed any corn during the summer months. It is heating, and oats do better.

We still hesitate to make the positive assertion that we have discovered the cause of this hitherto mysterious disease; but it certainly looks so, and we most earnestly urge upon all interested a patient trial of the same preventives; then, by the result, it will be demonstrated whether our most fatal Florida chicken disease is, or is not, solely produced by overheating and too sudden cooling of the blood.

It is well at all times to put in the drinking-fountain a dessertspoonful of Douglass' Mixture to a pint of water, at least twice a week; oftener, if there be any disease among the chickens. There is no better tonic than this, both as a preventive and an active agent. It is made as follows:

DOUGLASS' MIXTURE.

Place one pound of sulphate of iron (copperas) and one ounce of sulphuric acid in a two-gallon jug, fill half full with hot water, let it stand twenty-four hours, and then fill up with water.

This tonic is invaluable given to young chicks and to molting adults; it helps the latter through with an exhausting period, and hastens their return to the egg manufactory.

CHAPTER XXI. FIRING THE WOODS.

Permitted by Law for the Benefit of Cattle; but will soon be a Thing of the Past. A Most Pernicious Custom, Injurious to Soil and Property. How to Fight Fire.

For many, many years our stately pine woods have been devastated annually by an element which is most truly said to be "a better servant than master." And no one who has once witnessed the fierce Florida fires roaring and rushing through the woods, sweeping every thing before them in their fiery onset, but can realize the full force of this saying.

All over the State it is the custom to "fire the woods" early in the spring, so that the fine straw and old grass may be burned off, and new grass, the famous wire-grass, grow up, so that, forsooth, the roving stock may find plenty to eat without money and without price, so far as their owners are concerned.

No matter how much a man may desire to preserve every blade of grass and every leaf that grows on his land so that it may decay and eventually enrich the soil, his neighbor has his cattle to provide for, and so the latter goes out, torch in hand, and sets fire to the grass, and burns it up, every blade of it, deliberately robbing the owner of the land of all the rich humus and fertilizing material that nature had manufactured for that purpose.

"If," said a noted orange-grower, "I was offered two tracts of land, side by side, one where the grass had been burned off year after year, the other where it had been left to grow and to rot, and the one was offered at ten dollars per acre and the other at twenty, I would take the latter on the instant, because the difference in the quality of the soil would be more than equal to the difference in cost."

And there are many intelligent land-owners in the State who will indorse this opinion and who endeavor, but in vain, to preserve for their soil the humus it so much needs. But year after year they see it destroyed for the benefit of those very cattle who also destroy their crops. There is no redress; the law authorizes the theft of their best fertilizer, provided it is done according to certain prescribed rules.

It is terribly hard upon the poor, patiently toiling settler. Let any one glance over the columns of the Florida country papers, during the months from January to April, and he will realize the pressing urgency of this matter. The reports of fences, houses, groves, even lives destroyed by these wholesale burnings will reveal the true inwardness and culpability of a law which allows a practice so injurious to our State and to the common sense of its lawgivers. It is a law that stands side by side with that which protects the man who turns out his cattle and hogs to prey upon his neighbors' crops; they may have been just when they were enacted years ago, when Florida was little else than a vast grazing ground with houses and fields few and far between ; but times have changed, and such laws must, and speedily will be, changed.

Like the old Florida cow and its management, the forest fires and the fencing out of your neighbors' roving stock will soon be among the traditions of the past, and hardships that the coming settler will not be obliged to face. They have endured too long, but their end is near.

"What is the motive of those who thus fire the woods in the settlements?" you ask.

To illustrate: A thickly-settled neighborhood, owning valuable fences and groves, resolved to make a cordon around the settlement and "whip out" all approaching fires at a distance from their property. But they reckoned without their host; right in their midst dwelt the first comer in that region; he declined to part from old customs. "If the grass don't burn off around here the cows will be late comin' home at night, 'cause they'll have to wander to hunt fresh grass; and this here grass is goin' to be burnt, that's all about it!"

And so at sundown, one early spring day, fire began creeping out beyond the line of plowed ground he had run around his own fences, and the whole settlement was compelled to rush to the rescue of its property, and, with hoes, rakes, axes, and the tops of young pine trees, fight fire till daylight, even thus losing hundreds of rails, which loss threw open groves and fields to the inroads of stock for several days. And these thrifty, intelligent citizens had no redress against this one ignorant one!

The law, as it stands at present, allows fire to be put out into the woods during the months of January, February, March, and April; but decrees that the person so firing the woods shall give one or more days' notice of his intention to every one within one mile of his home.

It is hardly needful to say that this latter clause is generally disregarded; true, the penalty is heavy, liability for payment of all the damage done. But what matters a penalty, when no one can prove who started the fire?

Neighbor A. "'lows that old man B. did it." Old man B. reckons that C. mought a done it." But no one knows, so no one suffers except the innocent.

Even in the case we have just mentioned, while moral proof was strong, the act of firing was not seen, so there was no legal proof.

Our law-makers should have interfered in these premises long ago; but soon the people will settle it for themselves, for they are awakening to the injury these half-savage laws inflict upon an agricultural community.

Shut up the cattle on their owner's premises, and the temptation to destroy other people's property for their benefit will be removed.

The opening of spring brings with it months of anxious watching, by night and by day; no one knows where or when the inflammable pine straw will be fired, nor by whom, far or near, and the only warning is the rapid approach of the fierce-roaring flames, bellowing like a hundred bulls, leaping like an army of demons rejoicing over the destruction of all they may meet in their resistless rush, and even to the very lives of human beings!

Only a few years ago a hapless family, driving through a dense hammock where a wide wagon-track had been cut from amidst the heavy underbrush, were overtaken by an onrushing wall of roaring flames; they lashed their horses and fled onward; there was no turning to the right or left, even had there been no fire to bar the way. Close behind them rushed the fierce fire demons, gloating over the prey, for whom, alas! there was no escape. Vainly was the whip applied to the affrighted horses. Hammock roads are rough, full of palmetto roots, hills and hollows; and soon the poor beasts stumbled and fell; then the family alighted and fled on foot, the father snatching up two little children, the mother clasping her babe to her breast, and still another child, a boy of eight years, followed after them in deadly fear.

On came the flames with that horrible glow and that awful roar so familiar, more's the pity to the Florida settlers, and their pace was swifter than that of the wretched human beings fleeing before them. Soon the little boy tripped and fell headlong into a tiny pool of liquid mud in the center of the road; his forehead struck a root and he lay there unconscious as the flames swept by on either side, leaving him scorched and suffering, but alive.

Less fortunate were his parents. Burdened with the helpless little ones, the terrible flames caught them up and wrapped them all—father, mother, and three children—in their fiery arms; and so all that was left of the six human beings and two horses, that only an hour before had entered on that fatal road, full of life and hope, was a mass of charred bones, and one little boy.

And all this, not by any means a solitary instance, that a drove of cattle might be provided with a good supply of new, fresh grass!

Every fence outlying the open forest must, early in January, be "protected" by a line of ten or twelve consecutive furrows plowed entirely around it, and all tall grass or weeds, that might serve to carry fire across, carefully raked out. A still better plan is to plow another similar strip ten or fifteen feet, outside the first, and then burn off all the trash and grass between the two; this makes the safest possible barrier; but still the fire does sometimes cross it, so that even when thus guarded it behooves one to watch closely or mischief may ensue.

A fire may be met and conquered to all appearance, and yet several days thereafter it not unfrequently happens that, without a breath of warning, a thick, black cloud of smoke is seen, an angry roar of flames heard, and the settler rushes out to find his "protected" fence burning furiously almost at his door ; and no one can tell how it started, except on the theory that some smoldering log has been fanned into a flame by the breeze and a spark wafted across the line of furrows right into the dry grass along the fence.

Another cause of the recurrence of fires deemed extinguished is the tall pine trees, beneath whose bark the flames creep, creep, creep "out of sight, out of mind," till they burst out at the very top, and then, from a height of seventy or eighty feet, sparks sail slowly away in the air, dropping into the grass here and there in places not yet burned over—often at a distance of a hundred or more feet from the point of departure.

Wherever a fire has swept, the trees that stand within two hundred feet of grass uuburned should be closely examined, and, if the slightest signs of internal or external fire can be detected, let them be cut down on the -instant, before they have the chance to do mischief, and mischief too that is of the worst sort, because unsuspected until under full headway.

This has occurred in the writer's personal experience several times, and great damage done, just as it often happens that when one is feeling most secure the enemy appears in force upon the threshold "seeking what it may devour."

It is no light task to "fight fire," as we know to our cost. Many a time, during our Florida life, lack of help has compelled us to face the blinding smoke and scorching flames, armed with rake, hoe, and pine brush, with a threatened fence behind us at our very elbow, and the fierce flames leaping ten feet high on the other side of a narrow plowed strip, and often reaching out and almost spanning the barrier.

No, it is no light thing to fight fire, rushing here and there to check its advance, fighting with breathless haste, aching arms, weeping eyes, and choking lungs, to keep the warring foe at bay.

Many a time have the weak women of a household, during the absence of the stronger ones, been forced to rush out, drag down the heavy rails, so as to break the connection, and fight and struggle for hours to save their hard won property from destruction, often failing partially, if not entirely, in spite of the toil that not unfrequently lays them upon a sick-bed.

It is an every-day complaint, for three or four months every spring, that fences, trees, even houses, have been destroyed, and groves and fields thrown open to the ravages of the roving stock for whose benefit all this destruction is wantonly caused.

If it occurred only once in several years, that would be bad enough; but to go through the same scenes of toil, loss, and anxiety every year is almost more than mortal can endure.

"Let us have peace."

CHAPTER XXII. ALL ABOUT FENCES.

The Fence Law. Repeal Urgent. Injury done by allowing Stock to roam at Large, and compelling the Agriculturist to Fence against Them. How to Make Good and Cheap Fences. Wire Fences Made at Home

If there is one law more than another urgently required in Florida, at this present juncture, it is a law that shall compel each owner of cattle and those other "curous critters," called in local parlance "razor-backs," to keep his property on his own lands, and not send them abroad to raid and pillage his neighbors' substance, ruin his temper and encourage profanity.

Here is a reform in the Florida laws that is even more imperative if possible than that other we have looked into, the firing of the woods—and we refer to it now in detail, not so much that incoming settlers may see what is awaiting them, but rather that they may know what their predecessors have faced; for the days of roving stock are numbered, as, like those of the forest incendiaries, both belong to the "ancient *regime*" now swiftly passing away, as the tide of immigration sweeps onward, bringing improved methods and more thrifty, provident habits in its train.

These two laws have been Florida's most glaring drawbacks in the eyes of the industrious, common-sense settler; they are still alive though near dissolution, and in some sections already practically dead; and the sooner the official death-seal is placed upon them, once and forever, the more rapid will be the advance of the whole State.

We have seen how the firing of the forest works destruction, now let us look into this fence matter for future traditional reference.

The past and present law allows stock to roam at will over the property of every man who cannot afford to fence in his possessions in such a manner as shall effectually prevent the leaping over by horses or cattle, or the creeping under by the other obnoxious class of rovers.

That the law should actually decree that the property of one man worth, say twenty dollars, shall be free to destroy and raid upon the property of another man worth ten times as much, not counting the expenditure of time and labor in creating the latter, seems too barbarous to be credible in these enlightened days.

This law says that a planter must erect a fence nine rails high and above these rails affix others by "stake and rider." This is to keep roving cattle and horses from leaping over. Then the base of this fence must be laid in small rails, so that they may be close enough to deter 'razor-backs' from creeping under.

A few years ago we noted in one of our State papers an article from a prominent orange-grower, which is so apropos that we can not do better than quote from it.

"Myself and neighbors have done and still have to do considerable fencing. In fact the heaviest immediate outlay, when extending our groves or fields, is for the fences that we have to make to keep our neighbors' worthless 'razor-backs ' from destroying the result of our labors. Now, by a little figuring, I find that I could well afford to pay one hundred dollars, if thereby I could have the hogs shut up so that I should have only to fence against cattle. To have the cattle also fenced in would be worth at least another hundred dollars to me to-day, to say nothing of the great saving in the future by reason of not having to keep in repair the fences already built and by the increased fertility of my land if not burned off by the stockmen each year.

"While thinking this matter over, a neighbor, who has just cast his lot with us and purchased five acres of land, came along, and I asked him what he would give to have the hogs shut up to-day. He replied that he would willingly give fifty dollars, but that it would be worth much more than that to him.

"Soon another came by, and in reply to the same question, said two hundred dollars would not nearly pay for the fencing that he had got to do on account of the 'cussed critters.' Another set the figure at one hundred.

"It will cost each of us in the next two years much more than the sums named, in cash, to so fix things that we can plant a few dollars' worth of sweet potatoes, on our own land, with any hope of ever getting a bite of them. We are not alone. I feel sure that nine out of ten that I would meet in a day's ride would come down handsomely with money if thereby they could do away with this nuisance.

"After laying out fifty dollars and considerable labor to fence a small field of less than one and one half acres, I became foolish enough to put a small part of it in potatoes, thinking that that lot was safe from hogs, guarded as it was by six strands of barbed wire drawn taut with 'watch tackle,' so that the wire was pulled in two several times before completed, and with posts set near together. The potatoes came up nicely and did fine. When nearly ready to dig they came up again and were done fine—*too fine*. Nature's greatest mistake had them. I had my gun with me, well loaded with coarse shot. I saw several queer, limber things jerking about just above ground along my potato rows. They looked like uneasy snakes. Man usually kills the snakes he sees; but I knew they were not snakes. I knew from long experience that that kind of a quirk meant pig somewhere near. I sat my gun down against a palmetto tree and quietly drove them away, and said to the next man I met that the next office-seeker I voted for would help me on the fence question."

Now, this complaint was written two years ago, and, by way of pointing out the moral of our statement of a moment ago, we will add that in the neighborhood referred to, although the objectionable law is still in force, the thrifty settlers are no more troubled with the inroads of their four-footed enemies. It has been the experience there, as in many other localities (our own is one of them), that the owners of this lawless kind of stock were made to feel that it was somewhat unprofitable to find their "bunches," as they are termed, of 'razor-backs' gradually but surely disappearing without any return. Of course no one ever know what became of them. Certainly not: they simply departed and left no trace behind, unless sundry unusually thrifty growths, in spots, of trees or vegetables might serve as indications that some strong fertilizers had been buried close by.

So, finally, the owners concluded either to shut up their hogs and fatten them at home, or kill them once for all.

"Let us be thankful," we heard a justly irate settler exclaim one day, "Let us be thankful, at least, that the law allows us to go to all this expense to try to shut out those wretches, and don't compel us to open wide our gates for their benefit!"

And he used the word "try" advisedly too, because it is only a "try" after all; for, get inside they will in some way, in spite of the expensive "legal fence," whose erection and repairs bear heavily on purse or muscle.

And if, exasperated beyond endurance at the sight of his treasured potato patch trampled and uprooted, and his chief dependence for his family's subsistence destroyed before his eyes, the injured man ventures to punish the depredators (openly), or do ought else but turn them away without harm to them (as to himself and property, what matters that?), he is ignominiously summoned before a magistrate and sentenced to pay frequently more than the full market value of the marauder.

"You ought to make your fence hog and cattle -proof, and then you would not be annoyed."

Exactly! but it would take a genius to solve the problem of what is "hog and cattle proof."

Looking at those marvelous creatures, yclept "razorbacks," in sarcastic reference to the prominence of their vertebrae, let us see what they are equal to in the way of burglary.

When we first "came over" to Florida, we had only made acquaintance with pigs in the city markets, "drawn and quartered." We liked them very well there; they looked so fat, clean, and comfortable; no visions of the future marred our then complacency as regarded hogs. En route to our Florida home we passed on the road, or, more correctly, wagon track, a group of queer black objects, bodies long, lank, lean, with backs that looked like the inverted keel of a vessel, legs slim and suggestive of stilts; snouts sharp and pointed, eyes like beads, and tails in many instances destitute of the far-famed graceful curve of a "pig's tail."

"What are those things!" we exclaimed; "surely you don't call them hogs?"

"Well," replied our driver, slowly—he was a genuine "Cracker"—"I don't just rightly know. We calls 'em razor-backs. N-o, I. don't reckon they is hogs."

So, to this day, we too "don't reckon they is hogs;" we would not dare to bestow the title on these odd creatures, and then look their staid, respectable portly Northern congener's in the face.

That is how they look, and their actions are fully in accord with their unique appearance.

Between the house-lots of one of our neighbors and ourselves there were no fences, and the outer boundaries of the two (making an inclosure of about fifteen acres) were fenced with the then all-prevalent rail fence; the latter was not all new, and, as events proved, needed repairs.

Well, the very first morning that dawned on us in our new home was made lively by the squealing of pigs, the barking of a dog, and the shouts of men, as the whole party of pursued and pursuers dashed over our premises, here, there, every where; for full half an hour the chase was hot and heavy, a panel of fence being torn down first in one place, then in another, as hope grew brighter on the flight of the fugitives toward the one joint or the other; but at last they were cornered and driven out into the woods. They had done damage not a little, but the law made them sacred from the reward of evil-doers.

And then the forlorn and wearied victors, flushed, panting, covered from head to foot with sand-spurs, a luxuriant product of cultivated fields when neglected—sat down to pluck up their courage and to pick off the sharp spurs as best they might.

And the next thing was to make a tour of the whole inclosure, critically examine the fence and institute necessary repairs.

But the next day, and the next, and the next, the same impromptu performance was repeated. If a rotten rail could not be found at the bottom of the fence, the razorbacks would root a hole beneath and creep through; night after night they feasted upon our chufas, sweet potatoes, corn, and vegetables.

In the day-time they came just the same, nothing daunted by the daily chase; but then they could be seen and driven out before much more mischief was done.

On our neighbors' land, within ear-shot of our dwelling, was a small building, one room occupied by a woman and her five-year-old child; it was near this spot that the marauders usually found entrance, and the child acted as a detective. Often and often we would hear it cry out excitedly, "Mom, mom, pigs, pigs!" and then, as a hubbub of squeals, barks, and shouts shortly followed, we would think of David Copperfield's famous Aunt Betsey, and would softly murmur, "Janet, donkeys!"

Morning after morning we were roused from sleep by the grunts and squeals of the invading razor-backs and the barks and growls of a dog beneath our feet, the former taking refuge beneath the house (like all Florida houses, it was built upon blocks), and there holding their pursuers at bay.

Finally, in desperation, and with reluctance because of the increased expense, a close board fence, fondly deemed hog-proof, was erected in place of the rails; but still, alas! the razor-backs put in an appearance.

"The how and the where" of their entrance was a mystery. That it was on the line of the new fence was certain; for, when pursued, they invariably, after tacking back and forth over the fifteen-acre inclosure without either rhyme or reason for such maneuver, ended by finding exit in that direction.

Well, we watched, sorely perplexed. What, think you, did we finally discover?

Those wonderful razor-backs, not being permitted to "grub" under the new fence, had actually climbed over it! Standing on their hind legs, they hooked their fore legs over the second board from the base, raised their hind legs to the top of the base-board, and then the smaller ones pushed themselves through between the second and third boards, while the larger ones climbed all the way to the top of the fourth and last board, and came flying down on the inside!

The owner of these acrobatic creatures could not credit our statement until he saw for himself, and then, knowing that not even Florida law would punish the destruction of such arrant blockade-runners, he drove them out of our neighborhood— to torment some other unfortunates.

These were the same chicken-eating razor-backs to which we have referred elsewhere, and most thankful were we to see them disappear.

Then, as to making a fence "cattle-proof" (a rail fence which, until very recently, was the almost universal fence of Florida), that too was more easily said than done.

Our neighbors had roving herds of cattle, and they were always trespassing; we observed, too, that it was always a cow that led the rest of its companions into mischief, its sex being, as we all know, more energetic, persevering, and enterprising than the opposite.

One would suppose that a fence ten rails high, though not "staked and ridered," would be ample to prevent cows from leaping over; but they find a way to get inside and devastate fields of corn and cow-peas and vegetables, all the same. Did you ever see them go to work to overcome such trifling; difficulties as rail fences?

"No?" Well, this is how they do it. They have three ways of accomplishing their praiseworthy designs; either one is effectual, and bespeaks an intelligence worthy of a better cause.

One is to stand by the fence, lower the head, thrust the horns under the top rail and then to toss it to one side then to serve the next, and the next, and the next in the same manner, and by that time the fence is low enough to jump over with ease, so the leader "rises equal to the occasion," and "the herd follows."

A second method is for one cow to retire to a distance of twenty yards or so, then, head down, to run full tilt against the fence; down it topples, and over they all go, rejoicing.

The third way is to place their breasts against the rails, and by dint of bending their hind legs and pushing with all their might, over goes the fence, stake, rider and all. The stake and rider stops the first method, but is no hindrance to the second and third.

After this, let no one say that the native Florida cow is not intelligent. Our belief is, if she were sent to college, she would graduate at the head of her class with honors. She is brought up like the city street gamin, and, like the gamin, soon becomes preternaturally cunning in learning to take care of herself.

Oxen, too, soon learn the same lesson. A saw-mill, located near our dwelling at the time of our settlement, employed four of these patient, much-enduring animals; all day long they hauled heavy logs, but at night they were turned loose to wander at will and forage for themselves where they could, a large bell that discoursed any thing rather than "sweet music" being secured around their necks to give their owners notice of their whereabouts.

Not alone their owners, however, as we soon learned to our sorrow; night after night for long, weary weeks, we were compelled to rise from our beds, sometimes three or four times in one night, to drive away from beneath our windows these same oxen, of whose presence there, in the midst of our corn and cow-peas, the clashing bells gave warning.

It was impossible to raise the fence high enough or build it strong enough to resist their determined assaults; there was no remedy. Not only had we no wish to incur the enmity of their owners by shooting the trespassers, but humanity forbade us to injure the innocent animals who were unconscious of wrong-doing; only for this latter consideration it might have fared ill with them, for our fences complied with the fiction of a "lawful, cattle-proof" fence, and the owner could not have collected damages for the death of his oxen.

Now, looking at the right or wrong, at the justice or injustice of this important matter, how does it stand?

The common law is supposed to give equal rights to all; it is supposed to protect one neighbor from the depredations of another. If a man comes upon our land when he is warned to stay off of it, he becomes a trespasser, and is liable to answer at law. If he steals our property, he is a criminal, and the law decrees a severe punishment for such an offense; if he sends his servant to rob or assault us, he is held responsible for the acts of his servant.

This is the law of the land, the law of all civilized people; yet how is it in Florida ?

A neighbor may not trespass on our inclosed lands, or rob us without putting himself under the ban of the law; but he can send forth his cattle, his hogs, his sheep, his horses, to trespass on our property and steal the hard won fruits of our toil, and we dare not retaliate. If we do, the law will punish us for objecting to the theft or protecting our property.

In our own immediate locality this past season, one leaping, pushing "leader-cow," in a roaming herd, caused so much damage and expense to others than its owner, that deep and general indignation was aroused; but what good did that do?

The offending animal is still at liberty to teach and lead other cows to "go and do likewise." Within a radius of two miles that one cow, worth fifteen dollars, compelled fences to be raised higher, at a cost of over one hundred dollars, besides destroying ten acres of cow-peas and corn, and several patches of sweet potatoes and young cabbages, so that the families depending upon them for their winter supply were obliged to purchase.

Let us be devoutly thankful that these two unjust, discriminating laws (fire and cattle), must ere long become things of the past; where they are not actually and legally repealed, public opinion and the rapid, onward march of improvement in agriculture and in stock will, of themselves, cause their ignominious suppression and disuse. It will not pay to burn one's own fences and trees, nor will it pay to turn costly cattle out to shift for themselves; hence, there will be less incentive to fire the woods or to allow cattle to roam abroad.

Meantime let us be thankful for another thing that nowadays, in these times of far-reaching improvements, neither the Florida farmer (nor any other) need longer be at the mercy of rail—no, nor even of board fences.

Having been taught by the most accomplished teacher in the world, Experience, after a goodly amount of lessons no less painful than costly, that the prosaic question of fences is one of great and pressing importance to every one outside of cities, and to none more than to the farmer, stockraiser, and fruit-grower, we have given this subject special attention with a view to ascertaining not only the best but the cheapest kinds of fencing for such purposes.

It is not often that the "best" and "cheapest" are identical; but, thanks to the inventive genius of these progressive days, we have succeeded beyond our most sanguine expectations; we have found both combined, and henceforth it is the settler's own fault if he is longer at the mercy of cows, horses, oxen, fires, or, worse than all, razor-backs.

Had we possessed a fence of either of the kinds we shall presently point out, in those early days we have referred to, we would not have been harassed, body and temper, and damaged in our property; we should have laughed at the vain efforts of our four-footed foes to invade our premises and steal our produce, and have defied the forest-fires to burn our fences.

There is a fence which has been only recently introduced to public notice, yet has already won from all the highest praise, even enthusiasm; in four States alone, last year, over twenty-five thousand miles of this fence were sold, and from every purchaser came back the most satisfactory reports. It is being extensively used in nearly every State in the Union, and also in Canada, with the same gratifying results to its manufacturers, the Georgia Fence Company, 28 Peach-tree Street, Atlanta, Georgia.

The Committee of Agriculture of the General Assembly of Georgia were invited to examine this fence officially, and they unanimously pronounced it "the greatest fence ever made."

The experienced Commissioner of Agriculture of the same State gives it this strong official indorsement

"After a careful examination of the 'Combination Wire and Picket Fence,' made by the Georgia Fence Company, I am of opinion that it offers to the farmers of the State several very decided advantages. It is very strong, durable, cheap, to some extent ornamental, and free from the objection so generally urged against the barbed wire fence; it can not injure stock."

And the Assistant Commissioner follows suit : "The fence question is becoming a serious one for the farmer. Being a farmer myself, and needing fences, I have been investigating, and have decided that the Wire and Picket Fence made by the Georgia Fence Company is the most practical and economical ever introduced."

Says a well-known banker on the same subject: "I am more than pleased with the fencing. Have investigated the subject pretty thoroughly, and it is decidedly the best for all purposes I have ever seen. It will turn any kind of stock, from a pig to a bull—is easily stretched, saves and improves the land in appearance and value."

And another says: "It stands as firm as the Rock of Gibraltar."

And now, let us see exactly what this valuable fence is made of: five double strands of galvanized wire, that is, ten wires woven in and out around pickets or slats.

The "Standard Farm Fence," four feet high, painted, with the pickets two to two and a half inches apart, is sold at five cents a running foot, and at this price costs less than the ordinary picket fence. It comes in rolls of fifty to one hundred feet long. The posts are set sixteen to twenty feet apart. Here is another of its cheap points, for many more posts are needed for board or picket fences.

The fence is secured to the posts with staples, and when you want to move it, all you have to do is to draw the staples, roll up the pickets and carry them where the new line is to be run. Two men can put up a mile of this fencing in a day, and the process is so simple that any one can do it. This is one of the rarest and most valuable features a fence can have; a movable fence is worth ten times as much as any other.

By cutting the rolls apart, nailing on strips top and bottom, with a brace running from one to the other, gates, large and strong, may be made of this accommodating fence.

While the usual "Farm Fence" is four feet high, it can be made higher to order, or the same result may be obtained by placing a board at the bottom, an excellent plan, especially for vegetable gardens and poultry-yards; and then, if the posts are run up six inches or so above the top line, and a barbed wire stretched along from one to another, the fence at once becomes proof against boys and tramps, no small consideration where poultry, fruits, and vegetables are concerned.

While the "Farm Fence " is very neat and trim when painted, ornamental and lawn fences, costing from fifteen to twenty-five cents a foot, are made to order on the same machine.

To sum up, this fence is very strong, cheap, durable, no chance to rot out any where, can not be blown down, will keep out stray animals, even rabbits, and keep in your own.

We have dwelt thus at length upon this fence subject, because experience has taught us its importance. We are not quite done yet, either. There are two more fences that are well worthy of attention, not only from the fact that they are really "home-made," in the truest sense of the term, inasmuch as the right to make them can be bought for a mere trifle, while the possession of the "farm-right" will save hundreds of dollars in fencing expenses.

One of these two, also a wire and picket fence, is made by the " Fairburn-Hulbert Fence Machine," which not only uses any kind and number of wires, with any length, or size pickets, willows, or canes, but can also be used for stretching the wires of any other kind of fencing.

It is a simple little machine, with no cogs, no castings or wheels; so simple in fact, that any one who buys a firmright can, if he chooses, rather than pay $10 for the readymade machine, make one for himself, with about $2 worth of lumber, a saw, hatchet, and auger, and it will be just as good as the one made by the manufacturer.

The little machine, when set on the ground at work, looks not unlike a wooden frog frantically endeavoring to leap backward at the end of several wire tethers. It is a comical little affair, but, like some other small people, capable of wonderful work.

The farm-right gives to the purchaser license to use the machine on his own lands for seventeen years; it costs for forty acres or less, $2, eighty acres, $4, one hundred acres, $5, and so increases up to one thousand acres at a cost of $17.50. These terms are certainly liberal enough to suit any one, especially as any number of machines may be made and operated on the same land at the same time.

This little machine, to which was awarded the highest premium at the North Central and South American Exposition in 1886, is a godsend to those who want a good, durable, fireproof fence made at home. Once possessing the machine, the wire is the only outside expense, a very light one, as the pickets and posts can be made from one's own timber, and in many cases by one's own "strong right arm," and fencing made *ad libitum*.

The same manufacturer (A. G. Hulbert, 904 Olive Street, St. Louis, Missouri) owns also another patent for "Homemade Wire-netting," in other words, an all-wire fence.

This netting fence, with galvanized wire, which is the cheapest in the end, costs from twenty-five to fifty cents a rod (sixteen and one half feet) according to the size of the mesh, and the right to make it is sold on the same terms as that of the wire and picket fence.

The posts are set sixteen or more feet apart; the wires strung up on the posts at the desired distances apart, parallel, of course; the outer or selvedge edges drawn tight, the others left slack; two strips, with spikes set in them as far apart as the meshes are to be, are fastened to the selvedge edges, the slack wires resting on the spikes; with this basis to rest on, the meshes are formed by passing a perpendicular wire back and forth.

The manner of working is very simple, and any farmhand of ordinary intelligence could make the meshes, and make them rapidly too.

Every body likes an all-wire fence, but heretofore it has been beyond the reach of people of small means. Now, however, thanks to Mr. Hulbert, it is placed within the grasp of every one.

It is scarcely needful to remark that the netting can be made coarse, if only cattle are to be fenced, or fine enough to turn rabbits, poultry, gophers, or other such "small game," and with a barbed wire at the top from post to post, will effectually turn the "small boy" also. It is well worth while to send for a circular, and find out all about it, and about every other kind of iron fence as well.

In making ordinary farm-gates it is a frequent fault to make them too heavy. Where an ordinary board fence is used, boards five inches wide, top and bottom, are quite strong for a ten-foot gate; for the ends use the same, one on each side, well secured with screw-bolts; on these nail four or five slats according to the height of the gate; and last, but not least, nail on the brace from the upper hinge to the toe of the gate, just exactly the reverse way from the common custom. It is a curious fact that so simple a thing as this is so seldom done right, when it is just as easy as to do it wrong. Then, to finish up, put on three perpendicular slats on the opposite side from the brace, and you will have a gate that will endure for years upon years.

The directions for the brace, from upper hinge to toe, and the vertical pieces opposite, also hold good for the wire and picket and netting fence gates.

Another important point: A gate that will open but one way is only half a gate; it ought to swing freely both ways; look out for this in getting your hinges.

And still another point: No one wants gates that sag or swing sideways, yet nearly every one has them so. There is no necessity for it, and here is how to avoid it.

There is little use in expending extra labor on the gateposts to keep them upright ; set them firmly at the start, and then set the gate properly and there will be no trouble.

Let the toe of the gate rest always solidly, either when shut or open, on a stone or block; with this simple arrangement the gate will not "draw" the post, nor sag; without it, it will, no matter what you do to the post; then, by putting the latch or fastening near the top, the gate is prevented from ever getting that side twist that is so unsightly in the majority of gates.

And now, in closing, a few words about preserving the posts:

"Many farmers believe that fence-posts set top end down last longer than those set butts down. Professor Beal, of Michigan Agricultural College, in a report of his experiments in post-setting, says that the average results are not in favor of inverted posts; in a word, he found on a fair average the results the same, whether set top or butts down. Small or medium posts, other things being equal, last longer than large ones. Red cedar is the preferred timber for posts; yellow cedar also endures well. Catalpa has of late years been largely employed for posts. Farmers who have soft timber to deal with try various processes for preserving the same when used for posts. Coal-tar has proven effective in many cases for preserving the post beneath the ground and crude petroleum above the ground. Petroleum penetrates the pores of the wood freely. A good preparation is to soak the posts thoroughly with petroleum and then hold it by an exterior coat of coal-tar. Charring the surface of the post has been practiced with satisfactory effect, first covering the post with hot coal-tar sufficiently high to reach a few inches above ground. Coal-tar alone applied to that portion of the post immediately above ground does not seem to do much good. The action of the weather appears to neutralize its preservative effect."

CHAPTER XXIII. HOUSEHOLD HELP.

Housekeeper's Trials. Florida Negro Servants. Amusing Experiences. Importance of the Problem of Domestic Help. How it may be solved.

Of course there are trials to be met; there is no use in denying it; for no one with common sense would credit such a denial. But the greatest of these in Florida is servants.

Every housekeeper, North, South, East, or West, knows full well that her path is not strewn with roses, whether she has servants to do the work (or make more work), or whether to her duties, as wife and mother, must be added those of cook and maid-of-all-work.

This latter is a position, or rather a combination of positions, held, and held competently too, by hundreds of thousands of women in this weary world of ours, and we have yet to see the first man who would have the patience and energy to meet so many varied calls upon his time and temper, nerves and strength, or to master and control so many different branches of duty.

In no country is the housekeeper's place a sinecure, and we do not claim for Florida an exception to the universal rule, although for obvious reasons the general work of keeping the house clean is certainly less than in the North, where constant winter fires, mud, rain and slush, add heavy items to the sum total of work that was heavy enough before.

But even in genial Florida, with her sunny, mild winters, houses must be kept in order, meals must be cooked, and, worse than all, dishes, pots, and pans must be washed three times every day, twenty-one times every week, ninety times every month—nearly eleven hundred times every year!

Did you ever think of that, with its weary, dreary monotony? Let some of the grumbling husbands and fathers think of this one item of the home-life work, and they will drop their heads abashed.

This is only one single item; the business of a housekeeper is a complicated one; a hundred different branches of skilled labor massed into one—a piece of complex machinery, each part fitting into some other part, working smoothly so long as all are kept under control and oiled; but creating a terrible clashing and confusion so soon as one portion is thrown out of gear.

We have tried it in the North with servants, trained, competent servants; we have tried it in the South with servants—not trained, and without them—and our verdict is, that the life of a housekeeper is full of trials and tribulations.

The worst trial the Florida housekeeper has to encounter is the total absence of competent, reliable help in house or kitchen. To be sure, there are in most sections plenty of so-called "cooks" to be had, and, generally, the new-comer who can afford to pay from eight to ten dollars per month, and has never been accustomed to doing her own work, makes it her first business to secure one of these wonderful assistants immediately — we call them "wonderful" advisedly, as will presently appear.

And if the "lady of the house" has cherished dreams of the famous old plantation "aunties," so neat, so tidy, so faithful, so respectful, so competent to do all and everything, then "great is the fall thereof."

Of a far different class from the faithful old slaves of yore are the present generation of free-born colored ladies and gentlemen.

Not long since one of the former was hailed in the streets of Jacksonville.

"Hello, Chloe! where are you going so fast?"

"Goin'? I'se goin' to see the lady what washes for the woman what lives in dis yere house."

The said "woman" being one of the elite of Jacksonville.

We have had "gentlemen" call at our house, making inquiry "if the young lady was at home?" and the first time, in our innocence and ignorance, sent our sister to meet the caller, supposing he had been engaged without our knowledge, to cut wood "or such."

And we smiled audibly when investigation revealed the truth, that the "young lady" was the colored girl employed in our kitchen. More than once, too, has our "young gentleman" been asked for by other gentlemen of his own sable hue.

The above was not the only ludicrous mistake made before we settled down resignedly to the knowledge that the employers were only white men and women, while the colored people were the ladies and gentlemen of the community; but we know all about it now, though an occasional smile is still inevitable.

How the terms ever came to be thus confused and reversed, no one can say; but it is certainly a very uncommon thing for the Florida negroes to use them in the conventional way, whether speaking to the white people, or in ordinary conversation among themselves. Occasionally they use the prefix "culled" to gentleman or lady; but as a rule this is omitted, to the frequent confusion of the ignorant "white folks," who know no better.

The older ones, those who spent at least the earlier years of their lives as slaves and received some training, are very scarce in Florida; they have, for the most part, remained near their old homes in the older States, and the few who have found their way hither have settled on homesteads of their own, and are as a class well-to-do, industrious citizens, recognizing their proper place in the community, and quite content to render due respect to their white neighbors, though they look down upon the "poor white trash," and in many instances justly so. And in return they receive the respect and support of those around them.

We could name several within a radius of five miles of our present home, who are the owners of broad lands, a horse and wagon, great fields of cotton and corn, flourishing groves and a comfortable house; such a property and such a home as thousands of educated men in the North and West, and East and South, toil all their lives without attaining to one half their value and comfort.

And in the older Southern States there are many such examples as these of the "poor, down-trodden negroes of the South," who are so industriously held up to view and waved aloft by certain desperate politicians of the North.

The status and treatment of the negro, under the same circumstances, is far better in the South than in the North, and it is full time that this fact should be universally acknowledged, as it is already by many of that race themselves.

But these negroes of the better class are the exceptions in Florida, and are very rarely available for servants.

The younger generation only "hires out" for household work, and all are "cooks," no matter whether they know how to make a loaf of bread, a pie, a pudding, or even to cook an ordinary "meat and vegetable dinner," or not; and it is more frequently "not" than otherwise.

The housekeeper who engages the ordinary Florida cook must make up her mind to "endure all things," or do her own work. The probability is strong that after a time she will come to the conclusion that the latter alternative not only involves less expense, but less wear and tear to nerve, temper, and strength.

We can perhaps best illustrate our meaning by narrating some of our own experiences in this path; it was not strewn with roses, although there was an oasis of laughter here and there along the weary road, especially after the ruts were numbered among the things of the past.

When our new Florida life commenced, we found the routine of household work far from pleasant, having never before been without trained, competent city servants to do it all for us.

Especially did we grow desperately weary of the disagreeable monotony of washing dishes, pots, and pans, three times every day. It was all uninviting enough; but this was the worst feature, as every housekeeper knows.

So, when a little colored girl, about eleven years old, whom we will call the Goddess—since she bore the name of one of those classic deities—came one day, and made request that we would keep her "to wash dishes and do errands," we gladly accepted the offer.

We soon discovered, however, that we had a very fair specimen of a self-willed, untamed savage in our kitchen, and that the task of reducing the same to subjection would require no small amount of patience and perseverance.

The Goddess was gifted with more than the usual acumen of her race, and was capable of learning, if she wished to, which is more than can be said of the majority; but her temper was sullen and obstinate in the extreme.

We managed to teach her to read and to write, after a fashion of her own, and very proud she was, and fond of displaying her accomplishments.

Our chief troubles were to teach her the meaning of the words "obey," and "order," and the fact that china would not bear as rough usage as iron, ideas which it seemed impossible for her to comprehend.

She possessed the proverbial characteristic of the negro race to perfection, an utter carelessness in regard to property, whether her own or another's, and an utter absence of thought for the morrow.

Once, after "saving up," to buy a much-needed calico dress, she expended the money in a glass card-receiver, very pretty, it is true, and of course exceedingly useful to her, only she broke it before she left the store. She returned home sadder, but no wiser.

Again, her savings were expended in a viniagrette bottle, with gilded chains in a gay ribbon, which went into the washtub the next day, and a gaudy fan which soon helped to feed the kitchen fire.

And when these purchases were made, we had been trying to train the Goddess for over four years!

To go back to her several oddities, which caused us many trials and tribulations: One day we heard a terrible clatter of breaking china, and, stepping out to the kitchen, found the Goddess performing a jig in the midst of a mass of broken plates, singing as she danced,

"Once there was six, now there's two;
Hoo, hoo, hoo! hoo, hoo, boo!"

On another occasion, inquiry being made as to the disappearance of a handsome china bowl, her eyes twinkled and her teeth gleamed as she answered,

"'Pears like it hopped off de table, and went to 'Kingdom Come.'"

As it was at first, it continued to the last, a matter of perfect indifference as to how much destruction her rough handling caused.

She had a habit that became very annoying of asking for any thing she happened to take a fancy to, and answered every reproof with,

"I'd sooner ast than take;" and that was true—the Goddess was honest.

It was a great disadvantage to her well-being as well as to ours, that her family lived only a few miles away, and their influence and example were constantly drawing her back into her old ways.

Whenever allowed to visit her old home, even for one day, she would return with the buttons cut from her dress and pins inserted in their place, and every little article of adornment that had been given her, ribbons, collars, hats, handkerchiefs, shared the same fate. "Mom tuck 'em," was the explanation; even her dresses were carried off when "Mom" or her elder sisters came to see her.

Looking at the full moon one night, soon after she came into our household, through a powerful field-glass, her first experience of the kind, the Goddess startled us by a shriek, and dropping the glass, turned a summersault backward up the portico-steps, and lay there gasping with her eyes shut. Presently she opened them, and raised herself cautiously, looked up at the far-away luminary, then at us and the field-glass, in a ludicrously bewildered way, then drawing a long breath, exclaimed,

"Oh, Lawd! I done thought fur shure it was tumblin' on top of me! I was skeert most to death!"

Familiarity breeds contempt; finding that the dreaded luminary still remained at a safe distance, the Goddess proceeded to tell us about the man who lived up there; how once, long, long ago, a bad black man had gone out to pick up a load of wood on Sunday, when the Lord had told him not to, and how, to punish him, he had been sent to live alone in the moon, and forever walk about with a load of wood on his back; and how, ever since, he had been trying to make other folks bad so as to have some company.

This, we afterward found, was the negro explanation of the far-famed "man in the moon," one of their many superstitions.

Once a question was propounded to the Goddess apropos of the setting sun.

"How is it that the sun sets over there, in front of you, and rises in the east, behind you?"

A puzzled expression stole over those dark features, and the short, crinkly hair was rubbed up on end. The Goddess had put her thinking-cap on, and this was the result, triumphantly announced:

"Why, it done goes through a hole in the earth, and comes out on the other side. In course I knows that, pooh!"

Her expression of scorn was overwhelming; how could we have supposed her so ignorant? She knew, of course she did!

Our smile, though irrepressible, was rather grim. We had been training that "young idea how to shoot" for over two years, and this was a fair specimen of the result, except for the reading, which was more successful.

The Goddess had not so exalted an idea of her race as had some of her contemporaries. She had an unpleasant habit of throwing herself into all kinds of uncouth attitudes, and of twisting tongue and features to correspond.

On one especially exasperating occasion, the *mater* exclaimed, "Why will you act so like a monkey?"

On went the thinking-cap again, and out of its folds emerged this remark, made in all earnestness:

"Well, niggers is half-monkeys, anyway. I knows it; I s'pose that's the reason."

"Half monkeys! Goodness, child, what ever put that idea into your head?" was the amazed query.

"Seed 'em in Miss Helen's book; monkeys hangin' to trees, jest like niggers, only niggers aint got no tails; done chopped 'em off, I s'pose. Some of the monkeys had n't no tails; they was most all niggers."

The *mater* was worsted; she was no match for this unconscious Darwinian, this primitive evolutionist, and, hastily smoothing the corners of her mouth, beat a hasty retreat. A laugh "loves company" as well as misery.

For five years we labored patiently to make something better of the Goddess. Several times she was sent home in disgrace, but as often returned with the plea to be allowed one more trial.

She had some good qualities, and we sought to train her in the way she should go; but it was of no use. Early training and outside influences prevailed, and she went more and more in the way she should not go, until at last we were compelled to give her a final dismissal.

Then followed an interregnum of weary housework again, until we grew desperate enough to seek another assistant.

Then appeared a "cook" who did not even know how to fry potatoes, but was anxious to learn.

She could wash dishes and clothes, but took her lessons in cooking standing in the doorway with her back to the stove, while we watched the dinner; if a particle of fat flew or "spit" from the frying-pan, our cook fled from the kitchen; she "wasn't goin' to be burnt up 'fore her time, 'deed she was n't!"

Several times she took to her bed for several days, but entertained company gaily; and once, after we had waited on her and carried her meals to her, she arose, brought the dishes into the kitchen for us to wash, and departed to visit a neighbor.

We bore much for the sake of being spared the dishwashing and hunting up a washer-woman; but when, with the Christmas dinner on the stove, and stranger-guests in the parlor, we found the fire out, the kitchen deserted and our "cook" strolling in the woods picking flowers, we felt that even our patience had reached its limit.

She departed the next day, a much-abused victim.

Our next servant could cook plain dinners, with some superintendence; but we "wore her heart out a-washin' dishes," and she soon vanished.

"Mighty kind folks," was the verdict reported to us; "but, they'se got too much style for me; big plates for dinner, little plates fer termaterses, and more plates fer pudden; it jest wore the heart out o' me." For a family of four members, her heart appeared easily "wore out."

Our next cook really was a cook, and had acted as such in a Jacksonville hotel kitchen, and was competent to do all and more than all that was required of her, so we did not grudge her the $10 a month she asked, albeit her predecessors had been content with $8—and well they might!

So we drew a long breath of delighted relief; but, alas! it was short-lived.

A cook we had, it was true, but also an invalid; fully one third of the time she was in bed, with her work left for us to do, and herself to be waited on in addition.

She occupied the "servants' quarters," a detached room back of the kitchen; and the groanings and gruntings that issued thence were simply appalling. They were intermitting too; we soon discovered that when no one was supposed to be near the groans ceased, but were resumed the moment our footsteps proved us to be within hearing.

While remonstrated with concerning these unpleasant noises, her reply was, "The Lawd made some folkses to grunt when theyse sick, and some folkses not to grunt. I'se one o' the gruntin' sort. Must grunt—oh, Lawd! oh, oh!"

And she did, there was not the least doubt of that; she was a proficient, even a razor-back would have retired into a corner, *disgruntled*.

This was one of the crosses we had to bear with our new cook, and another was—her pipe; we succeeded in exiling it from the kitchen itself, but between whiles tobacco smoke reigned.

The end of it all was, that we finally concluded to be resigned and do our own work, as being the easiest method, having a woman to come in and do the washing and scrub floors or do extra work; and we have held to that resolve ever since; it is certainly more peaceful.

The washer-women, like the Florida cows and "cooks," are "curous critters;" they are usually moderately good washers, if watched; but it is very rare to find a good ironer among them; the housekeeper must, as a rule, makeup her mind to do her own ironing.

The charge for "a wash" is from fifty to seventy-five cents, and the same amount (it varies as to localities) is asked for a day's work. But a wash is "a wash," whether finished by noon or by night; in the latter case more pay may sometimes be expected; but in the former no deduction is made—that is a different case altogether.

Nor can they ever be depended upon to be punctual to any set day; like the majority of their race, and, unhappily, many of our own, they have no idea of the sanctity of a promise; they are quick to make one, and as quick to break it. It is almost useless to expect one to come on a Monday; they are usually "too sick"—cause, too much shouting and singing at church on Sunday, their evening meetings frequently being prolonged till nearly midnight.

Once, on a special occasion, we engaged a young negro girl to come and iron; she was a total stranger, a newcomer in the neighborhood, and we knew of her only by hearsay.

As she approached the house later than she should have been, she heard the sound of a piano in the parlor, and, instead of directing her footsteps to the kitchen, came in through the front door and startled the performer by suddenly appearing in the parlor. She did not even utter the usual greeting, "Howdy?" but stood silently beside the pianist, who was practicing a hymn.

"Pooh! I don't like that! Play something else right smart!" exclaimed this cool specimen, a self-satisfied graduate of the Atlanta Colored College, as we learned afterward.

The player turned round; it had taken her some time to recover from the bewilderment of the unexpected apparition.

"Your work is waiting for you out in the kitchen," she remarked, mildly. "Go out through the hall; the kitchen is across the piazza."

"Oh, yes, I know the way; but I aint in no hurry. I want you to play something real lively. I can play the pianny, a woman in Atlanta learned me."

The quiet, decisive closing of the piano was her reply, and she stalked away in dignified silence.

She had been at her ironing scarcely an hour, when a "lady" called to see her, and she left a half-ironed garment on the board while she strolled with her visitor to the gate; she was absent fully an hour, and then returned with the announcement that she "reckoned she wouldn't iron any more that day; for she wanted to take a walk."

It is needless to say she was given free permission to go, and to remain indefinitely.

Now, this girl was impudent of *malice prepense*; she considered herself a little better than white people, and intended to assert her opinions.

But, aside from the intentional transgressors, it is very curious to note the entire absence of all idea of the fitness of things, even in the most faithful and respectful of their class.

We have been frequently asked, "What do you ask for makin' a dress like that?" or, " Give me that sack you've got on, please ma'am."

The request to sell articles of dress, or furniture, or to make the former "on the machine," as if it were a very trifling favor, is of common occurrence.

No disrespect is intended; it is a relic of the by-gone slave days, when the mistress cut out and made the dresses for the slaves, gave them all that they had, and taught them all that they knew.

Verily, in the light of our own experience, we pity those old-time plantation mistresses from the bottom of our heart.

Many of the odd, familiar ways that shock our Northern notions are simply the remains of the old-time familiarity that necessarily existed between those brought up from their earliest childhood in daily and hourly contact, even though they occupied the relative positions of mistress and slave; the latter frequently was treated as an humble friend, and proved not unworthy of the trust.

What Northern servant would dream of entering her mistress's room uninvited and unannounced, and, because she had nothing else to do, it being evening, should throw herself at full length on the floor, and go to sleep there for an hour or two? Yet this is an experience passed through by the writer, who, though astonished and amused, knew full well that not the least disrespect, but the contrary, was the governing motive.

"My ole missus liked it; we was both on us lonesome," the unconscious culprit remarked.

Again, one colored woman we know, a hard-working respectable, sensible woman, recently remarked in good faith:

"I does wish you'd like to take my gal; you knows such heaps o' things, all of you; and you could show her lots. I'd like you to larn her to play on the pianny just like you does, and to sew on the merchine, and to do heaps o' things. My! but I does wish you wanted her!"

She was thoroughly in earnest and had not the least idea that any one could take exception to her words or wishes, or that they were in any way unreasonable.

Perhaps the most satisfactory—nay, we should more correctly say, the least unsatisfactory—help the Florida housekeeper can find among the native colored population, as at present generally constituted, is a "dish-washer," pure and simple; namely, a boy of about twelve or sixteen years of age, who can wash dishes, pots, and pans, prepare vegetables, make fires, carry wood, scour the floors, and at odd times do light out-of-door work, such as hoeing and weeding the flowers.

From three to five dollars a month are the wages usually paid the "dish-washer," and, if a good-tempered, obedient boy, who is above the average intelligence of his class, can be obtained, he will lighten the burden of housekeeping wonderfully. We tried two of them once; they were not of this latter kind, though.

One was a mulatto boy, who was bright enough, and easily taught his duties, but disobedient, indisposed to work and very sullen in disposition. He departed suddenly one day, by special permission, after threatening to horsewhip his mistress because she opined that the corners of the kitchen required sweeping as well as the center.

There is an odd incident connected with this promising youth, which so aptly illustrates the fondness of his race for high-sounding names, that we can not refrain from inserting it here.

He had two sisters. One, by the assistance of a fun-loving white neighbor, was named "E Pluribus Solus," to the intense delight and pride of her parents. The second one was called Jettica, and when, a little later, the baby's complexion promised to belie her name, proving yellow instead of jet, the misnomer was corrected by the same obliging neighbor, who made it still more striking by the addition of Errata.

E Pluribus Solus and Jettica Errata are now stylish "young ladies."

Our second dish-washer feared to go out in the rain, at least that was the excuse given for a four hours' absence on a near-by errand—marbles and two other boys constituting the "fear." He preferred fishing to working; loved to go to sleep in the wood-box, while the fire burned out; considered it a superfluity to wipe dishes after having washed them, or to wash the outside as well as the inside of pots or frying-pans; and finally, after secretly breaking and hiding a valuable tool, was "took very bad sick," and departed—to fish all the afternoon, remain away all night, and return the next morning, to be amazed at the mandate to take up his clothes and go forthwith to his home.

But still there are some reasonably satisfactory boys to be found, and we would advise our help-hunters to look for them, and not to be discouraged too easily. "If at first you don't succeed, try, try again," is a good adage to put in practice here, both with regard to the dish-washers and cooks; perseverance may reveal a treasure, rare as treasures always are.

As might well be anticipated, the code of morality here, as elsewhere, does not stand high among the majority of the colored race; and this fact, with all its consequences, the housekeeper must be prepared to face as an irremediable evil, and make the best of it.

Their ideas of some very important subjects are fairly and humorously illustrated by the following, taken from a current issue of the great Florida daily. *The Times Union*, of Jacksonville—an actual occurrence:

"Late yesterday afternoon a colored man went into the county clerk's office, and finding Mr. B. in charge, asked for a marriage license. The usual questions were asked him by Mr. B. as to the age of the woman he wanted to marry, and if her former husband was dead or alive.

"She's been divorced," replied the colored gentleman.

"'Well,' replied Mr. B., knowing as he does that frequently negroes separate without going through the form of getting a divorce, "have you got a certified certificate of her divorce? If not, I can not issue a license under the law until you get such certificate from the clerk of the county she came from."

"The negro replied in the negative, and went out in search of the woman to see if she had a certificate of divorce, being considerably wrought up. She went into the office with the man and was asked if she had the required certificate, to which she answered in the negative, when Mr. B. refused to grant the license. This angered the woman, and she railed out at Mr. B,:

"'I guess I knows dat I hab a 'vorce, and kin prove it, kase I hab had four childruns since I quit my husband."

"She thought that this statement would clear things up with Mr. B. Notwithstanding the children, the license was again refused, and the unhappy couple took their departure, a wiser but a badly disappointed pair."

We have now said enough to reveal the condition of household help as at present found in Florida, with rare exceptions.

In the "*old régime*" the South was famous for its good cooks; the wives and daughters of the planters vied with each other in making their homes attractive. They were wise in their generation and knew the royal road to a man's heart, so they taught the most promising of the slaves how to cook, and allowed them to do nothing else. Hence, with good teachers, their whole time, energy and thought, given up to the business of their lives, and with an unlimited amount of that practice which alone "makes perfect," it is not to be wondered at that the genuine old plantation cooks excelled in their art.

But after the *new régime* set in these cooks were scattered abroad, and there remained no one whose interest it was to train up the rising generation in the way of the "good cook."

The Florida State papers are full of horticultural discussions and plans for the furtherance of fruit culture, crops, freight rates, railroads, politics—every thing that concerns the sterner sex; but all the time there is one numerous and powerful class of their readers whose pressing needs they ignore almost entirely.

The question of more help and competent house servants for the Florida home is a grievous one, and bears heavily on every frail, educated, refined wife and daughter in the land, and should be earnestly heeded by every husband and father, even if only from the selfish considerations which actuated a certain German we once heard of.

He had paid a housekeeper for some years, and finally married her, explaining that he did so because he had found out that "A vife is cheaper dan a vomans; you has to pay de vomans to do sometiuks; but you no has to pay de vife to do ebery tinks."

We could point out to-day several men, who call themselves gentlemen, who not only leave their delicate wives without even the poor help that might be secured, but also expect them to cook, wash dishes, and wait on all the company it may suit their royal will to bring into the house, and to cook and wash dishes for the colored laborers whom they hire to do their own work for them.

Such men as these will ultimately discover, as the old German did, that "a vife is cheaper dan a vomans," and that a mother's love and care can not be duplicated for their children.

Out-door labor can be supplied readily enough. There are very few colored men who can not plow, chop wood, and readily earn the wages asked, from $15 to $20 a month. But, as we have seen, the in-door work wears a far different aspect: it is a problem that presses for a solution.

In Florida are thousands of housekeepers crying out, "Give us servants, or we die!" and in the frozen, crowded North and East are other thousands of intelligent, capable, respectable young women, crying out, "Give us work, or we die!"— American girls, the daughters of hard-working farmers or mechanics, who would fain help themselves and their parents if they could, who are quite willing to "go out to service," but whose better educated and more refined tastes shrink from close social contact with the rougher, uneducated, foreign class of servants, who at present have almost a monopoly of such work at the North.

Now, here in Florida we have just the very homes they are looking for, where the work is not too heavy, and where they would stand "alone in their glory," entirely free from any possible contact with the ordinary Northern servant; and how more than welcome would be the work of their neat, deft hands to the discouraged, overworked, worn-out housekeeper, who has been compelled to be "all things to every body" in the household. It is just this latter point that makes it so hard: not a wife only, not a mother only, not a chamber-maid only, not a maker and mender of garments only, not the caterer and caretaker only, not the cook and dish-washer only, but all these things combined. But how to bring them together, these two classes, who so sorely need each other, yet are blindly groping in the dark along two diverging roads?

We have thought much and seriously on this subject, for it deeply concerns the welfare and the happiness of every refined household in Florida; nay, even the very life of the delicate wife and mother, whose strength is not equal to the unaccustomed strain of "doing her own work," with all that it entails.

And we would respectfully submit for the earnest consideration of our Florida readers, the outcome of our meditations, in the hope that some one can suggest a better plan, and that it may be acted upon with all the energy and promptitude that the emergency demands.

In every county of the State there is, or will shortly be a Fruit-growers' Association, and the great majority of their members are husbands and fathers, who should certainly have the welfare of their families at heart.

Florida has also a State Fruit-growers' Association, and a Farmers' Alliance.

Let these, as bodies already organized and in working order, take this matter up and look into it until they fully realize its vital importance, not only to the community at large, but to each one of themselves as individuals; and then let them act promptly and efficiently in their official capacities.

Let these associations select as their agents, in each of the larger cities of the North and West, a well-established, thoroughly reliable Labor Bureau or Intelligence Office.

Having accomplished this, the preliminary step, let them notify the various County Associations that the secretary, or some other official specially appointed for the purpose, will receive and forward all applications from communities or families in need of servants.

The County Associations, in their turn, should publish in their local papers and at their meetings that they stand ready to receive such applications, not only from their own members, but from any responsible parties in their county, and that terms of service, qualifications, and wages offered, should be distinctly stated in all such applications, and guarantee of good faith given.

Then, if the agents appointed in the North and West would advertise largely in the cities and country towns, as Florida Service Bureaus, the problem of competent help, not only indoors but out-of-doors, would be solved.

The seeker and the sought would be brought together; thousands of needy, deserving persons, singly, or in families, provided with comfortable homes, and the life of the weary Florida housekeeper relieved of its worst trials and tribulations.

Of course there would be many points to settle, as to fees paid by applicants for servants, transportation for the latter and other necessary expenses; but these could be easily and smoothly arranged by the several associations acting together.

There is one point, however, that should be fully understood by both parties, the employer and the employee, for without such clear understanding from the outset, discontent and insubordination on the part of the servant are very likely to ensue; several such instances have come under our own observation.

The trouble is just here. When white servants, whether men or women, see neighbors whom they recognize to be no more educated or refined than themselves received as guests of the family, they are apt to rise up in rebellion and claim the same treatment for themselves.

They can not see that though they may really be the intellectual superiors of the rough neighbor, whose ways are not as their ways, yet the social status of the latter is different, inasmuch as a land-owner or householder, who is free to come and go of his own will, ranks higher than the hired servant in the house of the employer, to whom duty and obedience are due. Hence, trouble crops up, unless the servant is unusually reasonable and hard to spoil.

We know of one instance, where a man and wife were brought to Florida as servants; the man had been a small farmer and gardener, the woman had been brought up as a servant, and had been such in the family of a friend of their employer in the North. Many of the neighbors in their new home were of their own class; but a new country and sparse settlements are great levelers of "class," and when these servants saw people "no better than themselves" received as guests, they rebelled, and finally, when the humbler neighbors called on their mistress, they were either turned away from the house without the knowledge of the latter, who was an invalid, or else were invited into the kitchen and detained there under the same circumstances as kitchen company.

The result was the sore-offending of the neighbors, who were led to believe they were so treated by orders of the "grand folks."

And finally admittance to the family table being refused, the husband and wife helped themselves from the dishes about to be placed on the table, and sat down to their meals at the self-same moment that the family sat down to theirs—"no second table for them; no, indeed! "

"Up North" they had never dreamed of claiming equality; but here, with superior education and habits to many of the neighbors, who were treated as equals by courtesy, they became demoralized, till finally, when patience ceased to be a virtue and they were dismissed, they went about slandering the kindest, most considerate mistress that servant ever had, as well as her friends before mentioned, whom the woman had formerly served.

So let this point be fully set forth, that the white servant engaging to serve in a Florida home will be well and kindly cared for, but must be content to occupy the same status that he or she would occupy under the same conditions in the North, and not claim the privileges of a family guest.

This is a trouble that will gradually remedy itself as the number of white servants in the State increases, and, until that desirable period shall have arrived, the method we have outlined above must be applied.

For those who may prefer foreign servants, or desire to settle families or colonies near them, to serve as such on occasion, the Commissioners of Emigration of New York hold the door open.

The emigrants land at Castle Garden, New York, and here is established a Labor Bureau which finds employment for the thousands of emigrants who arrive in the United States without definite plans or destination, who desire employment, yet do not know how to obtain it.

Every year this Bureau settles thousands of house servants and farm hands in good comfortable homes. In 1885, for instance, it found employment for over fifteen thousand, over six thousand of whom were women, and here too Florida may find a partial solution of this labor problem.

Few Catholics, however, can be induced to make their homes in this State at present, because there are very few Catholic churches.

The wages usually contracted for range from eight to ten dollars a month for house servants, and from eleven to fourteen dollars for the farm hands during "the busy season," and this is always in Florida. The employer usually pays the transportation charges.

An application addressed to the "Labor Bureau, Castle Garden, New York," stating exactly what is wanted, and the terms offered, will seldom fail to find satisfactory reply.

CHAPTER XXIV. TRIALS AND TRIBULATIONS.

Insect Foes, and How to Eight Them. Harmless Lizards and Frogs. The "Bugaboo" of Snakes.

Servants are by no means the only trials encountered by the Florida housekeeper, any more than by her sisters in other sections.

There are some tribulations incident to all housekeeping, and others incident to country homes only, that is, to any extent.

Foremost among these are the numerous, all-pervading tribe of insects.

City housekeepers usually are comparatively free from them; but all country housekeepers are more or less annoyed by them during the summer season, and as, in Florida, this season practically includes three fourths of the year at least, of course the Florida housewife is seldom entirely free to lay down her weapons and rest from the conflict.

In the front rank of these household foes—these uninvited guests—not only in size, but in the universal repugnance they inspire, stand the roaches.

They are not the mild little intruders of the cities of the colder climates, the "water-back" guests of the kitchen range, or the so-called Croton-bugs of New York City, but of another family altogether. We have seen them occasionally in the country "up North," but never in a city home.

There are two distinct kinds: one, the larger, is a plump, well-conditioned fellow, with a shiny black coat; he is fat, but, unlike the majority of stout people, very active and full of works; whether good or bad we will not say, since we do not doubt that he acts up to "his lights," which is more than can be said of the great mass of human beings. This black beetle-like roach has a peculiarity all his own, a strong one, by which you may know when he has met with an accident and become damaged in a collision, whether it be with your own foot or some other weapon; when "crushed to earth," down-trodden and oppressed, he gives one the idea of having committed suicide by means of prussic acid, or oil of almonds, so powerful and all-pervading is that scent on the air.

We found out all about it, to our sorrow once, soon after our arrival in Florida.

We had not yet become inured to the big black "critters" that sometimes appeared suddenly from behind pictures, or brackets, or other dark places; and one evening, when the hall was filled with a band of serenaders, a member of our family instinctively attacked the enemy, and all too successfully, as a pungent odor of almonds presently informed the guests that a murder had been done. There was a good deal of fun made of the attacking party by those who had grown wiser from experience, and after that the big black was allowed to flee unmolested, especially if company was "to the fore."

The other roach is not a perfumer by profession, and hence less hesitation is felt in dispatching him at all times and seasons, provided you can catch him, for he is very like a flea, "you put your finger on him, and he isn't there."

Though innocent of manufacturing perfumery, he is even more exasperating than his brother; he is a "grower" of wings, and right well does he understand how to use them. He thinks nothing of making a catapult of his wings, and dashing his long, slender brown body at full speed across the room, caring not at all whether he alights on the wall, table, book, or your own shrinking head or shoulders.

Possibly it is strange, but it is none the less true that some people object to such flighty familiarity, and hastily vacate the premises, or else energetically summon a braver or more stolid companion to "kill that horrid flying roach." Many and many a time has the writer been thus summoned to the rescue, and usually returned from the fray with the triumphant exclamation, "We have met the enemy, and they are ours." Not always though; sometimes the chase is long, and finally unsuccessful.

These flying roaches live more generally out of doors, than do their big black brothers, but often manage to force their way in-doors, especially if there is a bright light to attract them; like the June or harvest-bugs of the North, they work their way into the house in spite of netted doors and windows, and no one can tell how they do it.

The perfumer, however, while found out of doors also, in rotten wood or piles of trash, makes his home by preference in the house, in dark closets and corners, and sallies out at night on foraging expeditions.

Meantime, during the day, he has a nice quiet luncheon in the closet, if it happens to be one in which provisions are carelessly left open, or in which clothes are hung.

Just here is a point of which our new Florida housekeeper should take heed, and perhaps some of the older ones too, for we did not discover it ourself for several years, and there may be some who have not yet done so. It is this, that a great deal of the damage done to clothing while hung up in dark closets, must be placed to the account of these same roaches.

Again and again we found clothing that was only used occasionally, yet frequently taken out, shaken, and aired, badly eaten here and there, sometimes the holes were small and round, again, large and irregular. We wondered how the moths found time to do it, when they were so often disturbed, and how it was that they continued so active even during the cool winter months; for of course we laid all such transgressions at the door of the poor moths, although we very seldom found any of the silky-web traces of their presence.

But by and by we began to notice that there were always roaches, young or old, close at hand, when we moved the clothing, and then we remembered that once upon a time, in Central America, we had been put to loss and annoyance in the same way, and that these same big black roaches abounded there even more than here.

Then we watched more closely, and finally detected a roach in the act of eating a hole in a mohair skirt.

One of the things that first led us to suspect the roaches were the real culprits was the fact that the holes were always made where something had been spilled on the garment, and were large or small according to the spot; and we knew that moths are perfectly indifferent to such delicacies as soiled garments; new ones taste just as good to them, and they prefer wool, while roaches like the taste of "old clothes" and are indifferent as to whether their delectable dish be served up on silk, wool, or cotton.

That had been another of our puzzles, why moths, for the first time in our experience, should eat cotton and silk; we had found no more trouble in keeping them at a distance from winter clothing, regularly put up for the summer, than we had in our Northern home. Little bits of raw cotton soaked in turpentine and placed here and there inside the packages and chests containing the clothing, served their purpose as effectually in the one place as in the other. Turpentine is the best safeguard against moths that we have ever known, the only one, in our experience, that has proved a perfect protection.

We were a long while, as we have said, in unearthing the real culprits, and if we had only suspected the truth sooner the loss of many a valuable garment could have been prevented.

Henceforth we fought the roaches more vigorously than ever, and kept a sharper watch on all our clothing not in daily use.

We would not, however, lead our readers to infer that the roaches of Florida are much if any more numerous than in the majority of country places; we have seen them, smaller in size, to be sure, but greater in numbers, in seaside hotels and other summer resorts, and sometimes even in farm-houses at the North.

The peculiar features in Florida are their size, their wings, pungent odor, and their fondness for clothing and books.

"Books?" Yes, even books, when placed on shelves, or in book-cases, and not frequently disturbed, will soon look as if they had the smallpox. The substance used by the binders in glazing the covers finds particular favor with the roach family, and they eat it off in spots here and there.

Stout paper covers should be put on all books that are placed on shelves, if a fresh, neat cover is desired; handsomely bound books for the parlor may, however, be put out on tables without fear; we have never seen one, left out in this way, that was touched by roaches, they prefer shelter to work in.

It was a long time before we discovered how to outwit the roaches and ants who foraged at will among our jellies and marmalades.

No matter how securely we deemed them pasted or tied up in strong paper covers, they ate through it. Then we tried pasting strong muslin over the tops of the jelly glasses in addition to the paper; result just the same. Next, we soaked the paper in alum-water. That checked the industrious little ant, but the big burly roach kept right on in the " even tenor of his way," and his way was a very bad and exasperating way for us.

But there seemed to be no help but to let him do as he would with such of our jellies and sweetmeats as could not be provided tin or cork tops.

At last, however, we had a happy idea. We had tried paper made stiff with paste, and paper without paste, and we had tried muslin pasted tight over the glasses, but all in vain; it remained to test muslin, pure and simple, tied over the mouth of jar or glass, without paste, white of egg, or any other addition. And this last experiment, to our comfort and relief, proved effective, and all annoyance from this source ceased at once; the addition of a paper cover under the muslin excludes all dust, and, if they are kept clean, no speck of the sweetmeat allowed to touch them, both roaches and ants will pass them by in silent contempt.

No Florida house need be "overrun" with roaches. There are several effective ways of waging war on them and keeping down the enemy, and no more annoyance need be experienced from their presence than one has been accustomed to in the old home.

Clean out the closets every three or four months, and dash plenty of scalding water over the shelves and into the cracks between the boards, if there are any. It is far better to see that there are no cracks there to form a harbor for your enemies. Even if the house is only a box house, and plaster or building-paper can not be afforded, we would at least urge that the closets should be lined with the latter; it would save far more in work and worry than it would cost in money.

In the mean time, between the scalding visitations—and here "mean time" designates all the time—keep powdered borax and sugar mixed together, standing about on the shelves and in the dark places; the lids of the round wooden match-boxes are very handy for this purpose. Roaches will not eat borax alone, but when sugar is mixed with it they certainly do, notwithstanding some statements we have seen to the contrary. We have seen them eating it, have seen them sauntering slowly along afterward in a weary, don't-care sort of manner, very different from their usual lively gait, and a little later have seen them calmly reposing on their shiny backs, their once active legs folded over their bosoms in a pathetic way, that ought to have made us sad, but we are fain to confess had rather the opposite effect.

So we know that the combination of borax and sugar is a powerful weapon, and as it is not injurious to children or pet animals, and is neat and cleanly to stand around on the shelves and in the closets, we would advise its being kept there all the time, in preference to any other of the numerous mixtures recommended for the same purpose, although we know two of them, "Sure-pop" and "Rough on Rats," to be good; but these, the latter especially, must be carefully handled, as they are poisons.

Persian insect-powder, occasionally blown from the little insect-powder guns that are sold by every druggist, costing about fifteen cents, is also very effective, puffed about in closets, bureau-drawers, and book-cases.

Well, we have dwelt long enough among the roaches; let us pass on to the other " insect pests," that Florida's foes love to elevate into veritable bug-bears.

"Fleas?" Yes, of course there are some fleas. Did you ever see a country home where there were not at some seasons more or less fleas ? We never have, at least; nay more, we have seen more fleas in New Jersey than we have ever seen in Florida.

They are not the scourges that many are led to believe.

During our nine years' residence in Florida we have been only very occasionally annoyed by fleas, and then only for a short time continuously.

For the major part of the year we would not even know that there were such creatures in existence, did not our memory serve to remind us of the fact, and during the very height of flea-life (the spring months) an occasional warm kiss from flea-lips is the height and breadth of their offending.

The worst of a flea is his ubiquity: he gives you a nip, you "put your finger on him, and he is n't there;" no, he is somewhere else, hard at work, looking up another nice, tender place for a second bite. You rub and scratch, and he immediately proves his non-relationship to a leopard by changing his spots; he changes them often, with bewildering frequency, and

> "The wonder was, and still the wonder grew,
> That one small" flea could so much damage do.

But when one has looked into the mysteries of flea-life, and has learned that it takes him but half a minute, or less, to digest the delicate drop of blood he robs you of and get ready for another, the wonder ceases, and it is easy to understand how one flea is just as good—or as bad—as a dozen.

But he has a conqueror, before a puff of whose breath he lies down and dies very quickly. Shoot him with the insect-powder gun, and you will have no further trouble.

Does he creep into the bed and nip your toes until they feel as if you had been walking in a bed of nettles? Put the little gun beneath your pillow, and puff the powder down under the covers; that will change the direction of his energies and terminate speedily the base attack on your understanding.

Does he crawl up your sleeve, or down your back, and adorn you with a cluster of lumps more pronounced than pleasant? Then shoot him once, again; let but the tiniest atom of the powder touch him, and his race is run.

So, even if the fleas ever do become troublesome, as they do sometimes in some sections, no one need dread them very much; keep the insect-powder and gun on hand for use when wanted, and the enemy is easily routed.

The powder used to be very expensive, and then its free use was a serious matter; but now that the pyrethrum is raised in the United States it has become much cheaper; instead of one dollar per pound, which was charged for the imported, we have recently seen it placed on sale by grocers and wholesale druggists at thirty-five cents a pound. It should be kept in light jars or bottles, and, when genuine, is so powerful that it will admit of being mixed with one third its bulk of flour, starch, or some other powdered medium, and yet be entirely effective.

Whether at home, North or South, in hotels, or in traveling, we would advise as a constant companion and frequent "friend in need" the little powder-gun, well loaded for use. Those who have not tried it can not conceive how much it adds to one's comfort, nor how much better one can sleep if a few puffs of powder are sent abroad among the bedding of the sleeping-car or steamer berths before stepping into them.

It is charged by some that the presence of dogs or cats in the house involves the presence of fleas also. That this is a "true bill," so far as dogs are concerned, can scarcely be doubted, unless, indeed, the animal is a pet and is frequently combed and washed. Fleas love dirt, and will breed industriously in the fur of a dog, if allowed to work their own sweet will; then, of course, the result is an excess of population, and internecine wars, during which the weaker are driven beyond the home borders to seek their living, just exactly on the same principle that the crowded European countries send their excess of population over to the United States to seek new fields for their enterprise.

And the enterprise of the flea family certainly exceeds that of the majority of the human family: they believe that the world owes them a living, and they take it wherever they find it.

But though this is a true bill that dogs do scatter fleas about the house, it is equally as true in other places as in Florida.

But as to the charge against cats in the household, we must file a demurrer. Cats, without exception, are the neatest and most cleanly of all animals, and one that is made a pet of and allowed the run of the house, will give its owner no trouble by importing fleas for general distribution; it will shelter very few in its clean, soft fur, and those few will stay at home. We have proved this fact thoroughly.

But fleas do love kittens, we must confess; nice, tender, plump little kittens are tid-bits for their delectation, and they make the most of their chance.

But even here we can exclaim, "We have met the enemy and they are ours."

During our residence in Florida we have "raised" several kittens, and the flea problem soon attracted attention, for the out-dwellers of the sands at once scented the little furry lumps awaiting them, and flocked to the feast.

We put our thinking-cap on our head, the kittens on a blanket, the roughest, most fuzzy blanket we could find, and then we puffed insect-powder over the kittens. How they kicked and sneezed! And how the wicked fleas followed suit as to the kicking, and directly dropped off on the blanket, and crawled languidly into the midst of the fuzzy nap—to take an eternal nap themselves. Some were lively enough at first to try to jump. We had anticipated that; hence the blanket. The harvest of dead fleas reaped from the kitten-field was wonderful.

About once a week, while the kittens were young and tender, we repeated this treatment, and soon it was curious to note the difference in the disposition of the two kittens, just as much as we see in two human brothers.

They very quickly learned what the blanket and powdergun portended. One, a glossy black fellow, with a snowy breast, would begin to kick and cry the moment he saw them, and we had no little trouble to hold him without hurting him, until his enemies were compelled to vacate the premises; the other one, a handsome buff and white kitten, seemed to understand, almost from the first, that there was no use in struggling—in fact, he made a virtue of necessity, instead of starting to run at the sight of the little gun, he would deliberately sit up on his haunches, droop his forepaws, shut his eyes, and wait to be shot with the powder, and then, when this infliction was over, lie down on the blanket and let himself be turned over and over without a struggle, a very personification of meekness.

By this simple method we kept the enemy under, even when a kitten feast was in view, and as the latter grew older the fleas became so very scarce that we omitted the powder altogether.

Dogs, if unwashed, and above all razor-backs, if allowed to approach near the house, will undoubtedly set free more or less fleas to torment its inmates; but a clean, dainty cat, never.

So we pass by the flea as giving but little annoyance in most localities, although in most of the towns, especially in the stores and hotels, they are apt to be more numerous than elsewhere; private houses, especially those in the country, can well afford to laugh at their visits, above all when armed with the gun that shoots powder and kills without a bullet.

We pass by the flea, then, and pursue our investigations in another direction, looking next at an insect that causes far more annoyance than the wicked flea, not only in Florida, but in many other countries, in every State in the Union, and even up in the far-away Polar regions.

Mosquitoes, of course. There are some places in Florida where these tantalizing songsters are as numerous as they are in many of the coast regions or swamps of the sister States, and that is saying a great deal; but, again, there are other sections, notably in the high, inland pine regions, where they are practically unknown.

Just as they are North, South, East and West, during the summer season—troublesome after dark, when one sits out on the porches—so are they in Florida as a rule; this thing we know, we were more annoyed by mosquitoes in our Northern village home, than we have ever been in our far South home.

With ordinary mosquito-bars in the windows, and wirenet doors to keep the insects out when attracted by a light, and with a net over the bed, the "mosquito nuisance" becomes a very small one in the piney-woods home; we have known it to be a much greater one outside of Florida.

We wish we could say as much for the whole State; but truth compels us to confess that we have heard of localities in the hammocks and along the saw-grass shores of the large lakes, where double nets were used at doors and windows and over beds, and where the housewife, in making up her bread or cakes, was fain to wrap a gauze veil over her face for protection from a horde of hungry mosquitoes, who were anxious to make the most of her otherwise defenseless condition.

We have heard, too, of large, light frames, with nets stretched over them, under which the family sat to eat their meals, to read, or to sew; and these—were not in Florida.

The coast regions of Florida are very attractive in many ways; the dancing blue billows are glorious to look upon, and to sail over, the fresh salt air pleasant and invigorating, the fish and oysters and clams yielded up in generous abundance by the sparkling waters form no small items of home comforts; but—the mosquitoes!

They love the salt air too. From the beautiful, healthful shores of Charlotte Harbor comes the report, in response to our inquiries:

"We must confess that for several months of the year the mosquitoes are very trying; but we keep them at bay pretty effectually with nets in our doors and windows, and double nets over our beds. But this plague passes over; and all the rest of the year it is so enjoyable here that we forget the brief 'reign of terror' of the mosquito regime."

And up from the Indian River country, on the opposite coast, a voice reaches us, the voice of a new Florida housekeeper:

"We are passing through an age of mosquitoes; they are almost unendurable for two or three months; yet we would rather have them, and do all our own work in addition, than deal with a willfully-obstinate 'human,' such as we have often encountered in South Carolina."

[It is not only the Florida "cooks" that try one's patience, you see.]

But, whether few or many, mosquitoes can be readily conquered by the use of the omnipotent insect-powder.

Putting a little of it in a paper cone, and setting fire to it, is one way to clear a room, not only of mosquitoes, but fleas and flies; puffing the powder toward the walls and ceilings is another way.

Still a third method of driving off mosquitoes is to place a piece of gum camphor in a tin cup, and hold it over a lamp until a vapor begins to rise (don't let it take fire) and then wave the cup to and fro about the room until the air smells strongly of camphor.

We have found both powder and camphor very effective, though we have fortunately seldom been compelled to resort to them, and never except from carelessness in leaving windows open and unprotected, with a bright light in the room.

Even in the worst places in Florida, and during the height of the mosquito season, no one need be driven to the last resort of the natives of Lower Senegal. They go to roost, literally. During the several months when mosquitoes are on the warpath in deadly earnest, the unlucky human beings of that region are taught their own insignificance, and are compelled to retreat before their tiny foe. They set up regular roosts, or platforms, built on high forked saplings, reached by ladders, and floored with branches, and under these lofty platforms perpetual fires are kept burning; here the poor people have to live night and day, constantly enveloped in a dense smoke.

Squatted on their roosts they receive their friends during the day, passing hurriedly from one roost to the other, and never venturing out of range of the smoke, least they be eaten up alive; at night they stretch themselves on their platform, and sleep in the midst of smoke and warm air, with the stars above them and a fire below them. Query: Suppose the children should roll out of bed? It would be something like, "out of the frying-pan into the fire," would it not?

And now, in bidding farewell to the mosquito question, we will quote from "Sketches of Travel in Singapore, Malacca, Java," by a well-known German traveler, F. Jäger—an extract that will be found very useful to all hunters, whether Florida or otherwise, since they are sure to invade the haunts where mosquitoes "most do congregate."

"A tincture prepared by macerating one part of *Pyrethrum roseum* in four parts of dilute alcohol, and, when diluted with ten times its bulk of water, applied to any part of the body, gives perfect security against mosquitoes and all other vermin. I often passed the night in my boat on the ill-reputed rivers of Siam without any other cover, even without the netting, and experienced not the slightest inconvenience. The 'buzzing,' at other times so great a disturber of sleep, becomes a harmless tune, and, in the feeling of security, a real cradle-song. In the chase, moistening the beard and hands protects the hunter against flies for at least twelve hours, even in spite of the largely increased respiration due to the climate."

The same traveler also refers to the power of the insect (pyrethrum) powder over ants; and, as these are another of our household foes, sometimes quite troublesome in their persistent visits to pantries and provision closets, we will quote our author once more.

"Especially interesting is its [pyrethrum powder] action on that plague of all tropical countries, the countless ants. Before the windows and surrounding the whole house where I lived at Albay, on Luzon, was fastened a board six inches in width, on which long caravans of ants were constantly moving in all directions, making it appear an almost uniformly black surface. A track of the powder several inches in width, strewed across the board, or some tincture sprinkled over it, proved an insurmountable barrier to these processions. The first who halted before it, were pushed on by the crowds behind; but immediately, on passing over, showed symptoms of narcosis and died in a minute or two, and in a short time the rest left the house altogether."

And it is quite true, all this that Herr Jäger has to say about the ants, as we have proved time and again in our provision and milk and butter closets.

Insect-powder scattered over the shelves will keep them at a respectful distance, whether the marauders be the small red ants or the large brown ones, whose nippers are made on the model of a lobster's, and are quite capable of snipping out bits of flesh very neatly. The small ants carry red-hot pincers concealed about their persons, and use them on occasion, when disturbed at their meals or otherwise offended; step into one of their dwellings while digging or weeding, and you will find out all about it.

Nevertheless, we were quite as much annoyed with ants in our Northern country home, as ever we have been in our Southern.

If you have in your store-room a barrel of sugar, and the ants make a raid on it, as they will (for Southern ants are not one whit more honest than Northern ones, and we have seen the latter thieving sugar), all you have to do is either to sprinkle insect-powder on the floor around it, rub some in a circle on the staves, or make a chalk line an inch wide on the barrel, using the common granular chalk.

Sometimes the large ants make a nice, cosy nest in a little-used box, or bureau-drawer, and fill it with shapely oblong eggs. Use the insect-powder among them, and they will each seize an egg and start off on a journey to more hospitable regions. If the powder is good, they will stagger and faint by the wayside—and the place that once knew them shall know them no more.

Now, as to flies: Our experience has been that they are not nearly so troublesome in the Florida piney-woods home as they are in most Northern homes. Of course they are more plentiful in the hammocks and on the coast, and also in the towns, where the well-filled stores invite them to come and to tarry.

Probably the most annoying and tantalizing of all the insects of Florida—at least we know it to be so in the pine lands—is a tiny fly, called in local parlance a "gnat," although, properly speaking, it is a mosquito, and belonging to the mosquito family only, should be so termed.

These little flies, miniatures of the ordinary house-flies, sing and buzz around one's ears, nose, mouth, and eyes, with a persistence worthy of a better cause, and an apparent aimlessness worthy of no cause at all.

For, they don't bite; or, if they do, we have not yet discovered it. We could feel more charity toward them if they tormented us while in search of their living. A mosquito stings—but it is an honest, legitimate sting; he wants a good meal, and means to get it as best he may. But as to this "horrid little gnat," all that he wants, so far as one can see, is to torment and annoy, and this he does with a vigor and industry that must be pleasing to the Father of Evil, if he deigns to notice a little fly at all.

We look back with a shiver of "holy horror" on certain experiences of our own in the cow-pen.

Until we came to Florida we had dwelt in a great city, and had never so much as seen a cow milked; but we speedily discovered that this was one of the many things that must be learned, self-taught too, unless we were willing to see our whole family deprived of that powerful factor in household comfort and economy, milk, with all its accompaniments.

As we have said, the art of milking was an unknown quantity to us, the cow-pen a foreign country; but at least we had some ideas on the subject that were less eccentric than those held by a relative of ours when a little girl.

Going with her sister one day to witness the interesting process of milking the "family friend" in the barn-yard, the milkmaid allowed the former, the elder of the two children, to try her hand at milking.

Children are a good deal like a flock of sheep; let the leader spring over an obstacle in his path, and though the obstacle be immediately removed, every one of the flock will leap at the spot—what one does, all want to do.

So it was now: Mary, sitting on the milking-stool, no sooner resigned her seat to its legitimate occupant, than eight-year old Maggie insisted on having her turn.

But the milker had no more time to waste, and the petition was refused. Maggie pouted and withdrew, resigned?

Not a bit of it! She merely retreated in order to outflank the enemy, and outwit her in her own stronghold.

Two strong hands were raining down two milk-white streams into the beautiful white foam that was rapidly filling the generous pail, when stealthily another hand, a tiny little hand, slipped in between the hind legs of the patient cow, and grasped a third teat.

This was too much for the gentle animal's equanimity; one hind leg sent Maggie in a backward summersault, the other deposited milkmaid, stool, and milk-pail in one confused heap on the ground.

Mary rolled upon the grass in a convulsion of mirth—the astonished milker rose up, with the milk dripping from her head downward, and Maggie, the dumbfounded culprit, scrambled to her feet, sobbing, "I didn't know 'ow, 'ow she cared, where you stood to—to milk her; I did n't!"

Now, we were more than eight years old when we first set foot in a Florida cow-pen, and we did know that a cow "cared where you to stood to milk her;" but further than that we knew little, except that it was a lesson to be learned. So we taught ourself how to milk; and it was well we did, or the milk famine would have continued indefinitely, for we found that we could very seldom count upon help other than our own.

Either our cooks, or "young genermen," were unable to milk at all, or else we soon discovered that our cows and calves were being badly treated, the former kicked, the latter beaten with heavy sticks until their slender little legs were swelled and bruised.

So, in common humanity, we were compelled to retain our distasteful task three fourths of the time.

We taught the Goddess how to milk, and as our pater accompanied her to the pen to guard the calves while she milked their mothers, this plan worked very well and to our great relief.

But one day we bought a new cow with a beautiful shiny black coat. Now, whether it was this similarity of color, or some other cause of jealous antipathy, is to this day a mystery, but certain it is that so far from allowing the Goddess to milk her, Stella, the new cow, resented her presence in the pen so strongly that the moment she was permitted to enter the inner pen, where her calf was awaiting her, she would lower her head and make a dash for the Goddess, who "stood not on the order of her going," but went by rapid transit, whether through the bars or over the fence it mattered not at all, only so that she escaped from those threatening horns.

We hoped for a while that Stella and the Goddess would eventually become, reconciled, but it was a vain hope. As it was at first, so it continued; the entrance of Stella into the cow-pen was the signal for the hasty exit of the Goddess, over or under or through the fence.

We were sorely tried, for it meant the giving up of a favorite cow, or the renewal of our cow-pen ball-and-chain; but for all that the sight was so ludicrous we had to laugh. We chose the lesser of two evils, picked up our ball-and-chain and went back into the pen, and there, as we intimated awhile ago, before we wandered off into this by-way of reminiscence, we met our worst experience with "those horrid gnats," as we have often heard them called, and justly so.

There, when we were helpless, and both hands occupied, these tiny imps of aggravation delighted to sing their loudest, and dance their liveliest around our ears and eyes and mouth.

They may always be found, during their season, swarming around the cows, and, perhaps resenting our presence, they nearly drove us frantic during the milking process. We used to wonder what particular attraction the cows had for them, since we were satisfied that they never stung them; but after watching them for a while the reason became plain enough, they were watching their chance to dine at the expense of the large horse-flies that rarely fail to be in close attendance on the cows.

These large flies are experts at searching out nice, full veins and tapping them with their sharp proboscis, and, when the bright red drop comes forth in response, the tiny gnats sit down fearlessly in company with flies that are giants in comparison with themselves, and fill their transparent bodies to repletion.

So, observing this impudent proceeding on the part of the little gnats, it was easy to understand their attraction toward the cow-pen and their close friendship for the cows, but why they should dance a "Highland fling" around the innocent milker remains to this day a mystery.

But let not the new settler congratulate himself on the idea that these industrious gnats confine their persecutions to the vicinity of the cow-pen, and that if he avoids that devoted spot he will also avoid the tribe of winged torments. There is nothing they like better than to assist at the family meals, especially if soups or meats are present on the board.

They waltz hither and thither, whispering now in one ear, now in the other; then they take a flying trip up your nose, and then come out to see what you think about it, and if you open your mouth to give your opinion on the subject (it is sure to be a very decided one too), you are just as likely as not to ingulf one or two of your tormentors. With a diabolical glee do they dance and circle around your head, and up and down, over and into your plate.

Now while this aggravating quadrille is in progress there are just two alternatives to be faced and made the best of, one is to go without your dinner—but we have never yet seen any one choose this alternative; the other is to eat your food with a few gnats thrown in, nay, dropped in, by way of

>"Pepper and spice,
>Which is [not] very nice."

For there is no use in denying the fact that these omnipresent gnats will fall into one's plate, with the practical effect, if not the intention, of ending their lives there; the warm vapors arising from the food exert an intoxicating effect on the lively little torments, and as they waltz' over your plate, they reel and pitch and tumble about like the drunken flies they are.

But for all this, we would not have our readers exaggerate the annoyances caused by these little gnats. They are not so bad but that they might be much worse; neither are they always, nor every where.

Moreover, the netting, or cheese-cloth, which ought to be in the windows and doors of every country home in the North or South, in England or in Europe, during the hot season, will keep these little nuisances at bay almost entirely. These we might call passive defenses, but there are others more active.

Here, again, the famous insect-powder comes to the fore, and a few puffs of it sent around the dining-room, with closed doors and windows, about fifteen minutes before sitting down to the table, will prove a very powerful weapon. Another remedy, that secures at least partial if not entire relief, is to rub spirits of camphor over the face and hands, or sprinkle it about the clothing.

And just here, while considering this safeguard, it may not be amiss to step outside the house for a moment and go down into the stable.

Those "dreadful little gnats" are there, too, waltzing with diabolical glee around your horse's eyes, and all that poor, helpless animal can do in reprisal is to wink at them; but, strange as it may seem, they do not seem one whit abashed by so mild a reproach.

But, never mind! there is a "friend in need" for the poor horse as well as for his master, and it is this relief that we have come to bring him, in the shape of an ointment, made of powdered camphor and lard, rubbed lightly around his eyes and forehead and nostrils; or you may tie a little bag filled with broken bits of gum camphor around his neck. Gnats object so strongly to the smell of camphor, that they will retire from its neighborhood in disgust—and so will mosquitoes.

And now let us go back to the house and see what other trials and tribulations there await the timid housekeeper.

We use the word "timid" advisedly, because the few trials remaining to be noted are such as would be little heeded by one of strong nerves.

We are done with the insect family, we have seen quite enough of them, and have happily learned that we are not entirely defenseless against their assaults.

And now let us interview certain little creatures that are very apt to intrude into Florida homes, especially new houses, built upon land recently cleared; such very little fellows, and innocent of all evil either in thought or deed, yet often creating the wildest confusion amidst the feminine population.

We ought to know all about it, for we have been hastily summoned time and again, even during this present writing, in a most energetic manner, to the rescue of our more nervous home companions:

"Oh! oh! here's one of those dreadful little frogs! Do come and catch it! It will jump on me; come quick!"

And then, with towel, or some similar weapon, in hand, we run, ready to pounce on the unconscious intruder as he hops serenely over the floor, or runs up the wall or window-curtains, intent upon one thought only, the sole object of his visit, which is to hunt for his dinner of flies and other small insects.

"A frog?" Aye, even so; a very mite of a frog, with a beautiful bright green coat, the brightest of bright eyes, the quickest of red tongues, and the most earnest resolve to catch flies and not be caught himself "on the fly."

He intends no harm, and he does none, except to the nerves of the new-comer who does not understand the perfect innocence of his character and intentions, or to the timid sisters who can never get used to such terrible monsters as roaches, bugs, frogs, or lizards.

There is nothing repulsive about his looks either; he is one of the daintiest, prettiest little frogs to be seen any where; sometimes his bright green coat is spotted with olive, and a grayish yellow streak runs from the eyes toward the sides until it merges in the general green color of his coat ; he wears a very white shirt-bosom, edged with black, and a beautiful crimson brooch under his chin, whose existence no one would suspect till in a particularly happy moment he lifts his head and puffs out the gay brooch beneath. Sometimes, too, his coat changes to a much darker hue, as though he had been essaying the lofty profession of a chimney-sweep, and a Florida chimney-sweep at that, such a dusty, untidy creature as he is at such times ! and do you know what it means?

Just this: that his coat has become old-fashioned, and he has ordered a new one, which, unlike our own clothing, is fitted on underneath the old, and some fine day, if you watch closely, you will surely see this comical little fellow deliberately pulling off his coat and—selling it to the old- clothes' man, do you suggest? No, not that; but—eating it!

Our green friend is a true tree-frog, and right well does he know how to sing when a rain is coming, and at other times too; he is a merry, happy creature, and can readily be tamed so as to come at a signal and eat flies or other insects from one's hand.

He is not easily abashed nor diverted from his course. We know of one little chirper who for months made it a point of honor to take up his residence on the spout of the toilet pitcher in our bed-room, and he did not care at all how many " scares" he gave one occupant of the room, nor how many hasty excursions to the rescue he inflicted on the writer; he merely twinkled his bright eyes at us, flung out his slender little legs in a futile leap as the enveloping towel descended over him, and then, when we dropped him out of the door, hopped indignantly away.

But for all that it would not be long before we heard a voice, and such a voice, issuing from inside the pitcher, deep or shallow, according to the water-line within. If it came from "down in the depths," the resonance of that voice was wonderful, and reminded us of the famous bull-frog who "lived in the well."

Sometimes he would go on a journey from his favorite pitcher into our study adjoining the bed-room, climb the desk, and hop serenely over books and papers, snapping up a fly or mosquito or marauding spider here and there; occasionally he had even the impudence to sit on our hand, a proceeding not much to our fancy, for our merry little frog, "Puck" we called him, was cold and clammy to the touch, and the tiny disks on his toes, which enabled him to cling to walls or ceilings, did not feel very pleasant.

We had not the heart to injure the pretty little creature (he was very small, like all his family, hardly half an inch long), and therefore handled him very gently. But one day, alas for Puck! a wicked trespasser, in the shape of a hen, saw him hopping under the window, returning from an out-door excursion to his beloved perch on our pitcher, saw him, pounced upon him and swallowed him!

It seemed almost ridiculous to feel regretful for a frog; but we did. And to this day we hope the unfortunate little fellow made that lawless marauding hen uncomfortable by kicking.

So you see this trial, the frog bugbear, is not very heavy to be borne. Even if a tiny frog does intrude once in a while, it is harmless, and only comes to help free you from troublesome insects.

We have been "taken in and done for" more than once in the course of our experience, but we were never more completely deceived than by one of these very same tiny green frogs.

It was soon after our arrival in Florida, and during that transition period to which we have already referred, when the free razor-back citizens of the Flowery State were devouring all our young chicks who strayed outside the poultry-yard fence.

A heavy summer shower was pouring down from the skies, such a shower as we have never seen elsewhere than in Florida and on the Isthmus of Panama—genuine tropical showers, solid sheets of rain that pelt and drench and blind the unlucky wight who is caught out in them without protection.

In the very midst of the down-pour we heard the pitiful cry of a little chick, one that had evidently strayed outside the fence, and was not only in imminent danger of being drowned or chilled to death by the rain, but also of being caught by one of a "bunch" of razor-backs that had been seen close by just before the shower.

We could not turn a deaf ear to that pitiful appeal for help, even though it was uttered only by a little chick, so we donned water-proof, rubber-cap, and rubber-shoes, and boldly went forth to the rescue, battling with wind and rain, and almost losing our breath in the struggle.

We followed the sound of that mournful "cheep, cheep, chee-eep," as best we could across a belt of sand-spur grass, across another of rough, plowed ground, and along the fence in the high grass, full of pity for the unhappy little wretch crying alone in the storm, wet, and frightened, and miserable as it must be.

The sad "cheep, cheep, chee-eep!" never faltered nor ceased, as we made our way toward it, and at last our perseverance, our errand of mercy, was rewarded—we found the poor little waif.

It was not crouching in the grass as we expected, far from it; the unhappy chicken was perched on a fence-post, and it was the queerest looking chick that we ever saw! It had four legs, and it had pulled out or the wind had blown away all its feathers, if ever it had any, which we very much doubt, and was dressed in a smooth coat of bright green.

And there it sat on the fence-post, utterly regardless of our dripping presence, singing its plaintive song of "cheep, cheep, chee-eep," and winking at us as if it knew all about it, and enjoyed the joke at our expense.

The "poor little chick" looked and acted so very like a frog, and seemed to chuckle over our "taking in" with such merry glee, that we just cast one reproachful glance at it and then retraced our steps to the house in a very dignified manner, a sadder, a wiser, and a very much wetter individual than the one who had set out so bravely to rescue an unhappy wanderer from an untimely death.

We laughed then, and we often laugh now at the recollection of that fruitless expedition; yet several times since then, we and others have been deceived (but never so totally) by the peculiar, chicken-like cry of the little tree-frog.

Once—yes, we must tell it, for misery loves company—our honored *mater* was victimized too.

We were then hatching our chickens in an incubator—the "Perfect Hatcher"—and raising them in a brooder to which a glass run was attached. There were nearly two hundred lively chicks to be looked after and guarded, and sometimes, after the run was closed for the night, a pitiful cry outside would reveal the fact that one of the flock was shut out.

This was the case one evening about dusk; the chicks were supposed to be all safely gone to bed beneath the warm, cosy "mother" inside the brooder, and so the run was closed in. Soon after, however, from outside, came the pitiful, mournful cry of a chicken in distress.

"Oh! we have shut out one of those poor little things!" exclaimed the *mater*, and together we hastened to the rescue. We unhooked the wire netting, and the *mater*, after a lively chase, finally picked up a little brown thing, that kept jumping against the glass sides. "Poor little wretch!" she cried, "how cold and wet it is; it must have tumbled into the drain—ugh! ugh! boo-ooh!" And down went the "poor little wretch" on the ground with much more celerity than it was picked up.

"It's—it's a—frog!" gasped the *mater*, "such a horrid sensation, I feel it crawling all over me!"

We are afraid that instead of sympathizing with the victim of this terrible mistake, we were unfeeling enough to drop down on the grass and laugh till our eyes were dim at the picture of disgust before us, until the latter joined in the fun, and a chorus of small, startled voices in the brooder gave point and emphasis to our impromptu glee club.

The "poor little wretch" in question, this time, was not one of the very small tree-frogs, but the large kind, for there are two, the larger ones are usually green, but have the power of changing their color at will, and as a rule, will be found matching in hue Whatever object they rest upon, through all the shades of green or brown.

And now let us pass on from this very froggy subject to another, but still within the "reptilean era."

Lizards: what a horror some of our Florida sisters have of these innocent, graceful creatures!

There is no harm in them, not a particle, even in the larger striped species that live altogether out of doors; they have no wish to attack any one, and if they had, could do no injury. In the first place, the very largest of them all are only a few inches in length; in the second place, they have no teeth to bite with. The utmost they can accomplish in the way of defense, when attacked, we have seen them do when our pet cat has come to us crying for help, with a striped three or four-inch lizard hanging to its under lip; it could not bite, but only pinch hard enough to sustain its own weight and to worry its assailant.

But the slender little chameleon lizard can not do even so much as this. The nearest approach to it that it is capable of we saw once when two of them fell to fighting right under our very eyes; they twitched their long tails about, ironed each other's coats with their toes for smoothing-irons, played "leap-frog or die" over one another, and finally locked their jaws together with so fierce a grip that a light touch from a twig made them fall apart.

So you see what very formidable adversaries they are for the human family to encounter.

They often venture inside the houses, seeking, like the tree-frogs, for flies, and it is curious to note how expert they are. They usually stay near the windows and remain perfectly quiet for five or ten minutes at a time, or until an unwary fly appears close by, then, with a dart like a flash, the chameleon proves that he can not only "change his skin," but "his spots" as well.

Some people, many people, we fear, will try to catch a poor little frog or chameleon, and kill it. Now that is a thing we can not understand.

"It is more blessed to give than to receive:" what then is it to take violently that which it is out of our power to give back again? What good does it do, what pleasure does it give to any one, to destroy an innocent, harmless life, even if it does belong to "only a frog or a lizard"? It is theirs, not ours, and the same Hand created them that created us; they come near us to help us in destroying the insects that really do annoy us, and we (some, not all of us) show our gratitude by robbing them of all they have, their innocent little lives.

There was a chameleon, a graceful, pretty creature who wore sometimes a green coat, sometimes a yellow, sometimes a brown, and at other times a spotted coat, who used for one whole summer and fall to come regularly every day to sit on our study window and catch flies. It was a timid, fearsome little thing at first, but we caught flies several times and dropped them near it on the sill, and bye and bye it seemed to understand that we were friendly; then we whistled to it and played soft music on a little mouth-harmonica.

Chameleons like music, even such simple music as this, and it was odd to note how intently our unbidden but not unwelcome guest would listen to it, its tail moving gently when the music was slow and in quick jerks when the notes were loud or fast; its head would turn from side to side, its bright eyes twinkle, and ever and anon its slender neck was uplifted and an odd ruby-colored sack under its throat swelled out to a wonderful extent; and just so long as we kept up the music just that long would it remain in the same spot in rapt attention, especially so if we were whistling.

But, alas! our pet chameleon went the way that one's pets do mostly go. After one unusually cold night, we found it lying stiff and still on the floor beneath the window, frozen to death, its bright eyes dim, its green coat turned to the sable hue of one in mourning.

But ever and anon, during the warm, sunny summer days, other chameleons come darting in to see us, and even though they jump on our desk we find nothing alarming about them. They are very like one of our young "dishwashers," who naively confessed, regarding a cat that showed its fear of him, "I'm mighty more skeered of the cat, than the cat's skeered of me !"

And thus, trusting that we have laid the bugbear of "those dreadful little lizards," we will take a flight in the air, and see how it is about the busy mud-wasps who adorn our ceilings and walls after their own fashion.

Veritable "busy-bodies" are they from the coming of the warm weather to the end thereof, buzzing in and out of doors and windows, carrying little bits of soft mud in their mouths, sticking them up on the walls behind pictures, inside of closets, on the ceilings, or any where else they may fancy for the future birthplace of their larvae. For that is the whole object of their mud-houses, and the skill with which they build them, with their numerous cubelike tunnels, is well worth noting, as is the ludicrous energy they expend in kneading and pummeling the mud with their heads, and then smoothing it over with their feet.

The places they choose for building-sites are sometimes exceedingly eccentric: glass jars, tea-pots, bonnet-boxes, trunks, old hats, clothing hanging long undisturbed, all these are commonplace and fade into insignificance when compared with the site chosen by one wildly eccentric wasp.

No one would ever guess where it was, for it was located on in no less a place than the clustering curls surrounding the head of that devoted member of our family already alluded to, as having a horror of roaches, ants, fleas, frogs, chameleons, wasps, and others of their numerous family, and therefore receiving their especial attentions.

This wasp, we might well call it a "crank," came flying in a window at which habitually sat our companion. It paused over her head, and then gently dropped on it the first bit of mud, the intended corner-stone of its projected building.

That was supposed, of course, to have been dropped by accident; but when the same thing was repeated several times, and on successive days, that charitable view of the matter became impossible, and finally we were compelled in self-defense, or rather in defense of another, to shoot the persevering intruder with the omnipotent powder-gun, and that put an end to the projected "castle in the (h)air." For, in all the great family of insects, there are none that succumb more quickly to a puff of the powder than the wasps.

Whenever we hear the peculiar "buzz, buzz," that tells the story of the hidden, muddy piece of work in progress behind a picture, in a closet or corner, we go there straightway, gun in hand, and send some of the powder flying, and if the least particle of it touches the wasp, as it invariably does, it ends the building of that particular mudhouse.

Neither is it difficult to keep the wasps at a distance; the netting with which the doors and windows of every country house should be provided, whether North or South, will prevent their entrance, except perhaps a stray one now and then.

Add to this that the mud-wasps never sting of *malice prepense*, but only when a hand is actually placed on them, and it will be seen that they need cause but little annoyance to the housekeeper.

The same is true of scorpions, of which so many persons have an exaggerated idea; they are seldom seen at all, and then usually in hasty flight. Like the wasps, they will strike back if you lay your hand on them; but are they to blame for that? our own laws justify self-defense.

"Snakes?" Well, they can hardly be classed under the especial head of a housekeeper's trials, and yet they are often one of her first and most "awful" tribulations.

We know of one who for weeks after being domiciled in Florida would not allow her children to leave the broad piazzas that surrounded the house, because of her fear of snakes ; but after watching for their dreaded appearance in vain, she came to the conclusion, arrived at by every one who lives in Florida and knows it as it is, that snakes are actually less numerous, especially in the pine lands, than they are in the fields and mountains of the Northern States.

It is entirely a work of supererogation to confine one's self or family to the piazzas in order to avoid snakes, for, if they are about and take a fancy to visit one there, they can easily do so.

How well we recollect, one day during our first summer, hearing an unearthly shriek, accompanied by a scampering over the porch. We rushed out, and there, dancing on the lofty summit of a tool-chest, with her skirts drawn tightly around her, we found our *mater*.

"A snake! there's a snake in the netting under my hammock. I stepped right on it. Oh! I'm cold all over!"

We looked, and there, sure enough, was a poor, frightened black-snake, about three feet long, quite as much "skeered" as the *mater* was, and in a great deal more danger; it was struggling vainly to escape from the folds of the ample net which hung over the hammock and lay on the floor beneath it, a net used much more for flies than mosquitoes.

There is no harm in these black-snakes, on the contrary they are our friends, and always on the watch to destroy those who are our real enemies.

It is not so generally known as it ought to be, that there are two of our Florida snakes which ought to be protected rather than destroyed, the black-snake and the king-snake, the latter being much the larger of the two.

Wherever they encounter a poisonous snake they give it battle, and, which is still more to the purpose, they invariably come out of it victorious. The utmost of harm that we have ever heard charged to their account (and we have never seen it verified) is that they occasionally steal eggs and young chickens. But even if this be so, what is this in comparison with the important service they render us?

We would rather encourage, than otherwise, the presence of a few black-snakes on our premises, knowing full well that they will do good service in destroying such of our real foes as may be lurking in the grass.

We have sometimes killed a black-snake—the largest we have ever seen in Florida in the pine lands measured four feet and was too slender to have swallowed any but a very young chicken—we have killed them, but it was with regret, and out of regard to others who could not conquer the innate aversion we all feel toward snakes.

Only very seldom is a moccasin or spread-adder met with. These are both slow, sluggish reptiles, and we have frequently heard it asserted that even teasing with a stick will not provoke them to strike.

The only real fear one need have with regard to these occasional visitors to our fields and groves lies in their sluggish nature. Other snakes, seeing or hearing a person approach, will dart away like a flash, these will merely lie still and look at you, and if you step on them they punish your temerity or carelessness.

The spread-adder will warn you to keep your distance by uttering a low hissing that can not be mistaken, like a locomotive blowing off steam in the far distance. Three times only, during all our long years of residence in Florida, have we come to close quarters- with the spread-adder, and each time it gave us the warning to "Beware!" and each time, also, we hastened away, and returned, exclaiming "Hoe!" as we brought that handy weapon down upon the enemy's back, and then used it to dig a little grave for his remains.

Yes, in nine years we have encountered near our piney-woods home just three spread-adders and five moccasins, and in each instance we could say, with Commodore Decatur, "We have met the enemy, and he is ours!"

With the simple, common-sense precaution of looking where you walk, no one need have any fear of snakes here; we have seen less of them, as an actual matter of fact, than we used to see during our summer outings at the North.

And so we bury the much exaggerated bugbear of snakes, and with them close our list of "trials and tribulations" likely to be met with by the Florida housekeeper.

CHAPTER XXV. MAKING THE BEST OF IT.

Compensations for Drawbacks. How to Make the New Home Happy.

If, during the perusal of the preceding pages, our readers have not come to realize the fact that the new Florida home and its surroundings must of necessity be full of changes from the old routine they have elsewhere been accustomed to, then have we failed in our purpose.

It is so much better to expect little and find more, than to expect much and find little, that we have endeavored to point out the disadvantages and drawbacks very plainly.

There are, of course, many of these as regards mere physical comforts and indulgences, in comparison with the surroundings of old settled communities; but, as compared with any other new country, the Florida home has very few, and none of them involving actual personal suffering such as must come to the Northern or Western pioneer, if only through the medium of the cold, bleak months that make up so large a portion of each year.

That the mild, genial climate of Florida offers great compensation for many minor drawbacks in the new home, few will deny, and those who come, resolved to stay and make the best of things, until they can be improved, will find the "drawbacks" true to their name, inasmuch as they will retire further into the background, until finally the question will arise, "Where and what are they?"

The settler, whether man or woman, who resolves to be contented and carve out a true home from such crude materials as may be obtainable, will surely find the task comparatively an easy one. The whole secret is in their starting right, and in coming here just as they would to any other State to settle.

To expect to find the same soil and conditions of life and society here as those left behind would be foolish indeed.

No man will find money growing on the bushes along the roadsides, vegetables that plant and cultivate themselves, or orange trees that come into bearing in two or three years from the seed; neither will he find desirable lands and bearing groves to be given away, as though of no value to the owner.

The settler who is well-to-do and seeks a Florida home, not to mend his broken fortunes, but simply for his own or his family's health, will have no difficulty in finding plenty of beautiful, healthful, desirable places, located near the cities or transportation facilities, where every comfort and luxury can be procured; but he will have to pay for these things just as he would any where else.

If he wants to farm and "turn the soil" to his profit, he must study its nature and capabilities, learn the ways and means of semi-tropical products, and not be above taking advice from his neighbors, even though they may possess but little of the book-learning which has served him elsewhere, but will prove here an insufficient guide.

If he wants to go into business or procure employment, he must go about it exactly as he would "up North," or any where else: look out for localities where there is business to be done of the kind he desires to enter into, and then, having found it, advertise the fact that he is there on the spot and ready to supply the demand.

These are the kind of settlers that Florida wants, as we have said elsewhere; not tramps, here to-day, there to-mor-row, nor wild enthusiasts mounting high on a hobby-horse, and then, after a brief gallop, plunging headlong into the "Slough of Despond."

We have recorded enough in these pages, and in those of a former work ("Florida Fruits and How to Raise Them"), to prove that our beautiful State has wonderful capabilities of climate, soil, and varied resources; but it needs money, pluck, common sense, and common industry to develop these advantages. Men and women must work for their living here as elsewhere, although here the chances for present comfort and ultimate success are greater than in any other State in the

Union, and opportunities for the safe and profitable investment of capital—not only moneyed but physical capital—can no where be excelled.

No industrious man of good habits and ordinary health, however lacking he may be in "worldly gear," need be without a cosy, comfortable home in Florida, neither his wife nor his children. And here too a large family of the latter ceases to be a burden, for there is much they can do to help.

The one tiling most needful is, the resolve to make the best of it, to accept one's surroundings without discontent, to meet the changed condition of things in the new home, and gradually evolve comfort out of discomfort and order out of disorder, with patience, and without that constant fretting and repining which will wear out one's own life and throw a heavy cloud over one's whole family.

Florida is pre-eminently a harbor of refuge, a shipyard where barques, beaten and battered on the stormy financial seas, have put into port for repairs. These repairs will come in due time, and the ship will sail again "as good as new," if the ship-builder is industrious and tempers his tools with judgment; but there must perforce be an interval of hardship and discomfort for the crew, and it has to be lived through somehow. The situation has to be faced: it would be a much harder one, remember, under the same circumstances in any other section of the country—it has to be faced, and there are two ways of doing it. The one is by perpetual and irritable complaint, fretfulness, despondency, and worry, which crushes all life, hope, and energy, and makes home not a home, but a miserable prisonhouse, whose inmates would be thankful to flee if they could from the jailor to whom they are chained, and who makes their lives almost unendurable and cheerfulness impossible.

The other way is to face the inevitable changes quietly and calmly; to consider the blessings surrounding the new home rather than those left behind in the old; to take each one of the present difficulties and shortcomings in detail, examine into cause and effect, and use whatever remedies may suggest themselves. If none can be found, why then let it go, and don't fret over it.

As we have noted in previous chapters, it is upon the women of the household, those who have been heretofore unaccustomed to work, that the difference in their surroundings weighs most heavily. Take any city-bred lady, whether of America or Europe, one who has lived all her life with every convenience and comfort so close at hand that they have become as it were component parts of that life, set her down suddenly in any country home, in the midst of farm-work and rough, hungry farm hands, and leave her to perform all the work consequent thereon, and if she does not feel the yoke to be even more galling if borne near her old home, with its bleak climate, than she would in far-away Florida with its genial winters—then are we much mistaken.

As a rule the wife and daughters of a farmer, be the scene of their labors where it may, live in a chronic state of weariness, and we are fain to say that a great deal of this is their own fault; and before turning finally from this phase of our subject we are going to have a little plain talk with our Florida sisters, both of the present and future, because we have seen again and again, and not alone in Florida, the wearing out and laying away of the wife and mother, simply because she had not learned to sacrifice the lower things to the higher.

First of all, we want to ask our sisters a few questions. When the plants are too thick in your flower-beds, what do you do? Thin them out, of course. When a fruit-tree sets fruit too thick? Thin it out again. Of course, that is the only proper thing to do; common sense teaches that.

Then why not apply common sense to something higher?

Do you rise in the morning feeling worn and tired, as if you had just completed your day's work, and were more than ready to rest?

Says a farmer, "If you should happen out our way, doctor, I wish you would just look in at my wife. She seems kind of out of sorts."

"What seems to be the trouble?"

"Well, seems as if she is n't so strong as she used to be. For instance, this morning, after she had milked the cows, and got breakfast for us men folks, and washed up the dishes and started in at the washin', she complained of feeling sort o' tired and weary like. I reckon her blood wants thinnin."

Oh! blind man, blinder than a bat! "Her blood needs thinning!" Rather does it need thickening, and yours the "thinning."

Some thinning is needed, it is true, needed at once, too. But it is the work, and not the blood, that must be thinned.

A wife and mother, tired at noonday, tired at night, tired in the morning, when you should be bright and buoyant, take heed!

Are you wasteful of food, of money? Nay, you are careful, you guard against waste; if the one is limited, you try to make the best of it; if the other is scarce, you seek to make it go as far as possible by living frugally and cutting down every possible expense.

Now tell US, sisters, would you wear a silk dress in the kitchen to save a calico one? Yet that is exactly what you are doing, and worse, when you are so frugal of food and money and so spendthrift of strength and life. The first two may be replaced, the latter never.

It is all right to cut down expenses, when money is running out too fast; but your strength is worth money, and more than money; yet you keep on wasting it as though you owned all the life, health and strength of the world.

Cut down your work, thin it out; search, and you will find any amount of it that had better be pulled up and castaway. Sit down and ask yourself, "How much of my toil is done for my neighbors? How many stitches do I take to be looked at and admired by others? How many ruffles do I put on my little girl's dresses that other people may see them? When one ruffle is neat and pretty, do I think the other two make her more comfortable? If I have a lot of fruit, I do not want to waste it; but is it not better to do that than to waste my strength? Is it not worth more than fruit. If I can myself with the berries, stiffen myself with the jellies, evaporate myself with the dried fruit; is all that true economy? Is not my work, my guidance, my advice, worth more to my family than all the ruffles and fruit put together; and can I give them my services if I trample on my health, stew my strength to shreds, and get myself into a broil generally?" Think it over: these are homely similes, but significant ones.

Keep clean for the sake of health and self-respect; but if there is only a little dust here and there, and it is going to be "the straw that breaks the camel's back" to get rid of that dust, shut your eyes and let it lie.

Do what is necessary for comfort, but if you will lop off all the unnecessaries, the concessions to Mrs. Grundy, there will be no trouble to thin out your work.

"Once upon a time" (our grandmother saw and told the incident) a fire broke out in a country town; two or three houses were burned, many others were in danger. In the midst of the excitement an old lady, Aunt Patsey, she was called, ran out from one of the threatened dwellings, bearing under one arm an old cracked toilet pitcher, under the other the basin belonging to it. She ran here and there, at last darted across the street, and set her precious load down on our grandmother's door-step. "There! Thank the Lord, that's safe, any how!" she panted. Then she vanished, and directly was seen to emerge from her house again, bearing the remainder of that valuable toilet set and her comb and brush. Too excited to remember where she had deposited her first load. Aunt Patsey finally placed the second in the gutter, and sat down on the curb to guard it, with a satisfied expression on her face, and a murmured "Thank the Lord!" even though she saw her house, with all its valuable contents, burning to the ground before her eyes. For the time, crazed with fright and excitement, she was contented to have saved the old toilet set, where she might have saved the old family silver plate.

Sisters, are all the Aunt Patseys dead yet?

Learn ye to sacrifice the lower things to the higher.

"Make the best of it " in this way, and add to the systematic thinning out of household duties a resolve to be bright and cheerful, and to search out blessings rather than the reverse, and then you need not fear being unhappy in the new home, or finding its few drawbacks too heavy to be borne. After all they are only such as are found more or less in every country home where means or neighbors are restricted, except that the genial glow of a mild climate is always present in Florida.

CHAPTER XXVI. HELPFUL HINTS.

How to Paint Houses. Recipes for Cheap Paints. About Horses, Wagons, and Harness. How to Renovate Carriages. Home-made Furniture, Rugs, and Refrigerators. To Preserve Food.

And now, in conclusion, let us point out some of the practical ways of making the best of whatever means and surroundings the Florida settler may possess.

Taking it for granted, as is usually the case, that money is not plentiful, it behooves the settler to help himself without the expenditure of money, so far as it is possible.

With a little skill and knowledge many things can be done and made at home, that are usually either dispensed with or obtained by hired labor which can be ill-afforded.

First of all, let us see how the expense of hiring a painter can be avoided. In "Shopell's Modern Houses"—a quarterly magazine devoted to views and building plans for modern dwellings, and of great value to intending builders, published by the Co-operative Building-plan Association, 191 Broadway, New York, at $1 a volume—we find the following common-sense directions for

THE AMATEUR HOUSE PAINTER.

"For one who wishes to do his own painting, the best plan in most cases is to buy ready mixed paints, of which there are a number of good brands in the market; he can select his colors from the sample cards furnished, or order them as specified by the architects. In this way he obtains the colors desired and avoids the difficulties of mixing.

"If he prefers to mix the colors, thereby effecting a saving of money, he can have the pigments ground to the desired tints, then by adding the oil (raw linseed is the best) bring the paints to the proper consistency for using.

"White lead is good to lighten any color, and also makes the best body for white paint and some other colors.

"When using dry lampblack, saturate it with spirits of turpentine and there will be no difficulty in mixing it with oil afterward; no more turpentine should be used than is necessary to make a paste, as turpentine is bad for outside work. A small amount of lampblack is good to set the olive greens and make them durable.

"It is important that the work to be painted be perfectly clean and free from grease, oil or tar spots. All knots should be covered with a coat of strong shellac varnish before priming. If the work is new let the priming stand a week or two before laying on the second coat.

"The following will be found useful in computing the amount of paint required:

"Quantities required to paint one hundred square yards: For priming, if tinted white lead is used, there will be required twenty pounds of lead and five quarts of raw linseed oil. For second coat twenty pounds of lead and one gallon of oil.

"If three-coat work is intended, the amount of material required for priming and completing the work will average fifty pounds of lead and two and a half gallons of oil to cover one hundred square yards, or about one half pound lead per square yard. As painting is sometimes measured by the 'square' of 10x10 feet (or one hundred square feet), we give the following rule for computing the quantities required, viz., five pounds of lead and one quart of oil to the ' square' for three-coat work.

"When paint is already mixed and ready for the brush there is required one gallon per coat for each twenty-five square yards.

"Putty for stopping nail-holes, etc., one half pound to the square, or four to five pounds for each one hundred yards.

"In regard to the brushes required: It is economy to have enough brushes so that there will be one for each color, besides a few sash tools with which to touch up and for use in small spaces and corners. It is a waste of time and an annoyance to be obliged to wash or rub out brushes in changing from one color to another. No brush should be washed with soap and water; it destroys its elasticity and usefulness. If water is to be used in cleaning a brush, let it be well mixed with ammonia and used as warm as is comfortable to the touch. If brushes are washed in turpentine or benzine, they must be cleansed from same and laid out for a little time to allow the spirits to evaporate before painting is resumed. Turpentine endangers the durability of paint.

"One who does his own painting is not likely to be stinted in time, and consequently will not need to spend money for such large brushes as painters generally use. Brushes made with a selected quality of Russia bristles and bound with wire are considered the best, though there are very good brushes bound with cord or twine.

"A very good kind of flat brush, like a kalsomine or whitewash brush, can be obtained, that answers quite well for painting or oiling shingles or large surfaces; they are cheap and quite substantial, being bound in a patent rubber composition, and need no extra binding or ' bridling.'

"For laying on the body colors a round brush, not less than 0000 in size, should be used, one for each color, also one for the trim."

No better firm for the purchase of building supplies of all kinds, and oils, paints, varnishes, can be found than that of S. B. Hubbard & Co., of Jacksonville, Florida.

Not every one is able to afford oil paints, however, and to very many the cheap yet durable paints given below will prove of great value.

MILK PAINT.

"The cheapest and best farmer's paint that I have any knowledge of," says a well-known agriculturist, "is nothing but sweet skimmed milk and water-lime (cement). The chemical union that takes place between the lime and the caseine of the milk probably produces the film of stone which endures the weather in this country for years. I built a building in 1859, or 1860, for a carriage-house, stable, and granary, of well-sawed, unplaned lumber—stock boards one foot wide, battened with square, undressed two-inch battens—put two coats of this paint on the body of the building, and painted the trimmings (the base, cornice, door and window-frames) with peroxide of iron and oil, a reddish brown, and it was not until last year that I thought it needed another coating of the same, which cost me, for brown paint, oil, and putting on, $4.50; for skimmed milk, water-lime, and putting on, $3.25; total, S7.75.

"The building is fifty-two feet front and twenty-four feet deep, and high gables with sixteen-feet side posts."

The water-lime and skimmed milk are mixed together to a proper consistency to apply with a brush. This paint adheres well to wood, whether rough or smooth—to stone, mortar, or brick, where oil has not previously been used — and forms a very hard substance, as durable as the best oil paint ; any color may be given to it by using colors of the tint desired. If a red is preferred, mix Venetian red with the milk, not using any lime. It will look well for fifteen years, and is too cheap to estimate.

ANOTHER DURABLE PAINT

For outside work: Take two parts (in bulk) of water-lime, ground fine; one part (in bulk) of white lead in oil; mix them thoroughly by adding the best boiled linseed oil, enough to prepare it to pass through a paint-mill, after which, temper with oil till it can be applied with a common paint-brush. Make any color to suit. It is said that this will last three times as long as lead paint.

FIRE-PROOF PAINT.

Take six quarts of finely sifted slacked lime, one quart rock salt, and one gallon of water. Boil all together, and stir well; when boiled take off the scum and dirt that rises, add one pound alum and eight ounces copperas, finely pulverized, and mix in slowly, while stirring, twelve ounces powdered potash, and finally add four pounds wood ashes, well sifted. This becomes quite hard after it has been applied with a brush, and will do for wood or iron.

THE HORSE AND ITS ADJUNCTS.

Among the very first purchases that should be made by the settler are a horse and a wagon. They are so nearly a necessity of Florida life that they ought to be secured, even if some other desirable things must be sacrificed in order to obtain them.

To undertake to make a grove, or raise vegetables or fruit of any sort, without a horse, is like trying to raise a heavy load with one's hands tied. And of little less importance is the wagon. Without it, how can the family provisions be brought from the neighboring towns, a distance, most likely, of several miles?

Without a horse and wagon, the settler is compelled to wait upon the comings and goings of a neighborly neighbor, if such there be, or else all the family food must be carried in a basket on one's arm. We have seen that tried, and it was a terrible strain on a strong man to walk through the summer sun and yielding sand for four miles, two of them the return trip, with a heavy basket on his arm.

No, the horse and wagon must be bought, if within the bounds of possibility, even if the house has to be a little smaller or rougher, or the outside improvements less extensive in consequence; neither the property nor the family can be properly cared for if these two adjuncts are missing.

Horses, good, strong, sturdy horses can be purchased in most sections of the State for from $125 to $150, large horses, either imported from some of the Southern or Western States, or the offspring of such, born in Florida. If the latter, they are thoroughly acclimated and there is no fear for their health, if they are treated with the consideration that should be given them, whether in Florida or elsewhere. If the former, ascertain, if possible, how long they have been in the State. It is running a risk to buy a horse "just brought over" the border, except, indeed, from Southern Georgia, whose climate and forage plants are so like those of Florida as to be practically the same.

The time is not distant when the "Land of Flowers" will be able to boast of her horse as well as cattle ranches; and meantime she has already at least two reliable and extensive breeders of trotting and running horses, Schrader Brothers and Captain Patrick Houston, both of Tallahassee, to whom we have already referred as breeders of Durham, Jersey, and Guernsey cattle. Then there are the ordinary "Florida ponies," a breed of horses rather smaller than those in common use at the North, where heavy draft animals are required, yet strong and sturdy, requiring less feed to keep them in good condition than do the larger horses. While less able to haul heavy loads than the latter, they have quite as much, if not more, endurance, and are well fitted for all the ordinary hauling and cultivation of the farm or grove, or for driving purposes.

These Florida ponies can usually be purchased for from $80 to $125.

Be certain, before concluding the bargain, that the animal has been broken not only to the saddle and plow, but also to pull a cart or top-wagon. We have known more than one too-ready purchaser who found himself the dismayed owner of a horse who declined to pull cart or wagon, or, if all right on these points, would refuse to allow itself to be geared to a top-buggy; occasionally they are not even trained to the plow. As a general thing they are broken to all these uses; but it is well to be on the watch for the exceptions that "prove the rule." It all depends upon who trained the horses, and with what object in view; for some unambitious or lazy owners are quite content to break their colts to the saddle only, depending on the older animals for use on the farm and road.

And now as to a vehicle. Strange as it may appear, there is hardly any other manufactured article, especially one in such common use, of which the majority of people know so little as to what goes to make up its true value as the every-day wagon or carriage. Considering their cost and the heavy amount of wear and tear they must necessarily endure, people are very careless, as a rule, in their purchases in this line, and there is too much of what we may call random buying of unknown irresponsible builders.

To be serviceable and durable, nay, even to be safe, a vehicle, whether wagon, cart, or carriage, should be made throughout of the best materials and best workmanship; these can only be assured by purchasing direct from a well-known manufacturer who has a reputation to sustain, and hence, for his own sake, is sure to see that his name is connected only with honest, well-made articles.

A large, expensive establishment, where thousands upon thousands of dollars are at stake, can not afford to risk the loss of the business on which so large an amount is dependent, and hence can not safely deal otherwise than honestly.

We have seen so many badly built "rattle-traps" in Florida, so-called "cheap," but to our mind very dear, at $40 to $50, that we have taken especial pains to look about among the old reliable firms for vehicles suitable for our sandy State — their first cost more than the sums named above, but their ultimate cost far less. And we have found in the great manufactory of Bradley & Co., Syracuse, New York, two vehicles especially adapted for Florida use. One of these is a wagon, six feet in body length and thirty-two inches wide, aptly named the "Handy Wagon," "because," say the manufacturers, "it is something for the multitude, correct in principle, simple in construction, with great strength in proportion to its weight; it hangs low and is adapted to a greater variety of uses than any vehicle ever introduced."

Solid steel axles are used in this wagon, and the body rests on a half-elliptical spring, so that the weight of the load is brought near the ends of the axles; that is why it is so strong. Then, instead of the body being perched high up in the air, so that it requires a complicated gymnastic feat to climb into it, it hangs low, only thirty-one inches from the ground, so that it is easy to load or unload, a feature that he who handles fruit or vegetable crates will know how to appreciate; as a matter of course there is a drop tail-board to further facilitate loading or unloading.

So much for the business view of the wagon. Looking at it now from the social side, we note that it has two comfortable, movable seats, both full-back if desired, English corduroy or imitation leather; an oil-carpet in the bottom, carriage-step, and, if a canopy top were added, one that could be put on or off at pleasure, no one need want a more comfortable, easy-riding family carriage than this very "handy wagon," which weighs, with the two seats, about three hundred and fifty pounds.

It is not an expensive vehicle either; in fact, considering its durable qualities and good workmanship, it is very low in price, on the principle of "large sales and small profits." Here are the prices given: wagons with one seat $70, with two seats, one full-back, $75, or with two fullback seats $77.50. These prices are with shafts only; for a double team, the pole complete costs $10 more.

The above description applies also to a smaller size of Handy Wagon, only live feet long and with one (movable) seat. This is a lighter wagon than the two-seat, and for one horse would be even better for our Florida roads, since if more than the one seat was occasionally required, a cushioned board laid across from side to side would suffice.

There are carts and carts; and if ever there was one country more than another where that popular little carriage, the "road-cart," is in place, it is Florida.

The old-style buggy is all very well where the roads are firm and straight; but even there we like the road-cart best, for it is just as pleasant to ride in, just as roomy and a great deal easier on the horse.

We would like to see the buggy banished from our Florida roads. They are for the most part sandy, and where there is much travel, soft and yielding, and four wheels for the horse to pull through the sand are just two more than are necessary.

In driving here and there through the country, where, as is the case throughout the State, the roads are little more than wagon-tracks, and very eccentric ones at that, winding in and out around fallen trees, it frequently becomes necessary to turn short and "about face," as *cul-de-sacs* are not uncommon. Right here is one great advantage of the two wheels over the four in a carriage; another is, that if the horse becomes frightened and wheels about, there is no upsetting, as there is with the four wheels, with danger to life and limb.

The first of these carriage-carts that were introduced were not easy to ride in, and hence a prejudice was excited against them, and not unjustly either, for certainly the jogging horse-motion was far from pleasant.

In the present dainty "Bradley Two-wheeler," however, this objectionable motion is entirely overcome and the carriage is as easy to ride in as the easiest buggy, there is absolutely no horse-motion at all.

These two-wheelers are handsome little vehicles, just the very things to gear a pony to and "flee as a bird" over the country.

There are several styles of the Bradley two-wheelers, with buggy tops, with canopy tops, or without either, buggy bodies or phaeton bodies, bodies swung higher or lower, as desired; the latter is best for ladies or children.

We cannot conceive a more perfect carriage for two persons than these two-wheelers. They are not only just the thing to go visiting in, but they are roomy enough to carry ordinary packages, whether dry goods or light groceries. The prices range from $80, without top or lamps, to $145 with both.

There is one point we have not yet mentioned, and it is a very important one: in common humanity let the wheels of every vehicle you use, whether cart, wagon, or two-wheeler have broad tires. Do not use the ordinary narrow ones employed on the hard turnpiked Northern roads or paved streets; remember that Florida roads are sandy roads, and be merciful to your horse.

For cart or wagon the tires should be three inches wide, then the horse will be able to pull twice as much with half the fatigue; for the buggy or two-wheeler, two inches will be wide enough. Do not overlook this point, or you will regret it; we know whereof we speak from personal experience; We have used broad tires and noted their value.

Another thing: do not trust the care of your vehicles to ignorant farm hands; above all, look after the greasing of the wheels yourself, for of this you may be certain, if you do not, they will either be totally neglected, to their own injury and that of the horse, or else "smothered" to the extent of clogging. In this case, as in many others, "enough is better than a feast."

After your carriage or wagon has been used a year or two (or even longer if they have been cared for as they should be), they will look a little the worse for wear so far as paint and polish go. Then they should be done up.

"Can't afford it. No coach-painter near."

Well, you think so, doubtless. But we dispute both assertions. You can afford it, and there is a coach-painter near. He is as close as your own good right arm; you can do it yourself, when once you know how.

How to renovate the carriage or wagon: Let us suppose the body to be black, the wheels and running-gear red.

First procure the following materials: One pound of drop-black ground in Japan; if you can not get it ground in Japan, get it in linseed oil; one pound of Indian red, for the wheels and running-gear; one quart of good varnish, several sheets of number one and a half sand-paper, and number five and a quarter ground pumice-stone (very fine).

Rub the body first with sand-paper, then mix your drop-black with turpentine and varnish, and paint the body; when thoroughly dry, rub it well with the pumice-stone and water on a rag; then paint again, and when thoroughly dry varnish with clear varnish, without the drop-black added.

Mix the Indian red with linseed oil and turpentine, and paint the wheels and running-gear; when thoroughly dry varnish with clear varnish.

It is best to do this work during the winter months, when there are no small insects to light upon it and impair its appearance, which will be equal to new. If there is a patent-leather dasher to be looked after, rub in two or three coats of castor oil, or sweet oil, and, after it is well dried, a coat of varnish.

You will also find, if you try, that you can re-stuff and cover cushions, line curtains, and "fix up" your vehicles generally, not only improving their appearance, but contributing to their longevity.

A thrifty farmer can also avoid having unsafe wheels, by soaking them thoroughly once a year with hot linseed oil, laid on with a paint-brush; keep it as hot as possible while using it—a small iron pot set on top of glowing embers is the best way. Wheels treated in this simple manner will last a life-time, and shrunken spokes and loose tires will be things obsolete.

Of scarcely, if any, less importance than a good vehicle is harness of a similar character. From faults in these two particulars come more than half the accidents on the road that we see chronicled from time to time. Thanks to defective harness which gave way, frightening the horse, the writer was once thrown from a cart and dragged beneath it, holding fast to the reins, until the runaway brought up against a tree, as a Florida 'runaway is certain to do sooner or later. Yet that harness was supposed to be of excellent quality; but it was not, as what might have been a fatal experience proved; and so many like instances have come to our knowledge that we deem it a duty to our readers to put them on guard, and advise the purchase of harness direct from reliable manufacturers who have reputations to lose by sending out faulty harness.

That there are many who come under this head we have no doubt; but, personally, we only know of one, and are quite satisfied; and, as the State Granges of New Hampshire, Vermont, Massachusetts, and Connecticut give their unqualified indorsement of the manufacturing firm of King & Co., of Owego, New York, we feel no hesitation in following in their lead, as, both for quality and low prices, we have been unable to find their equal.

"A reliable firm and offering specially good advantages to purchasers," says the committee of these Grangers; and our Florida settlers who do not know where to turn for a good honest set of harness, that is sure, to be all that is claimed for it, will be wise to send to the manufacturers for their catalogue.

"Every body knows," or ought to know, that goods bought direct from the manufacturer, whose whole fortune rests upon his reputation for fair dealing, are sure to be honest and their prices lower than when sold at second or third hand, where each handler has to make his profit from the purchaser. King & Co. make harness of all kinds, for carts and carriages, wagons and drays, single or double; also saddles and bridles, and in all of these their retail prices are lower than can be found elsewhere for an inferior article offered as "the best."

In ordering harness, do not make the mistake of selecting the breast-strap instead of the collar and hames; the former is suitable only for firm, smooth roads where the labor of pulling is light and easy, but is entirely out of place on sandy highways, bruising the muscles of the breast and crippling the horse. Neither draw the check-rein tight; that is a needless cruelty at any time, but especially so where the animal needs full freedom of every muscle in order to haul with the least fatigue. Tie your own head back and then try to pull a loaded wheelbarrow behind you, the wearisome strain of the muscles of the neck and shoulders will soon teach you something of the unnecessary cross borne by the faithful horse who is tight-reined. We would dispense with the check-rein entirely, or else use the overdraw check very loose.

So, also, whether in Florida or any where else on the face of the globe, would we consign those barbarous "blinkers," "winkers," or "blinders," to the tomb of the past. The latter of these several names is literally the true one; blinders they are in every sense of the word; and the idea that a horse will be less frightened if he hears a noise without seeing its origin is simply ridiculous. Apply it to yourself: Are you more courageous in the dark, hearing a noise you can not understand, than if you were to see its cause?

We most heartily indorse the paragraph below, written by the eminent naturalist, the Kev. J. G. Wood:

"I unhesitatingly condemn blinkers as being among the silliest of the silly devices whereby man has contrived to lessen the powers of the horse. The notion that horses are guarded by them from taking fright at alarming objects is utterly absurd, the horse being nervously timid when its senses are partially obscured, and dauntlessly courageous when facing a known danger. The horses employed on the Midland Railway wear no blinkers, and yet they walk about among the screaming whistles, snorting and puffing engines, as composedly as if they were in their own stables, not even requiring to be led. To be consistent, the horse's ears ought to be furnished with stoppers, so as to prevent the animal from hearing any sound that might frighten it. The only excuse for blinkers that has the least sense in it is, that they may possibly save the eyes of horses from the whips of brutal drivers. But as no man who would flog a horse about the head ought to be intrusted with a horse, even this very lame defense breaks down."

The proper care of harness is another point upon which every one is not well informed, and it is an important one too, involving its long-continued usefulness.

TO PRESERVE HARNESS.

There is nothing that looks nicer in its way than a clean, bright-looking set of harness, nor is there any thing more quickly damaged by neglect. Harness should be washed and oiled frequently. To do this effectually the straps should be unbuckled and detached and then washed with soft water and Castile soap, or crown soap, and hung by a slow fire or in the sun until nearly dry, then coated with a mixture of neatsfoot oil and tallow, and allowed to remain for several hours until perfectly dry, then rubbed thoroughly with a woolen rag. The rubbing is important, as it, in addition to removing the surplus oil and grease, tends to close the pores and gives a finish to the leather. In hanging harness long wooden pegs should be provided and the straps allowed to hang always at their full length; twisting up the traces, for instance, is a bad practice.

HOME-MADE FURNITURE.

Among our Florida settlers, as elsewhere, the money is frequently lacking to supply such household goods as refined taste would dictate, and packing-boxes and lumber from the neighboring saw-mill are often the only resources available. Many, however, are able to purchase, and for these we can point with pride to the firm of Cleaveland & Son, Jacksonville, dealers in furniture and bedding, as the largest and oldest house in the State of Florida, and the only one issuing a complete illustrated catalogue. Not only can we heartily indorse this house as being an honorable one, and its prices wonderfully low, but of late it has made a specialty of supplying incoming settlers, whether in colonies or as individuals, with goods sold on the popular installment plan. This inducement, coupled with the low prices at which they are placed, effectually disposes of the question we have frequently been asked, "Is it cheaper to bring one's furniture, or to buy it in Florida?" If purchased of Cleaveland & Son, we believe the balance of expense would be in favor of "buying it in Florida," excepting only such special pieces of furniture as are valued for association's sake.

For stoves and other hardware, S. B. Hubbard & Co. will be found ready to meet every call satisfactorily.

But for those who must trust to making the most of the materials at hand, the following directions will be found invaluable in creating order out of disorder, comfort out of discomfort, softness and beauty out of hard, angular ugliness, and plenty out of scant materials.

And now let us see how to go to work to do all this.

BED-ROOM FURNITURE.

Suppose you have no bed — well, make one. Go out to the nearest hammock and get some strong, pliable saplings, hickory or oak, two for the sides of the bedstead, two for the ends; for the legs you want thicker saplings, sawed off to the height you wish the posts to be; if you want a headboard, let the posts run up accordingly. Of course the bark must be peeled off from the saplings before they are fit to use. Into one side of each post cut a notch at the height from the floor that you desire your bed to be—remembering to allow for the height of the mattress—of such a size as to allow the side and end saplings to fit neatly within them, then a few nails or screws will render them secure, and if you have a firm foundation to work upon, if the posts are stout enough, and if you can get an auger that will bore a hole through them large enough for the saplings to slip into, so much the better; in this case, use hot glue in the holes liberally before putting in the side and end pieces. A light hempen rope run in and out in a net-work from one end of the frame-work to the other, tightly drawn, makes a first-rate spring. This is for a "tural-lural" bedstead that need not cost a penny, unless it is for rope and cutting the saplings; but if you prefer to procure lumber from a mill, the bedstead can be made on the same plan; in this case the rope can be dispensed with, the side pieces made deeper, a slat nailed on the bottom and battens laid across from side to side to support the mattress. But this would not give as much spring as the rope. If you have a fence made of pickets and wires, go and look at it and get an idea. There is a good deal of spring in that, and by driving staples in the ends of your home-made bedstead, weaving some pliable wire in and out around the laths or battens, and twisting the ends of the wires through the staples, you will have a veritable springbed. All cracks can be filled up with common brown soap, and then there will be no trouble about vermin.

About the head-board: If you are making the rustic bedstead, stretch tightly across from post to post (a slat nailed across at the top is an improvement) a piece of muslin, satin or calico, plain satteen or muslin, a floral design worked on it in outline stitch in the center makes a very neat finish. If, however, the bedstead is made of our Florida pine lumber, a pretty head-board could be made from selected pieces nailed across from post to post, and the top board could be sawed into an arched form, then, if oiled and varnished, or stained with walnut stain, no one need wish for a neater looking bedstead.

The mattress: Florida moss, pine needles, palmetto leaves, or excelsior, are all good materials for the filling. The moss should be buried for a month or more, then washed and dried; the pine needles should be washed and then thoroughly dried, this is all the preparation they need; for palmetto, procure the green leaves, cut them from the midrib and strip each blade, a three-tined fork is a good implement to use, let them dry thoroughly. Of these three home products we prefer the latter, it makes a clean, sweet, springy mattress that will last for years, so that the trouble of gathering and preparing them is fully repaid. If you have excelsior at hand, this, also, will serve the purpose, either by itself, or used in connection with one of the other stuffing materials; but it is the least desirable.

As to the making of the mattress, here are directions furnished by one of our Florida housekeepers, which have borne the test of eight years' experience: "Make the tick for a double bed in two sections, it is so much easier to handle, and then there is never any sagging or ridge in the middle of the bed. If possible, buy a good article of ticking, for, if properly made, it should last a life-time. In cutting, allow a good margin both in length and breadth, else it will draw up in the stuffing, and be too short and too narrow.

"Cut out and sew up, box shape—a glance at a ready-made mattress will show you how; put the seams inside to avoid harbors for insects; leave one end half open in the middle of the seam. Have ready strong tape or strips of ticking cut in lengths of about six inches; sew these to the wrong side of the tick with stout thread, about nine inches apart; place a folded bit of the ticking or bright-colored cloth or leather on the top side, and sew through all very securely. Be very careful that each strip on the top-side is exactly opposite the corresponding one on the bottom side. Now, keeping your tick wrong side out, or rather, turned back to the first row of strings, stuff the interval between these and the end with your moss or palmetto, or whatever else you use, and do not spare it, stuff in all you possibly can—remember it will settle with use; then tie the strings securely, slip the ticking along to the next row of strings, and proceed as before, and so continue until the stuffing is completed; then sew up the end, and your mattress is an accomplished fact."

In lieu of springs, an under-ticking may be made, leaving one half the seam open in the middle of the top, and filled with pine needles. The odor of the pine is very pleasant and healthful, and by pushing a broom-stick in the open slit the needles are stirred up and kept from packing.

The great advantage of this method of making the ticking lies in the facility with which it may be emptied, the contents picked over and replaced, making each time a "good as new" mattress, without the labor of a new ticking; there is no ripping to be done except at the end which was sewed up last, only the strings to untie and tie again.

Bolsters and pillows: For bolsters and pillows, the same materials as for the mattress—pine needles, palmetto, moss, shavings—are often used; but for those who can procure them, feathers are far preferable, especially for the pillows. They need not be geese feathers to be comfortable; those of chickens, killed for the table, are good enough if properly cured, and this is a simple matter; scalding does not hurt them; all that is necessary is to dry them very thoroughly. A good way is to put them in a bag and lay them in a moderately warm oven; the small feathers are all right, but the pen-feathers (wings and tail) need to be stripped.

The bureau: For the bureau, a box of suitable size is just the thing, and four blocks glued and nailed at the corners will make the feet; if you have casters, so much the better; always use them, if possible, on heavy furniture, it saves all around, the furniture itself, the floor, the carpet and, more than all, your own strength. Many a woman has made herself an invalid for life by pushing or pulling or lifting heavy furniture. Sisters, don't do it; if you can not have casters, let the dirt be; better that than injure your health.

Instead of drawers, which are difficult for an amateur to fit properly, put in shelves. Strips nailed on the inside of the box for the shelving to rest on are best; it is best, too, not to fasten the shelves, but slip them in, so that they can be readily taken out to clean. A front nailed on the outer side of the shelves, three or four inches high, will keep clothing and small articles from falling out, while a neat curtain, parting in the center, will conceal the shelves and their contents. The same material can be tacked smoothly on the sides, or the latter can be painted, varnished, or stained with walnut stain. If one is skillful enough to make doors for the bureau, so much the better. Then, if a mirror is forthcoming, make a frame that will fit around it, the two side pieces running down and being screwed to the back of the bureau. To fasten the glass to the uprights, put a strip across the back, screwed to the frame of the mirror and also to the uprights. The top can be finished like a pointed arch or straight across, as preferred. The uprights should be at least three inches wide, and this will allow a small bracket to be fastened to each one to hold candles, toilet bottles, vases or jewel boxes.

The washstand : As good a washstand as one need want can be made from a box stood on end, with a top made of boards, if not large enough without. Around the top nail a strip that shall project about half an inch above the surface, so as to form a ledge, omitting it in front of course. A narrow shelf, raised up a little, running across the back, furnishes a good resting-place for the soap-cup, tooth-brush holder and cup, leaving the top free for pitcher and basin. One or two shelves fitted inside the box make a nice closet for medicine bottles, salve, old linen handkerchiefs (handy for binding up the "wounded heroes" of the family), and other odds and ends of a like nature.

Toilet table: A barrel with a couple of boards nailed across will make an excellent foundation for a toilet table. The top, if planed, may be painted or varnished; if rough, some kind of cloth or muslin should be drawn smoothly over it and tacked at the edges; then full around it material to match, and you will have a very pretty toilet table.

A mirror, if you prefer it here instead of on the bureau, adds very much to its appearance, especially if set off by a "half-circle shelf" above it, fastened to the wall, from which depends some graceful drapery, parted in the center and sweeping to either side of the table. A square hole cut in the front or side of the barrel at the base, makes a convenient receptacle for shoes or a hat-box, which is entirely concealed by the drapery.

THE ROSS NOVELTY RUG MACHINE.

This is a subject that excites our enthusiasm, and well it may, as we look around us upon the handsome rugs of woolen yarn and rags, and the silk chair covers, and table covers, that our household owes to this little wonder-worker.

With this simple machine in hand (it is so very simple that a child can use it), there is not a scrap of cotton, silk, or woolen rags, old coats, merino stockings or dresses, that can not be utilized, with ease, and converted into handsome, durable rugs, mats, chair, ottoman, lounge or table covers; and the lighter shades of these otherwise "waste pieces" can be readily dyed by the aniline dyes of any color or shade desired.

The Ross Novelty Machine costs but one dollar by mail (Ross & Co., Toledo, Ohio, are the manufacturers), but the number of dollars that may be saved by its use are infinite. Let us see how it works.

The first thing after getting your machine ("first catch your hare") is to get a frame, a very simple affair, four strips, one and a half inches wide, one inch thick; two of the four strips should be six or seven feet long—the latter is safer, if you want large rugs—and the other two, three feet long; bore auger-holes through them, about three inches apart, of a size to fit the four common iron bolts, with nuts, which complete the frame; if stained with black walnut, the latter will look very neat; yellow pine, however, will only need to be sand-papered and varnished. Of course, having the frame made this way, it can be put together, by means of the bolts, to suit any size rug desired.

The manufacturers supply regular patterns for rugs, laprobes, and foot-stools, stamped upon burlap all ready for working, and also carpet yarn of the proper colors. These make soft, thick, beautiful rugs serviceable enough for door-mats, handsome enough for the parlor, and they are not expensive either. At the same time, it is not necessary to purchase these; armed with the little machine, and an oat or corn sack, and some woolen rags cut about a quarter of an inch wide (not sewed), you can make as handsome a rug as any one need desire, without its costing one cent. Turn the edges of the oat sack, stitch them down to make them strong, then set the frame so that it will be about an inch larger than the prepared piece, and then with strong twine, fastening the four corners first, and a stout needle, a sail-needle or short upholsterer's needle, sew in the sacking, drawing it as tight and straight as possible. Then you are ready to go to work, having your rags cut and handy in a basket at your side. Nearly all the work can be done sitting in a chair; neither is there any hard pushing, but just a quiet simple motion of the hand pushing the needle and loop in and out; the stitch is automatic, the same size each time.

You can work the colors just as they come, "hit or miss," or you can lay the sacking on the floor after it is stretched and draw on it any design you fancy; work right on the pattern, it will be thrown out on the other, or right side, and also turn the hemmed-down edge toward you, so that the right side will be smooth, no ravelings to work up and spoil the neatness of the rug.

The writer has made rugs on the stamped burlap patterns, using woolen rags, and the result is almost if not quite equal to the effect of the carpet yarn. A pattern one yard long and half as wide costs forty cents and makes a good-sized rug, the yarn for this costs ninety cents; a rug pattern one yard and three quarters by one and a half yards costs seventy-five cents, and the yarn about two dollars and a half. Of course the yarns are nicer for parlor use if they can be afforded, but if not, the woolen rags, especially if some silk be mixed with them, are almost as handsome.

Armed with this little rug machine, oat sacks, and rags, the work of brightening up the floors and covering the furniture of the plainest houses will not only be easy but pleasant. The work is really fascinating. For ten cents, the manufacturers send a little book of colored patterns from which to order.

We find so much rest and relief for mind and body, and so much profit for our home surroundings, in this light, pleasant occupation, that can be taken up or dropped at a moment's notice, the frame and chairs standing always ready, that we feel grateful to the little rug machine, and would like to see one in every home all over the land; no better investment could be made of a dollar.

The making of rugs and covers by no means exhausts the list of its virtues; added to these are tidies, lap-robes for carriages, lamp-mats, wrist-warmers, winter caps for girls and boys, slippers, warm smoking caps for men, and nice mittens; for these last and the caps the manufacturers furnish patterns. In fact, there seems to be hardly any limit to the articles that may be made with this little machine, with its two working parts, the needle and loop-holder.

We have heard of a crumb-cloth and stair-carpet being made with it; but that seems a waste of time, when they can be bought so cheaply; a silk bed-spread could be made, however, one that would be very handsome and durable.

THE BARREL CHAIR.

No list of home-made furniture would be complete without the famous old-time barrel chair, which is really, if properly made, one of the most cosy resting-places imaginable.

You want a good, strong barrel for the foundation, sugar barrel for instance, and the first thing to do is to nail the central hoop firmly to the staves, clinch nails are best to use; then secure the bottom hoop half way across the barrel intact, to serve as a back, which can be varied in height and shape as desired, and made with arms or without. The seat is formed by nailing stout pieces of wood to the sides of the barrel of the proper height to reach from the bottom to the seat, when placed on end; three or four placed at equal distances around the inside will make a good foundation for nailing across stout strips of webbing, two or three each way interwoven. If you have not got the webbing, strips of strong ticking, doubled and stitched, from two to three inches wide, will do as well. Over this tack strong bagging—an oat sack will do very well.

Make sure that this is not slighted, for it is not conducive to comfort or good temper to sit down on an empty space, as sometimes happens if the seat of a chair is not securely made.

The next step is to make a cushion of the same shape as the back, and another for the seat, and tack them in place. Then cover the rest of the chair neatly with the same material, chintz or cretonne are best. If one is willing to take the trouble to tuft the cushions, they will be all the more comfortable, and the chair will look like an expensive, regularly upholstered piece of furniture.

Two or three of these barrel chairs will be found very cosy in the family sitting-room, and half-barrels, treated the same way, make comfortable chairs for the little folks.

Strong packing-boxes also can be transformed into very desirable chairs, by sawing them into the proper shape and then proceeding as with the barrels. If the bottom of the box as it stands in position for the chair is left intact, and the seat made of solid board and hinged, a first-class shoe or hat-box results. The cushion should be tacked to the lid so as not to be displaced.

"Rockers?" Why, yes, of course you can have rockers. They can be sawed out from a thick board, and made as good as a "bought rocker."

A divan, as pretty as it is comfortable, may be easily made if you have a spare mattress, and if you have not it will pay to make one, only, in this case, it might be as well to make it in two sections, the one for the back, the other for the seat.

But supposing that you have the spare mattress on hand, this is the way to make the divan: place the mattress so that one third of it rests against the wall, then fold the other part over toward it, and fasten the folded parts in proper positions, the back and seat at right angles. If you can place it on a box or platform about a foot high, so much the better, but it will do very well without. With a pretty cover of some cheap material and one or two square pillows to match, you will find that you have one of the most cosy resting-places imaginable.

A HOME-MADE REFRIGERATOR.

Obtain two common dry-goods boxes, of such sizes that the smaller one will be large enough to hold the ice and food you wish to keep within it, and the other will be about four inches larger around. The smaller one must be lined with zinc, or it will absorb moisture from the ice and soon make trouble. Near one corner of the bottom of the smaller box bore a hole an inch in diameter, and, when the box is lined with zinc, have a tube about seven inches long securely fastened in this hole. There must be no crevice into which the water can soak. A cover, which also should be zinc-lined, must be fitted to the box. Then procure some charcoal, broken finely, and fill the larger box (in which a hole has first been bored to receive the tube from the inner box) with the powdered charcoal to a depth of about four inches. Place the smaller box on the charcoal, and fill the space between the sides of the two boxes with the charcoal, up even with the inner box, and cover the space with a neat strip of board. This will give you a box with double bottom and sides filled with charcoal, the very best of non-conductors. With an outer cover, the size of the larger box, and four blocks to raise the whole from the floor, so that a pan may be placed under the tube to catch the water which comes from the melted ice, the whole will be done, except to add shelves as desired.

An improvement on this plan could be made by arranging the boxes so that the ice would be at the top, with the shelves below, the outer cover becoming a door, and the top hinged to admit the ice.

How to preserve food with sulphur is another good thing to know, especially where ice is not obtainable.

It is very simple, yet effective. Take an ordinary wooden box, make the joints air-tight, hinge the lid and make that also air-tight ; then bore a series of holes around the sides, inside, not through, but deep enough to drive wooden pegs into. On these pegs hang any meat, fish or game, that you wish to keep; place in the box a tin plate with some sand and a few live coals, sprinkle on the latter a little sulphur, close the box and the work is done. Food, cooked or raw, can be kept in this way for a week or more. There is no taste or smell.

www.ingramcontent.com/pod-product-compliance
Lightning Source LLC
Chambersburg PA
CBHW070604170426
43200CB00012B/2583